HARVARD HISTORICAL MONOGRAPHS

Published under the direction
of the Department of History
from the income of the
Robert Louis Stroock Fund

Volume LXXIII

"Begging Friars, Granada," from John F. Lewis, *Sketches of Spain and Spanish Character made during his tour in that country in the years 1833–1834* (London, n.d.)

Church, Politics, and Society in Spain, 1750–1874

William J. Callahan

Harvard University Press
Cambridge, Massachusetts
and London, England
1984

Library of Congress Cataloging in Publication Data

Callahan, William James, 1937–

   Church, politics, and society in Spain, 1750–1874.
   (Harvard historical monographs ; v. 73)
   Includes index.
   1. Catholic Church—Spain—History. 2. Spain—Church
history. I. Title. II. Series.
BX1585.C214   1984   282'.46   83-26503
ISBN 0-674-13125-8 (alk. paper)

For my parents

Preface

Few subjects have aroused more controversy in the history of modern Spain than that of the Church. Intimately involved in the great political struggles and social conflicts of the twentieth century, it has long been the focus of polemic on the parts of both defenders and detractors. Recent advances in the study of the Spanish Church by ecclesiastical historians, moved by a vigorous spirit of archival inquiry, and by the new generation of social and economic historians have made possible a more rational assessment of the Church's role than could have been undertaken just a few years ago.

I am indebted to the staffs of the Archivo Histórico Nacional, the Biblioteca Nacional, the Hemerotecas Municipal and Nacional, and the Jesuit Library in Madrid for assistance in gathering materials for this book. Cambridge University Press granted me permission to use portions of my essay from the volume *Church and Society in Catholic Europe of the Eighteenth Century* (ed. W. J. Callahan and D. C. Higgs). Sage Publications, publishers of the *European Studies Review*, and the editors of *Historical Reflections* allowed me to reproduce parts of my articles from their journals. I owe a special debt to Solita and Juan Marichal and to Mercedes and Trinidad Aboitiz, who provided constant encouragement during my research and writing. Several colleagues gave me generous assistance and critical comment, particularly David Higgs, Olwen Hufton, C. C. Noël, who kindly allowed me to consult his dissertation, J. H. Galloway, and Paul Grendler. Financial support was provided by the Social Sciences and Research Council of Canada. I also owe thanks to Eva Hollander and Sandra McAuslan for their patience in typing the manuscript, to Hedy Later for preparing the maps, and to Elizabeth Suttell of Harvard University Press for her expert editorial assistance.

Contents

Tables

Maps

Church, Politics, and Society in Spain, 1750–1874

1 / The Organization of the Church, 1750–1790

Few institutions have played so central a role in the history of a people as has the Spanish Church. From the Middle Ages to the twentieth century the Church, for good or for ill, has been closely identified with the great issues of Spain's past. The contribution of religion to the *Reconquista*, the centuries-old effort to conquer the Moorish kingdoms of Iberia for Christian arms; the activities of the Inquisition from the late fifteenth century onward; the massive campaigns of evangelization among the Indians of the New World; the sixteenth-century flowering of mysticism and spirituality; the virulent anticlericalism of the nineteenth and twentieth centuries; and the support given by the Church to Francisco Franco during the civil war of the 1930's—all testify to the historical importance of an institution praised by some and attacked by others, but ignored by few.

This study begins with the Church of the later eighteenth century not because of an intention to ignore the richness and complexity of ecclesiastical history in earlier times. But the purpose of this book is to reveal the origins of the problem of the Church in modern Spain. It has been fashionable to consider the history of the Spanish Church as a long continuum from the time of Ferdinand and Isabella to the years before and during the civil war of 1936–1939. However, the organization, economic base, and mentality of the Church as it developed in the nineteenth and twentieth centuries were very different from those during the Old Regime. It was, indeed, the collapse of the Church of the eighteenth century, identified with absolute monarchy and possessed of immense privileges within a hierarchical and agrarian society, that transformed the role of the Church and made it a focus of conflict until our own time.

The eighteenth-century Church was not the heroic and mystical Church of the late fifteenth and sixteenth centuries. It produced no Saint Teresa of Ávila, no Saint John of the Cross, no spectacular missionary achievements in distant and exotic lands. Even the Inquisition went about its work with a desultory spirit that would have shocked the harsh inquisitors of an earlier age. But the Church of the eighteenth century, though it lacked the vitality of its predecessors, continued to be a rich and powerful institution in a nation where religious practice was deeply rooted and luxuriant in its variety. Moreover, the Church impressed itself on the fabric of social life more deeply then than in a later age. Through its religious mission it held a nearly magical hold over the peasant masses, who lived uneducated and isolated in an often unforgiving natural environment. As supreme moral censor, the Church imposed its standards of conduct on the entire range of society, from aristocrat to agricultural laborer. Through its control of charity and education, it exercised a social function that later would become the prerogative of the State. As a landowner and recipient of the tithe, the Church possessed the financial resources necessary to maintain an elaborate ecclesiastical organization touching the lives of all Spaniards in one way or another. The eighteenth-century Church was omnipresent; no one escaped its influence.

A Royal Church

Few nations have seen their national fortunes grow and decline as spectacularly as Spain did between the late fifteenth and the eighteenth centuries. The great age of imperial expansion begun under Ferdinand and Isabella and carried forward by Charles V and Philip II was followed by a century of military defeat, economic depression, and inadequate political leadership. Although the succession to the throne of Philip V, the first Bourbon king of Spain, in 1700 did not immediately transform the kingdom, it introduced a period of equilibrium that would endure until the 1790's. The Bourbon monarchs, Philip V (1700–1746), Ferdinand VI (1746–1759), and Charles III (1759–1788), failed to resolve the nation's fundamental problems, but their attempt to reform antiquated political, social, and economic structures brought Spain closer to the more advanced states of Europe than it would be at any time until the twentieth century. The process of reform, though begun by Philip V and his ministers, reached its height during the reign of Charles III. In this silver age of political stability and modest economic and intellectual progress, the king, assisted by a competent ministerial bureaucracy, attempted to stimulate economic development, update the curricula of the schools, reform an archaic and inefficient tax system, and implement measures designed to bring the kingdom into the modern world.[1]

The Church partially owed its preeminence to its historic relationship with the State. For centuries the secular and ecclesiastical worlds depended on each other and in the process became so close that even today it is difficult to disentangle them. Church and monarchy were different aspects of absolute power applied to the religious and secular worlds. The Church was linked to Rome by doctrinal ties, but the increasingly weak papacies of Benedict XIV (1740–1758), Clement XIII (1758–1769), Clement XIV (1769–1774), and Pius VI (1775–1799) were incapable of exercising decisive influence over the administration of the Spanish Church. This was above all a royal Church, molded by the Bourbons to suit their policies. Spanish monarchs had long attempted to control the Church at the expense of Rome, but it was only in the eighteenth century that the "Catholic Kings" successfully minimized the power of the papacy in Spain. The victory took the form of the Concordat of 1753, which bestowed on the Crown nearly universal patronage over the most important ecclesiastical benefices, a right hitherto shared in an uncomfortable relationship with Rome.[2] Favoritism and influence played their parts in the ecclesiastical patronage of the Bourbons, but during the reign of Charles III the State used its powers to form a clerical establishment that accepted in large measure the royal vision of the Church's role in the reforming program.

A few bishops were uneasy about the degree of state control, but Madrid would brook no opposition to its expanding authority over ecclesiastical affairs. When the aged bishop of Cuenca, José Carvajal y Lancaster, expressed reservations about the changing balance of the civil-ecclesiastical relationship in 1766, he received an abrupt summons to the capital, where he was given a humiliating dressing down by royal bureaucrats.[3] The central administration moved with equal firmness against one of the most prominent clerical reformers of the late eighteenth century, José Climent, the bishop of Barcelona. Climent's impressive pastoral record at the head of his diocese could not save him from Madrid's anger when he fell under suspicion—quite unjustified—of supporting separatist aspirations in Catalonia. Determined to remove Climent from Barcelona and also to avoid public scandal, the royal administration offered him promotion to a non-Catalan diocese, but the prelate, true to his principles, refused and resigned his post.[4] In general, however, the Church through its bishops accepted the increasing use of the ecclesiastical establishment as a royal instrument. From 1750 on clerics outdid one another in their exaltation of the Bourbon monarchy, which they compared in Old Testament language to the kingship of David and Solomon; in their view it possessed nearly divine attributes. Francisco Bocanegra, archbishop of Santiago, was even moved to make the distinctly untheological statement, "if we imitate our King, we all shall be perfect."[5]

Enlightened absolutism as it developed after 1750 suffered from internal contradictions. Absolute monarchy pressed forward to centralize power, eliminate the archaic, and devise policies capable of transforming the administration of the State and the economy; but it would not, indeed could not, tamper with a traditional social structure dominated by aristocratic and corporate privilege. In the end, the reforming initiatives of the Bourbons resulted in only a superficial resolution of national problems, but the utilitarian spirit with which the Crown and its bureaucracy approached reform influenced the State's ecclesiastical policies.

Kings and ministers frequently testified to their Catholicism. Charles III, the most persistent royal patron of change during the century, led a personal life of piety. The monarch participated in the activities of pious associations, such as the Franciscan Third Order, and alighted from his carriage and knelt on the ground as willingly as any commoner whenever a priest passed carrying the Eucharist to the dying. The personal Catholicism of the king and his ministers was not, however, the religion of elaborate ceremonial and "superstitious" practice so widespread in eighteenth-century Spain. The public self-flagellation of penitents, the musical bands and papier-mâché giants dancing about the processions celebrating liturgical feasts, the indecent Christmas carols sung by the gypsies of Seville on Christmas Eve before the archbishop—all were foreign to the more austere Catholicism that the king and his ministers observed and wished to see spread throughout the Church.

The State profited from its control over clerical personnel and wealth, but it hoped to reform abuses within the Church by eliminating what it saw as superstition, establishing a more rational ecclesiastical administration, and improving the quality of seminaries—in short, creating a Church more attentive to pastoral responsibilities. In October 1767 the Council of Castile, the institution responsible for internal government of the kingdom, dispatched a circular to the bishops ordering them to curb abuses and superstition in their dioceses. After 1766 the government of Charles III encouraged the creation of diocesan seminaries to improve the lamentable education of the parish clergy, and it curbed devotional excesses, such as flagellation in penitential processions. The State intervened directly in ecclesiastical discipline and religious practice to realize its ideal of a pastoral Church.

The reforming ministers of Charles III did not intend to confine the Church to the purely spiritual. Royal bureaucrats proposed to employ it in the modernization of the kingdom. They expected the clergy, from bishops to parish priests, to cooperate with the reforming impulse coming from the Crown. "Public utility," declared one of the most enthusiastic clerical advocates of a civic-minded Church, "is one of the objects of our religion, its maxims lead to the good of souls and to the happiness and tranquillity of peoples."[6] The clergy were seen as agents of the State promoting economic development, improving education, building public works, and, in general, advancing the utilitarian policies formulated in Madrid. They were to be "the philosopher's stone which will enrich towns and villages and make them happy."[7] This modernizing role for the Church reflected the increasingly secular emphasis of the Bourbon monarchy, but at the same time it reinforced the ties between Throne and Altar by blurring still further the already hazy line dividing Church from State. The clergy were to become a kind of religious civil service closely identified with the task of national improvement.

Bishops and Priests

To improve the efficiency of the Church in its spiritual mission and to make it an instrument of secular reform would have been difficult enough had it possessed a simple organization with clearly marked lines of authority. But the eighteenth-century Church was a complex institution with an administrative structure determined more by historical circumstance than by rational planning. The ecclesiastical map showed a patchwork of unequal divisions.[8] The number of dioceses, sixty by the end of the century, was not excessive by European standards, but three of the eight archdiocesan sees—Toledo, Santiago, and Tarragona—were located in stagnating provincial towns, while Madrid, a city of nearly 200,000 inhabitants and the capital of a world empire, lacked episcopal status. Barcelona, experiencing an economic and demographic expansion that established it as the commercial and industrial center of the kingdom, was only a suffragan diocese to the archbishopric in the sleepy town of Tarragona. Other towns—Sigüenza, Calahorra, and Tarazona—had acquired bishops centuries before, when they were cities of some importance. By the eighteenth century they were scarcely more than overgrown villages, but they continued as diocesan seats. Bilbao, already an important commercial town, would lack a bishop until 1949. The diocese of Sigüenza provides the most glaring example of acquired historical right taking precedence over reality. Located in a depopulated zone of New Castile beyond Guadalajara, the diocesan capital contained only 4,000 inhabitants in the midst of an impoverished countryside. Yet it was one of the richer dioceses of the Church.

Nor was there logic behind the division of the Church's metropolitan provinces, each presided over by an archbishop. The archbishop of Toledo, primate of Spain, headed an ecclesiastical province of eight dioceses ranging from Valladolid in Old Castile to Córdoba, Jaén, and Murcia; in contrast, the archbishop of Granada had as suffragan bishops only the prelates of Guadix and Almería. Differences in territorial size among the dioceses were accompanied by severe disparities of income. The archbishop of Toledo enjoyed annual revenues amounting to 3 million reales; the bishops of Albarracín, Barbastro, Tudela, Tuy, and Valladolid survived on less than 100,000 reales.

The ecclesiastical map of the eighteenth-century Church demanded rationalization, but the difficulty of overcoming acquired interests prevented any substantial changes in territorial demarcation of dioceses. Four new sees were established during the eighteenth century—Santander, Tudela, Ibiza, and Menorca—but only the first was located in an important town. The effort to separate Santander from the diocese of Burgos, begun by Philip II in the sixteenth century, ended only in 1754. The struggle was so troublesome it left even the reforming Bourbons with little enthusiasm for the rationalization of diocesan boundaries.

Unequal territorial divisions and the uneven distribution of wealth provide glaring examples of the imbalance and confusion characteristic of the Church's administrative structure. Bishops did not exercise supreme authority over their dioceses. They clashed frequently with cathedral chapters, the communities of canons charged with providing liturgical services in episcopal churches. The accumulation of privileges from Crown and pope over the centuries endowed chapters with a quasi-autonomous position in relation to their bishops. The unfortunate prelate quarreling with his chapter might be unwelcome in his own cathedral. Archbishop Yermo y Santiváñez of Santiago (1727–1737) suffered the misfortune of falling out with his chapter in a dispute over precedence on the very day he took possession of his see. In succeeding years the unforgiving canons seized every opportunity to frustrate the prelate's administration.[9] Further, bishops exercised little or no authority, depending on circumstances, over the religious orders. Episcopal authority over the great monastic foundations of the Benedictines, Cistercians, and Carthusians was nonexistent. The great Spanish monasteries, whether Silos in Old Castile or Poblet in Catalonia, formed minidioceses for all practical purposes, with jurisdiction over parishes in the surrounding countryside. The bishops' ability to control the mendicant orders, such as the Franciscans and Dominicans, was greater, but over them too they found it difficult to impose their authority.

In theory, the Spanish Church of the eighteenth century was governed by the twin principles of authority and hierarchy. In fact, lack of clear jurisdictional lines, maldistribution of ecclesiastical wealth, and uneven territorial boundaries created an institution without strong cohesion. Eighteenth-century clerical writers correctly referred not to the Spanish Church but to the Spanish "churches." Bishops, for example, rarely came in personal contact with one another, a circumstance noted by the English traveler Joseph Townsend in the 1780's: "the meeting of two prelates is a phenomenon in Spain, because the moment a minister of the altar accepts a mitre, he devotes his life wholly to the duties of his office and confines himself altogether to his diocese."[10] The "churches" lacked an institutional means of developing an independent stance against either king or pope. The ancient Congregation of the Churches of Castile and León, founded in the reign of Ferdinand and Isabella, had once represented the financial interests of the Church in negotiations with the Crown and Rome. But by the end of the seventeenth century, the institution was no longer important. Without a collective means of expression and with an incoherent internal structure, the Church accepted the direction marked for it by the Bourbon monarchy.

To foreigners visiting Spain for the first time, the number of priests, monks, friars, and nuns appeared "prodigious."[11] A massive clerical presence was obvious in the major towns. Barcelona alone had a cathedral, eighty-two churches and chapels, twenty-six religious houses of men, eighteen of women, two oratories, a seminary, a tribunal of the Inquisition, and several smaller foundations. In Valencia 2,610 priests and religious lived in a population of approximately 80,000; in Seville the religious orders were so numerous that they could marshal 1,600 members to participate in the processions of Holy Week and Corpus Christi. But the impression of a nation overrun by priests, friars, and nuns is misleading. The census of 1797 showed an ecclesiastical population of 182,778 in a total population of 10.5 million. But recent studies of ecclesiastical demography have noted that this figure includes a certain number of lay employees of the Church, such as sacristans and administrators. An adjusted total of 148,409, or approximately 1.5 percent of the general population, was not excessive; in some Catholic countries the proportion was higher.[12] Although there is little reliable evidence for estimating the size of the clerical population early in the century, it appears to have remained stable between 1700 and 1800, with perhaps a slight decline at the century's close.

Within the ecclesiastical establishment the secular clergy numbered 70,840; male religious, 53,098; and nuns, 24,471. But these figures also must be adjusted. The secular clergy included over 10,000 clerics who had received only minor orders. Many had entered the Church not to seek ordination but to qualify for benefices left by pious benefactors. The tendency of both the regular and secular clergy to concentrate in towns and cities also magnified the clerical presence, for in a rural and agrarian society the Church was urban. The secular clergy flocked to the towns, where the religious orders also preferred to establish their houses; at the same time country parishes, especially in poor districts, often lacked priests. The 1797 census reveals that nearly 3,000 parishes lacked incumbents; the highest vacancy rates were in the impoverished regions of Galicia, Extremadura, and Soria.[13]

Functional and geographic imbalances in the distribution of clergy further hindered the Church in its pastoral mission. Only a minority of the secular clergy, approximately 22,000 of a total of 60,000 ordained priests, were active in parish work as either rectors or assistants.[14] The majority of the secular clergy survived on benefices, the endowments established by pious benefactors; chaplaincies in noble households, cathedrals, and hospitals; and the stipends received for conducting religious services. Many benefice holders performed liturgical duties and thereby contributed to the pastoral life of the Church, but because they, too, preferred the cities to the countryside, they did little to alleviate the lack of clergy in rural districts. Benefices attracted priests into an unseemly careerism that often conflicted with their sacerdotal character and gave rise to criticism by secular and ecclesiastical writers. There was no shortage of secular clergy in eighteenth-century Spain, but their distribution also favored the cities and often left poor country parishes without priests. The Council of Castile frequently received desperate requests from rural villages without clergy. In 1800, for example, three small towns—Cubillos, Posadina, and Cubillinos—told the council that for twenty years they had lacked "spiritual nourishment . . . because there was no income to support a priest in the sacred ministry."[15]

The geographic distribution of the secular clergy with cure of souls was uneven and already reflected the classic north-south division between areas where religious practice was more deeply rooted and those where it was not. On a national scale, there was one priest with cure of souls for every 497 parishioners. The regions well staffed with clergy were concentrated in the north and northeast: Álava, 1:153; León, 1:170; Toro, 1:268; Valladolid, 1:345; Aragón, 1:441; and Catalonia, 1:403. But in the south, the center of dechristianized Spain in the nineteenth and twentieth centuries, the ratio of priests to parishioners was significantly higher: Córdoba, 1:1,115; Murcia, 1:1,721; and Seville, 1:1,332. The disparity between southern and northern dioceses arose in part from the historic development of parochial organizations. Parishes in the south were extremely large compared with those in the north. In the administrative region called the kingdom of Seville, 303 parishes served a population of over 750,000. But in Catalonia, with more than 800,000 inhabitants, there were 2,738 parishes.[16] In some southern dioceses parishes could reach gigantic size; in Cádiz a single parish located in the cathedral served a population of 57,000, although chapels in monasteries and convents in the city also provided services.[17]

Day-to-day government of the Spanish "churches" rested with eight archbishops—at Toledo, Seville, Santiago de Compostela, Granada, Burgos, Tarragona, Zaragoza, and Valencia—and fifty-two bishops. The bishops were aptly described by Cardinal Lorenzana of Toledo as "prelates placed upon a high lookout point" who combined the duties of "shepherd, citizen, good vassal of the King and good neighbor."[18] Bishops held responsibility for implementing in their dioceses directives emanating from the Crown and, to a lesser extent, those from the papal nuncio in Madrid. They formed a clerical elite necessary for the orderly functioning of the Church. The State, recognizing the importance of the bishop's role, developed elaborate procedures through a chamber of the Council of Castile to ensure the selection of "men of honor and reputation" for episcopal office.[19]

Eighteenth-century observers and later historians agree that the quality of the hierarchy, especially during the second half of the century, was high. Townsend said of the Spanish bishops: "these venerable men, from all that I could hear and from what I saw in the near approach to which they graciously admitted me, for piety, and for zeal, can never be sufficiently admired."[20] The praise of this perceptive Protestant cleric was echoed later by the Frenchman Alexandre Laborde: "the superior orders of the Spanish clergy . . . are, for the most part, exempt from the irregularities which are charged (not altogether without reason) on the clergy of other countries."[21] To be sure, there were occasional abuses, concentrated largely in the first half of the century. The eight-year-old son of Philip V, Luis de Borbón, received the temporal administration of the rich archdioceses of Seville and Toledo. Already a cardinal at fifteen, though unordained, the young prelate was installed as archbishop of Seville in 1742 with extravagant ceremony. But such abuses were rare during the reign of Charles III, when the *Cámara* of Castile suggested to the Crown prelates of known ability and probity. The most able prelates of Charles's reign, Cardinal Francisco Lorenzana of Toledo, Archbishop Francisco Fabián y Fuero of Valencia, and Bishop Felipe Bertrán of Salamanca, were perfect examples of what the absolutist State expected of its bishops.[22] Men of culture and education, assiduous in the fulfillment of their pastoral duties, they were at the same time prelates who cooperated actively with the Crown's reforming policies by establishing schools, seminaries, and even manufactures.

The Spanish episcopacy of the eighteenth century, unlike its counterpart in France, was not an aristocratic preserve. Some bishops were drawn from wealthy and distinguished noble families, such as Francisco de Solís Folch Cardona, the son of a grandee of Spain and a baron in his own right who served as archbishop of Seville from 1755 to 1775. But the number of prelates from the great nobility was modest. Episcopal recruitment, however, was neither democratic nor based on merit and service. For all practical purposes the kingdom's 22,000 priests with cure of souls had little hope of becoming bishops. Whatever the quality of the episcopacy, the system of recruitment reflected the inequalities of a social structure in which access to high office, whether in the State or the Church, belonged to a privileged minority. The secular clergy, from whose ranks the vast majority of the bishops came, was divided into two unequal groups, a small elite who possessed the most lucrative benefices, and the great mass of clergy, parish priests, curates, and a large number of clerics without any living at all. The size of the ecclesiastical establishment is difficult to establish, but it included the bishops; 2,300 canons in cathedral and the closely related collegiate chapters; and a minority of the kingdom's 15,000 benefice holders, a group, perhaps, of 5,000.

Advancement rested on education—more precisely on training in the theological, philosophical, and law faculties of the universities. The clerical elite formed a highly educated group within Spanish society. Bishops and canons frequently held doctorates in theology, philosophy, canon law, and even civil law. Progress through the ranks of the secular clergy depended in part on academic accomplishment, for it was critical for the ecclesiastical careerist to gain admission either to a university faculty or to a cathedral chapter. Through the Spanish academic procedure known as *oposiciones*, candidates for canonries had to pass examinations in ethics, theology, and canon law.[23] Because membership in a chapter gave access to the most important episcopal recruiting ground, only candidates with the requisite academic credentials could hope to win the coveted prize. Priests educated in seminaries, where the quality of education was inferior to that of the universities, rarely bothered to apply for vacancies. Many secular clerics received an even more rudimentary education, which excluded them completely from any prospect of advancement. The division of the secular clergy through academic streaming was complicated by the nobility's dominance in the kingdom's clerical elite. Commoners could become bishops, but the hierarchy was the preserve of the numerous lesser nobility, who had respectable but economically modest backgrounds. Bishops and cathedral canons often came from noble families, which traditionally had sent their sons into the service of the State and the Church. For centuries these hidalgo families sought higher education for their sons to provide them with the academic qualifications for successful ecclesiastical careers.

The bishops of the eighteenth-century Church did more or less what was expected of them. They carried out pastoral visits to the parishes of their dioceses with remarkable diligence in an age when poor communications and transport made this a burdensome task. Bishop Amador Merino Malaguilla of Badajoz visited all the towns of his diocese at least five times during his tenure of office.[24] Bishops promoted the founding of seminaries and ecclesiastical conferences to improve the education of the rural clergy. Many distributed charity to the poor with a largess that evoked the disapproving wonder of foreign visitors such as Townsend, who complained of the bishop of Córdoba, who had given alms to 7,000 people. This example was not unusual. Bishops established charity schools to educate the poor, and, following the directives of the State, they participated actively in the work of social and economic improvement. Cardinal Lorenzana of Toledo tried to revive the decaying silk industry of his diocesan seat and established a charity hospice for the poor. Felipe Bertrán of Salamanca created a vocational school to train goldsmiths; the archbishop of Tarragona, Santiyán y Valdivielso, restored the city's ancient Roman aqueduct. Other prelates built bridges and town gates, planted trees, and in general contributed to the physical improvement of their diocesan seats.[25]

In spite of the personal piety and responsibility of the vast majority of prelates, there was a fundamental contradiction in the position of the eighteenth-century bishop. The bishops formed a privileged minority within the Church and were part of a privileged social elite in the broader society. Whether personally noble or not, the eighteenth-century bishop possessed the education, wealth, and culture that set him apart from the poorer and less educated clergy of the countryside. Cardinal Lorenzana of Toledo donated generously to charity but also spent lavishly to acquire a library of rare books. An archbishop of Granada distributed alms daily to thousands of poor gathered outside his palace gates and provided wet nurses for 400 children. According to Townsend, "his bounty to the poor is such, that we can scarcely conceive his income to equal his expenditure." Yet the good archbishop also lived "in some degree of splendor," with his meals prepared according to the rules of "French cookery" and served on silver plate.[26] The bishops of the eighteenth century did not on the whole spend wantonly, but they lived comfortably when many of their clergy did not. The eighteenth-century episcopacy existing within the traditional social structure of the Old Regime established a kind of equilibrium between the bishop as pastor and the bishop as a noble seigneur. But the vast social and cultural differences between bishops and priests remained a serious weakness in the eighteenth-century Church.

Below the bishops stood 2,300 canons in cathedral and collegiate chapters.[27] The canons lived in a world as diverse and colorful as any within the Church. Chapters were large or small depending on the size and wealth of individual dioceses. The Oviedo chapter had thirty-six members, but the wealthy chapter of Seville numbered over sixty. Canons in richer dioceses enjoyed handsome revenues that sometimes exceeded those of bishops of poor sees. Eleven canons of Seville received over 60,000 reales a year, approximately the salary of a government minister; another forty received a comfortable 40,000 reales a year. Elaborate styles of ecclesiastical dress distinguished the canons of one chapter from those of another. The canons of Zaragoza wore a black cassock covered by a mantle of violet silk; the canons of Barcelona, a scarlet cassock covered by a surplice trimmed in ermine. Members of the chapters fulfilled a variety of responsibilities, which included chanting the divine office daily in the cathedral and supervising the elaborate ceremonies of the liturgical year. They also spent much of their time maintaining the extensive properties and endowments that belonged to the cathedrals. Possessing an exaggerated sense of their corporate dignity and enjoying revenues of their own, chapters often jousted with their bishops and the civil authorities over rights of precedence and the extent of episcopal control over their affairs.

The life of eighteenth-century canons left ample time for study and reflection, although most chose to languish comfortably and simply perform their modest duties. But from the ranks of canons came bishops of superior quality. Canons also took an active part in the reforming efforts of Charles III. Antonio de Paramo, a canon of the cathedral of Santiago de Compostela, traveled widely abroad, built a fine library and numismatic collection, and studied natural history. He formed the most admired "cabinet" on that subject in Santiago, a collection that he donated to the royal economic society of the town. Jerónimo de Róo, dean of the chapter in Las Palmas during the 1770's and 1780's, founded a school of design, promoted the foundation of an academy of architecture, and became an active member of the royal economic society, which had been founded in 1777 with the encouragement of the Crown to stimulate the economic development of the Canaries.[28]

As did the bishops above them, however, canons formed a privileged minority within the Church. Although they led lives free from scandal, and many were men of cultural refinement, they were even further removed than the bishops from the difficult

pastoral work of city and country parishes. The endowments enjoyed by many chapters were often held at the expense of the
parochial clergy. In Córdoba, for example, the cathedral chapter
had the right to collect and retain the tithes originally destined to
support the parochial clergy. Toward the end of the century in
the diocese of Segovia, parish priests received only 28 percent of
the tithes, even though they formed the most numerous group
in the clergy. The small body of cathedral canons took about 16
percent for its share, and the local bishop received 14 percent.[29]
Everywhere chapters and diocesan administrations drained resources away from the lower clergy.

The kingdom's nearly 19,000 parishes formed the strongest as
well as the weakest link in the Church's organization. The parishes
and their priests touched the lives of the population more closely
than the local bishop, who might make a pastoral visit once a
decade, or the diocesan canons, who rarely left their cathedral
towns. In isolated country villages the parish was the center of all
social life, and the *cura* presided over the ceremonial recording
of the basic stages of human existence. To the parish clergy fell
the awesome task of teaching the elementary truths of religion to
an illiterate rural population who had little or no contact with the
educated clerical elite of the cities. In an agrarian society few
groups in the Church should have been more carefully trained
and generously treated. In fact, the 22,000 priests with cure of
souls faced their task with often inadequate pastoral training and
financial circumstances distinctly inferior to those of bishops and
canons.

Eighteenth-century clerics believed that the quality of the clergy
was one of the gravest problems facing the Church. An examiner
of candidates for parish appointments in the diocese of Mondo-
ñedo complained of priests who, having been taught to read and
speak Latin "like parrots," said Mass "without understanding what
they were saying."[30] Complaints of priests saying Mass hastily and
"with little reverence" were common.[31] The Jesuit Pedro de Calatayud, who traveled indefatigably on preaching campaigns through
the rural villages of central and northern Spain at midcentury,
has left a devastating indictment of the parish clergy with whom
he came in contact. He found some who never taught Christian
doctrine from their pulpits and whose parishes included adoles-

cents who had never received Holy Communion. He met others who devoted their time to illicit business dealings and still others who had lived for years with their mistresses and yet dared "to go from the arms of Venus to the altar."[32] Decades later the vicar of Ciudad Real stated that in his district "many priests were to be found who were so stupified and ignorant that it was a triumph for them to understand the canon of the Mass."[33]

Serious problems in recruitment and education of the parish clergy existed, but they were by no means universal, and any explanation of them must go beyond the ignoble personal motivations that eighteenth-century critics believed were responsible for the Church's difficulties with its priests. A study of the clergy of the Toledo archdiocese (one of the largest in territory) during the last years of the Old Regime shows that the problem of negligent parish priests was closely linked to the imbalanced financial and administrative structure of the Church, even at the diocesan level. The flow of ecclesiastical income from the countryside into the cities and larger towns that was characteristic of the Church as a whole also occurred in Toledo. The best-endowed parishes (a few with incomes higher than some bishoprics) were located in Madrid, Toledo, and towns where diocesan administrators had their seats. In contrast, the poorest parishes were in isolated rural districts in the Montes de Toledo, Extremadura, and La Mancha. The ecclesiastical authorities believed that 55 percent of the archdiocese's parishes lacked the minimum income (5,000 reales) judged necessary for modest sustenance of the parochial clergy.[34]

The maldistribution of parish income in the Toledo archdiocese inevitably meant that the best-qualified clergy moved into cities and towns, where they would receive a comfortable income and the possibility of further preferment. The rest of the parochial clergy were left to struggle with the inadequate revenues provided by country parishes. And it was there that the most serious abuses took place, although regional differences existed within the archdiocese. The vicars and visitors responsible for maintaining discipline among the rural clergy of Toledo thus found the parish priests of the Andalusian vicarates of Huescar and Cazorla to be among the most intractable. An inspection of the vicarates carried out early in the nineteenth century found numerous priests living with their mistresses. Others were addicted to gambling and hunting; still others engaged in contraband and business dealings. The inquiry found many priests who even refused to wear clerical dress as they performed their duties.[35]

During the second half of the eighteenth century, the State undertook several initiatives to remedy abuses and improve the quality of the parish clergy. In 1766 Charles III issued a decree designed to encourage the foundation of seminaries on a larger scale and to improve the standard of instruction in those already established.[36] Seminaries had existed since the time of the Council of Trent in some dioceses, but they operated under the control of cathedral canons, who regarded their students as sources of free labor to arrange chairs, pump organs, and otherwise assist in the liturgical services of the cathedral to which they were attached. The seminary of Cádiz even refused to admit candidates who could not sing well on the grounds that it required good voices for the cathedral choir. Moreover, these early seminaries were rent by disputes among different schools of scholastic philosophy that often made orderly instruction impossible.

Charles III attempted to reform the seminaries by converting them into quasi-universities, freeing them from the control of cathedral chapters, and eliminating contention among philosophical schools. Seminary expansion and reform were also designed to put an end to the training of priests in local Latin schools, where candidates for the priesthood received a rudimentary education that scarcely went beyond the catechism and the form of saying Mass and administering the sacraments. How many clergy entered the priesthood through Latin schools is difficult to estimate, although there are indications that the number may not have been as great as ecclesiastical critics of the time imagined. Only 18 percent of those applying for parish vacancies in Toledo, for example, lacked university degrees.[37] It is at least certain that the poorly educated clerics coming from these schools were doomed to spend their lives in impoverished country parishes.

Charles III's efforts to increase the number of seminaries were successful to the extent that ten were founded during his reign. But the reforms the State promoted failed to improve significantly the educational level of the lower clergy; most of them continued to acquire whatever knowledge they needed for their ministry in the traditional manner. Nor were the seminaries able to match the prestige of university faculties in theology and philosophy. By 1800 many seminaries were caught in serious financial difficulties and were being disrupted again by internal disputes that often led to disturbances. In Murcia, for example, clerical students rioted in 1803 against the attempt of the cathedral chapter to intervene in the seminary's affairs.

The civil and ecclesiastical authorities also attempted to raise the quality of the parish clergy through a system of competitive examinations, *los concursos de curatos*, designed to weed out clerics unsuitable for pastoral work. Developed and refined in the archdiocese of Toledo, the *concurso* system was extended to all dioceses by royal order in 1784.[38] In theory, the *concursos* were to recruit the best-qualified clergy for parish vacancies. Priests throughout the kingdom with three years' parish experience could apply, and the archdiocese sent circulars to the universities of Salamanca, Valladolid, and Alcalá de Henares hoping to attract well-educated clerics. The examinations were elaborately organized under the direction of the diocesan vicar general.

The success of the *concurso* system varied from diocese to diocese. In Toledo it functioned with limited success, but in Osma, according to a complaint of the bishop in 1790, only four of twenty-one candidates appearing for the competition were judged competent. The bishop had to appoint eight of the failed candidates, lamenting that this would be "prejudicial to the parishes which will be filled with unsuitable ministers and the entire diocese with ignorance."[39] Even in Toledo the results of the *concursos* were disappointing. A survey of the condition of the diocesan clergy near the turn of the century drew a bleak picture of "absenteeism, a lack of interest in studies, and concubinage" as well as a general failure in preaching and catechetical work.[40] The *concursos*, which in one form or another survived into the twentieth century, also encouraged ecclesiastical careerism that resulted in constant turnover of clergy hoping to move up from poor parishes to more comfortable situations. In Toledo the youngest successful candidates were given the least desirable parishes, which later would be left vacant as their priests moved up the ecclesiastical ladder, or would be held by clergymen without the ambition or education to continue their upward mobility.

The difficulties the Church experienced with some parish priests were real enough, but it would be unfair to tar the entire parochial clergy with the brush of negligence and irregular behavior. Priests in charge of impoverished rural areas far from the vigilant eye of diocesan authorities were the most likely to engage in improper activities. The geographic extent and topography of a diocese helped determine, either favorably or unfavorably, the quality of its clergy. The vast extent of the Toledo archdiocese, ranging from Old Castile to Extremadura, La Mancha, and Andalusia, presented a handful of diocesan administrators with an impossible task. Occasional inspections, such as that carried out in the remote vicarates of Andalusia, never succeeded in reforming clerical habits developed over years of isolation. Bishops of more compact dioceses with easier communications were in a better position. Bishop José Climent of Barcelona, a former parish priest himself, paid special attention to the quality of his parochial clergy through pastoral visits and supervision of the examination process. Within the modest territorial limits of his diocese he was able to maintain close contact with his priests. Although Climent held an austere view of the qualities required of a priest and quickly censured those failing to live up to their responsibilities, he believed that the vast majority of his clerics were faithfully performing their pastoral duties.[41]

It is also evident that the quality of the parish clergy in the cities and larger towns was far higher than in the countryside. The well-endowed parishes of urban centers attracted well-educated priests, many with doctorates in theology or canon law, who were aware of their obligations. Francisco Celma, doctor in theology and parish priest of Catí near Castellón for more than fifty years, provides an example. Celma enthusiastically promoted devotion to the Eucharist and the Sacred Heart, contributed actively to the town's charities, and worked to spread knowledge of doctrine among his parishioners through the publication of several popular catechisms written in Catalan. And he was by no means unusual.[42]

The civil and ecclesiastical authorities viewed the problem of the parish clergy as one of education and recruitment, hence their emphasis on seminaries, competitive examinations for parish appointments, and the periodic spiritual conferences so often con-voked by eighteenth-century bishops for their priests. But the problem had deeper roots. The parish priest stood at the bottom of an ecclesiastical ladder heavy with the wealth, prestige, culture, and education of a privileged minority.

It is difficult to establish with any precision the financial situation of the parish clergy over the kingdom as a whole. Conditions varied from region to region; they depended in part on the number of parishes in a diocese and on the size of parochial endowments. Within dioceses there also were substantial differences of income among parishes.

In some dioceses the general economic prosperity of the Church between 1750 and 1790 filtered down to the parish clergy. In the diocese of Segovia parish priests received an average of 982 reales a year in surplice fees, approximately the yearly wages of an unskilled workman, in addition to their basic source of income, the tithe. Overall, the incomes of a majority of the diocese's parochial clergy compared favorably with those of highly skilled artisans and minor royal officials in the area.[43] Over the kingdom as a whole, however, the existence of 3,000 parish vacancies, in spite of a recruiting pool of 60,000 secular priests, suggests that many parishes, particularly in poorer rural districts, could not offer sufficient financial rewards to attract clergy, even from a large body of unbeneficed churchmen desperately in need of employment.

In the minds of the civil and ecclesiastical reformers of the eighteenth century the inadequacy of the parochial organization, the alienation of parish tithes, and the financial situation of the parish clergy demanded immediate remedies. Although there were some attempts to create new and properly endowed parishes, these often foundered on opposition from within the Church itself. When the bishop of Cádiz proposed to erect six new parishes in the city, he aroused the hostility of his canons, who felt that dividing the city's one parish, located in the cathedral, threatened to diminish the chapter's influence over the local clergy. Any substantial readjustment of parish structures would have required a massive transfer of funds from bishoprics and chapters to parishes, and this the privileged elite dominating the Church would not accept. The weakness of the parish and of its clergy constituted one of the most serious inadequacies of the eighteenth-century Church.

The Religious Orders

To compensate for the deficiencies of the parochial clergy, the Church might have turned to the approximately 50,000 priests and members of the male religious orders. Distributed in 2,052 houses, according to the census of 1797, the regulars far outnumbered the secular clergy with cure of souls. But their contribution to the religious mission of the Church was uneven. Like the elite of the secular clergy, the orders preferred the cities to the countryside. The exceptions were the great monastic foundations, such as the Benedictines and Cistercians, who traditionally established their monasteries in rural areas. In Andalusia, where the large size of parishes raised an obstacle to pastoral efficiency, the cities were filled with monasteries and convents of both men and women. The regular clergy outnumbered the secular in Seville, where eighty-four monasteries and friaries occupied a more important place in the city's religious life than its thirty parishes. The orders, moreover, avoided poorer regions, which in turn had the greatest number of parish vacancies. In Galicia, where 28 percent of the parishes lacked priests in 1797, the orders composed approximately 24 percent of the total number of clergy; in Seville they represented 59 percent. The orders were poorly represented in Galicia; the Basque Provinces; and the less wealthy provinces of Old Castile, León, Burgos, and Extremadura; but they were well represented in Madrid, Córdoba, Murcia, Seville, and Granada, and along the Mediterranean littoral, especially in Catalonia and Valencia. The regular clergy suffered from the same maldistribution of personnel as its secular counterpart.

For the orders the eighteenth century was a period of stability and prosperity. The seventeenth century had seen a spectacular increase in recruitment and the proliferation of new houses; the eighteenth was an era of consolidation and material progress. A few communities, notably among the Franciscans, were so deluged by candidates for admission that the order drafted a plan to limit the number of novices in 1768.[44] The comfortable prosperity of the regulars disguised inertia, sterile routine, and a lack of intellectual and spiritual vitality. The decline was most evident in the great monasteries of the Benedictines, Cistercians, Carthusians, and Hieronymites. These houses were theoretically devoted to contemplation and prayer, but more worldly concerns consumed their energies.

The Cistercian monastery of Poblet in Catalonia provides an example of the deterioration of monastic life during the century. This foundation, possessing extensive properties and seigneurial rights in the surrounding region, spent so much time enforcing its claims on the local population through a barrage of lawsuits that at one point in the early 1770's it was nearly bankrupt because of excessive legal costs. Relations between the monastery and the residents of the neighboring town of Vimbodí, over which Poblet held jurisdiction, finally became so strained that the monks sent armed bands including lay brothers with "pistols around the waist" to threaten the villagers.[45] Nor were conditions within the monastery walls any better. After 1760 the monks divided into warring factions, which left the house in a state of undeclared civil war. Disputes arose over the election of abbots and also from periodic attempts by religious superiors to force the monks to observe the order's rules. In 1764 the monastery's reforming administration issued a decree revealing the low standard of monastic observance. It forbade monks from attending bullfights and comedies; from spending nights outside the monastery; from using silk, silver, and gold in their dress; and from entering the houses of persons "of ill repute."[46]

The state of the Carthusian monastery of Santa María de las Cuevas in Seville was no better. Its administration spent generously on ecclesiastical decoration and lavish entertainments, as in 1749 when it regaled the visiting archbishop with "splendid banquets and agreeable refreshments." The monastery suffered, too, from the curse of internal dissension, which became so severe on occasion that the monks retained a special prison for the recalcitrant. But to judge from the frequent reports of escapes, the holy jail was not effective. And like all monasteries, Santa María engaged in a perpetual round of legal jousting with the city and individuals it suspected of encroaching upon its property and rights.[47]

Monasteries contributed to the Church's pastoral mission insofar as they often held responsibility for parishes in their vicinity, but this usually meant that a monastery collected parochial tithes and paid a miserable salary to a secular clergyman serving as vicar. There were, however, some bright spots in this bleak picture. The Premonstratensian monastery of Santa María de Belpuig in Catalonia developed a flourishing intellectual life and produced a group of capable historians and archivists, such as Jaime Caresmar. The Benedictines included one of the great figures in the intellectual history of eighteenth-century Spain, Benito Feijóo, and their abbey of Silos in Old Castile imitated in a modest way the scholarly work of the French monastery Saint Maur.[48] More typical of the intellectual poverty of the monasteries was the case of Luis José de Urebal, a monk at Santa María de las Cuevas in Seville, who spent his life writing thirty-three dreary volumes on philosophy and theology that never saw the light of day. The routine, extravagance, and intellectual mediocrity of the monastic orders served the Church badly. The number of monks was not great, only 10 percent of the regular clergy, but the enormous wealth sustaining the kingdom's monasteries and their small populations added another element of imbalance to the eighteenth-century Church.

The nonmonastic orders, particularly the mendicants and the communities of canons regular—Franciscans, Dominicans, Carmelites, Trinitarians, Augustinians, and others—occupied a more important place in the Church. The Franciscans, though divided into several branches, formed the largest group within the regular clergy—over 17,000 members according to the census of 1797—far exceeding the 4,393 of the second-place Dominicans. Unlike the monastic orders, the mendicants usually established themselves in cities and towns and carried on active lives of preaching and teaching.

Yet it is difficult to assess the role of the mendicants within the Church or in the broader society. Already in the eighteenth century they were regarded with little favor and considerable hostility by the elite of the secular clergy and the royal bureaucracy. Denounced by one critic as "the Pharisees of our time," the mendicants and the canons regular seemed an excessively numerous body of clergy contributing little to the pastoral mission of the Church. Friars appeared to many as propagators of crude religious devotion bordering on superstition.[49] But this picture is too simply drawn. The mendicants esteemed education as much as the secular clergy. Every order maintained colleges and houses of study for the education of its members and of laymen as well. The Capuchins, for example, maintained arts colleges in thirty-three of thirty-nine friaries in their province of Cartagena and in twenty of their thirty-eight houses in Andalusia.[50] Moreover, the foundations maintained by the mendicants in the university towns of Salamanca, Alcalá de Henares, and Santiago de Compostela were minifaculties of theology and philosophy; their professors often competed for chairs in neighboring university faculties. A high degree of education was as indispensable for advancement in the orders as in the secular clergy. Most of the administrators (provincials) of the Franciscan province of Santiago de Compostela during the eighteenth century held doctorates in theology, philosophy, or canon law, and this was the pattern among other orders as well.[51] The intellectual quality of the elite of the mendicants and canons regular was not overpowering, but the orders produced some figures of distinction, such as the noted Augustinian historian and archivist Enrique Flórez.

The problem of the nonmonastic orders was similar to that of the secular clergy. An elite of well-educated priests monopolizing high administrative and teaching posts presided over a more numerous body of clerics, whose intellectual quality and religious commitment left much to be desired. Some clerics taught in arts colleges, novitiates, and theological and philosophical faculties; others, particularly the "apostolic missionaries," who moved through the kingdom in campaigns of popular evangelization devoted themselves to preaching. But the orders had too many members to provide full-time pastoral and educational employment for all. The Franciscan friary of Barcelona, for example, had 150 friars in residence at the end of the century; another 60 resided in two smaller houses.[52] The orders, moreover, recruited members indiscriminately from every social class. A respectable family and educational background counted a good deal in the internal careerism of the regulars, but the orders were willing to accept any reasonable candidate for admission. In 1750 the Franciscan province of Santiago observed that it had so many friars that "it did not know where to put them or to find the means to feed them."[53]

With only a minority of their members occupied completely with pastoral or educational work, the orders sustained the remainder through the liturgical ceremonies and special devotions promoted in their churches. The Augustinian community of Agreda survived by maintaining a small arts college and conducting a perpetual round of services in the town; processions and novenas succeeded one another without interruption.[54] The Capuchins everywhere promoted the cult of the Virgen de la Pastora in their churches; other orders encouraged particular devotions such as that of the Sacred Heart, which was identified with the Jesuits. Emphasis on ceremonial and devotional pursuits could not disguise the fact that the orders did not have enough to do, even though pastoral needs were near at hand. This produced an atmosphere of routine and religious formalism, as in Cádiz, where the Capuchins rang matins each morning but stayed comfortably in their beds. The provincial visitor of the Clerics Minor of Andalusia found that conditions in the houses of the order had slipped so far below a minimal standard that he forbade the clergy from coming to choir in silk hats, smoking in the house's environs, lending money to laymen, and decorating their cells with English wallpaper.[55] Some attempts were made to revive the waning fervor and austerity of the orders. Beginning in 1764 the Capuchins established a series of friaries of "common life," where the religious observed austere discipline. But such reforming movements were rare among the orders of the eighteenth-century Church.[56] In general, their members lived routine existences untouched by either great scandal or deep religious commitment.

The mendicants and canons regular suffered from the same internal dissension that made life intolerable in some of the kingdom's monasteries. Squabbling might be initiated by clerics defying their superiors, as in the case of an Oratorian priest in Granada accused by the order of spreading "hatred and rancor" in his house. Ecclesiastical politics created a more serious problem and often disturbed the tranquillity of cloisters. In 1788 the Discalced Franciscans quarreled over an attempt by the visitor, Antonio José Salinas, to appoint provincial administrators if he believed that the friars in their chapters had elected "unworthy and useless subjects" to be superiors. Throughout the eighteenth century the Franciscan province of Santiago de Compostela was troubled by bitter dissension between friars from Galicia and Castile. Similar tension in the order's province of Extremadura finally forced it to be divided in two, with the Tagus River as the demarcation line.[57] Dissension in the orders became marked as the century progressed, especially during the 1780's, when royal efforts to assert greater control over the regular clergy often began undeclared civil wars among friars of different factions.

Moved by a desire to use the ecclesiastical population to advance its social and economic policies, the enlightened State of the second half of the eighteenth century did not view the orders sympathetically. Occasional examples of opposition to the Crown's reforming policies among the regulars irritated the authorities. In 1786 in Zaragoza, the Capuchin Fray Diego de Cádiz, the most celebrated preacher of the day, set off a national uproar by denouncing the materialism of the local economic society to the Inquisition. The society, an association of notables interested in promoting economic development that had been founded with royal encouragement, immediately appealed to the highest councils of government for redress in the midst of acrimonious controversy. The orders generally pursued a more prudent course, realizing that the State was always willing and able to interfere in their affairs. The Carthusian monastery of Las Cuevas in Seville, for example, made a generous donation to the local economic society just as Fray Diego was fulminating against its counterpart in Zaragoza.

The fundamental objection of the enlightened monarchy to the regulars arose from the conviction that they were not contributing to either the spiritual or material improvement of the kingdom. The emphasis of the orders on "long prayers and the scrupulous observance of certain exterior ceremonies" led them, in the opinion of one critic, to ignore "works of piety and mercy," undertakings that would specifically contribute to material as well as spiritual progress.[58] The orders, he believed, should produce architects and engineers to build bridges and roads as well as priests and teachers.

The State, although unhappy with the orders' failure to contribute to its utilitarian program, was unable to redefine their role or to undertake the kind of reform, already advocated by some critics, that would substantially reduce the number of religious and redirect their energies into useful educational and charitable pursuits. Under Charles III the State contented itself with efforts to assert as much control as possible over the orders. In 1776 the Crown forced the appointment of a national vicar for the Franciscans to limit the authority of the order's headquarters in Rome. This measure was extended to the Trinitarians in 1782, the Carthusians in 1784, and the Augustinians in 1786. Royal authority over the regulars expanded, but it failed to bring about significant change. Increased governmental control tended to aggravate factionalism, as monks and friars fell into the habit of appealing to the Council of Castile for resolution of internal conflicts.

The kingdom's 24,000 nuns fulfilled a different role from that of their male counterparts. The vast majority of the nuns lived in contemplative communities. Although there are some examples of educational and charitable activity among orders of women, in general active work was not common. Significantly, the Sisters of Charity, an order involved in hospital and charity work, experienced the greatest difficulty establishing itself in Spain. The first community did not appear until the 1780's, and even then the order spread slowly. One reason for the lack of active communities during the Old Regime was the long monastic tradition of the women's religious orders in Spain; another reason may have been the special social function convents played in the structured society of the Old Regime. Not every convent was a refuge for genteel women who could not be supported economically in the outside world, but the activities of the contemplative orders, however harsh and austere they might have become on occasion, fit into a widespread mentality that such activities were proper for women and that employment in hospitals and orphanages—work among the lowest classes of society—was not.

The organization of the regular clergy remained unchanged during the eighteenth century with two exceptions. In 1787 the State suppressed the Order of San Antonio Abad because it lacked patients for its leper hospitals, the principal reason for its existence. More spectacular was the expulsion from Spain in 1767 of the Jesuits and the subsequent extinction of the order itself by Pope Clement XIV in 1773 at the instigation of the Spanish court.

Few orders were more closely identified with Spain than the Society of Jesus. Founded by a Spaniard, Ignatius of Loyola, and numbering prominent Spaniards among their early recruits, the Jesuits became the glory of the Counter-Reformation Church and one of Spain's most influential orders. The order's militancy, commitment, rigorous recruitment, and training program created a powerful and effective instrument for the revival of sixteenth- and seventeenth-century Catholicism. But by the eighteenth century the order had lost much of its earlier élan. The Spanish Jesuits, numbering fewer than 3,000 on the eve of the expulsion, suffered from many of the problems troubling other orders.[59] Although the educational level of its members was high, the order produced only a few figures of intellectual distinction, the historian and archivist Andrés Burriel, the Basque grammarian Manuel de Larramendi, the historian of the Jesuit missions in Paraguay Pedro Lozano, and the author of the celebrated satirical novel *Fray Gerundio*, José Francisco de Isla. Theological and philosophical studies in the order suffered from the same meaningless and trivial emphasis on disputation that characterized ecclesiastical learning elsewhere in the eighteenth-century Church.

The Jesuits, however, continued to play an important role in secondary school teaching through 117 *colegios* and two of the kingdom's most distinguished institutions of learning for the nobility: the Colegio Imperial and the Seminario de Nobles in Madrid. But the order by no means confined itself to education of the nation's elite. Along with the Capuchins, the Jesuits provided the personnel for perhaps the single most important religious initiative of the century—the vast missionary campaign that saw clerics, such as the Jesuit Pedro de Calatayud, traverse the kingdom in a determined effort to spread knowledge of religious doctrine to an illiterate and isolated rural population. The Jesuits also continued their missionary activity in the dominions of the Spanish Empire, particularly in Paraguay, where their missions among the Guaraní Indians were extraordinarily successful.

The Jesuits of eighteenth-century Spain were no longer the tough and disciplined religious shock troops of the sixteenth century, but they were influential. Through their schools they dom-

inated the intellectual formation of the nation's social elite; through
their influence at court, where the royal confessor was invariably
a Jesuit, and through their connections with prominent families,
they achieved an envied place in the ecclesiastical establishment.
But they were not popular within the Church. They shared with
the other orders a readiness to enter into combat over theological
and philosophical issues. Jesuits and Augustinians thus struggled
for nearly a century over the questions of free will and predes-
tination.[60] Clerical polemicists delighted in attacking their opponents with the vehemence formerly reserved for heretics. But
differences between the Jesuits and other orders were more than
intellectual. The orders resented the influence of the Jesuit royal
confessor over ecclesiastical politics. Father Rávago, the confessor
of Ferdinand VI, acquired extraordinary influence in the murky
world of clerical patronage and created resentment in the process.
Some Jesuits became adept intriguers in court politics during the
early 1750's with the emergence of the pro-Jesuit marqués de
Ensenada as Ferdinand VI's most important minister. Ensenada's
fall from grace in 1754 was a setback, but the king continued to
show his favor to the order.

The succession of Charles III to the Spanish throne in 1759
opened a dangerous period for the Jesuits, culminating in the
expulsion of 1767. The new monarch, though exemplary in his
personal piety, had absorbed the strong regalist traditions in vogue
in the kingdom of Naples, where he had ruled for twenty-one
years before becoming king of Spain. Charles assembled about
him ministers whose vision of a Spanish royal Church left no place
for the Jesuits. Objections to the order included an alleged attempt
to convert the Paraguay missions into Christian republics free of
royal control; its persistent opposition to one of the king's favorite
schemes—the canonization of an anti-Jesuit seventeenth-century
Mexican bishop, Palafox; its known sympathy for Ensenada's return to power; and the widespread suspicion, not entirely justified,
that it opposed the vigorous regalism of the king and his new
ministers. All these made the order the decisive religious issue of
the early 1760's.

A series of riots in Madrid beginning on Palm Sunday 1766
against a reforming minister, the marqués de Esquilache, was the
catalyst. The State accused the Jesuits of fomenting the disorders

as part of a plot to bring about ministerial change, though the causes of the disturbances are not clear even today, in spite of the attention they have received from historians. The king named a special tribunal of the Council of Castile to assess responsibility. This body, on which five bishops sat, placed the blame squarely on the Jesuits: "the riot of Madrid was certainly their work with the purpose of placing the government entirely at its disposition," said the archbishop of Burgos, Rodríguez de Arellano.[61] There was no convincing evidence behind the accusation, but regalist-minded ministers and clerics believed firmly in the theory of Jesuit conspiracy.

The Esquilache riots furnished the State with an excuse to eliminate an order that did not conform with its plans for the Spanish Church. The order's prestige and suspected political influence aroused resentment in the government and the ecclesiastical establishment. Further, the Jesuits' principal activities were not the kind of utilitarian pursuits so highly esteemed by the enlightened monarchy of Charles III. Classical education provided to a largely noble elite in the Jesuit schools seemed anachronistic to royal bureaucrats, who wished to shift the emphasis of Spanish secondary and university education to the sciences, mathematics, and economic concerns. Moreover, the Jesuits' gentler interpretation of the rigorous precepts of Catholic moral theology did not sit well with the harsh code of conduct accepted by the king, his ministers, and the anti-Jesuit faction within the Church. Accusations of laxity in resolving problems of moral theology revealed that the Jesuits were out of touch with the reforming spirit that had begun to develop in the Church after 1750. This movement, denounced as "Jansenist" by the Jesuits, received wide support among the clerical elite of Charles III's royal Church. It vigorously attempted to curb the excesses of "popular" religion and to impose on the faithful an austere, puritanical code of morality. The Jesuits' expressed opposition to the so-called Jansenists made the order appear to be an obstacle to reform in the Church.

The Jesuits' expulsion was welcomed by the hierarchy and the religious orders. Opportunism and ecclesiastical careerism undoubtedly inclined some clerics to support the State's action, but many ecclesiastics believed the Crown was contributing to the Church's welfare by expelling the Society of Jesus. Forty-two of the kingdom's bishops supported the expulsion; many published pastoral letters extolling the king's initiative. The superiors of the religious orders also welcomed the expulsion with ill-disguised satisfaction.

However, the reaction within the Church and the use to which Jesuit property and endowments were put by the State reveal that the motive of the expulsion was not antireligious. The Crown ordered that the order's houses and income be used for religious and educational purposes. The confiscation of Jesuit property allowed the State to found new seminaries for the improvement of the parish clergy, to establish new schools under religious auspices but with more advanced curricula, and to create charitable institutions under clerical direction.

The Inquisition

One institution still occupied a special place within Church and State, the Inquisition. Founded by Ferdinand and Isabella in 1478, the Council of the Supreme and General Inquisition, although established by papal decree, was in fact a royal body whose head was named by the Crown. Originally created to punish converted Jews or their descendants (*conversos*) suspected of secretly observing their old faith, the Inquisition gradually expanded its activity to include censorship and the punishment of heresy; witchcraft; sorcery; magic; superstitious practices; moral offenses, such as bigamy and homosexuality; and immorality among the clergy. The Inquisition of the late fifteenth, sixteenth, and seventeenth centuries went implacably about its work of enforcing orthodoxy and morality. With its secret procedures, its ability to confiscate the property of its victims, and its enormous jurisdictional powers over laymen and clerics alike, it could act whenever and wherever it pleased. Its celebrated sixteenth-century victims included an archbishop of Toledo and primate of Spain, Bartolomé Carranza, who stood accused of Lutheranism; and the poet, theologian, and mystic Fray Luis de León, who spent years in inquisitorial prisons before being released.

The terrible force of the Inquisition was not primarily in its ability to have its victims burned at the stake in the elaborate public ceremonies of the *autos de fe*. A recent examination of 50,000 cases between 1560 and 1700 shows that only 1 percent of those accused suffered the ultimate penalty; the incidence of execution was far higher in the Inquisition's first twenty years than at any later time.[62] Secrecy coupled with the ability to strike at any moment, confiscate the property of the condemned, and destroy a career for even minor offenses conspired to create the pervasive psychology of fear that lay behind the institution's ruthless effectiveness as a guardian of orthodoxy and morality. So successfully did the Inquisition instill fear in the population at large that the vast majority of denunciations it received came not from its agents but from relatives, friends, and acquaintances of the accused. The Inquisition did not select its victims capriciously. According to its own lights it pronounced judgment only after careful examination of the evidence. Anyone summoned before the Holy Tribunal might well have trembled with fear and terror, but it was possible to be absolved. And there were occasional examples of common sense overriding popular passions, as in Navarra in the early seventeenth century, when the Inquisition effectively ended Spain's witch craze after a searching examination into accusations produced by mass hysteria.[63]

The history of the Inquisition in the eighteenth century has not been widely studied, and for good reason. After a flurry of activity against *conversos* (often Portuguese merchants who had settled in Spain between 1720 and 1730), the cases coming before the Holy Office declined to the lowest levels in its existence. Thus, the Inquisition of Toledo (one of fourteen provincial tribunals) heard an average of 200 cases a year during the middle of the sixteenth century, 30 a year during the early seventeenth century, and only 3 or 4 a year by the end of the eighteenth.[64] Moreover, charges showed a dramatic shift away from the most serious accusations of Judaism and Protestantism toward those focusing on superstition, morality, and erroneous and heretical "propositions" that fell short of formal heresy. A survey of more than 4,000 cases taken to the Supreme Council during the eighteenth century shows that 43.5 percent dealt with "propositions" (compared with 19.4 percent in the seventeenth century) and less than 10 percent dealt with Judaism and Protestantism (compared with 48.6 percent in the preceding century.)[65] The changing pattern of accusations also corresponds with the less frequent exaction of the death penalty, which was carried out only in 1714, 1725, 1763, and 1781. The Inquisition's last victim, Dolores of Seville, provoked inquisitorial wrath because of her claim that she maintained contact with the Virgin and had released millions of souls from purgatory.

The Inquisition's reduced activity during the second half of the eighteenth century also reflected the efforts of Charles III and his enlightened ministers to impose limits on the exercise of inquisitorial authority, which on occasion seemed to threaten that of the government itself. Although a royal council, the Inquisition had acquired over time a sense of its own autonomy clearly unacceptable to a monarchy obsessed with the preservation and expansion of its own power.

In 1761 the decision of Inquisitor General Manuel Quintano Bonifaz to publish a papal bull condemning a Jansenist book without seeking prior approval from the king provoked a crisis. Charles III, irritated at seeing a work condemned that he had approved as king of Naples, exiled the inquisitor general from Madrid and allowed him to return only after exacting a statement of submission. The king followed with a decree (January 18, 1762) forbidding the publication not only of any papal bull but even of the edicts of the Inquisition until they received royal authorization. Although this measure was suspended a few months later, in 1768 the Council of Castile proposed unheard-of restrictions on the Inquisition's censoring powers and repeated the terms of the 1762 decree on the publication of its edicts. The crown attorneys (*fiscales*) who commented on the proposal affirmed the absolute right of the king "to watch over the use which the Inquisition makes of its jurisdiction, to enlighten it, to reform its abuses, to impose limitations on it and even to suppress it if this should be demanded by necessity and public utility."[66]

The audacious proposal of 1768 did not lead, however, to the severe restrictions on the Inquisition that its authors had in mind. Charles III, with his characteristic prudence, chose instead to guide the Inquisition in a more moderate direction through the appointment of inquisitors general sympathetic to the reforming spirit prevalent in the government. The king's decision to appoint Felipe Bertrán, bishop of Salamanca and a leading episcopal reformer, to be inquisitor general in 1774 opened a period of moderation, particularly in the field of censorship, that would last until

1790.[67] By the mid-1780's the Inquisition's reputation had so improved that even Joseph Townsend, the English clergyman who visited Spain during these years, could say: "I am inclined to think that in proportion as light has been diffused in Europe, even inquisitors have learnt humanity."[68]

It was, paradoxically, during Bertrán's tenure as inquisitor general that the Inquisition aroused itself from its apparent lethargy to strike a spectacular blow reminiscent of the heady days of old. The arrest in 1776, trial, and subsequent condemnation of a prominent royal official, Pablo de Olavide, on a charge of formal heresy shocked enlightened circles in Spain and Europe. That the former royal governor of the extensive province of Seville and superintendent of one of the king's favorite schemes (the creation of new settlements in the Sierra Morena) should disappear into the prisons of the Inquisition for two years without a trace and should then appear in the peaked cap and smock of the condemned to hear himself sentenced to eight years of confinement to a monastery and the confiscation of his property seemed to herald the beginning of a new age of inquisitorial fanaticism.

Sensational as it was, however, the case did not lead to a general campaign of persecution against the enlightened circles of government and society with whom Olavide was identified. But it did reveal that the Inquisition was still capable of baring its teeth. The charge of formal heresy against Olavide rested on a series of dubious accusations levied by the numerous enemies he had made during his tenure in Seville (1769–1776). Although Olavide was personally devout (witnesses testified that he knelt in prayer beside his bed each night before retiring), he disliked the extravagant and superstitious practices he believed were characteristic of Spanish Catholicism. And, what was more dangerous, he did not shirk from expressing these objections publicly. "Gentlemen," he once told a gathering of local noblemen about to spend a vast sum to decorate a shrine, "you would do far better assisting your neighbor to use this money to develop agriculture and increase the value of your properties and thus give sustenance to the poor who are perishing, that would be good devotion."[69] Olavide's view of religion—that it should emphasize interior spiritual development rather than external ceremony—was not significantly different from that expressed by so-called "enlightened" Catholics elsewhere in Europe and within Spain itself. But to express such views in an urban society dominated by a conservative clergy and nobility invited trouble. Olavide, moreover, alienated the local oligarchy by introducing reforms that sought to eliminate the corrupt deals made possible through its control of municipal government. Olavide's most redoubtable enemy, however, proved to be the superior of the Capuchin friars, who had been brought in to provide religious services to the new towns of the Sierra Morena. The governor's efforts to prevent the friars from introducing what he believed to be the worst excesses of popular piety led in the end to the denunciation that destroyed him.

Given the importance of the accused, the Supreme Council of the Inquisition quickly assumed jurisdiction over the case. Because little is known of the discussions in the council, it is difficult to establish whether its professional inquisitors saw the process against Olavide as the symbolic weapon that would allow the institution to recover its old free-wheeling autonomy at a stroke. But the case could not have proceeded without the support of the inquisitor general, a churchman known for his moderate views, and the authorization of Charles III, who was kept fully informed at every stage. Whether Bertrán endorsed prosecution of Olavide out of conviction or timidity before the pressure of his fellow councillors is unclear.[70] It is equally uncertain whether the king allowed the case to continue because his own deeply held piety took offense at the charges against Olavide or because he dared not halt a process into which the Inquisition threw all its energy. But if the Inquisition believed that its spectacular initiative would substantially alter the royal policy designed to curb its excesses, it was mistaken. Until the end of his reign Charles III continued his policy of controlling the Inquisition through the appointment of moderate, reform-minded ecclesiastics to the post of inquisitor general.

If the Inquisition failed to capitalize on the Olavide affair as it had hoped, neither did it face extinction. Cautious to a fault, Charles III never seriously considered suppression. The historic relationship between the Crown and the Inquisition, which for centuries contributed to the latter's power, was weakened during

Charles's rule. However, following the king's death in 1788 and
the outbreak of revolution in France during the summer of 1789,
the old relationship was reestablished, albeit incompletely and in
somewhat different form.

The ministers of Charles IV (1788–1808), particularly the conde
de Floridablanca, believed that the French Revolution threatened
the survival of absolute monarchy in Spain. Measures were taken
to isolate the kingdom from the contagion of revolutionary ideas.
The censoring powers of the Inquisition (to which royal officials
had often objected in the past) offered the government a useful
tool in the effort to keep the nation free of subversive opinion.
In 1789 the Spanish ambassador to France advised Floridablanca
that "a secret agreement between the Court and the Inquisition
would be the best way of rooting out this evil."[71] In 1792 the
government and the inquisitor general worked out an arrangement designed not merely to censor suspected works but to exclude them entirely from the country through rigorous inspection
at the frontiers and confiscation of books that had already made
their way into the peninsula. The Inquisition threw itself into the
task with unaccustomed fervor. Of all the condemnations of French
books between 1747 and 1807, fully one-half fell in the fifteen
years after the outbreak of the French Revolution. The Inquisition
had always condemned books judged dangerous to faith and mor-
als, but its censoring role took on a more immediately political
purpose as it sought, according to the inquisitor general, to remove "the difficulties which could result from the introduction of
seditious books and papers."[72]

The revived alliance between an absolute monarchy concerned
with its survival and the Inquisition did not mean that the latter
abandoned its traditional preoccupation with questions of doctrine and morality, nor did it mean that the State gave the Inquisition a blank check to do as it wished. The tension characterizing
relations between the government and the Holy Tribunal in the
reign of Charles III did not disappear. By the end of the 1790's
influential ministers were advocating outright suppression as a
result of new conflicts with the Inquisition. But by then the economic and political difficulties of the monarchy prevented decisive
action. The ambiguous relationship between the Crown and the

Inquisition would continue until the end of the Old Regime, because each institution believed that it needed the support of the
other.

After the skirmishing of the 1760's, the organization, personnel,
and institutions of the Caroline Church followed the road that
the king and his ministers had marked for it. The weaknesses
inherent in the structure of the eighteenth-century Church were
disguised by the reforming ecclesiastical policies of the Crown.
An ineffectual papacy offered no serious opposition to the State's
direction of the Church, and a carefully selected hierarchy accepted, sometimes quietly, sometimes enthusiastically, its assigned
role. The Church, in its relations with the Crown and in its internal
life, achieved an equilibrium of sorts. The period 1750–1790 was
one of prosperity, stability, and general calm for the ecclesiastical
establishment. But in the end the equilibrium of the Caroline
Church proved no firmer than that of absolute monarchy.

2 / Prosperity and Religion, 1750–1790

In the four decades after 1750 the Spanish Church enjoyed for the last time a flourishing material prosperity built upon its centuries-old accumulation of resources. As the wealthiest single institution in the kingdom, the Church received the immense revenues necessary to maintain a public cult of extraordinary variety and splendor and to play a comprehensive social role in an agrarian society dominated by ecclesiastical and noble privilege. The end of that society was not far off, and with its disintegration the Church found itself deprived for the first time in centuries of the economic base that had sustained it as one of the nation's fundamental social and religious institutions.

Wealth

The complex organization of the eighteenth-century Church rested on solid economic foundations. Through legacies, donations, and purchase it had acquired over time the land and agricultural income necessary for the prosperity of any institution, secular or religious, within a predominantly agrarian society. The variety of the Church's resources, the complexities of land tenure in the Old Regime, and the drain on ecclesiastical funds created by fiscal obligations toward the State make an accurate assessment of the extent of clerical wealth difficult. There are, however, partial indications of the immense weight of the Church in the Spanish economy of the time. The only cadastral survey of the period, carried out in 1749 at the order of the marqués de Ensenada, provides information on the extent of clerical wealth in the twenty-two provinces of Castile.[1] The figures provided are, of course, approximate given the extraordinary difficulty of gathering the data, but they show beyond any doubt that the Church was one of the kingdom's most powerful economic institutions.

Ownership of land provided the foundation of ecclesiastical wealth. The Church possessed nearly 15 percent of the property in the provinces surveyed, although there were significant regional variations (Table 1). The proportion of land owned by clerical institutions ranged from a low of 5 percent in Galicia to a high of 27 percent in Zamora. The presence of the Church as landowner was strongest south of the Guadarrama Mountains, and in Salamanca, Palencia, and Zamora in the north. In the provinces of Toledo, La Mancha, Extremadura, and Seville the Church possessed at least 20 percent of the land. In the provinces of Old Castile and León its share of land was somewhat less but still

Table 1. Ecclesiastical land holdings in the provinces of Castile, 1749.

Province	Ecclesiastical Land Holdings (percent)
Ávila	19.8
Burgos	16.7
Córdoba	20.0
Cuenca	10.0
Extremadura	21.0
Galicia	5.1
Granada	17.2
Guadalajara	13.0
Jaén	15.5
La Mancha	27.2
León	12.5
Madrid (less city)	17.6
Murcia	12.3
Palencia	20.2
Salamanca	26.5
Segovia	13.1
Seville	20.0
Soria	9.4
Toledo	20.2
Toro	18.7
Valladolid	19.1
Zamora	27.3

Source: "Resumen general de tierras, población, ganados y colmenas de León y Castilla a mediados del siglo XVIII, según las averiguaciones realizadas para el establecimiento de la única contribución," in Antonio Matilla Tascón, *La única contribución y el Catastro de Ensenada* (Madrid, 1947), appendix 34.

substantial, with the exception of Soria, where its holdings were
less than 10 percent.

The extent of ecclesiastical land holding, however, tells only
part of the story. The share of agricultural wealth the Church
derived from its property was significantly higher than the proportion of land it owned. Thus, in Córdoba, where ecclesiastical
institutions owned 20 percent of the land, the Church received
nearly 30 percent of the agricultural income. This pattern prevailed in the other provinces as well, with the exception of Galicia,
where the share of agricultural income received by the clergy was
only marginally higher than the extent of its property. The higher
profitability of ecclesiastical holdings reflected their superior quality, as in Córdoba, where Church lands were concentrated in the
fertile areas bordering the Guadalquivir River rather than in the
poorer hill districts.

Income from agricultural property furnished the Church with
its largest single source of revenue (Table 2). Ecclesiastical insti-

Table 2. Principal sources of annual income (secular and ecclesiastical) in Castile,
1749 (in reales).

Source of Income	Ecclesiastical	Secular	Total	Percentage Ecclesiastical
Agricultural holdings	259,654,410	816,666,797	1,076,321,207	24.10
Tithes, urban property, etc.	136,419,500	169,958,177	306,377,677	44.50
Loans (censos)	26,852,134	11,446,924	38,299,058	70.10
Industry	9,858,758	475,368,519	485,227,277	0.02
Livestock	21,934,599	197,922,217	219,856,816	9.90
Total	454,719,401	1,671,362,634	2,126,082,035	21.40

Source: "Resumen general de tierras, población, ganados y colmenas de León
y Castilla a mediados del siglo XVIII, según las averiguaciones realizadas para
el establecimiento de la única contribución," in Antonio Matilla Tascón, La única
contribución y el Catastro de Ensenada (Madrid, 1947), 535–43. The ecclesiastical
figures include both the income of church institutions and that from the clergy's
personal property. The latter forms approximately 15 percent of the clerical
total.

tutions received nearly one-quarter of Castile's annual income from the agrarian sector of the economy. In addition, the Church received nearly one-half of the income generated by tithe payments, certain dues, and the rents produced by urban property. And clerical institutions held a quasi-monopoly over a kind of mortgage loan (*censo*) that was the single most important credit instrument for the upper classes. The Church also profited from the ownership of 2,725,842 head of grazing stock. Only in the area of manufacturing and artisan income did its share decline to insignificant proportions. The Church, then, received just over one-fifth of all the income produced by the leading sectors of the economy, according to the Ensenada survey. It enjoyed other sources of income as well, such as the stipends paid for funerals, marriages, and baptisms. In a detailed study of the eighteenth-century economy, Gonzalo Anes estimated that the total income of the Church in Castile may have reached the substantial proportion of nearly 28 percent of the gross income of all economic sectors.[2]

Not all these funds remained in the coffers of ecclesiastical institutions; the Church paid dearly for its privileged relationship with the State. The king had the right to claim part of the income of benefices falling under royal patronage through a variety of special levies, such as the *mesada* and the *media annata*, and he received the income from all benefices left vacant by the death or transfer of the incumbent (*espolios y vacantes*). Other royal imposts on the Church (the *excusado* and *subsidio*) augmented the State's treasury, as did the Crown's right to receive two-ninths of the amount collected from tithe payments. The tithe was further diminished in certain regions, such as Galicia, by the claims of secular patrons of parish churches. And there were other encumbrances on ecclesiastical income. Clerical institutions often paid pensions to fulfill the terms of wills leaving property to the Church, and they frequently had to pay the interest on loans assumed to finance building and decoration. It is not possible to estimate with precision the amount lost through these obligations. But what remained provided a generous income.

The eighteenth-century Church was urban, but the source of its wealth lay in the countryside. Ecclesiastical institutions possessed the kingdom's best land, whether in the fertile Campiña of

Andalusia or in the productive cereal lands around Estella and Tafalla in distant Navarra. Religious institutions, however, placed only a small proportion of their property under direct cultivation. In the diocese of Segovia, for example, the Church cultivated only 26 percent of its land directly; the remainder it leased to private individuals under a variety of rental arrangements.[3] Some cultivation was carried on by monasteries and convents, which were often models of efficient agricultural management. Laborde thus admired the fields worked by the Carthusian monks of La Concepción near Zaragoza, where "the most attentive cultivation assists its various products."[4] More impressive still were the gardens of the Carmelites of Ugarte in Vizcaya, where the friars reclaimed saline marshlands and planted 6,000 fruit trees deemed so precious that a unanimous vote of the community was required to cut a single one.[5]

The land of the Church, whether tilled directly or rented, did not take the form of large estates, even in Andalusia, the region of the great latifundia. Institutions rented out their property as they received it, whether through purchase or donation—hence the fragmented character of Church property throughout the kingdom. Only 59 of the 107 religious communities possessing land in the province of Seville had more than 200 hectares. The secular and regular clergy between them possessed more than 5,000 separate pieces of rural property, which were rented in turn to small tenants. Nearly 64 percent of those leasing Church land in the region rented plots of less than 15 hectares, though there were a few larger holdings of 125 hectares or more.[6] This pattern of distribution also prevailed elsewhere. The richest friary in Toledo, the Dominican house of San Pedro Martir, received its income from numerous small farms rented out in the surrounding countryside.[7] Though chapters and monasteries tried to squeeze as much as possible from their property, the scattered nature of individual institutions' holdings prevented the Church from taking full advantage of its landed wealth. Institutions maintained a small army of administrators, lawyers, and rent collectors to keep their numerous tenants in line, but economies of scale were not possible.

Religious institutions also possessed real estate in urban areas. In cities where the Church dominated economic life, these holdings could reach impressive proportions, as in Toledo, where the cathedral chapter, monasteries, and convents controlled more than half the city's building stock.[8] The proportion was not as high in larger towns, but it was still substantial. In Madrid the Hermandad del Refugio, the capital's most important charitable organization operating under religious auspices, financed its activity from the rents paid by tenants in the forty buildings it owned in the city. But urban real estate was less lucrative than rural property. The necessity of making costly repairs to shoddily constructed buildings as well as the obligation of royal taxes on city property reduced the return on investment to a modest 1–2 percent.[9] Few ecclesiastical institutions were willing to pour money into the improvement of their urban real estate. The return was too low, and it was next to impossible to evict tenants who fell behind in their rents. Religious institutions served, indeed, as eighteenth-century versions of modern slum landlords. The houses they possessed in Madrid late in the century, four- and five-story tenements in poor condition, were let out at low rents to servants, washerwomen, small tradesmen, and unskilled artisans. The return on another important source of Church income, the interest on loans (*censos*) made to individuals and institutions who could offer suitable collateral, was also modest, from 2.5 to 3.0 percent during the late eighteenth century.

Revenues produced by real estate, the tithe, *censos*, and other sources can be classified as Church income, but this simply means the accumulated income of a multitude of ecclesiastical institutions—bishoprics, monasteries, convents, and charitable and pious associations. Clerical wealth was fragmented in its origins and its distribution. The income of the kingdom's bishops at the end of the Old Regime thus ranged from the 34,534 reales received annually by the prelate of Ibiza to the 3,550,874 reales of the archbishop of Toledo. The distribution of episcopal revenues reveals the disparities of income not only over the nation as a whole but within its ecclesiastical provinces (Map 1). The archbishop of Santiago's revenues of 1,527,176 reales made him one of the wealthiest prelates of the Spanish Church; his neighbor in Tuy, with 97,343 reales, was one of the poorest. With the exception of the dioceses of Coria in Extremadura, Guadix in Andalusia, and Segorbe in the Levante, the poorest sees were concentrated in Galicia

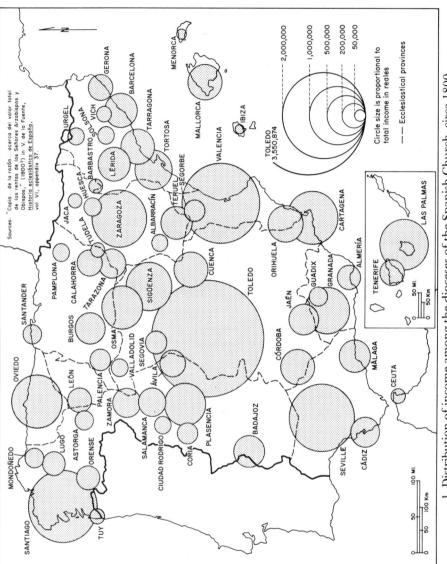

1. Distribution of income among the dioceses of the Spanish Church, circa 1800.

(save for Santiago), Aragón (save for Zaragoza), and rural Catalonia. In coastal Catalonia, southern Old Castile, New Castile,
Andalusia, and the Levante the bishops enjoyed comfortable incomes; the wealthiest were the archbishops of Toledo, Seville, and
Valencia.

In spite of the imbalanced distribution of resources, the drain
on ecclesiastical income created by financial obligations, and the
problems arising from the fragmented character of religious property, there is no doubt that the Church was wealthy and that it
maintained its economic position as the century progressed. A
steady rise in agricultural prices, especially of wheat and other
grains, in the years after 1750 benefited those owning property
and receiving payments in kind. Christian Hermann's study of
the income of episcopal households in the Kingdom of Castile
shows that their revenues, derived largely from payments made
in grain, approximately doubled between the 1730's and the 1780's
(Table 3). The growth of income was less spectacular in the dioceses
of the Crown of Aragón, save for the bishopric of Barcelona,
which saw its revenues increase more than twofold between 1765
and 1738.[10] The strong inflationary pressures of the later eighteenth century diminished the real value of these increases, but,

Table 3. Index of revenues of episcopal households by diocese, 1729–1793 (base
= 1).

Diocese	1729–1758	1777–1793
Toledo	1.18	—
Seville	1.35	2.66
Santiago	1.37	2.85
Málaga	1.38	2.75
Cuenca	1.15	2.15
Sigüenza	1.04	—
Granada	1.20	2.26
Córdoba	1.19	2.07
Cartagena	1.64	3.04
Jaén	0.89	1.90

Source: Christian Hermann, "Les revenus des évêques espagnols au dix-huitème
siècle (1650–1830)," Mélanges de la Casa de Velázquez, 10 (1974), 188.

as an institution receiving large payments in the form of agricultural products, the Church clearly held its own in a time of rapid inflation.

Ecclesiastical institutions did not neglect the opportunities for profit produced by the rising demand for agricultural products. Numerous complaints came before the Council of Castile beginning in the 1760's from tenants of cathedral chapters who suddenly found their rents doubled and tripled. There is evidence that some chapters were not above using their control over grain stocks accumulated through the tithe to create artificial shortages and drive up prices. In 1754 the chapter of Toledo, the wealthiest in the kingdom, deliberately maintained the price of bread at a high level even though it held grain supplies that could have lowered the cost for the local population.[11] Moreover, the pressure some ecclesiastical institutions exerted on the peasantry through high prices for agricultural products was in addition to the tithe.

Analysis of Church income according to the Ensenada survey in terms of the per capita contribution of the population shows that every resident of the twenty-two provinces of Castile paid— albeit in theory—more than 90,000 reales a year to ecclesiastical institutions. There were some regional variations, but the differences among the provinces were not extreme. Only Galicia, with an average annual payment per capita of 17,000 reales, fell significantly outside the pattern. The economic weight of the Church bore down on the population of the Kingdom of Castile with relentless uniformity.

Consumption and Charity

The disproportionate share of the national income received by ecclesiastical institutions allowed the eighteenth-century Church the luxury of sustaining its archaic organization. In spite of the limited religious knowledge of much of the urban and rural population, no thought was given to efficient use of resources for pastoral needs. Apart from the funds used for physical sustenance of the clergy, religious institutions spent heavily on building, decoration, and what was euphemistically called the "splendor of the cult."

The eighteenth century witnessed an orgy of construction by

the secular and regular clergy. Some were massive projects, such as the great Baroque facade of the basilica of Santiago de Compostela, built between 1738 and 1747, and the cathedral of Cádiz, begun in 1722. Wealthy monasteries engaged in a round of new construction or reconstruction of old facilities. The Benedictines of Silos spent a fortune between 1751 and 1792 constructing a new church to replace the Romanesque edifice that had served them for centuries. The Carthusians of Santa María de las Cuevas of Seville at midcentury engaged the most famous craftsmen of the city to cast a statue of their founder, Saint Bruno, in silver and poured thousands of reales into the purchase of vestments and other liturgical ornaments. Enough remained for the monastery to spend more than 100,000 reales in the same year on repairs to a stable, a brick kiln, and a barn for livestock. At Santiago de Compostela the cathedral chapter let out a three-year contract to a local silversmith for a hundred candelabra. Chapters, especially in the wealthier sees, maintained large staffs for the conduct of services. The cathedral of Toledo employed 237 canons, chaplains, choristers, musicians, and vergers; its staff was second only to Saint Peter's in Rome. Even in Ávila, a relatively poor diocese, services in the cathedral were conducted by a staff of more than a hundred.

These generous expenditures made the Church one of the kingdom's most important consumers. The preindustrial character of the economy, with isolated pockets of commerce and manufacturing and an expanding population straining the productive limits of agriculture, enhanced the Church's economic role in regions and cities with many religious institutions. The constant drain of revenues from countryside to town created by its organization enhanced the eighteenth-century Church's urban nature and made ecclesiastical institutions indispensable to local economies. In the great cathedral towns of Santiago, Toledo, Tarragona, and Seville, where industrial and commercial activity was poorly developed, communities of silversmiths, roofers, carpenters, candlemakers, and musicians depended on the employment the Church provided. Ecclesiastical spending did not flow into the productive channels of an emerging capitalist economy, but it made the Church a major force in a traditional economic system that would be transformed only with the industrial revolution of the nineteenth century. The Church, moreover, obtained important social benefits from its economic function within an Old Regime society. By providing employment the Church contributed to the maintenance of social equilibrium in the cities and to the survival of its own privileged situation.

The employment provided by bishops, chapters, and monasteries could not, however, resolve a more fundamental problem—a large population living either in poverty or on its margins. Massive poverty arose from the weaknesses of an economy without sufficient agricultural and industrial productivity to provide for a constantly expanding population. Though some estimate that as much as 50 percent of the population was unable to afford food, shelter, and clothing, accurate assessment is difficult. But the poor were everywhere, and their presence in both town and country was an accepted fact of life. The archbishop of Granada on one occasion in the 1780's counted more than 5,000 paupers waiting at his palace gates for the daily distribution of alms. Joseph Townsend complained of "the multitude of beggars, infesting every street" in Málaga and the swarms of mendicants roaming Alicante in search of assistance.[12] In Burgos beggars circulating through the cathedral constantly upset the decorum of services with their loud appeals for alms.

Responsibility for poor relief fell primarily upon the Church, which accepted and fulfilled the obligation with reasonable success. Theology and tradition dictated that the Church should come to the aid of the impoverished. A vague social contract existed between the Church and the poor. The former realized that it was under "rigorous obligation," according to the archbishop of Santiago, to help the impoverished; the latter turned naturally to the Church in times of distress.[13] Moreover, the Church enjoyed surplus revenues, which made it the only social institution capable of relieving popular misery.

Churchmen did not speak of relief or public assistance; they spoke of charity—the distribution of alms to save the souls of donor and recipient alike.[14] The charity dispensed by religious institutions, however, was very different from the assistance such groups would provide later. Few religious orders worked directly in hospitals, orphanages, and asylums. Charitable activity in the modern sense was not an important concern of either the secular or regular clergy and certainly not of the orders of nuns. Hospitals and other charitable institutions operated under ecclesiastical auspices, but religious personnel rarely worked directly with the unfortunate. The charity of the Old Regime Church was more diffuse and yet more comprehensive. Bishops, cathedral chapters, monasteries, and convents distributed food, clothing, and alms—in many cases on a daily basis—to all who appeared in need.

How much the Church spent on its charitable efforts is impossible to say given the fragmented way assistance was distributed. But there are indications that during the eighteenth century the charitable expenditures of religious institutions reached an unprecedented level. The income of Madrid's most important charitable group, the Hermandad del Refugio, was six times greater in 1800 than in 1700, a significant increase, even taking into account the effect of inflation.[15] In the 1780's the bishop of Málaga spent half his annual income on the poor. And an eighteenth-century account of the charity of the archbishop of Granada declared: "besides private pensions to families and occasional relief in seasons of distress, he provides nurses in the country for 440 orphans and deserted children; he sends poor patients to the hot baths at the distance of eight leagues from Granada, where he actually maintains fourscore, and he daily distributes bread to the poor, who assemble at his doors . . . In this bounty he is imitated by forty convents at which are distributed bread and broth without discrimination to all who present themselves."[16]

Charity served an important purpose during the periodic agrarian crises, which exposed both urban and rural populations to widespread misery and hunger. In 1768–69, for example, heavy rains destroyed the harvest in Galicia and drove the price of grain to unheard-of levels; thousands of starving peasants filled Santiago de Compostela and besieged the city's civil and ecclesiastical authorities for help. A relief effort organized by Archbishop Rajoy y Losada and the cathedral chapter raised funds to buy eighteen shiploads of grain in southern France for sale at a subsidized price to the needy.[17] In Seville, during the tenure of Archbishop Delgado y Venegas (1776–1781), the diocesan authorities distributed 23,000 bushels of wheat to peasants whose crops had been ruined by hailstones.

The Church fulfilled a similar function in the towns, where no scene was more familiar than crowds of the indigent clustered around monastery and convent doors awaiting the daily ration of bread and soup. In urban areas pious associations operating under religious auspices served as primitive versions of modern social agencies. In Madrid the Hermandad de San Fernando gathered beggars from the streets and furnished them with food and lodging; the Congregation of San Felipe Neri, composed of prominent members of the nobility, sent its members to work every Sunday in the city's charity hospitals; and the Hermandad del Refugio assisted more than 5,000 people a year between 1750 and 1785 with weekly gifts of alms.[18] The Church thus provided eighteenth-century society with a critical mechanism for the preservation of social peace. The vagaries of agriculture subject to frequent natural disasters, the limitations on production imposed by the inequalities of the land tenure system, and the inadequate base of urban economies meant that unemployment, distress, and in some cases hunger were widespread at all times and massive in periods of economic dislocation. Moreover, these crises occurred with greater frequency as the century progressed.

The Church's charitable role should not be exaggerated. The assistance distributed by religious institutions was massive, but it was not well organized or particularly efficient. The fragmentation of charitable undertakings among a host of institutions prevented development of a coordinated scheme of relief for the poor. At best, the Church provided temporary assistance to the numerous victims of the agrarian economy of the Old Regime. Left by the State with the principal responsibility for poor relief, the Church was able to fulfill its charitable role effectively, even in the midst of recurring agrarian crises after 1748. It did so because rising agricultural prices paradoxically increased the numbers of those requiring assistance while endowing religious institutions with the revenues to provide that help. Ecclesiastical prosperity between 1750 and 1790 allowed the Church to fulfill the terms of its social contract with the poor. Vast sums were spent on buildings, statues, vestments, and decoration, but the Church understood that these expenditures must be accompanied by generous spending on the impoverished. The vague social contract or trade-off between the Church and the poor served the interests of the religious establishment. The charity practiced by ecclesiastical institutions buttressed the Church's popularity in an age when the social equilibrium of a traditional society was still sheltered from revolutionary attack.

The Old Regime Church contributed far less of its resources to education than to charity. A well-developed network of Church schools teaching large numbers of pupils would not appear until the mid and late nineteenth century. Local primary schools were numerous enough in the eighteenth century (more than 11,000 in 1797), but they taught few students (approximately 400,000) relative to the total population of 10 million.[19] The Church or, more precisely, the religious orders paid little attention to elementary instruction in country villages. Education in the countryside was left in the hands of ill-paid and badly trained schoolmasters, who were given a miserable wage by local authorities.[20] Instruction in the catechism figured prominently in the curriculum of primary schools, but with little effect, to judge by clerical complaints about the religious ignorance of the rural population. The urban character of the Church meant that its institutional role in education was greater in the cities and larger towns, primarily because of the instruction offered by the religious orders. Secondary education, in the sense of institutions devoted exclusively to the training of youth (in contrast to the large number of monastery schools designed to educate religious but also open to lay students), was dominated by the Jesuits until their expulsion in 1767. With more than a hundred schools, the Jesuits concentrated their efforts on the education of local elites through instruction that emphasized the Greek, Roman, and Spanish classics as well as literary and social graces. The Seminario de Nobles of Barcelona, serving the Catalan elite, maintained two dancing masters, three music teachers, and a fencing instructor in addition to an academic staff. And its students were warned that "they must not develop friendships . . . with boys of low birth."[21]

The expulsion of the Jesuits gave the State an opportunity to reform secondary education. New schools, such as the Reales Estudios de San Isidro and the Asturian Institute established by Gaspar de Jovellanos at Gijón in 1794, developed more secular and utilitarian curricula, although the teaching of religion remained an important concern. A similar reform of university education ordered by Charles III instilled new life into a curriculum previously dominated by a narrow and pedantic scholasticism. Charles III moved Spanish higher education in a more secular direction, but even the reformers regarded religious studies as necessary for the secondary school and university student. Moreover, the religious orders continued to dominate secondary education and were still represented on university faculties as the eighteenth century drew to a close.[22]

Religious Practice and Reform

The real strength of the Church lay in its spiritual hold over the population, from aristocrat to peasant. That Spain was Catholic in the eighteenth century, at least in a formal sense, seems beyond dispute. The Inquisition, performing its appointed task with methodical efficiency, had eliminated religious dissent. To the casual observer, the influence of the Church appeared to pervade every aspect of life. Peasants and city dwellers set their schedules on the tolling of church bells; religious processions filled city streets on the great festivals of the Christian year. The basic stages of human existence—birth, marriage, and death—were surrounded by sacramental ritual. Even the pattern of leisure activity was determined by more than ninety holy days, on which the population did not have to work.

Yet the religious condition of Bourbon Spain is not easily established. To assess the quality of faith among a population divided by deep economic, social, regional, and cultural differences presents serious difficulties, which students of the question have never successfully resolved. It is at least possible, thanks to the efforts of Gabriel Le Bras and other religious sociologists, to use the incidence of practice—attendance at Sunday Mass, reception of the sacraments, and so on—as an external sign of conformity to the Church's authority. What the level of observance says about the depth of religious commitment is less certain.

The few studies of this kind available for the Old Regime tend to confirm the image of a Catholic Spain at the level of practice and minimal doctrinal knowledge. A study of evangelical efforts in New Castile between 1540 and 1650 shows that the Church was remarkably successful in spreading a basic but highly limited body of religious knowledge and commitment to practice among the population as a whole.[23] Based on the responses of witnesses in inquisitorial cases who were asked if they attended Mass regularly, confessed, and knew certain prayers—such as the Our Father and the Hail Mary—the study discovered a high degree of religious ignorance in 1540; only 40 percent of those questioned could meet the minimal requirements of the Church. By the early seventeenth century this situation had changed dramatically. Nearly all those examined knew the basic prayers, attended Sunday Mass, and confessed regularly. There were, to be sure, some exceptions, generally itinerant tradesmen and artisans, and it is clear that this limited religious knowledge was based on rote learning rather than catechetical techniques concerned with the meaning of doctrine. In spite of these limitations, however, the christianization of the urban and rural populations in New Castile had made significant progress.

The limited information available for the eighteenth century suggests a continuation of this pattern. Pastoral registers recording baptisms in Bilbao between 1724 and 1734 show that the ceremony took place in the vast majority of cases on the day of birth—a clear sign of christianization according to students of religious practice. Surveys of the Easter Communion obligation in the Catalan town of Vimbodí in 1772 and in the diocese of Pamplona in 1801 again indicate that observance was virtually universal in these rural districts, and a catechetical campaign launched in the middle of the eighteenth century on Mallorca— a region known then and now for its Catholicism—shows that most of the population at least knew the Our Father, the Hail Mary, and the Ten Commandments.[24]

The limited research carried out on religious practice in the eighteenth century does not permit an accurate map of observance. It is likely that external conformity to the basic requirements of the Church was generally high, but it is not yet possible to perceive the regional and local variations that would make such a map meaningful, particularly in light of the massive nineteenth-century dechristianization in the industrial cities and the southern countryside. There were already in the eighteenth century tenuous signs of urban disaffection with the Church—an early indication of the dechristianizing process according to religious sociologists. The English traveler Joseph Townsend noted that in

the Madrid of the 1780's the resourceful were able to avoid the
Easter Communion obligation by purchasing the certificates of
compliance demanded by the ecclesiastical authorities.[25] The certificates, bearing no names or signatures, were easily obtained in
the churches, often by prostitutes, who did a brisk trade selling
them to the public.

There were also signs of decline among the pious associations
or confraternities characteristic of urban social life during the Old
Regime. In Seville, a city known for the number, wealth, and
splendor of its associations, the decline is evident after 1750. The
Confraternity of the Holy Trinity, founded in 1535, ceased participation in the great Holy Week processions for which Seville
was celebrated after 1778, and it was by no means the only example.[26] In Gerona toward the close of the century, the city authorities found so few artisan guilds willing to join religious
processions that they had to order them to appear. Even so, many
guild members fled to the countryside rather than take their traditional places in the line of march.[27] The decline of the urban
confraternity, although related to many causes—including government hostility and the deterioration of the guilds' economic
and social position—signaled, however weakly, a diminution of
religious fervor in the cities.

It would be premature to suggest that later dechristianization
in an age of rapid city expansion bore any relation to the few
signs of dissatisfaction observed at the end of the eighteenth century, but it may have had some relation to the growth of urban
anticlericalism clearly evident by the revolution of 1820. It would
also be useful to know whether the dechristianization of the Andalusian countryside in the nineteenth century emerged only as
a result of the harsh economic and social conditions prevailing
among the landless of the time, or whether it had deeper historic
roots. It is at least possible that the glaring inadequacy of parish
organization in the south prevented the kind of effective christianization that had taken root in New Castile by 1650. As late as
1958 and after two decades of intense proselytizing activity in an
age of easy communications, the Church in Franco's Spain still
found itself unable to minister to isolated villages in Andalusia,
where the clergy scarcely ever appeared.[28] The history of dechristianization in Spain, however, save for the very recent past,

has not yet been satisfactorily explored. The examination of its historic origins awaits further research.

The means the Church used to convey its message to a diverse and often unlettered population were many. There were, first of all, the official rituals marking the distinct phases of the liturgical year and the celebration of the sacraments. The "splendor of the cult" occupied a far more important place in the ceremonial life of the Church than would be thought appropriate in a later age. In wealthy cathedral towns liturgical ceremony reached heights of costly magnificence difficult to imagine today. The cathedral of Seville, for example, contained eighty-two altars on which 500 Masses were said daily. In the course of a single year the cathedral consumed 24,195 liters of wine, 10,040 liters of oil, and 11,500 kilograms of wax. Its extensive body of canons were assisted by twenty chanters, two vergers, a master of ceremonies and assistant, thirty-six choirboys, twenty-three musicians, several music directors, nineteen chaplains, and several other salaried priests for a total staff of 235.[29]

The celebrations held in the city in 1761 to mark the proclamation of Mary of the Immaculate Conception as official patroness of Spain testified to the grandeur of Baroque ritual. For three days and nights the bells of more than a hundred churches rang out at regular intervals as thousands of candles illuminated religious buildings. A great banner embroidered in gold and silver hung from the famous tower of the cathedral, the Giralda, while 4,000 candles lit its Gothic facade. On the final day the pious associations of the city, accompanied by choirs, musical bands, and hundreds of priests, moved in solemn procession through the streets carrying a statue of the Virgin with a priceless crown of gold and jewels.

The "splendor of the cult" attained its greatest magnificence in cathedrals and churches able to pay for it, which meant for all practical purposes that it was confined to the cities, although wealthy monasteries in the countryside also indulged their expensive liturgical tastes. The clergy suffered no embarrassment over conducting costly services, which were seen as eloquent testimony to God's power and majesty.

A second manifestation of urban religious sentiment used by the Church served a more didactic purpose. The processions held on certain great feast days of the liturgical year, particularly during Holy Week and on Corpus Christi, attempted to evoke intense religious feeling among participants and spectators alike through visual effect. During Holy Week, for example, statues of extraordinary realism depicting the Passion and death of Christ conveyed a message of repentance and resurrection that even the most unlettered onlooker could comprehend. The statues were carried by members of religious confraternities. Some bore heavy crosses; others, belonging to the "confraternities of blood," scourged themselves as the procession followed its route. Joseph Townsend has left a detailed description of such a procession in Barcelona during the 1780's:

The last supper of Christ with his disciples, the treachery of Judas, attended by priests, together with the guards, the flagellation, the crucifixion, the taking from the cross, the anointing of the body and the burial . . . were represented by images large as life, placed in proper order on lofty stages . . . This procession was preceded by Roman centurions clothed in their proper armour, and the soldiers of the garrison brought up the rear. The intermediate space was occupied by the groups of images above described, attended by eight hundred burgesses clothed in black buckram, with flowing trains, each carrying a flambeau in his hand. Besides these one hundred and four score penitents engaged my attention . . . These were followed by twenty others, who walked in the procession bare footed, dragging heavy chains, and bearing large crosses on their shoulders . . . immediately after them followed the sacred corpse, placed in a glass coffin, and attended by twenty-five priests. Near the body a well chosen band with hautboys, clarinets, French horns and flutes, played the softest and most solemn music.[30]

Not all processions took on this somber, penitential character. Their atmosphere varied with the feast being celebrated and often with the region. Processions marking the feast of Corpus Christi in June were marked by solemnity combined with the airs of a joyous secular festival. In Seville and Valencia the processions of the Corpus were led by papier-mâché giants dancing about the streets to the vast amusement of the populace, who coined nicknames for their favorite figures. The procession held in Valencia to celebrate the city's patron saint, Vincent Ferrer, blurred still more the distinction between the religious and the secular. Eight mobile stages, on which were presented scenes from the lives of the Virgin and the local patron, were attended by an astonishing array of picturesque figures: "two men dressed as Moorish kings, with great beards and royal crowns on their heads, carried banners, a great number of children, some dressed as shepherds, others as sailors, others in a costume which cannot be defined, shook their tambourines, dancing and leaping about, twelve men dressed in white, played the castanets . . . a great number of others, in white breeches and waistcoats with red mantles on their shoulders, masks upon their faces and long white sticks in their hands, repeatedly throwing the stick[s] into the air."[31]

The elaborate processions characteristic of urban Catholicism conveyed knowledge of the faith simply and directly to the population, and for this reason the Church valued them. But there were aspects of these manifestations of faith that did not sit well with the ecclesiastical and civil authorities. Public flagellation in the processions of Holy Week was seen as an example of excessive zeal that distracted onlookers from contemplating the sacred scenes passing before their eyes. Clerical pressure finally persuaded the State to forbid the practice in 1780, although the prohibition was often ignored. And to many churchmen the joyful character of other processions seemed to have degenerated into simple frivolity. In 1768 the bishop of Ciudad Rodrigo was so incensed by the funds a local confraternity spent on bullfights, comedies, meals, and refreshments during the feast of Corpus Christi that he called on the government to initiate a general inquiry into the condition of pious associations in the entire kingdom.[32]

The vitality of the procession as an instrument of religious instruction depended in no small measure on the participation of the numerous confraternities abounding in every Spanish city. Seville and its region contained more than a thousand, according to a survey of the early 1770's.[33] Although such pious associations were common in medieval Europe, the period of their greatest growth in Spain corresponded to the sixteenth and seventeenth centuries. Every confraternity served a religious purpose, for each took the name of the Lord, the Virgin, or a saint and conducted services in its patron's honor during the year. But there were several distinct types of associations. Some were primarily charitable institutions engaged in the distribution of poor relief; others served as mutual benefit associations providing minimal health, unemployment, and burial assistance to their members. The vast majority, however, were devotional in purpose; in simple terms this meant that the brothers gathered each year, often at a special altar in a particular church, to celebrate the feast day of their patron. Membership in the confraternities reflected the social divisions of an urban hierarchical society. The groups were open in theory to all displaying a sincere religious intent. In fact, entry into confraternities was often restricted. Thus, in Seville noblemen belonged to an association of their own, as did lawyers; artisans gathered in confraternities according to their craft. Each association also possessed a distinctive and colorful form of dress for use in public ceremonies.

In spite of their importance in urban social and religious life, the Spanish confraternities have not received the attention they deserve. There is no doubt, however, that they provided the Church with a useful means of focusing religious sentiment among the population of the cities. The pious associations were not primarily ecclesiastical institutions. Each conducted its internal affairs with considerable autonomy, subject only to occasional inspection by the civil and religious authorities. The corporate autonomy of the confraternities, particularly in financial matters, attracted the unfavorable attention of the reforming president of the Council of Castile between 1766 and 1773, the conde de Aranda. Supported by enlightened opinion at court, Aranda ordered a general inquiry into the state of pious associations because of allegations that many were wasting their funds on frivolous pursuits or costly religious services.

The brunt of Aranda's attack fell not on associations actively engaged in charitable work but on those with a primarily devotional purpose. Reports received from the kingdom's intendants confirmed the central government's view that something had to be done about the devotional associations. The intendant of Segovia reported to Madrid that in his province the officers of confraternities spent lavishly from their own pockets and often ruined themselves in the process because they wished "to outdo their predecessors in extravagance." The intendant also observed that confraternities in his region often competed with one another to see which could place the greatest number of candles on the altars of their respective patrons. This competition, he complained, resulted from "pure vanity" and cost immense sums to import wax from outside the country.[34] The offensive of the enlightened State against the confraternities did not lead to their suppression. But Aranda was close to the truth in his perception that many had strayed from their devotional origins to become little more than social clubs. The clear signs of decadence by the late eighteenth century indicated that this traditional form of religious life was gradually losing its vigor.

The eighteenth-century Church did not devote to pastoral work the resources it consumed maintaining the "splendor of the cult." Reforming bishops, such as Climent of Barcelona and Bertrán of Salamanca, exalted the parish as the fundamental institution of popular evangelization. Upon the parish priest fell the primary obligation of providing "a continuous explanation of Christian doctrine and of the maxims of the Gospel" to the faithful.[35] These high hopes could not be easily fulfilled, however. The imbalanced distribution of ecclesiastical wealth and the uneven quality of the parochial clergy raised serious obstacles to a vital parish life. Complaints of parish priests who failed to instruct their congregations even through the Sunday sermon were common. The Jesuit missionary Father Pedro de Calatayud noted that the clergy of rural parishes in the districts where he traveled "neither instructed . . . nor drew poor countrymen from their crass ignorance." Decades later the vicar of Alcaraz in the Toledo archdiocese declared that "although the number of secular priests is excessive, the Christian people do not receive the spiritual nourishment which is necessary."[36] Bishop Bertrán of Salamanca felt called upon to remind his parish priests that the obligation to provide instruction in doctrine was not simply "a work of supererogation and a simple counsel" but "a specific and important obligation."[37] Father Calatayud also attacked the assumption he declared was widespread among the parochial clergy in towns with monasteries that they had no need to preach because that task was being carried out by monks and friars.

This is not to say, though, that parish priests everywhere neglected their responsibilities. There is evidence that in dioceses where a town's parochial clergy formed communities of *cabildos parroquiales* roughly similar in structure to cathedral chapters, the degree of pastoral responsibility was considerably higher. The success of Francisco Celma, the model parish priest of Catí, arose in part from the vitality of the parochial community to which he had belonged almost since the day of his ordination.

The parish could not fulfill the important role envisaged by its promoters for the simple reason that it did not enjoy a religious monopoly, save in the smallest villages. Church law required that the faithful be baptized in their parish and that parishioners receive the obligatory Easter Communion in their local church. The bishops expected congregations to appear for the principal Sunday Mass to receive instruction through the sermon. But there was nothing to prevent the residents of a town from attending Mass at the churches and chapels of the religious orders and confraternities or, in the case of the wealthy urban elite, in the oratories established in private houses. Cardinal de Borbón of Toledo complained that the competition of the latter, where religious instruction was rarely given, seriously undermined the parish: "Oratories have been converted into parishes by the indiscreet devout. They are the cause of much Christian doctrine being ignored, for their supporters look with indifference if not with disaffection upon the parishes."[38] In a society abounding in churches, chapels, and oratories, the task of elaborating effective pastoral techniques that touched the lives of all parishioners was difficult if not impossible.

To encourage popular piety the Church also relied on a variety of religious devotions. The eighteenth century formed a transitional period in the history of devotional practice. Alongside the traditional processions and religious services of the confraternities—with their emphasis on external, collective manifestations of pious sentiment—there existed another world of devotion stressing the individual and his relationship to God. This formal piety, unlike certain religious practices that escaped clerical control, was stimulated and directed by the Church itself. The great propagators of the new devotions in Europe—notably Saint Alphonsus Liguori (1696–1787) and Saint Francis de Sales (1567–1622)—emphasized the spiritual, the personal, and the affective in their devotions. From the viewpoint of the Church these devotions, untouched by popular excesses, provided an effective technique for spreading religion among the masses without the dangers inherent in totally free expressions of personal piety.

The new devotions originated outside Spain, particularly in late-seventeenth-century France, but they soon spread to the Iberian Peninsula. The cult of the Sacred Heart, which enjoyed wide popularity in France through the efforts of Saint Francis de Sales, Saint John Eudes (1601–1680), and Saint Margaret Alacoque (1647–1690), was introduced into Spain by the Jesuit Bernardo de Hoyos in the early 1730's.[39] The new cult stressed the love of Christ for men and the necessity of personal spiritual development. It differed in many ways from the collective, community-oriented piety promoted by the traditional religious confraternities. The Jesuits made the cult of the Sacred Heart their own and worked to spread it throughout the kingdom.[40] Jesuit missionary preachers founded pious associations known as congregations in the parishes they visited. The congregations, unlike the older confraternities, devoted themselves entirely to spiritual exercises. Thus, the congregation founded in 1746 at Deva in the Basque Provinces met several times a year exclusively for devotions to improve the spiritual condition of its members.[41] Although devotion to the Sacred Heart fell under suspicion with the attack on the Jesuits in the 1760's, it received wide support from bishops during the 1740's and 1750's and became the most important new cult in the kingdom. There were others, such as that of the Virgin as Shepherdess of Souls promoted by the Capuchins, but none equaled the Sacred Heart in popularity.

The spread of the new devotions strengthened the faith among a population that at best commanded a minimal knowledge of doctrine. The Church also sought to encourage a basic knowledge of the faith through the distribution of the old but still popular catechisms of Gaspar Astete (1599) and Jerónimo Ripalda (1618). Their effectiveness was limited both by widespread illiteracy, particularly in the countryside, and by the absence of any catechetical technique save the simple memorization of questions and answers. Although some bishops introduced the more sophisticated catechism of the abbé Fleury, the Spanish Church failed to produce an effective catechetical text of its own until the mid nineteenth century.

An abundant literature devoted to more detailed exposition of doctrine and the norms of moral conduct served the kingdom's educated minority. Works such as *La familia regulada* by the Fran-

ciscan Antonio Arbiol, or the *Promptuario de la theología moral* by
the Dominican Francisco Larraga, were to be found in even the
smallest personal libraries.[42] These guides to the proper Christian
life were meant for those with a certain degree of formal education. The texts were invariably long; Arbiol wrote nearly 600
pages; Larraga outdid him with more than 700. Moreover, each
page contained appropriate scriptural citations and references to
theologians and philosophers, which only the formally educated
could comprehend. These works were not directed to the cultivation of spirituality within the great tradition of Spanish religious
writing. They were rather manuals emphasizing in a narrow, legalistic way the obligations of the Christian and the diverse means
by which he might fall from the standard demanded of him. In
a general discussion of the sacraments, for example, Larraga devoted more pages to penance (86) and matrimony (48) than to
the equally important sacraments of the Eucharist (23) and baptism (18). And for good measure he allotted nearly 200 pages to
the numerous sins that could be committed against each of the
Ten Commandments.

The norms of conduct expected of the faithful according to
this literature reflected secular as well as religious concerns. Within
the framework of an absolute monarchy and a hierarchical society
dominated by the nobility, it is not surprising that authors emphasized the obligation of submission and obedience to authority.
In his explanation of the fourth commandment Larraga stressed
that respect and obedience must be rendered not only to one's
parents but also to the ecclesiastical authorities and "to the other
superiors who govern us," from kings to teachers. This duty was
further linked to the structure of society, for each individual was
bound to observe "the obligations which correspond to his estate
and occupation."[43]

The manuals devoted considerable attention to family life. Here
too the principle of authority was rigorously upheld. Antonio
Arbiol affirmed that "Married women are subject to their
spouses . . . because the man is the head of his wife just as Christ
Our Lord is the head of his Holy Church; . . . thus, women must
be subjected to their husbands in all things."[44] Larraga observed
that the obligation of obedience to the father was so great within
a family that "the son who does not obey his father in matters

involving the government of the household and good customs commits a mortal sin."[45] On the terrain of morality the manuals took pains to underline the numerous temptations of the flesh threatening the stability of the family. This literature, however, was not exclusively concerned with questions of personal morality. The manuals invariably exhorted their readers to practice charity both to save their souls and to preserve a hierarchical society, which was thought to rest on organic links based on the mutual obligations of all its members, from king to beggar. How deeply these manuals influenced their readers is impossible to say. Their continued popularity throughout the eighteenth century does indicate that they were being read by a wide public and that they continued to be useful as a means of communicating knowledge of doctrine and the Church's teaching on moral questions.

An instrument of popular evangelization was also used by the Church with some success. Since the Council of Trent the Church throughout Europe had relied on groups of priests, drawn generally from the regular clergy, to revive religious fervor and spread knowledge of basic doctrine through the preaching of popular missions. The missions of the seventeenth and eighteenth centuries produced a number of extraordinary figures, whose instinctive grasp of mass psychology and communications techniques made them highly effective preachers. Saint Vincent de Paul (1580–1660) and Saint John Eudes in France, and Saint Alphonsus Liguori and Saint Leonard of Port Maurice (1676-1751) in Italy were among the most successful practitioners of the missionary art.[46] The Spanish Church produced no one of similar magnitude and organizational skills, but the missions of the eighteenth century allowed it to instill a measure of religious fervor in a population whose pastoral needs were often badly served.

Missionary campaigns carried on by the orders, especially the Jesuits and the Capuchins, were examples of mass evangelization that any modern preacher might envy. The missionaries, chosen for their oratorical skills, planned their activities with care and precision, first arousing local interest with placards, leaflets, and processions and then conducting the services of the mission itself. Continuing from eight to fifteen days, a successful mission produced an atmosphere of terror, fervor, and repentance that could combine into an explosive emotional mixture capable of sweeping an entire town into a wave of religious exaltation. Thus, Father Pedro de Calatayud, the most famous missionary of midcentury, placed his congregations in a receptive mood through an opening sermon on the words of the prophet Jonas, "In Forty Days Nineveh will be destroyed," as he painted a dark picture of the fate awaiting unrepentant sinners.[47] The missionaries, who regarded themselves as prophets preaching in a wilderness of moral corruption, spared their hearers nothing in their threatening sermons. The Capuchin Fray Diego de Cádiz, described by a contemporary biographer as "a prophet whose lips were purified with a burning coal," preached with such emotion against comedies in Antequera toward the end of the century that those present shouted spontaneously that they "hated them and wished to destroy them," which, indeed, they did at the close of the service by pulling the local theater to the ground.[48] The emotions aroused by Fray Diego, the most popular missionary preacher of the late eighteenth century, were so intense that he had to be protected against the zeal of his admirers, who would have pulled his clerical habit to shreds in the hope of obtaining a remembrance and future relic.

The missions were not simply occasional outbursts of religious enthusiasm. The missionaries stressed communication of the basic truths of the faith in their sermons and endeavored to establish devotions and pious associations where they preached in the hope of preserving the fervor they had aroused. The Capuchins, for example, identified with devotion to the Stations of the Cross, spread the cult throughout the kingdom; the Jesuits established congregations of the Sacred Heart during their missions. Some clerics doubted the effectiveness of the missions, and in one sense they were correct. Though carried on across the length of Spain, the missions did not bring about a religious transformation. But they may well have allowed the Church to hold its own, particularly in those areas, such as Andalusia, where parish structures were inadequate. The most significant pastoral contribution of the religious orders to the eighteenth-century Church lay in the small groups of missionary clergy who fanned out through rural Spain in these periodic evangelical campaigns. Thus, the Capuchins alone preached missions in more than a hundred villages in the archdiocese of Toledo during 1769 and 1770.[49]

Civil and ecclesiastical authorities regarded the missions as necessary for the preservation of the faith, and hence gave them moral and financial support. But the mentality of the missionaries, the emotional fervor with which they preached, and their vision of the world as a morass of moral corruption existed uneasily with the emphasis of the royal Church's elite on personal spiritual development and simple liturgical practice. The missionaries were if nothing else combative; they believed that their task, in the words of Fray Diego de Cádiz, was "to expose libertines face to face."[50] The State, moreover, found it difficult to control the preaching of the missionaries, who exercised a freedom of expression not found elsewhere in the Church. Fray Diego frequently found himself in difficulty with the authorities for sermons touching raw official nerves.[51] In Écija he upbraided a congregation of stunned municipal councillors for their corruption and neglect of the needs of the poor; his attack on the economic society of Zaragoza came perilously close to an unheard-of questioning of royal policy.

The concerns of the missionaries, fervor and repentance, were far removed from the preoccupations of many bishops with the State's projects to modernize Spain. Regarding the material world as corrupt, the missionaries essentially rejected the secular role assigned to the Church by the Bourbon monarchy. Father Pedro de Calatayud thus attacked the commercial practices of the merchant guild (*consulado*) of Bilbao, a body highly regarded by the State, reproaching it for exploiting the peasantry in a dispute that the Council of Castile finally had to resolve.[52] The missionary mentality, based on a theocratic vision of human existence, would in the end make the missions an instrument of conservative reaction to the reforms promoted by the secular authorities.

Alongside the official liturgy and clerically promoted devotions existed a variegated and luxuriant array of religious practices that largely escaped from ecclesiastical scrutiny. What has been called "popular" or, most recently, "local" religion is difficult to define within the context of formal religious belief. In a recent study William Christian argued that these relatively uncontrolled religious customs, observed by all levels of society from peasants to aristocrats in both town and country, arose from the deep need for assurance when confronted with the fragility of human exis-

tence. Death, disease, locusts, droughts, storms, and a variety of
other natural catastrophes gave to all an immediate sense of the
precariousness of the human condition and of life itself.[53] Thus
there developed a world of vows, shrines, and religious images
designed not to win the grace necessary for salvation, of which
the theologians spoke, but to protect man from earthly disaster,
bring him good fortune in this life, and secure intercessors for
the life hereafter. Religion at this level served as a protective
talisman, for it rested on a bargain or contract with God, the
Blessed Virgin, and the saints—all of whom were represented in
immediate and physical terms by sacred places, statues, and intercessory rites.

Whether "popular" or "local" religion existed as autonomously
from the official liturgy of the Church as Christian suggested is
not entirely clear. It is at least certain that during the eighteenth
century this varied and often extravagant form of religious practice persisted. The prospect or fact of natural disasters invariably
resulted in intercessory rites designed to win the support of particular saints whose efforts were thought to be efficacious in specific calamities. In 1758, when locusts and ants invaded the fields
of Andalusia, the head of Saint Gregory Ostiense, who was esteemed for protection against natural plagues, was brought to the
afflicted regions from distant Pamplona. Representatives from
country towns filled the cathedral of Seville to venerate the sacred
relic and to obtain holy water that had touched the head to sprinkle
on their fields as they returned home. Natural disasters frequently
involved the formal participation of the clergy. When the earthquake of 1755 struck Seville, thousands rushed to the streets
"pleading for confession and mercy" as the clergy organized
processions through the city to persuade the population to repent
in that dark hour which seemed to herald the end of the world.[54]
Other intercessory rites were designed to win good fortune, as in
Oviedo when thousands of peasants from the surrounding countryside filled the cathedral each year for the exposition of a holy
shroud imprinted with the image of Christ. The congregation
raised baskets filled with bread and cakes as high as possible when
the shroud was raised "in the full persuasion that these cakes, thus
exposed, would acquire virtue to cure or to alleviate all diseases."[55]

There was little liturgical purity and even less decorum in the many examples of popular piety that have come to light. In Talavera de la Reina, for example, a high Mass was sung in a local church on each of the nine days before Christmas for the town's children. They arrived "furnished with whistles . . . As soon as the Mass begins the vaulted roofs of the church resound with the strong and shrill sound of innumerable whistles; they accompany the singing of the priests with this disorderly noise at the elevation of the host, the communion and the prayers at the end of Mass."[56] Such picturesque activities received grudging tolerance from the Church. But the clergy viewed others with open hostility. The festival of Las Mondas held in Talavera after Easter evoked intense clerical opposition. In a ceremony with origins in a remote and perhaps pagan past, peasants moved through the town carrying "corn, wine, oil, fruits and flowers" and leading "lambs, sheep, asses, and hogs" into the church itself, where they were offered to the Virgin.[57] In 1802 the clergy of the town declared that they would not attend the ceremony, because in their judgment it was entirely profane and unsuitable from a religious point of view.[58] The authorities of the archdiocese of Toledo took even more vigorous action to eradicate a custom that had taken root in the town of Torrijos. At vespers on the feast of San Gil, a bull was introduced into the parish church and led to the altar as the priest intoned the Magnificat. The animal was then taken to the local hospital so patients could kiss the rope with which it had been led and benefit from its miraculous qualities.[59]

The Church had long sought to eradicate or at least control religious practices it judged superstitious. These efforts became particularly intense after 1750. Bishop Felipe Bertrán of Salamanca summed up the attitude of many of his episcopal colleagues before customs he believed were irregular and damaging to the faith. Such practices, he held, were "so opposed to the simplicity of the Gospel of Jesus Christ" that they threatened "to suffocate the seed of true and healthy doctrine."[60] Ironically, bishops such as Bertrán and Climent, esteemed for their commitment to pastoral work and numbered among the most enlightened members of the hierarchy, attacked "popular" religion most vigorously. In Barcelona Climent worked tirelessly against such practices, as did

Francisco Lorenzana in Toledo, Francisco Fabián y Fuero in Valencia, and Bertrán in Salamanca.[61] These efforts, however, did not succeed in eliminating customs that had taken deep root in patterns of local sociability. Climent's admonitions to parish priests of churches where "the most horrible abuses" were thought to be taking place reveal that the clergy was not particularly willing to reform practices that continued to enjoy wide popularity.[62]

The opposition of bishops, such as Bertrán and Climent, to "superstitious" practices was one aspect of the reforming movement that swept through the elite of the Spanish Church after 1750. The reformers were committed to a purity of belief and practice incompatible with both the extravagances of the official cult and the practices of "popular" religion. The reformers, although labeled Jansenists by their enemies and enlightened Catholics by recent historiographical admirers, did not constitute a tightly knit group committed to the realization of a specific program of change within the Church.[63] The movement rested on its supporters' perception that religious ignorance, superstition, and moral corruption made Spain Catholic in name only, and that the problems facing the Church required critical examination and rational solutions.

The intellectual origins of the reforming movement were extremely diverse, ranging from the Gallican French reformers, notably Bishop Bossuet and the abbé Claude Fleury, to the Tuscan reformers gathered around the bishop of Pistoia in the 1780's, Scipione de' Ricci. Many of the ecclesiastics identified with reform in Spain also looked back to the brilliant humanistic culture that had developed in the sixteenth century under the influence of Erasmus. The concerns of these "new humanists" of the eighteenth century were similar to those of their sixteenth-century predecessors, whose aversion to the narrow world of scholasticism and religious formalism they shared. The reforming movement in the eighteenth-century Church was, moreover, a significant intellectual phenomenon in the secular culture of the period. Figures such as Francisco Pérez Bayer, the biblical scholar; Enrique Flórez, the archivist and historian; and others testify to the solidity of its cultural foundations.

The reforming movement, although it did not rest on a co-

herent set of philosophical and theological assumptions, did attempt to study the obvious problems the Spanish Church faced
with a rational and humanistic spirit. The emphasis was not doctrinal but practical and pastoral, hence the wide differences of
opinion that often separated the reformers on specific issues. But
between 1750 and 1785 suggestions for reform in certain areas
received wide support from bishops such as Climent of Barcelona,
Bertrán of Salamanca, Lorenzana of Toledo, and Fabián y Fuero
of Valencia as well as from canons in cathedral chapters and priests
holding university chairs. Those pressing for reform formed a
minority of the clerical elite, but their education, intellectual gifts,
and religious commitment produced a vital ecclesiastical culture
that the Spanish Church would never know again.

The issues attracting the reformers' attention in the three decades after 1750 were primarily pastoral. Prelates, such as Bertrán
in Salamanca, painfully aware of the intellectual poverty of their
clergy, worked actively to promote the foundation of new seminaries and urged their priests to participate in periodic spiritual
conferences. The extravagant language and theatrical gestures
common to Spanish preaching until the middle of the century
evoked severe disapproval. The preacher holding a lantern in
front of him in a darkened church to search for lost souls, carrying
chains that he clattered to illustrate the fate of the damned, flut-
tering a white handkerchief to hold the attention of his congregation, or using elaborate language incomprehensible to most of
his hearers—all were censured by the reformers. Particularly in
the 1770's and 1780's, a reform designed to make sacred oratory
more effective through simplicity of language and gesture was
encouraged.[64]

The great enemy of the reformers was what they saw as superstition and the vast range of popular devotions, which they
believed hindered the faithful from practicing their religion with
the purity the reformers felt it merited. Through their influence
public flagellation and dancing giants in processions were forbidden, and other devotions were subjected to scrutiny. The reformers had little use for the new piety embodied in cults such as the
Sacred Heart and the Virgin as Shepherdess of Souls. After the
expulsion of the Jesuits, reforming bishops worked actively to

eliminate devotion to the Sacred Heart from their dioceses on the grounds that it detracted from the central object of liturgical devotion, the Mass.[65] The reformers also encouraged biblical study, and in 1783 the Inquisition took the unheard-of step of allowing the Bible to be read in the vernacular. This initiative led to the first complete Castilian translation of the Bible, published in Valencia between 1790 and 1793 by Father Felipe Scio. The ideal of the reforming movement was an intellectual religion in which the faithful understood the truths of the faith, practiced the liturgy with simplicity, and advanced on the road of personal spiritual perfection.

The success of ecclesiastical reform was closely tied to the support it received from the State during the reign of Charles III. A close alliance existed between reform and regalism; clerics interested in promoting change endorsed expanding royal intervention in Church affairs even at the level of discipline. Reforming ecclesiastics welcomed the expulsion of the Jesuits, the royal foundation of new seminaries, and the intervention of public authorities against the excesses of "popular" religion. Moreover, the interests of reformers and royal bureaucrats coincided on such issues as the power of the bishops in relation to the papacy and episcopal control over the religious orders. But some clerics, Bishop Climent of Barcelona, for example, feared the consequences of excessive state control. In general, however, reforming churchmen looked to the State because they perceived that it alone had the authority necessary to grapple with both Rome and deeply entrenched religious custom.

Between 1750 and 1780 the reforming movement, with its primarily pastoral and educational emphasis, received broad support from the elite of the Caroline Church. During the 1780's, however, reform began to move toward a more vigorous program, which envisaged deeper changes within the Church and a sharper challenge to papal authority on the issue of episcopal jurisdiction. The emergence of a new generation of reformers, who exemplified the vitality of ecclesiastical culture in the 1770's and 1780's, and the influence of the ambitious reforms proclaimed in Italy by the diocesan Synod of Pistoia in 1786 with the support of Bishop Ricci and the grand duke of Tuscany, opened new perspectives of change.[66] The new reformers—Archdeacon Palafox of Cuenca; Antonio Tavira, later a leading reforming bishop; Juan Antonio Llorente, canon of Valencia; and others—viewed the problems of the Church in sharper focus and pressed for change more aggressively. Their hostility to the religious orders and the Inquisition as well as their determination to reduce papal authority over the Spanish Church were viewed with sympathy by the royal bureaucracy. But by 1790 a growing number of clerics, including some of the old reformers of the 1760's and 1770's, regarded these views with increasing suspicion.

Whether in its first or second phase, the reforming movement of the second half of the eighteenth century shows that a cultural vitality closely tied to the intellectual currents of the age was present in a select minority of the ecclesiastical establishment. How deeply reform penetrated through the dense mass of ritual and popular religious practices is another question. Even the real achievements of the reformers aroused opposition within the Church. The decision to allow the reading of the Bible in the vernacular, for example, was not greeted with uniform enthusiasm by the clergy. "It is unbelievable," said Canon Joaquín Lorenzo Villanueva, one of the advocates of the reform, that such "fears and suspicions" should persist among priests who were afraid of the faithful reading the Scriptures.[67]

The reforming movement failed to produce the transformation its supporters so ardently preached. Although the post–Vatican II world might view many of the reforming initiatives of the eighteenth century with approval, the emphases on a more personal, interior religion, on knowledge of religious truth, and on the practice of a simple liturgy had little appeal to a population for whom religion meant emotion and ceremony and rested at a popular level on a mixture of faith and folk belief.

The reforming movement, moreover, emerged from a small, cultivated clerical elite that owed its very existence to the unjust and imbalanced structure of the eighteenth-century Church. The reformers advocated improving the financial lot of the lowly parish priest, and in general wished to see a reduction in the number of monks and friars, but they did not propose any fundamental restructuring of the Church to redistribute personnel and resources and allow it to fulfill its pastoral mission more effectively. The chasm between the reforming ideal and the social reality of the Church was never bridged.

The appeal of traditional forms of religious expression and the organizational weaknesses of the Church prevented the religious transformation of the kingdom. The Spanish Church arrived at the end of the reign of Charles III (1788) in the same form and with the same problems that had troubled it thirty years before. Its weaknesses—organizational, material, and pastoral—had been held in check by the quality of civil and ecclesiastical leadership and by economic circumstances, which had made the four decades after 1750 perhaps the most prosperous in the history of the Spanish Church. But in the 1790's Church and monarchy alike entered a new and dangerous phase, which over the long term would transform their places within the social and political order.

3 / The First Shocks, 1790–1814

The final decade of the eighteenth century opened a long period of institutional decline for the Spanish Church that would end in the destruction of its wealth and the constraint of its privileges. By 1840 the Church had lost much of its property and was on the verge of losing the remainder; it had seen the suppression of the male religious orders and faced a challenge to its interpretation of social standards and culture from the nineteenth-century secularizing revolution associated with the rise of liberalism. Between 1790 and 1808 the Church saw the erosion of its financial resources and its once comfortable relationship with absolute monarchy. It confronted for the first time the danger posed by revolutionary upheaval, and after 1808 it reeled under the material devastation that followed Napoleon's intervention in Spanish affairs. The convocation of Spain's first modern parliamentary assembly, which met at Cádiz between 1810 and 1813, effectively ended the absolute monarchy of the eighteenth century. The Cortes of Cádiz introduced a new political order involving limitations on royal power, the creation of parliamentary institutions, and the undermining of social privilege, which the vast majority of churchmen refused to accept. There thus began the long conflict between liberalism and the Church that characterized Spain's nineteenth-century history. The struggle was not easily resolved, for the Church emerged from the crisis that began in 1790 with a harsh and theocratic view of its role in society. This would make its task of adaptation to new social and political forces impossible over the short term and painful over the long.

The Church in Crisis, 1790–1808

The opening of the period of crisis coincided with the death of Charles III, the most successful architect of the royal Church,

in 1788 and the outbreak of the French Revolution in 1789. Both
events would alter the course of Spanish history and exercise a
profound effect on the Church's future.

The succession of Charles IV (1788–1808) did not promise
substantial changes in the enlightened absolute monarchy that had
functioned well during the preceding reign. The new king's limited intellectual abilities, indecisiveness, and preference for car-
pentry and collecting clocks over attending to the affairs of the
State were already well known. But the ministers of Charles III,
particularly the conde de Floridablanca, were kept in office, and
there was every indication that government policy would continue
on the same course. The ministerial stability so prized by Charles
III did not long survive the court intrigues and vacillating character of the new king, however. Few periods in Spain's history
demanded a higher degree of statesmanship than the two turbulent decades following the accession of Charles IV. The emergence of an aggressive France during the Revolutionary and
Napoleonic periods and a series of economic and fiscal crises, each
deeper than the preceding, would have tested the survival of the
kingdom's absolute monarchy in the best of circumstances. The
direction of the State after 1792, however, rested with a royal
favorite, a young ex-officer who had won the favor of the king
and queen. Manuel de Godoy would dominate the kingdom's
political history, except during the years 1797–1800 until 1808.
Although often ridiculed by his political opponents and blamed
for Spain's subsequent misfortunes, Godoy possessed a quick if
superficial intelligence that reflected the traditional concerns of
the eighteenth-century royal bureaucrat. His policies were not
very different from his predecessors', although his opportunism,
lack of administrative experience, and personal greed impeded
the continuation of effective reforms.

The policy of the State toward the Church appeared to follow
the pattern laid down by Charles III. But the royal Church that
fit so smoothly into the projects of enlightened absolutism began
to suffer new strains. The prudence that had allowed Charles III
to convert the Church into a useful instrument of royal policy
yielded to more direct pressures under Charles IV. Favoritism in
ecclesiastical appointments, though not lacking during the pre-

ceding reign, became widespread, as evidenced by the large number of bishops appointed from Godoy's native Extremadura and
by his open intervention on behalf of certain monks and friars
for appointment as national vicars of their orders.[1] Although Godoy
continued the practice of extending state authority over every
aspect of ecclesiastical life, it became clear that the ideal of a royal
Church took second place to manipulation designed to buttress
the favorite's personal power.

Prelates daring to question the State's expanding hold over the
Church, particularly in ecclesiastical finances, aroused a violent
reaction in Madrid. Symbolic of the changing character of the
relationship between Throne and Altar was the fate of a model
bishop of the royal Church of Charles III. Francisco Fabián y
Fuero as bishop of Puebla (Mexico) had supported the expulsion
of the Jesuits before returning to Spain as archbishop of Valencia
in 1773. Few prelates of the Caroline Church came closer to the
ideal of the cultured, public-spirited, and pastoral bishop. None
was more loyal to Charles III's design for the Church. But even
the Valencian archbishop became uneasy over the demands of
the Crown in the 1790's. An order issued in 1795 by the city's
captain general commanding a group of French Ursulines to leave
Valencia provoked an episcopal protest that prompted the wrath
of Godoy. Accused by the Council of Castile of having acted "in
direct contradiction to the orders of His Majesty," Fabián y Fuero
was forced to resign his see in the midst of a controversy that
showed how far Madrid was prepared to go to eliminate any
challenge to its authority.[2]

Prelates such as Cardinal Lorenzana of Toledo who showed
concern over the direction of state policy were eased from their
positions. Lorenzana, primate of the Spanish Church since 1772
and, like Fabián y Fuero, a model of the enlightened bishop, found
himself expendable as Queen Maria Luisa and Godoy intrigued
at court to secure the appointment to the Toledo archdiocese
of a member of the royal family, the Infante Luis de Borbón,
whose pliable character contrasted with that of the more determined incumbent. The eliminations of Fabián y Fuero and
Lorenzana did not provoke widespread opposition within the
Church, but they stimulated an undercurrent of dissatisfaction

among clerics who were growing uneasy over the degree of state control.

The aggressive ecclesiastical policies of the State after 1792 served Godoy's political interests; they also won support from influential groups in the royal bureaucracy that wished to eliminate remaining papal control over the Spanish Church and reinforce the authority of the bishops. The new regalism of the 1790's reflected the growing influence in official circles of the program of ecclesiastical reform developed at the 1786 Synod of Pistoia.

The departure of Godoy as principal minister in 1797 and the installation of the most progressive ministry of the century saw the State attempt to extend its authority over the Church.[3] The new ministry, dominated by enlightened figures such as Gaspar de Jovellanos and Mariano Luis de Urquijo, did not intend to undermine the privileged position of the Church, but it believed that in certain areas of ecclesiastical policy changes were necessary. The opposition of conservative ecclesiastics prevented the adoption of significant reforms, but the new government skirmished with the Inquisition, and in 1799 it issued a controversial decree ordering that matrimonial dispensations previously accorded by Rome should be granted by the bishops.[4] The decree, another unilateral extension of royal authority over the Church, aroused the apprehensions of leading members of the hierarchy. The archbishops of Santiago, Burgos, Tarragona, and Valencia saw the beginnings of a schism between Rome and the Spanish Church in the government's action. A few prelates, notably Bishop Tavira of Salamanca and Cardinal de Borbón of Toledo, supported the State's initiative because it reinforced the authority of the episcopacy, but others kept silent. Although the attitude of the bishops revealed divisions within the Church, for the first time in over four decades a significant minority of the hierarchy began to look to Rome as a possible counterweight to the pressures of absolute monarchy.

The equilibrium between Throne and Altar was also upset during the 1790's by the royal treasury's demands on ecclesiastical revenues. The government of Charles III had appropriated a considerable portion of clerical wealth for secular purposes, but the general prosperity of the Church after 1750 allowed ecclesiastical institutions to bear that financial burden. Although evidence suggests that revenues, particularly for institutions receiving payments in kind, rose during the last decade of the century, state financial pressure on the Church increased more rapidly.[5] The kingdom's archaic tax structure, inefficient in the best of circumstances, could not produce the funds required to support heavy military spending for the war with revolutionary France. Spain's precarious international situation in subsequent years meant a continuing drain on the treasury for military expenses and pushed the State close to bankruptcy. Moreoever, a series of agrarian crises in 1793–1794, 1797–1798, and 1803–1805 created an unfavorable economic climate.

Desperate for new sources of revenue, the State turned to a variety of expedients, including massive issuance of interest-bearing notes, the *vales reales,* and forced loans and special levies imposed on civil and ecclesiastical institutions.[6] Bishoprics, cathedral chapters, monasteries, and convents were expected to contribute generously to the royal treasury. The outbreak of war with France in 1793 set off a wave of clerical giving. Initially, ecclesiastical institutions donated generously in a burst of patriotic fervor. In 1793 the cathedral chapter of Santiago de Compostela offered Charles IV a gift of 2.5 million reales; the archbishop of Seville, Antonio Marcos de Llanos, donated 750,000 reales and promised an additional 300,000 a year for the duration of the conflict. But the war and state finances went badly, and in 1795 the royal treasury had been so reduced that the king ordered cathedral chapters throughout Spain to forward gold and silver ornaments not being used for liturgical services to the mints of Seville and Madrid.

With the coming of peace, disastrous though it was for Spain, the financial crisis eased. But it revived again in 1798, when the kingdom found itself at war with England because of the alliance with France that had been part of the 1795 settlement. Again the State turned to the Church for assistance, but ecclesiastics responded with less enthusiasm. The chapter of Santiago grumbled that "it had exhausted its possibilities" when it received the request for funds, but it raised 500,000 reales for the State and donated an additional 500,000 to the captain general of Galicia for defense

of the region against possible English attack.[7] The State also resorted to more forceful measures. A decree of 1798 ordered ecclesiastical and charitable institutions to invest certain endowments
in a redemption fund for the *vales reales* in return for 3 percent
annual interest.

The insatiable appetite of the royal treasury did not directly
threaten Church property, but conservative churchmen became
apprehensive over the State's intentions. In 1795 Gaspar de Jovellanos published, with the support of Godoy, a *Report on an
Agrarian Law* that was openly hostile to the Church's accumulation
of property through entail. Although the proposals of Jovellanos
were never put into effect, they aroused the suspicions of the
Inquisition. It was, however, the fiscal exigencies of 1798 that
forced the State into a drastic action, which—though it did not
attack ecclesiastical property—seemed to establish a dangerous
precedent. On September 15, 1798, Charles IV ordered the sale
of the property of charitable institutions, hospitals, orphanages,
and certain pious foundations at public auction. In theory, the
State did not order an expropriation; the funds realized from the
sale were to be deposited in the *vales* redemption fund in return
for annual interest. In fact, the weakness of royal finances between
1798 and 1808 meant that the interest was paid sporadically and
often not at all. The sale of charitable property moved slowly at
first, but progressed rapidly from 1805 on and reached substantial
proportions by 1808.

Implementation of the 1798 decree affected the charitable
function of the Church. The erosion of revenues and sale of the
property of institutions engaged in poor relief diminished resources just when economic difficulties increased the number of
poor requiring assistance. However, the distribution of charity
under religious auspices did not disappear; monasteries, convents,
chapters, and bishoprics continued to dispense alms, and some
charitable institutions managed to retain their property. But by
1800 the traditional system of charity was in crisis; the Church
found it more and more difficult to fulfill the terms of its social
contract with the poor. The royal Church survived intact until the
great upheaval produced by the Napoleonic intervention of 1808.
But by 1800 the State's aggressive regalism and its pressing fi-

nancial demands had already strained the once comfortable relationship between Throne and Altar.

Regalism, Revolution, and Reform, 1790–1808

The mistrust of state policy felt by some clerics was linked to the serious divisions emerging within the Church over the character and direction of the movement for ecclesiastical reform. During the 1790's the reformers, supported by elements of the state bureaucracy, began to press their demands more vigorously. Progressive clerics for the first time found themselves well placed to propagate their views and influence government policy. Figures sympathetic to the reforming cause—Juan Antonio Llorente, secretary general of the Inquisition and Bishops Antonio Tavira, Agustín Abad y Lasierra, and the latter's brother, Manuel, who was appointed inquisitor general in 1792—promoted works endorsing ecclesiastical reform. Theological and philosophical books recommended by the Synod of Pistoia found an eager audience in the universities, where antischolasticism became fashionable.[8] The reformers' intellectual offensive, however, was not matched by practical achievement. No synod similar to Pistoia was ever held in Spain, although bishops favoring reform introduced modest changes into their dioceses.

Determined opposition to the reforming movement appeared for the first time during the 1790's. Expressions of support for organizational changes within the Church, particularly those designed to improve the status of parish priests and reduce the influence of the religious orders, aroused the suspicions of some clerics, who perceived a threat to the Church in its traditional form. The religious backlash of the 1790's produced the first assault on the reforming movement, although it did not arise suddenly or inexplicably.

Martínez Albiach's study of the eighteenth-century ecclesiastical mentality has called attention to the pessimism that gripped the clergy, especially monks and friars, after 1750.[9] Both reformers and traditionalists started from the same perception—that everywhere about them existed unbelief and immorality. For both Spain seemed a more pagan than Christian nation. The reformers of the 1760's and 1770's stressed the necessity of pastoral work to reeducate Spaniards in the faith. To other clerics the task was not one of education but of rooting out vices they held responsible for the moral decay of the kingdom. The restoration of the faith through pastoral work was secondary to purging what the traditionalists called "libertinism," the indulgence of individual passions.[10] For the early generation of reformers, the seminary, the sermon, and the Scriptures were weapons in the struggle to revive the simple faith of early Christianity; but for traditionalists it was not reason that mattered but rather an emotional, spiritual awakening preached with the fire of the Old Testament prophets. Celebrated missionary preachers of the 1790's, such as Fray Diego de Cádiz, saw repentance and moral fervor as the key to a national religious revival. Many reformers attacked "libertinism" as vigorously as any missionary friar. But there was a fundamental difference. The reforming movement saw institutional reform as the only means of transforming the Church so that it might conduct its spiritual mission more effectively. For the traditionalists, on the other hand, the cause of the Church's difficulties was not the corruption of ecclesiastical institutions but the moral perversity of men.

This vague sense of impending doom grew more intense and specific after 1790. The radical course of the French Revolution, especially after the execution of Louis XVI in January 1793, appeared to many ecclesiastics as the clear sign of the triumph of libertinism abroad, which had cast down Throne and Altar, the bulwarks of a Christian society. The vengeful spirit with which preachers aroused popular emotions against the French, "impious enemies of God and country," represented a new phase of the traditionalist campaign for moral regeneration at home. The disasters visited on Spain between 1793 and 1808—military defeat, a weak and incompetent king dominated by a corrupt favorite, the round of ever more frequent food shortages culminating in the great hunger of 1803–1805, the devastating epidemics of yellow fever that swept through southern Spain in 1800—all confirmed some clerics' vision of a world threatened with destruction by an impatient deity weary of a nation's moral dissolution.

In 1800 when Fray José Arnau preached in Valencia, which was threatened by the epidemic already ravaging Cádiz, he told his congregation that the cause of their misfortunes was "the liberty in vice, the unbelief, the arrogance, the vainglory, the corruption of youth, the injustice, the intemperance and the lasciviousness" reigning in the city.[11] Arnau's appeal for moral reform led by the clergy was echoed by countless preachers during these years, and it provides one of the keys to understanding the Church's role during this period of national disintegration. Spain could be saved by purging its own corruption under the direction of the Church. This was not to be a moderate Church, but one led by priests who regarded themselves as modern prophets charged with bringing the people of God back to their senses to recreate a theocratic society in which religious and moral values were paramount. Preachers dwelt on the comparison between Spaniards and the stiff-necked people of Israel in the Old Testament: "The Lord has punished you for your sins. Oh Spain! do you not think that you are as deserving as Judea of punishment? Have you not provoked the just wrath of the Lord with your sins and crimes? This is the cause of your calamities and misfortunes."[12]

The prophetic and theocratic tone of traditionalist thought after 1793 was incompatible with the plans of the ecclesiastical reformers for a Church more rationally organized and attentive to pastoral responsibilities. For clerics opposed to change, the Church and its institutions formed the last line of defense against the forces threatening to overwhelm Christian Spain. But it was an aggressive and militant spirit, raising as its symbol the spiritual patron of Catholic Spain's long struggle against the Moors, Saint James, that inspired this view of the Church's role. The battle to save Christian Spain from what preachers called the "execrable philosophy" of the eighteenth century and from the secularism and "libertinism" propagated by the French Revolution was for many clerics a modern crusade out of which a morally regenerated Spain would emerge.

This crusade was directed not only against the enemy without but increasingly against one within the Church itself. The more radical direction of the reforming movement and the rising suspicions of conservative ecclesiastics plunged the Church into a state of civil war. The first skirmishes between reformers and traditionalists occurred with the promulgation of the papal bull *Auctorem Fidei* (1794) which condemned the propositions of the

Synod of Pistoia. The Inquisition had begun an inquiry into the orthodoxy of the Spanish version of the Synod's proceedings published in 1788, but it had taken no action and had virtually dropped its investigation during the tenure of the reforming inquisitor general Manuel Abad y Lasierra (1792–1794).[13] This changed with the appointment of Cardinal Lorenzana to the inquisitorial post in 1794. Lorenzana, in spite of his earlier sympathy for aspects of the reforming movement, was hostile to the program of Pistoia and urged the Council of Castile to approve the bull's publication. Opponents of *Auctorem Fidei*, however, enjoyed enough influence to prevent its publication in Spain until 1801. What is significant about the decade-long conflict over the bull is less the ecclesiastical and bureaucratic infighting than the fact that it moved the debate over reform to a polemical stage in which hope of compromise steadily diminished.

As controversy intensified between 1793 and 1808, it revealed the full extent of divisions within the Church. For traditionalists, the survival of a Catholic society depended on the maintenance of the institutions and privileges of the Church before the threat of internal and external enemies. For reformers, who also doubted the ability of Catholic Spain to survive, the Church needed to adjust its organization and methods to new realities. No differences of doctrine separated the opposing forces. Although the reformers adopted a more moderate attitude, for example on the question of censorship, they firmly maintained their commitment to Catholicism as the official religion of the State. It was a sign of the widening breach within the Church that the traditionalist counterattack took the form of an indictment charging the advocates of change with heresy.

In 1798 a Spanish translation of an antireform work originally published in 1789 by an Italian ex-Jesuit, Rocco Bonola appeared; his *League of Modern Theology with Modern Philosophy* provided traditionalists with the specific line of attack they would use over and over again during the next three decades. Bonola attacked what he called the "new theology" as an expression of the rational, "secular" philosophy of the eighteenth century, which was bent on the destruction of the Church and the creation of a "natural" religion based on reason. He declared that the time had come to expose "the pernicious doctrines appearing in the books of many modern theologians who are furiously combatting the Catholic Church under the specious pretext of reforming it." For Bonola, clerical advocates of reform were co-conspirators with modern "philosophers" in a subtle plot to undermine the unity and power of the Church from within.[14] The Church had allowed these corrupt theories to develop, and although Bonola did not provide a specific plan of action, his implication was clear: reform had to be eliminated if the Church was to regain the strength and discipline necessary to survive the threat to its existence.

Neither side triumphed in the continuing and increasingly bitter debate over reform before 1808. The balance of forces shifted constantly, to the reformers between 1790 and 1792, to the traditionalists between 1793 and 1795, to reform again during the progressive ministry of 1797–1800, and then in the other direction with the promulgation of *Auctorem Fidei* in 1801. Given the range of opinion in both camps, it is difficult to establish precise lines of division. The regular clergy and a majority of the hierarchy, though circumspect, were either hostile to or at least uneasy about aspects of the movement for change. Reform drew its strength less from the hierarchy—in spite of the support of several prelates, such as Bishop Tavira—than from the secondary levels of the Church's elite—cathedral canons, ecclesiastical bureaucrats, and university professors. They were the cultivated clerical intelligentsia formed at Salamanca and other universities where the ideas of Pistoia had exercised a profound intellectual effect since the mid-1780's. The mass of the secular clergy, living isolated in country parishes, scarcely participated in the struggle. Among those involved, traditionalists composed a clear majority, but the reformers enjoyed a significant advantage; their ideas on change and their acceptance of secular intervention in ecclesiastical affairs won the support, firm or weak depending on prevailing political circumstances, of the strongly regalist state administration. But neither side was able to win a total victory by the eve of Napoleon's intervention in Spanish affairs.

The civil war within the Church between 1790 and 1808, the State's aggressive regalism, financial demands on ecclesiastical institutions, and the militant and theocratic mentality encouraged by the French Revolution upset the equilibrium that Charles III had imposed on the Church. The Caroline formula, based on a high degree of state control designed to promote the enlightened objectives of absolute monarchy, proved increasingly unworkable as the kingdom entered a period of political, economic, military, and diplomatic crisis. By 1808 it was clear that many churchmen were disenchanted with the monarchy of Charles IV and the government of Godoy. There was no question of the Church assuming a direct political role because of its own divisions and the State's enormous power over ecclesiastical affairs. But simmering clerical resentment against the royal favorite and a monarchy whose fiscal demands and interference were becoming more onerous, as well as the conviction that Spain was submerged in a morass of spiritual degradation and libertinism, created a mood of frustration and suspicion that made the Caroline ideal of a pastoral and public-spirited Church impossible. For the majority of the clergy, only lightly touched by the critical introspection of the progressive elements of the ecclesiastical elite, reform receded before a deep and primitive sense that the Church was about to enter a final struggle between Christianity and irreligion.

In these circumstances there was no possibility of bringing about either ecclesiastical reform or the spiritual regeneration desired by both reformers and traditionalists. The fundamental problems of the Church grew more serious. Between 1790 and 1808, a period of rampant inflation, the economic situation of the parish clergy deteriorated significantly. The *cura* of Boceguillas in Segovia complained that parochial revenues had declined so severely between 1796 and 1805 that many parish priests of the diocese lacked the funds "either to feed or dress themselves decently."[15] The clerical elite and the regular clergy, though affected adversely by the financial demands of the State, survived with their wealth largely intact; the distance between the upper and regular clergy and parish priests widened.

The orders, in fact, experienced an increase in vocations between 1800 and 1808.[16] This was not, however, accompanied by any reform of the factionalism and lack of religious commitment characteristic of the regulars during the eighteenth century. Dissension within the orders reached epidemic proportions just before 1808. Accusations against tyrannical superiors poured into the Council of Castile from monks and friars throughout the kingdom. In 1804, for example, the Franciscans of Ledesma complained against "an inhuman and despotic" superior whose arbitrary conduct had left the friary on the verge of open revolt.[17] Godoy regarded the problem of the orders as so serious that in 1804 he secured a brief from Pius VII authorizing a general inspection of the regular clergy as a prelude to reform, but nothing was done. The Spanish Church thus arrived at the critical year of 1808 with none of its problems solved, some aggravated, and new ones created.

A New Crusade, 1808–1814

By 1808 the monarchy of Charles IV had drifted toward the final stages of disintegration. Years of economic and financial crisis, widespread dissatisfaction with the French alliance Godoy had accepted, and mounting resentment against the favorite among supporters of the heir to the throne, Ferdinand, finally produced the explosion that ended for all practical purposes the absolute monarchy of the eighteenth century. Godoy began to fear Napoleon's intentions. Although French garrisons across northern Spain were ostensibly stationed to maintain communications with the Napoleonic army fighting the English in Portugal, they were not docile guests. Godoy's suspicion of them led him to transfer the court to the royal palace at Aranjuez south of Madrid as a prelude to a further move either to southern Spain or perhaps to one of the American colonies. Seizing the opportunity created by the apprehension and confusion surrounding the court's removal, supporters of Ferdinand, whose relations with his father and Godoy had been strained for years, played on popular fears to provoke a riot. The Tumult of Aranjuez (March 17–19, 1808) brought about the fall and arrest of Godoy and forced a frightened Charles IV to abdicate in his son's favor.

The accession of Ferdinand VII was welcomed by the Church save for a few clerics, such as the archbishop of Zaragoza, Ramón de Arce, who owed his career to the favorite's influence. Throughout the kingdom the clergy held services of thanksgiving for the new monarch, while denunciations of Godoy for having "degraded and debased" Spain poured from clerical pens.[18] But national rejoicing was short-lived. Napoleon, whose troops were established in the important cities of the north and in Madrid itself, had no intention of accepting Ferdinand as king. Although the emperor did not name his brother Joseph to the Spanish throne until June 6, after compelling Charles and Ferdinand to renounce their rights, it was becoming evident that the French had arrived to stay.

Growing resentment against the presence of what was seen as an army of occupation exploded in the patriotic rising against the French in Madrid on May 2, 1808. The revolt was easily quelled, but news of it spread quickly. *Juntas de defensa* were formed in numerous cities during May and June to rule, theoretically in the name of the absent Ferdinand. Although many bishops had accepted the change of dynasty with little or no protest, the widespread nature of the rising moved the ecclesiastical establishment to active participation. Bishops served as presidents of local juntas in Cuenca, Santander, Toledo, Seville, Zamora, and other cities, while in Cádiz, Valencia, Murcia, and Huesca they attended as members.[19] In Santiago de Compostela the local junta was composed of twenty-one members, including Archbishop Rafael de Múzquiz as president, a canon of the cathedral as vice-president, and several other ecclesiastics. The archbishop donated 300,000 reales to the junta, as did prelates of many other dioceses.

Surprised by unexpected resistance, the recently installed monarchy of Joseph Napoleon seemed doomed when a French army under Dupont suffered a humiliating defeat at Bailén in Andalusia on July 19, 1808. The disaster forced the new king to abandon his capital and endangered the French presence in the Iberian Peninsula. The triumph at Bailén, however, marked the beginning of a long struggle. Napoleon himself came to Spain to command his armies, and by December the French has reoccupied Madrid. In 1809 they pushed southward in a victorious campaign that by early 1810 left only the city of Cádiz, protected by its natural site, and the Balearics, guarded by an English fleet, free of French control. Guerrilla warfare continued, however, in the occupied zone.

The 1808 Constitution of Bayonne, the fundamental document of the Bonaparte monarchy in Spain, proclaimed Catholicism as the official religion of the State. Napoleon himself appreciated the importance of not provoking the Church, at least as far as the secular clergy were concerned. The new regime hoped to establish

normal relations with the hierarchy. But bishops who had supported the rising of 1808 through pastoral letters and donations
fled their dioceses as the French armies advanced in late 1808 and
throughout 1809. Even the eighty-year-old bishop of Segovia, José
Sáenz, left his diocese in the dead of winter and crossed the snowy
Guadarrama Mountains to escape. Bishop Aguiriano of Calahorra
dressed as a simple priest fled his diocese in a region of intense
military campaigning and moved on foot over back roads toward
Murcia in the south, while Archbishop Múzquiz of Santiago and
Bishop Pedro Quevedo y Quintana of Orense abandoned their
sees in Galicia for Portugal. The steady progress of the French
advance kept the bishops on the move, although most proceeded
in the end either to Cádiz or Mallorca.

The episcopal exodus prevented normalization of the Church's
position in regions dominated by French arms, and this included
most of the kingdom by the end of 1809. The new regime tried
unsuccessfully to persuade prelates such as Quevedo y Quintana
to remain in their dioceses and then turned to the few churchmen
sympathetic to the monarchy of Joseph Napoleon. In May–June
1810 the secretary of state, Mariano Urquijo, deposed the bishops
of Osma, Calahorra, Astorga, and Toledo, who had all left their
dioceses to support the national rising. Their nominated replace-
ments included Fray Miguel de Santander, once auxiliary bishop
to Ramón de Arce in Zaragoza, for Seville; Alfonso Aguado, auxiliary bishop of Madrid, for Calahorra; and Félix Amat, one of
the most distinguished intellectual figures among clerical reformers, for Osma.

This policy, however, proved unworkable. The nominee for
Astorga declined; Amat expressed reservations about his appointment; and Fray Miguel de Santander, though willing to accept his
elevation to Seville, never occupied the diocese. The fate of Aguado,
one of the few prelates who attempted to take up his appointment,
revealed how little control the government exercised over the
Church, even in regions under its power. From his sanctuary in
the south, the deposed bishop, Aguiriano, was able to maintain
contact with his cathedral chapter through messengers. When the
new prelate arrived in Calahorra, he found a recalcitrant chapter
refusing cooperation and the financial support he needed to live
as well as popular hostility. Recognizing that his position was hope-

less, the new bishop finally abandoned the city. The government in Madrid, realizing that its policy had been a failure, revoked its episcopal nominations in the summer of 1811.[20]

Joseph Napoleon's government attempted to come to terms with the hierarchy, but its policy toward the regular clergy was openly hostile. From its early days monks and friars had taken an active part in the resistance against the French. Indeed, no group was more vehement and determined in its opposition to the new regime—hence the term *frailada*, applied by historians to the resistance of the orders. Throughout the kingdom members of the regular clergy supported the initial risings of May and June 1808. In Catalonia the Franciscans served as members of local juntas in Lérida, Reus, Tarragona, and Gerona. In La Coruña the order opened its friary to conspirators plotting against the French. In churches where the Catalan friars preached against the invaders, congregations became so aroused that they shouted: "Long live Jesus! Death to anything contrary to his Divine Love!"[21]

During the military campaigns of late 1808 and 1809 religious played a significant part as support troops and soldiers in the heroic defenses of Zaragoza and Gerona. In the siege of Gerona the Franciscans, the most numerous order in the city, assumed defense of the Merced Fort and repulsed numerous attacks. As the French armies advanced southward, members of the regular clergy joined the irregular army of guerrillas harassing French lines. In Baeza the superior of the Franciscan friary and a lecturer in theology took to the hills and commanded a unit of guerrillas; in Galicia another member of the order, "Lieutenant" Pego, won fame for his military exploits.[22] The orders also served as effective instruments of propaganda against the French. A Dominican chronicler writing shortly after the war thus recalled with satisfaction: "in the sacrament of penance and in their sermons, the friars aroused the greatest hatred against our enemies by showing that they had violated the religion of our fathers and persecuted the Church of Jesus Christ."[23]

The new regime was in any event hostile to the orders. The Spanish ministers of Joseph Napoleon, such as Urquijo, who had been a member of the reforming government of 1797–1800, shared the aversion to the regulars already widespread in official circles. As the French secured their position in 1809, the government dealt with the regular clergy. On February 11 Urquijo instructed religious superiors to dismiss all novices. On August 18 the State ordered the suppression of monasteries and friaries. In September monks and friars began to leave their houses, although some, the Benedictines of Samos and the Franciscans of El Ferrol, survived throughout the war. The suppression, however, proved counterproductive. Living in their residences, monks and friars could be controlled to a limited extent, but in the autumn of 1809 they moved through the countryside, spreading opposition to the government in towns and villages. The Franciscans of Montblanch in Catalonia, according to a contemporary account, "withdrew to the neighboring hills and fanned the flames of that holy war in the towns they passed through." They were imitated by other friars of the province ousted from their houses.[24] And the suppression aroused the regulars to new heights of fury against the French. The prior of the Carmelites in Logroño thus exhorted his friars to become "religious warriors" prepared to give up their lives "on the battlefield of a Holy Crusade."[25]

For the majority of the secular and regular clergy, the struggle against Napoleon was a sacred war, a "Holy Crusade" against an invader for whom no epithet was too harsh. Churchmen poured out a stream of violent rhetoric depicting the emperor as worse than the infidels and heretics of old. He was "the thief of Europe, the Attila of the present century, the enemy of God and of his Holy Church," "the most heretical of all heretics."[26] Spaniards taking arms in the holy cause under the banner of the Virgin of the Pillar, officially proclaimed commander in chief of the armies, were assured of a celestial reward. Preaching in Málaga at a funeral service for the dead of Bailén, a friar thus addressed the fallen: "you who have died on the field of battle have flown from there to be united to God . . . to receive the eternal prize in the home of the just." For good measure he called upon the Lord to cover "the arid bones, the corrupted cadavers of the conquerors of Marengo, Jena and Austerlitz . . . with opprobrium and ignominy."[27] Such rhetorical flights were common between 1808 and 1813 and revealed the depths of clerical hostility toward Napoleon and the Bonaparte monarchy in Spain.

In retrospect, these assaults seem excessive. Whatever the emperor's own religious convictions, he believed that the Church was

necessary in a stable social order; he had reestablished the link
between Church and State in France after the break imposed by
the Revolution. In Spain Joseph Napoleon realized the importance of winning ecclesiastical support. Even the suppression of
the regular clergy, though a radical step, was not moved by antireligious sentiment. But a realistic perception of the Napoleonic
regime's attitude toward the Church never entered the minds of
ecclesiastics, who had developed a distinct moral and philosophical
interpretation of the place of France and the French in the modern world. For many, the French Enlightenment began the process
of undermining faith, and the excesses against the Church during
the Revolution represented the triumph of corrupt philosophy
and moral license. Bishop Aguiriano of Calahorra put the issue
simply in 1809: "From France all evil, all pestilence, all ruin has
come to us. We should have no communication with that country . . . and we must eliminate the French language from our soil
and forbid its teaching."[28] Moreover, churchmen perceived Napoleon's fundamental indifference to religion and his conviction
that the individual should not be persecuted for his beliefs as long
as the interests of the State were protected. How could "the man
of all religions" be "the conservator of our religion," asked one
preacher. The Napoleonic commitment to maintain Catholicism
as the only religion in Spain was dismissed as the promise of a
"sophist imposter."[29] Preachers suggested that the new regime
would introduce religious toleration, a prospect they attacked in
no uncertain terms.

Specific grievances against the French encouraged clerical resistance, but as Martínez Albiach has shown in his brilliant study
of the ecclesiastical mentality during these years, the attitude of
many churchmen toward Spain's national crisis reflected a theological interpretation of the kingdom's history. In one sense, Napoleon was only the accidental agent of an impatient deity striking
down a people who refused to repent of their sins. "Spain is
suffering the lash of punishment because it provoked against itself
the terrible hand of God," stated a preacher in a sermon given in
the cathedral of Valencia in 1809.[30]

Long before the war clerics had believed that the nation was
sinking into moral dissolution. Refusing to heed the first signs of
divine wrath—the great epidemics of yellow fever in 1803 and

1804, which were considered the "first sparks of the consuming fire"—Spaniards had rushed on blindly until the final catastrophe, for "far from appeasing the anger of God, they acted to provoke it." But if Providence had acted to punish, it also offered the chance of repentance. "The Most High, who is the God of fury and vengeance, is reaching out anew to Spaniards to convert them," declared a preacher stressing a theme repeated over and over again in the sermons of 1809. Despite all the kingdom's trials and tribulations, the war offered an opportunity for spiritual regeneration. For many churchmen the conflict seemed a purifying instrument that opened the prospect of a new age of morality and religion linked to a glorious national revival. Preaching in Cervera in 1809 at a service for the victims of the second of May, Agustín Torres told his congregation, "Spain . . . will fix its attention on the foundations of a new order, generation and century; it will improve its laws and correct the vices which have led it to the precipice; . . . it will erect a wall of bronze against the greed, vices and perfidy of our wicked neighbour [France] and will proscribe its dress, fashions, customs and impiety . . . In the midst of most confused and terrible convulsions, a golden century of prosperity and grandeur will be born. May God finish this great work."

Ideas on sin and repentance, and spiritual and national renovation inspired the extravagant and violent rhetoric against Napoleon and the Bonaparte monarchy in Spain. Many churchmen were convinced that Joseph Napoleon and the French army had to be driven out if the religious and national "revolution" they preached was to succeed. Clerics were vague about the specific content of the revolution, but they saw the Church as the directing force in a great national transformation. Customs were to be reformed, moral corruption extirpated, philosophical dissent suppressed, and religious values exalted. Society was to be transformed along theocratic lines so that a repentant nation might fulfill its destiny as the "chosen people" of the New Testament.

Theocracy and Liberalism, 1810–1813

Realization of this emotional and messianic vision was not to be easy. Political circumstances in unoccupied Spain during 1808 and 1809, particularly the weakness of the Junta Central as a national government, resulted in the convocation in 1809 of Spain's traditional but long dormant parliamentary assembly, the Cortes. The election of a Cortes to save the nation from the disasters multiplying on all sides initially won support even from those committed to the survival of the traditional monarchy. Responses of ecclesiastical notables to a questionnaire dispatched to the kingdom's civil and religious elite in 1809 revealed strong support for the summoning of a Cortes. The clerics felt it would prevent what they considered abuses committed by absolute monarchy under the influence of Godoy. The bishop of Orihuela stressed the necessity of imposing restraints on capricious and arbitrary government through a Cortes in which "all the deputies should possess entire liberty to speak and petition the King not only with respect to . . . the reforms necessary in their respective provinces . . . but also in that which touches upon . . . the Government of the King and his Ministers."[31]

The ecclesiastical responses also show that the Church expected the reformed monarchy to free it from the regalist controls imposed by successive Bourbon monarchs—controls that had reduced the bishops to being "deaf and dumb dogs" according to the prelate of Orihuela.[32] Bishops and cathedral chapters also expressed resentment at the disamortizing legislation of Charles IV directed against pious and charitable endowments in which the Church had a large interest. The responses of 1809 were straws in the wind indicating that the Church had a clear idea not of the nature of political reform but of what it expected its own position to be under the new order.

The later differences between the Church and the Cortes could only be dimly perceived in 1809, for as the elections took place it was unclear what specific direction the new assembly would take. Every group could nourish the hope that the Cortes would satisfy its wishes. But even before the Cortes met at Cádiz in 1810, defenders of the Church as a highly privileged corporation within the framework of absolute monarchy suffered a setback. The Cortes was not divided into chambers representing the hierarchical estates of Old Regime society. It took the form of a unicameral assembly of deputies elected through a complicated system of indirect voting by a single group of voters. These arrangements diminished the electoral possibilities of the bishops, only three of whom won election. One of the most influential groups in the Church, the regular clergy, was excluded entirely; they complained that they had been denied what "the most lowly of the populace and the mulattos of America" were given.[33] Ecclesiastical participation in the Cortes, however, was substantial; 97 priests from the ranks of the secular clergy were elected among the 308 deputies. The majority of the clerical deputies were drawn from the secondary levels of the ecclesiastical elite—particularly from the ranks of university professors and cathedral canons, whose education and prominence had converted them into political notables in the confusing circumstances of 1808 and 1809.

The ecclesiastical deputies, however, did not form a monolithic block. Some of the leading clerical figures identified with ecclesiastical reform over the preceding decades won election. Joaquín Lorenzo Villanueva, former professor of theology in Salamanca, member of the Royal Academy of History, and chaplain of honor to Charles IV, won a seat and became a persistent advocate for reforming the abuses of the eighteenth-century Church. Diego Muñoz Torrero, former professor of philosophy and rector of the University of Salamanca, emerged early in the sessions as a leading partisan of political and ecclesiastical change. But, as the later crucial votes on the fate of the Inquisition and liberty of expression would reveal, clerical deputies committed to far-reaching political and ecclesiastical reform were a distinct minority among their fellow clergymen. Priests determined to defend the Church's traditional privileges—Inguanzo, Ostolaza, Cañedo, Ros, Aguiriano, and others—became the leading opponents of the liberal revolution elaborated by the Cortes of Cádiz between 1810 and 1813.[34]

The election of deputies took place in the midst of the French offensive that pushed the Spanish army southward throughout 1809. The resulting confusion as well as the indirect system of voting allowed the election of a parliamentary majority that rejected the fundamental principles on which the eighteenth-century State and society had rested. Formal political parties in the modern sense did not exist at Cádiz. The first manifestation of what came to be known as liberalism arose from a broad and sometimes shifting alliance in the Cortes that was willing to support profound change in the traditional order. Deputies drawn from the civil administration (36.5 percent of the membership) and the military (13.6 percent) were joined by a minority from the clergy to form the basis of a liberal majority.[35] The political origins of liberalism at Cádiz arose from diverse sources—the utilitarian emphasis of state reform during the eighteenth century, the critical spirit that had swept through educated opinion from the 1780's on, the influence of the French revolutionary constitution of 1791, simple disgust with the performance of absolute monarchy in its recent history, and more individualist patterns of economic thought. All these contributed to the creation of a powerful sentiment in favor of fundamental changes in government and the development of society.

The Cortes of Cádiz did not challenge the existence of the monarchy itself. It early recognized Ferdinand VII as the kingdom's legitimate sovereign. But the assembly undermined the basis of absolute monarchy and the hierarchical social structure of the Old Regime through legislation. The Cortes proclaimed the doctrine of national sovereignty, abolished seigneurial and jurisdictional privileges held by the nobility and the Church, established the principle of equality before the law, and ended legal privileges based on social class. In 1812 the Cortes passed a constitution that severely limited the authority of the executive power vested in the king and established a clear division of powers, giving the legislature a dominant voice in the conduct of political affairs.

The legislation of the Cortes represented the triumph of those educated groups within Old Regime society that had been excluded from direct participation in political power and from the benefits enjoyed by a small minority of the socially privileged. The liberal revolution was radical insofar as it dismantled absolute monarchy and the hierarchical society associated with it; it was conservative in its determination to avoid creating an open-ended political system with significant popular participation.

The relationship of the liberal revolution to the Church would influence the course of Spanish history into the twentieth century. In the eyes of generations of clerical apologists, the decisions of the Cortes on ecclesiastical matters began the erosion of the Church's influence. In spite of the brickbats hurled at the liberal deputies of Cádiz even before the assembly dissolved, nothing was further from their minds than a program designed to undermine the place of religion in Spanish life. Villanueva expressed the sentiments of the proreform deputies in a motion presented in October 1810: "we are Catholics and we must give proof ot it." He moved that the session should open with the hymn *Veni Creator* and prayers to the Holy Spirit.[36] Shortly later, a motion worthy of the most zealous missionary preacher of the eighteenth century was passed. Proposed by the bishop of León, it called for a campaign to improve public morality in which prostitution and gambling would be forbidden; it demanded further that women should dress properly so "that sins and public scandals" might be avoided.[37] Moreover, Article 12 of the Constitution of 1812 (approved unanimously) declared without equivocation: "the religion of the Spanish nation is and will be forever the Catholic, Apostolic and Roman, the only true religion."[38]

In spite of this clear affirmation, conflict with the Church was inevitable. The liberal reformers and their largely clerical opponents in the Cortes expected very different consequences from the parliamentary process begun in 1810. The Church, long resentful over the degree of control exercised by the Bourbon State before 1808, saw in the summoning of a Cortes an opportunity to secure freedom from government interference while maintaining the legal and financial privileges it had enjoyed for centuries. The liberal majority never presented a comprehensive plan of ecclesiastical reform. Its concerns with expelling the French and drafting a constitution were more than enough to occupy its time. However, liberal policies in three important areas—the status of the Inquisition, the question of liberty of expression, and the future of the religious orders—posed a direct challenge to clerical interests determined to defend the privileged Church of the Old Regime. The question posed at Cádiz and repeated in the later history of liberal Spain was never whether the Church should or should not exist, nor whether it should be separated from its official relationship with the State. The question was whether the kingdom's ecclesiastical elite would accept a redefinition of the Church's role within a new political society molded by a Catholic, educated middle class with a more secular and individualistic ideology than that underlying the old monarchical and hierarchical order.

The attitude of the liberal majority—both lay and clerical deputies—in its conflict with the Church did not rest on any new and radical perception of the Church's role. Liberal ecclesiastical policies can be traced directly to the regalist tradition of the Bourbon monarchy, which had clearly established the right of the State to exercise significant control over Church affairs save in the realm of doctrine. These policies reflected, too, the alliance between regalism and the movement toward ecclesiastical reform that had developed within the eighteenth-century Church, particularly after 1780. Many of the liberal deputies at Cádiz had studied in Spanish universities during the 1790's, when the regalist-reform program as embodied by the Synod of Pistoia was widely considered as a model of what might be accomplished by effective cooperation between government and an enlightened clergy.[39] The emphases of Pistoia on pastoral concerns, on the exaltation of the parish clergy, and on the corresponding diminution of the religious orders' role exercised a powerful appeal in a country where serious problems were evident in all three areas. This is not to say that practical considerations were lacking among the liberal deputies. The continued existence of the Inquisition seemed an obstacle to true national sovereignty, and the property of the religious orders offered a tempting way out of the financial exigencies created by the war against the French.

Whether the Church would accept limited reform imposed by legislative decree was not entirely clear in 1810. From the beginning some ecclesiastics were uneasy about the direction of the Cortes. In October 1810 Bishop Quevedo y Quintana of Orense refused to take the obligatory oath of loyalty to the Cortes because of his doubts over whether sovereignty should reside in the nation rather than in the king. The cardinal primate, Luis de Borbón, however, warmly accepted this revolutionary decision and swore the oath in a public session of the assembly. The other bishops in Cádiz took the oath with a noticeable lack of enthusiasm. Ecclesiastical concern deepened with a decree of November 15, 1810, that appropriated the income of vacant benefices and one-half the revenues from the tithes of bishoprics, cathedral chapters, and monasteries. The unease was only somewhat tempered by the decree's character as an emergency measure to raise money for defense.

Ecclesiastical irritation with the new regime, although evident in 1810 and 1811, did not grow into outright hostility until 1812 and 1813. The drift from vague disaffection to opposition did not come from any particular outburst against the Constitution of 1812. The constitution's affirmation of the Catholic nature of the State and its designation of four ecclesiastics to sit on the forty-member Council of State assuaged the clerical establishment. The bishops of Jaén and Ávila issued pastoral letters urging their flocks to accept the constitution; the archbishop of Santiago ordered a Te Deum sung in his cathedral to celebrate proclamation of the constitutional text. Only one bishop openly rejected the constitution by refusing to take the oath to uphold it. Quevedo y Quintana of Orense, already suspect in the eyes of the liberal deputies, provoked them still further by instructing his cathedral chapter that swearing the oath did not signify approval of the constitution. The liberal majority, after declaring the bishop "unworthy to be considered a Spaniard" ordered him dismissed from his post, and the prelate fled to Portugal.[40] Members of the regular clergy took the oath either reluctantly or not at all. In Catalonia, according to a Franciscan chronicler, the friars, who believed the constitution contained provisions "contrary to religion," made it "an object of execration and covered it with a hatred which was never extinguished."[41]

Clerical disenchantment with the new regime deepened in the spring of 1812 in the face of what conservative churchmen saw as unbridled discussion in books, newspapers, and pamphlets of the fate of the kingdom. Ecclesiastics supporting the restoration of absolute monarchy were scandalized by the liberty of political debate. In March 1812 the bishops resident in Cádiz complained to the Cortes of "the scandalous torrent of pernicious opinions" appearing in the local press.[42] Clerical anger intensified in the following month with the publication of a biting satire against the Church written by the librarian of the Cortes. The bishops living on Mallorca issued a pastoral letter calling the book "impious, blasphemous, sacriligious, impure" and heretical "in spirit and letter"; other churchmen called on the Cortes to take action against the author.[43] The decision of the Cortes in favor of legislation establishing freedom of the press, although with certain limits, further alienated defenders of the Old Regime Church.

The decisive break between the majority of the Cortes and the kingdom's ecclesiastical elite occurred over the question of the Inquisition.[44] Hostility toward the Holy Tribunal was not new. Reform-minded ecclesiastics of the eighteenth century had disliked its ability to operate outside episcopal jurisdiction; secular reformers, such as Gaspar de Jovellanos, saw the Inquisition as an obstacle to cultural progress. But the inertia of the absolute monarchy under Charles IV as well as the State's increasing reliance on the Inquisition as a kind of political police kept the institution alive. The enormous disruption created by the French occupation in most of the kingdom by early 1810 destroyed the Inquisition as a functioning body over the national territory. The liberal deputies of Cádiz could be grateful to the French for having destroyed the institutional power that time and time again had allowed the Inquisition to act with a high degree of autonomy and resist measures designed to weaken its authority.

No longer having to fear inquisitorial reprisal, the liberal majority at Cádiz was free to debate whether the Holy Tribunal should be fully restored upon the conclusion of hostilities. A parliamentary commission presented a report advocating abolition to the full Cortes in April 1812. Clerical deputies defending the Inquisition attacked the proposal at every turn; twenty-two bishops and thirty-two cathedral chapters petitioned the Cortes for a restoration. The arguments advanced by the Inquisition's foes were many and varied. In a long speech on January 9, 1813, the assembly's most brilliant orator, Agustín Argüelles, stated them all. He rejected the argument that the Inquisition was necessary to preserve religion because the faith had survived without difficulty for fifteen centuries before the fateful decision of Ferdinand and Isabella. He maintained that the Cortes had every right to decide on the Inquisition's fate because it had originally been imposed on Castile by Crown and papacy without consulting the Cortes. He attacked its intolerance against the *conversos* of an earlier age and called it an institution that had won "the universal hatred of enlightened man." But for Argüelles the question of the Inquisition was more straightforward. "The Government of the nation is not a theocracy," he declared, and the Cortes, "using the right inherent in its sovereign authority," could decide "to abolish or not the Tribunal of the Inquisition."[45] The Cortes could not permit, in effect, the existence of a state within a state. In the heated debates other liberal deputies expressed their views bluntly. The conde de Toreno declared, "the very name of the Inquisition . . . must be erased from among us."[46]

In the end it was the belief of the liberal deputies that the Inquisition was incompatible with the new constitutional order that justified abolition. The bishop of Calahorra sought to counter this argument by alleging that Article 12 of the constitution supported the Inquisition's survival because it was an institution engaged in protecting religion. In an increasingly embittered atmosphere the crucial vote was taken on January 22, 1813. Of the 150 deputies present, 90 voted for abolition, 60 against. Of the ecclesiastical deputies in the chamber, 32 voted against the motion, only 11 in favor, a clear sign of diminishing clerical support for the regime.[47]

The bishops deluged the Cortes with letters of protest, although most grudgingly fulfilled an order of February 23 commanding that the decree of abolition be read from the pulpit of every church. But the foot-dragging of the archbishop of Santiago, who delayed until May and then refused to announce the abolition in his diocese, led the Cortes to order his arrest and eventually condemn him to exile. From Portugal the bishop of Orense forbade his chapter from publishing the decree, but the authorities acted vigorously in that case too, arresting the entire chapter and ripping the bishop's edict from church doors. The bishops of Santander, Oviedo, and Astorga chose to abandon their dioceses rather than publish the decree of abolition. There was also resistance among the regular clergy, one of whom declared that he would leave his church in the middle of Mass rather than announce the decree to his congregation. In the end the Cortes broke the resistance of conservative churchmen, but at the price of strengthening clerical hostility against the liberal constitutional system.

The suppression of the Inquisition angered the traditionalist clerical elite, which had come to look upon its restoration as indispensable to the realization of the religious revolution of which it dreamed. The abolition of the Holy Tribunal did not, however, threaten the organization and wealth of the Old Regime Church. The Bourbon State had always taken its share of ecclesiastical revenues and had even ventured onto the dangerous ground of disamortization under Charles IV. But the vast property holdings of the secular and regular clergy were left untouched. The circumstances of the war against the French created an entirely new situation. The suppression of monasteries, friaries, and convents by the government of Joseph Napoleon in occupied Spain raised the question of what ought to be done with their property as more of the national territory was freed from the enemy. For the Cortes the question took on immediate urgency because of the desperate condition of state finances.

These fiscal considerations, moreover, were joined for the first time to pressures for the reform of the regulars. Criticism of the religious orders had long figured in the program of ecclesiastical reformers. But eighteenth-century suggestions for change focused on reducing numbers, directing religious into socially useful pursuits such as education and charity, and improving the quality of religious life in monasteries and convents. No royal official or clerical reformer dared to suggest that reform should include massive closing of religious houses and the sale of their property for the benefit of the State.

Any suggestion that the reform of the regulars should be tied to dispositions relative to their property was rejected out of hand by conservative deputies. Simón López, later to serve as archbishop of Valencia, summed up the unalterable opposition of the Church to any changes in this area: "As far as the few or many properties of the regulars are concerned, it is no business of Your Majesty [the Cortes] to dispose of them . . . these are ecclesiastical possessions, dedicated to the cult, consecrated to God . . . they are the possessions of God."[48] In spite of the efforts of traditionalist deputies to halt discussion of the question, extensive debate took place in parliamentary committees during 1811 and 1812 about a comprehensive program of reform for the regulars. The arguments that had been used by advocates of reform for decades were again brought forward. Manuel Cano, who served as the secretary of grace and justice for the Cortes, argued that the number of religious should be tied closely to the kingdom's pastoral, educational, and charitable needs. Orders not meeting this utilitarian test, particularly the purely monastic foundations and the mendicants, were clearly to suffer. Cano also advocated the suppression of religious houses with fewer than twelve professed members and declared that no order should have more than one establishment in any given town. And mindful of the orders' role in opposition to the new constitutional order, Cano urged that no monastery or convent be reestablished until its political conduct had been examined and legal proceedings begun against "the treasonous."[49]

A special committee on reform of the regular clergy presented its report to the full Cortes in 1813. It called for limits on the number of convents of women (350) and monasteries (60) and stipulated that the number of houses of the nonmonastic orders such as the Franciscans should depend on the size of a town's population and the quantity of its secular clergy. The report broke new ground in the long debate over the role of the regulars by forbidding authorized religious houses from acquiring new property. It went further by recommending that the property of the suppressed foundations under the plan "be used for the benefit of the State until the Cortes should decide that it is convenient to arrange the appraisal and sale of said property."[50]

Political circumstances during 1813 prevented the Cortes from addressing the committee's proposal. The Cortes dealt with the regulars, who expected to recover their property and revenues as the French abandoned the country, on a piecemeal basis. The authorities found it difficult to carry out the terms of a law passed September 13, 1813, that ordered sale of the property of monasteries and convents in a ruinous state as a result of the war. Efforts to prevent the reoccupation of religious houses, whether ruined or not, failed with few exceptions as the regulars began to return to their residences, often in defiance of government officials. The reestablishment of religious communities soon led to disputes between the returning regulars and the residents of cities and towns, who resented the reimposition of monastic rights and dues from which they had been free for years. The municipality of Ripoll thus protested to the Cortes against the return of the Benedictines to their monastery in the town. It objected particularly to the order's intention to resume collection of the tithe.[51] These disputes were common in 1813 and were examples of rising feeling against the regulars, which would surface later with a vengeance.

Proposals for the reform of the secular clergy did not receive the same attention given to those focusing on the regulars. Yet suggestions were advanced that would figure in the programs of later liberal governments. The Asturian deputy Calello, after noting "the poverty and misery of most parish priests," urged the abolition of surplice fees (the charges exacted for baptisms, marriages, funerals, and so on) and the redirection of tithes away from the ecclesiastical elite to the parochial clergy.[52] Calello further urged a fundamental parish reorganization that would guarantee every parish priest a decent income and would provide improved religious services to the population. Discussion also took place in the Cortes and in the press about the necessity of a thorough reform of Church financing. One deputy suggested that the State had every right to use the Church's immense wealth for the public good "because Jesus Christ himself said that his kingdom was not of this world." Several liberal political writers went further and advocated the sale of Church property to reduce the national debt, although on condition that other means be found to pay the clergy. Such suggestions never reached the stage of serious parliamentary discussion, but their mere appearance led to clerical counterattacks. The Cortes had no right "to rob God Himself," declared one defender of the Church.[53]

The achievements of the Cortes of Cádiz in ecclesiastical affairs were essentially negative. The destruction of the Inquisition and of the Church's traditional right to control intellectual life as well as the uncompleted reform of the regulars predominated over those aspects of the old regalist-reform program that looked to improve the quality of the kingdom's religious life. Liberal deputies at Cádiz, such as Villanueva, did not abandon their concerns for improving religion in Spain, but the fierce resistance of defenders of the Old Regime Church made comprehensive reform, both organizational and moral, an impossible task. It was only after liberal governments in succeeding decades had broken the institutional back of the privileged eighteenth-century Church that the ecclesiastical establishment accepted a limited degree of internal reform. The struggle would be long and difficult and would leave a legacy of bitterness toward the liberal State among many clerics that would endure into the twentieth century.

A Weakened Church, 1808–1814

The prospect of Ferdinand VII's restoration led conservative ecclesiastics to look on the return of the king as the salvation of the religious revival they had been preaching. Clerical anger once directed against the French was now turned on the liberals of the Cortes. Far from being seen as moving the kingdom toward repentance and religion, the liberals were accused of being accomplices in spiritual degeneration. Preaching in La Coruña in May 1813, a friar posed a question often repeated in later years: "Spaniards! Where do we stand? In a Catholic nation or among deserters of the gospels? Our unfortunate nation is covered by impious newspapers and other writings designed to rob us of our religion in exchange for deceitful liberty."[54]

The campaign against liberalism was as violent and emotional as the one against the French—and for the same reasons. The new constitutional system and its adherents appeared as obstacles to realization of the grand providential design for Spain. Churchmen thus exalted Ferdinand VII as an avenging angel who would purify the nation of its corruption and allow the Church to proceed with its spiritual revolution. With the arrival of the king, declared one preacher: "these philosophers who have declared war on the Church, persecuted its ministers, hated friars, corrupted morality and shown aversion to its dogmas will no longer walk upon the earth."[55] Clerics, however, did not wish to see the restoration of a royal Church subject to state control at every level of administration and discipline. The Crown had once used the Church for its own ends, but the Church proposed to turn the tables and manipulate the restored monarchy to create a theocratic society. Religious values would be paramount, and the Church would function with independence. By 1813 the absent Ferdinand appeared as a savior for an angry Church frustrated in its grandiose plans.

In March 1814 Ferdinand VII returned from exile in France. Once the king perceived that he could count on popular support and elements of the army for a coup d'etat, he undid the work of the Cortes of Cádiz. His return was everywhere greeted with jubilation by churchmen expecting a new age of piety. The Church, however, was ill prepared to undertake a vast movement of spiritual revival. The war had exacted a heavy material toll.

Unfortunately, there are no studies of the impact of the war on ecclesiastical finances, but the evidence suggests that it was enormous. Both sides in the conflict turned to clerical wealth as a source of revenue. In each zone the government appropriated most of the tithes of the secular clergy.[56] Whatever was left proved impossible to collect because of military conditions and the resistance of the peasantry, who easily evaded payment without the pressure of the agents and lawyers once employed to keep them in line. Both governments also extracted large amounts from the clergy. In 1808 the numerous donations of bishops and chapters to the national rising were followed by the heavy impositions of the French. In March 1809 the government of Joseph Napoleon imposed a loan on the secular and regular clergy of Galicia of 10 million reales and followed it with other demands in the spring and summer. The authorities also seized the gold and silver ornaments of the regulars' churches in Barcelona in the summer of 1810. Suppression of the religious orders in the French zone forced abandonment of numerous monasteries and friaries and led to substantial material destruction.[57] Monasteries were converted into stables, barracks, and munitions dumps or simply allowed to fall into decay. The destruction, however, was not universal. In Catalonia some monasteries, such as the Benedictine abbey of San Pedro de Besalu, were completely ruined, but another house of the order, San Pedro de Comprodon, escaped unscathed. Although the regular clergy paid the heaviest price, the entire financial structure of the Old Regime Church was undermined by the war. Declining revenues and the closing of monasteries led to the collapse of the traditional system of charity and prevented the Church from providing employment to urban artisans.

Together with declining resources between 1808 and 1814, the Church experienced a decline in ecclesiastical population. Accurate numbers are not available for the period, but one authority has estimated the loss at more than a third from the figures reported in the 1797 census. The decline may not have been this disastrous, but it was nonetheless extensive, particularly among the regular clergy. The Dominican province of Aragón lost one-fourth of its members during the war, with deaths outnumbering new entrants by two to one. The Franciscans of Andalusia saw their numbers fall from 1,544 in 1808 to 520 by 1820, with most of the loss occurring during the war; a similar decline took place in the order's province of Cartagena.[58] Monasteries and friaries in Andalusia, an area well populated with religious houses, suffered more than elsewhere because of the epidemics of yellow fever that swept through that region and the Mediterranean littoral as far as Valencia in 1811 and 1812. The Carmelites of Orihuela were annihilated: "all perished in the epidemic even the servants who tolled the bells," recorded the order's chronicler.[59]

There is less precise information on the secular clergy, but they too suffered losses. In Zamora many parishes had no priest. The bishop of Lérida declared that in his diocese "the number of secular priests has declined notably."[60] The demographic crisis also affected the hierarchy, although for other reasons. The pope's refusal to approve the episcopal appointments of either Joseph Napoleon or the Cortes of Cádiz created twenty-one vacancies by 1814, and it fell to Ferdinand VII to make the nominations. He did so by appointing bishops—Arias Tejeiro, Inguanzo, Creus, Strauch, and others—who were among the most active opponents of the liberal revolution and were far removed from the model bishop of the eighteenth-century royal Church. Bishops appointed before the war survived, of course, but the king created a new episcopal generation whose concerns differed from those of the prelates of Charles III. The new bishops looked to the regular and secular clergy to be the shock troops of the long-heralded religious revival, but the clerical army was no longer the militia of apostles and prophets that had crusaded against the French and the Cortes of Cádiz. It was a tired, aging, and impoverished force capable of vindictiveness but not of evangelization.

How greatly the war affected traditional patterns of religious practice is difficult to establish. It is at least clear, though, that for the first time in centuries pastoral routine and ecclesiastics' ability to exercise moral control over their flocks suffered disruption. The bishops of many dioceses fled from their sees during the

French occupation; parish priests, who generally remained at their posts, consumed much of their energy trying to survive in difficult economic circumstances. The suppression of the regulars in Napoleonic Spain brought to an end the missionary campaigns so important to the Church of the eighteenth century. At the close of hostilities the bishops were convinced that the weakening of clerical vigilance caused by the war had led to widespread immorality. The bishops attacked the "relaxation of customs" they believed to be universal throughout the kingdom. The king himself summed up the moral effects of the war as he saw them in a royal order of 1815 designed to restore the old standards of conduct. Public scandals caused by "the voluntary separation of married couples and the licentious life of either one or the other partner, . . . by the inobservance of religious feast days, obscene words, injuries to the ministers of religion, . . . irreverences in the churches,"—were to be punished by the civil authorities working with parish priests.[61]

The diminished institutional presence of the Church as a result of the war may have allowed some individuals to indulge in behavior that once would have led to prompt clerical censure. But ecclesiastical laments about the spread of impiety and immorality must be taken with a grain of salt. There is no evidence that the peasant regions of the north, esteemed for their Catholicism, were inundated by a wave of irreligion and moral depravity. Even Bishop Arias Teijeiro of Pamplona, one of the most vociferous accusers of the war's destructive moral effects, admitted that in his diocese the population had given repeated proof of "its docility and constant religion."[62] The reproaches of the clergy in many cases were directed not against the population as a whole but against the minority of intellectuals, progressive noblemen, journalists, lawyers, and their clerical allies who had made the liberal revolution.

The liberal deputies of Cádiz proclaimed Catholicism the official religion of the State. Conservative ecclesiastics dismissed this declaration as a subtle ruse disguising a plot to undermine the Church and destroy religion. Clerical suspicions were unfounded, although extreme liberal apologists expressed anticlerical and, in some cases, vaguely antireligious sentiments. These ideas did not circulate widely beyond the liberal elite, although there are indications that in the large cities, Madrid and Barcelona particularly, anticlerical and skeptical opinion had made progress among groups such as merchants, government employees, physicians, military cadets, and a handful of artisans. An inquiry carried out in 1815 and 1816 by the reestablished Inquisition led to accusations of "offenses against religion" against a small number of persons, including a tailor, a library worker, a physician, a surgeon, two sergeants and a captain in the Cantabrian regiment, and several others from urban groups sympathetic to the liberal cause. Most of the accused had done nothing more than make irreverent remarks about the clergy: "all Capuchins are superstitious" and "friars beg alms so that they can keep women." But a few had expressed skepticism about religious belief: "confession is useless," "there is no hell," "our souls are like those of dogs which perish with the body." Such statements scandalized churchmen and confirmed their view of the growth of irreligion.[63] These cases were not numerous and in any event were confined to the cities, although they did indicate a drift away from the Church in urban centers.

Between 1808 and 1814 the Church also failed to repair the division between ecclesiastical reformers and traditionalists. Clerical progressives supporting the limited reforms of the Cortes of Cádiz aroused the hostility of conservative churchmen. In a pastoral letter of December 1812 the bishops declared that Spain was not only engaged in a battle against a foreign enemy but also in an "internal war." They lashed out against "ecclesiastics who presume themselves reformers . . . this class of tonsured philosophers."[64] And in the same year an apologist of the Old Regime Church took up the charges laid against reforming clerics by Bonola years before. Priests advocating change within the Church were accused of participating in a great "philosophical" conspiracy of secularism, materialism, and libertinism that had arisen first in France and then elsewhere to destroy Catholicism. This made the ecclesiastical reformers all the more dangerous. They were, in the words of one preacher, "rapacious wolves propagating perverse dogmas, false doctors promising liberty when they are slaves of corruption."[65]

As the Anglo-Spanish armies freed more of the national territory in 1812 and 1813, the civil war within the Church spread from Cádiz to the liberated areas. In Seville during the autumn of 1812, reformers led by the cathedral dean, López Cepero, attacked the friars flocking back to the city as an idle class of slackers and criticized the excessive riches of monasteries. Conservative clerics replied in kind, accusing the reformers of plotting "to hang friars and burn inquisitors, thereby ending the misfortunes of Spain and, as a result, bring enlightenment to the villages, improve the arts, [and] purify morality under the cover of every kind of insult to religion and its dogmas."[66]

The struggle within the Church changed its character during the war of independence. The reforming movement in its first and second phases had arisen from a vital clerical culture tied to the broader intellectual currents of the age. Pressure for reform came from a vigorous minority in the Church. Reform had always been tied to state intervention, even during the reign of Charles III, and this tendency became more pronounced under Charles IV, as clerical reformers looked increasingly to the State rather than the Church for support. With the Cortes of Cádiz advocates of change identified the cause of ecclesiastical reform with the liberal State, hence the violence of the attacks on churchmen who supported the modest reforms instituted between 1810 and 1813. The identification of reform with liberalism, however, signaled the decline of the movement for change within the Church. The militant ideology of the conservative Church backed the reformers into a corner. The bishops and most of the clergy, even those once vaguely sympathetic to reform, were swept up in the fervor of the crusade first against the French and then against the liberals. Enthusiasm for renovation fell by the wayside except among a diminishing minority who, ironically, turned to the liberal State to save reform just as traditionalist clergymen looked to Ferdinand VII to rescue their spiritual revolution. Reform, once a manifestation of the intellectual vitality of a progressive minority within the Church, became primarily a political issue caught up in the conflict between the liberal State and absolutism.

Few periods were more critical for the development of the

modern Spanish Church than the years between 1808 and 1814. The material prosperity and relative internal peace of the royal Church of Charles III eroded under his successor, and events during the war of independence accelerated institutional decline. By 1814 the great royal Church of the eighteenth century had ceased to exist, although some of its external trappings remained.

4 / The Struggle Intensifies, 1814–1833

The end of the liberal experiment in 1814 did not resolve the fundamental constitutional and ecclesiastical questions posed for the first time at the Cortes of Cádiz. The struggle between liberalism, determined to mold the Church to fit the demands of a new secular outlook within the framework of a parliamentary system, and ecclesiastical interests, as firmly committed to recover every particle of clerical authority and privilege, continued with even more intensity. The balance shifted first to the Church, during the initial period of Ferdinand VII's absolute rule from 1814 to 1820, and then against it during the second liberal revolution from 1820 to 1823. Although the Church recovered its position following the second restoration of Ferdinand, political and dynastic circumstances between 1823 and the king's death in 1833 finally ended ecclesiastical hopes for the reestablishment of the Old Regime Church in all its splendor. The clergy, at least the vast majority, struggled to recreate the past with the same fierce energy it had directed against the French and the constitutionalists of Cádiz. But the consensus that had sustained the eighteenth-century monarchy and the Church itself could not be resurrected. The Church threw its resources into a losing contest for which it would pay a heavy price.

The Church Restored, 1814–1820

After the return of Ferdinand VII ecclesiastics vied with one another to exalt the sovereign and his presumed commitment to a religious restoration. With his accession, said a preacher in the cathedral of Seville: "religion has triumphed over the horrendous monster of impiety." A Carmelite friar declared: "Oh! sweet Ferdinand! . . . our beloved Ferdinand! . . . We owe everything to Ferdinand . . . Long live the King for the greater brilliance and

splendor of the Catholic religion!"[1] The clergy looked to the king
to realize the theocratic revolution it had been preaching and to
free the Church from its traditional dependence on the State.
During the years of Ferdinand's enforced exile in France, conservative ecclesiastics were able to embroider their fantasies without considering whether the king accepted them. Between 1814
and 1820, the first period of Ferdinand's absolute rule, however,
the king showed that he was his own man, and that he could use
the Church to buttress his own power as effectively as any monarch
before him.

Few sovereigns were called upon to rule in more difficult circumstances.[2] The war of independence against the French ended
victoriously, but in 1814 the general condition of the realm bordered on the catastrophic. The economic and financial decline of
the nation that had begun in the 1790's accelerated during the war
and continued after its close. Commerce with the overseas empire,
once the foundation of the kingdom's economy, had collapsed,
and the independence movement in the colonies, although not
yet completely successful, had built a momentum the mother country
was unable to halt. At home the purges, exiles, and prison terms
inflicted on liberals did not eliminate political opposition; several
conspiracies took place between 1814 and 1820. Ferdinand VII
lacked the character and intelligence to dominate the situation,
but he did possess a certain cunning, which enabled him to survive
exile, plotting, and a revolution to die in bed still an absolute
monarch in 1833.

In 1814 Ferdinand reestablished the administrative institutions
of the eighteenth-century State, but their restoration was more
nominal than real. The political, social, and economic changes of
the preceding two decades made revival of the Old Regime monarchy a difficult if not impossible task, a fact that Ferdinand realized with the primitive intuition which always saved him from
losing the power he cherished. Between 1814 and 1820, in spite
of the institutional forms of the past, the monarchy of Ferdinand
was a personal, albeit royal dictatorship. The king paid little attention to the institutions he had restored, relying instead on a
small group of personal advisers. Power rested neither in the
constitutional consensus that had supported the eighteenth-century
monarchy nor in the overwhelming prestige of the royal institu-

tion itself, but in a combination of forces—conservative elements
in the army, the Church, ambitious politicians, and ideological
zealots who believed the survival of absolute power would serve
their interests.

Ferdinand was a popular monarch, although in a very personal
way. His aversion to the aristocracy and the elaborate ceremony
of his father's court, as well as his modest style of life and general
accessibility, kept him from being isolated from his subjects by the
social trappings of the old monarchy. However, the king lacked
a clear vision of what he wished to do with the power that had
become his in 1814. The government's record between 1814 and
1820 was a sorry one. But Ferdinand managed to hold together
the disparate forces supporting him until the revolution of 1820
returned the liberals to power.

The king, realizing that his survival partially depended on the
support of the Church, quickly abrogated the ecclesiastical legislation of the Cortes of Cádiz. The religious orders were allowed
to reoccupy their houses if they had not already done so. A decree
of July 21, 1814, ordered the restoration of the Inquisition; another on May 29, 1815, authorized the reestablishment of the
Jesuits.[3] In 1814 and 1815 royal orders dealing with the improvement of moral standards and the necessity of evangelization campaigns set in motion a vast effort to end what the bishop of Pamplona
called "an era of confusion, disorder and crimes."[4] At royal command, bishops organized missions in their dioceses and enlisted
the services of the religious, who sallied forth, according to a
Franciscan chronicler, "with a truly apostolic spirit as they ripped
from the ground most of the seeds which evil genius had sown
in towns and villages."[5] The clergy thundered against the "relaxation of customs" and dissent from the doctrines of the Church,
which they believed had spread during the period of liberal rule.
The realization of the theocratic revolution seemed near at hand,
and ecclesiastics joyfully celebrated the coming triumph. When
the archbishop of Santiago reentered his diocese in 1814 after
having been exiled by the Cortes of Cádiz, he arrived in a solemn
procession including two groups dressed in sinister garb, chained,
and carrying placards labeled "Impiety and Heresy," "Iniquity
and Persecution."[6]

Ferdinand's campaign against liberalism and the Church's determination to destroy what it saw as libertinism provided the common ground for a new alliance between Throne and Altar. The revived Inquisition went about its business with a political as much as a religious purpose. In July 1815 it prohibited a series of books of no doctrinal significance on the grounds that it was necessary "to root out as soon as possible every kind of publication in any way contrary to the doctrine of holy religion and to the fidelity owed to the Sovereign."[7] The Church showed its loyalty to Ferdinand more concretely during the abortive liberal risings of these years. When Brigadier Porlier attempted to induce the garrisons of Galicia to rebel in 1815, the cathedral chapter of Santiago donated 50,000 reales to the governor and celebrated a Te Deum after the revolt's suppression. In Barcelona a timely gift from Bishop Pablo de Sichar to the captain general, whose unpaid troops appeared ready to desert to General Lacy's revolt, saved the day for the royalist forces.

Cooperation between the king and conservative ecclesiastics extended to the purging of clerics who had supported or simply shown sympathy for the reforms of Cádiz. In a decree of May 1814, Ferdinand ordered that competition for benefices should be confined to persons free of "dangerous and erroneous" opinions who had given proof of "their adhesion to healthy principles."[8] Cathedral chapters were purged of canons suspected of supporting liberalism. The most fortunate escaped abroad, but others, such as Joaquín Lorenzo Villanueva, one of the most prominent clerical reformers at Cádiz, suffered the harsher fate of arrest and imprisonment.[9]

Both Throne and Altar profited from the alliance against liberalism and libertinism, but Ferdinand got the better of the bargain. The king never intended to install the kind of theocratic regime clerical visionaries had conjured up during the war of independence. He had not acquired absolute power to relinquish it to the Church.[10] He insisted on retaining the rights traditionally held by the Crown over ecclesiastical appointments and revenues. Ferdinand used his powers of patronage to fill the episcopacy and cathedral chapters with clerics sympathetic to his rule and hostile to liberalism. Between 1814 and 1820 the king was presented with an unrivaled opportunity to exercise his right of appointment. He named sixty bishops and converted the hierarchy into a responsive

protector of his personal power.[11] The appointment of Fray Rafael
de Vélez, author of a celebrated defense of the alliance between
the Church and Crown, to the bishopric of Ceuta in 1817 symbolized the new episcopacy completely identified with the interests
of the absolutist State. Although the average age of the new prelates was sixty-three, Ferdinand appointed a number of younger
bishops on whom he could count in the future, and he turned
increasingly to the regular clergy, whose antiliberalism was proverbial, as an episcopal recruiting ground.[12] The personal quality
and educational level of the hierarchy was not far below the
eighteenth-century standard, but the direct use of royal patronage
on a massive scale for an immediate political purpose endowed
the Church for a generation with an episcopacy ill prepared to
grapple with ecclesiastical problems.

The clergy expected the restored monarchy to rebuild the economic foundations on which the eighteenth-century Church's
prosperity had rested. There are few studies of ecclesiastical wealth
for this period, but the evidence suggests that the decline which
had begun early in the century was irreversible. The agricultural
and commercial depression, which had deepened during the war,
continued unabated; the State was close to bankruptcy. Revenues
from the tithe, dependent on a flourishing agriculture, did not
reach prewar levels. Moreover, peasant evasion of the tithe continued in spite of the efforts of civil and ecclesiastical authorities.
An inquiry of 1817 in the diocese of Cartagena revealed such
deep hostility to the tithe among the peasantry that collection
agents dared not press their demands too aggressively. Peasant
resistance could be broken, declared one collector, only if the State
made examples of the recalcitrant through vigorous judicial action.[13] A similar pattern of resistance prevailed among those owing
money to the Church through the loans known as *censos*. The
Church received virtually nothing from this source during the
war and found it difficult to reestablish its claims after 1814 because of the complexity of these financial arrangements. No overall
figures document the decline in wealth, but the income of the
kingdom's bishoprics fell from 52,042,000 reales in 1802 to
34,274,279 by 1820.[14]

The Church's financial problems were aggravated by the demands of the State. The desperate condition of the royal treasury

forced the king to turn to ecclesiastical revenues as extensively as had both his father and the Cortes of Cádiz. In 1815 Ferdinand appropriated the income of benefices held by absentee clerics and forbade bishops from granting pensions on their incomes so that any surplus could be assigned to the treasury. In 1817 the king imposed a special levy of 30 million reales on the secular and regular clergy to be paid over a six-year period. The financial pressure of the Crown on the archdiocese of Santiago was so great that 60 percent of its revenues between 1814 and 1820 went into the State's coffers. Royal policy in other areas also affected the financial situation of ecclesiastical institutions. In 1814, for example, Ferdinand's suppression of feudal baronies in Catalonia led to a decline in income among the great monastic houses of the region such as Poblet, which depended in part on the payments from the surrounding countryside over which it exercised jurisdiction. The subjects of Poblet welcomed the abolition of the monastery's rights with jubilation and for good measure refused to pay the tithe and other obligations they had traditionally paid to the monks.[15]

Economic conditions and the financial demands of the State also affected the regular clergy. Josep Fontana's study of monastic revenues in Menorca and Catalonia between 1814 and 1820 has called attention to the crisis suffered by religious houses forced to consider selling some of their property to raise badly needed income.[16] Whether the crisis was general among the communities of religious is less certain. In Catalonia monasteries dependent on the tithe and other payments in kind were caught in difficult circumstances. But the mendicant orders, particularly the Franciscans, the most numerous in the region, fared better. When the provincial chapter met in 1818 it noted with satisfaction that "in only six years the province had been restored to a very flourishing condition" and that the extensive material damage suffered during the war had been entirely repaired.[17] Even the Carthusian monastery of las Cuevas in Seville, which had seen its fertile, irrigated gardens destroyed during the war, managed to secure enough income to rebuild its ruined church and enjoy a brief prosperity between 1818 and 1820. Although the recovery of the orders was uneven, resources committed to rebuilding as well as the pressures exerted by monasteries and convents on local populations to recover income in a time of general economic stagnation may well have contributed to the popular hostility to the orders, which would take violent form between 1820 and 1823.

Caught between economic problems and the political cunning of Ferdinand VII, the Church was as far from realizing its dreams in 1820 as in 1814. Clerical hopes outstripped the reality of the Church's position in Fernandine Spain. The persecution of religious and political dissent was no doubt satisfying, but it was not the great spiritual revolution expected from the restoration of the "Desired One" to the throne.

The weaknesses of the eighteenth-century Church remained, whether in the form of an archaic organizational framework or the imbalanced distribution of material resources. Conservative ecclesiastics displayed some interest in reform, but their obsession with the danger of a liberal revolution and the purging of reformers within the Church meant for all practical purposes the abandonment of any prospect for change. One of Ferdinand's earliest actions had been to secure a brief from Pius VII revoking the authorization of 1804 that had ordered a general inquiry into the state of the regular clergy as a prelude to necessary reform. In 1816 the bishop of Jaén complained to the king of "the lamentable state of monastic observance" he had found after an inspection of the monasteries and convents of his diocese. The state of the secular clergy seemed no better to the bishop of Calahorra, who issued a scathing indictment of his priests in the same year. Some had earned "public infamy" for living with their housekeepers or female servants; others were "drunkards and dealers at fairs and markets." Although the bishop admitted that only a minority of the clergy were guilty of such conduct, he claimed that many of their better-living fellows said Mass "without devotion or any awareness of what they were doing" and were "idlers . . . who never took a spiritual book in hand, nor even knew that such works existed."[18]

The economic difficulties of ecclesiastical institutions also undermined the Church's traditional social role. Bishops, chapters, and monasteries gradually resumed distribution of charitable assistance, but on a reduced scale. Limited resources meant that the massive charity efforts of the eighteenth century were no longer possible. Moreover, the number of vocations between 1814 and

1820, especially among the regular clergy, failed to replace the losses suffered during the war. By 1820 the bishops were lamenting the crisis in recruitment as one of their gravest problems, although the pastoral problems could have been resolved through efficient use of existing personnel.[19] And within the Church the purge of reforming clerics did not eliminate sympathy for change. The reformers, although silenced, did not disappear, and they would emerge again with the triumph of the liberal revolution. By 1820 the Church had failed to resolve its problems in spite of the alliance between Throne and Altar. A conservative ecclesiastical leadership produced no new initiatives and tied the fate of the Church to the fortunes of Ferdinand VII.

Christ or the Constitution, 1820–1823

Repression and the ineptness of the liberal opposition allowed the king to cling to power, but the government's lack of coherent policies, the continued deterioration of the State's finances, and the persistence of unfavorable economic conditions, combined with frustration among officers of the expeditionary army Ferdinand assembled to recover Spain's disintegrating American empire, finally produced the revolution that restored the Constitution of 1812. Discontent among young officers and the rank and file, reluctant to abandon their quarters in the province of Cádiz for the bloody battlefields of Venezuela and New Granada, combined with the conspiratorial activity of the masonic lodges that had proliferated both in the army and in the city of Cádiz to launch the second liberal revolution of the nineteenth century.

On January 1, 1820, the young commander of the regiment of Asturias, Rafael de Riego, proclaimed the restoration of the Constitution of 1812 and attempted to rally the officers and men of the expeditionary army to the revolutionary cause. The rising initially followed the same dismal course that had led to the failure of earlier attempts to restore the liberal regime, but the king's indecisiveness, the opportunism of his high command, and the spread of the revolution to other regions—particularly Zaragoza and Barcelona—forced the monarch, anxious to preserve his throne at any cost, to announce on March 7 that he would accept the constitution. Two days later Ferdinand took the oath to the constitution he had refused to accept in 1814, and on March 22 a provisional government called for elections to a new Cortes, which would meet on July 9.

The success of the revolution of 1820 caught the Church by surprise. Only the bishop of Cádiz, Francisco Javier Cienfuegos, came forward to condemn the conspirators and to assure his flock that their loyalty to the king would be rewarded with "peace and tranquility in this life and eternal life in the next."[20] The sudden triumph of the revolution, the king's decision to accept the constitution, and the appointment of a moderate liberal ministry dominated by former members of the Cortes of Cádiz led the hierarchy to view the new regime with something less than the hostility that might have been expected. In April, May, and June the bishops published pastoral letters urging the faithful to "observe the law of Jesus Christ, to trust in the constituted authorities," and to live "beneath the sweet empire of the Constitution," while diocesan authorities everywhere ordered the celebration of Te Deums.[21]

The abrupt about-face of a Church that had lavished praise on absolute monarchy was understandable. Ferdinand VII's acceptance of the new order deprived the Church of the ideological ammunition it had once fired against liberalism. Moreover, the spring and early summer of 1820 corresponded in some respects to the situation in 1809 and 1810 before the meeting of the Cortes of Cádiz. A moderate government ruled, and the direction of the new Cortes was as yet unclear. But the substantially different political circumstances of 1820 ensured that the Cortes would be able to undertake a more comprehensive program of reform than had been possible ten years before. The revolutionary government held firm control over the national territory, and the liberals' superior political tactics gave them a dominance in the assembly they had not enjoyed at Cádiz. The stunning and sudden success of the revolution as well as the opposition of upholders of absolute monarchy to participation in the new regime reduced the traditionalist representation in the Cortes.[22] The eloquent defenders of the old order who had directed steady fire against reform at Cádiz were missing in the parliament of 1820.

It was not clear in the early days of the revolution how far the new regime would go in its efforts to reform the Church. On March 9 the government decreed the abolition of the Inquisition, but with nothing like the passionate debate that had taken place in 1813. Even the clerical leadership reacted with unusual torpor. The bishop of Tortosa, Manuel Ros de Medrano, a committed supporter of absolutism at Cádiz, informed his diocese that the suppression of the Holy Tribunal should not be interpreted as a blow against the faith because Catholicism had survived in Spain for centuries before the Inquisition's creation. His argument was similar to that advanced by the liberal Argüelles in the parliamentary debate of 1813. The archbishop of Toledo and primate of Spain, Luis de Borbón, whose moderation had earned him the enmity of Ferdinand VII, went further and welcomed abolition because it reinforced episcopal authority within the Church.

Tension developed between the civil and ecclesiastical authorities over the State's insistence that all members of the secular and regular clergy should take an oath to uphold the constitution and that the parish clergy should explain it to their congregations during Mass. Most of the hierarchy swore the oath, though without enthusiasm, as did the superiors of the religious orders. Cirilo de la Alameda, the general of the Franciscans, told his friars that they must accept "the new principles of the new government."[23] Two bishops, Pedro Inguanzo of Zamora and Alonso Cañedo of Málaga, resisted but ceded in the end before the counsel of the papal nuncio, Giacomo Giustiniani.[24] The nuncio's moderation reflected the attitude of Pius VII, who published a brief on April 30 urging the Spanish Church to preserve its tranquillity before the political changes. But members of the regular clergy and some parish priests were not as cooperative. Among the Franciscans of Catalonia news of the revolution's triumph so shocked some friars that they took to their beds in fits of melancholy; the able-bodied absented themselves from their friaries on the day the oath was to be administered or kept silence when the fatal words of loyalty were pronounced.[25] The issues of the oath and the teaching of the constitution from the pulpit, however, were only irritants in a generally calm situation.

Ecclesiastical prudence in the face of changing political circumstances was also dictated by the reemergence of the liberal Church. Partisans of reform along the lines of the Synod of Pistoia, such as Joaquín Lorenzo Villanueva, Félix Amat, José d'Espiga, and others, returned from retirement, exile, or imprisonment to lead

discussion on the Church's fate. The basic outline of reform had
changed little since the 1790's. Advocates of change still looked
to the civil authorities and an alliance between Constitution and
Altar to impose reform on the Church. Issues such as the size and
role of the regular clergy, improvement in the status of the parish
priest, and reduction of papal authority in favor of the bishops
formed the core of the reforming program, as they had for three
decades. Reform received limited support from the episcopacy.
Some prelates—the cardinal primate, Luis de Borbón; Pedro González Vallejo, the former bishop of Mallorca deposed by Ferdinand
VII; and the auxiliary bishop of Madrid, Luis López del Castrillo—favored change, but the majority of the episcopacy remained firm in its opposition. As before, the strength of the
reformers was concentrated in the secondary levels of the ecclesiastical elite, among cathedral canons and university professors.
With the election to the Cortes of fifty-four priests, including the
leading figures of the reforming movement, a moderate program
of ecclesiastical renovation seemed close to realization.

The issue of Church reform surfaced in the Cortes scarcely a
week after its opening. Clerical deputies called for legislation to
improve the economic condition of the parish clergy, who lived
"in shameful misery" compared with the "unmeasured opulence"
of the clerical elite.[26] On August 20 the Cortes named a parliamentary committee to draft reform legislation for the Church.
Although some lay deputies sat on the committee, it was dominated by priests long identified with reform, such as Villanueva,
Diego Muñoz Torrero, Pedro González Vallejo, and others. They
worked for four months to produce a plan of reform that would
"conciliate the decorum of our holy religion and the necessary
endowment of its ministers" with "the kingdom's state of poverty."[27] The committee produced a series of legislative proposals
that represented a common-sense compromise which recognized
political and financial reality while attempting to buttress the position of the parish clergy. It made clear at the outset that its
projects would guarantee to "the ecclesiastical ministry in all its
ranks that it would be assisted and provided for by the Spanish
people, as it has been until now."[28] In one set of proposals the
committee recommended that the enormous disparities of income
among the kingdom's bishops be eliminated through a simplified

system of episcopal salaries that would depend on the size and importance of each diocese. It called for a reduction in the number of cathedral canons and urged that one-half the places in chapters be reserved for parish priests with at least twelve years' parochial service.

The committee directed particular attention to improving the condition and income of the parish clergy. Its recommendations, far more complete than anything discussed at Cádiz, sought to endow parish priests with what the reformers believed to be their rightful place within the organization of the Church. The committee thus called for a restructuring of the parochial system to create parishes that reflected the size of local populations; it proposed the elimination of benefices unconnected to pastoral work; and it suggested a range of salaries to provide the parish clergy with decent incomes. The proposals attached equal importance to improving the quality of the parochial clergy. Parish priests' obligation to teach knowledge of the faith to their congregations was stressed. The committee also stipulated that in the Balearic Islands, Catalonia, Valencia, Navarra, and the Basque Provinces parish priests and their assistants would be required to know and speak the languages of their regions.[29]

The parliamentary committee on ecclesiastical reform addressed the fundamental problems arising from the imbalanced organizational structure of the Old Regime Church. Its proposals were not radical or extreme, but their acceptance by the kingdom's bishops and endorsement by the papacy were doubtful. Some of the committee's recommendations, such as that on the parish clergy, eventually became law. The initiative for implementing the law's provisions, however, rarely came from the Church itself. In Barcelona, for example, municipal authorities undertook to rationalize the organization of parishes. New parishes were created to serve districts that had been badly served; some parishes in districts with too many churches were suppressed. The reform won at worst the open hostility of the diocesan administrators, at best their unenthusiastic tolerance.[30]

The tense but workable spirit of accommodation between a conservative Church and the liberal State began to sour when, on August 15, 1820, the Cortes ordered the suppression of the Jesuits and the sale of their property to benefit the public treasury. The

Jesuits had not recovered their old preeminence, but their special loyalty to the king, whom they regarded as a savior, and the traditional hostility of progressive opinion sealed their fate.[31] The radical elements of the liberal press began attacking the order in the spring, and the first signs of the popular anticlericalism that characterized urban society in nineteenth-century Spain surfaced against the Jesuits. Cries of "Death to the Jesuits!" were heard on the streets of Madrid; members of the order venturing out were insulted by angry crowds.[32] Although the Cortes treated ex-members of the order more gently than had Charles III, allowing them to remain in the kingdom with government pensions, the suppression elicited an angry protest from Pius VII and moved the Church closer to a break with the new regime.

The Cortes of 1820 also took up the question of reforming the regular clergy. A parliamentary committee including Bishop Castrillo produced a legislative proposal for the full Cortes in September. There was nothing particularly new in the project, which reflected many of the ideas that had circulated at Cádiz. But the proposal went beyond earlier suggestions for reform in calling for the suppression of all monasteries (that is the foundations of the strictly monastic orders, such as the Benedictines and Cistercians) save eight to be reserved for monks unable to become secular priests because of age or infirmity. Opposition to the monasteries arose from the widespread belief that these communities, devoted to contemplation and prayer, contributed nothing to the pastoral or economic benefit of the kingdom. The nonmonastic orders, particularly the mendicants, were treated more leniently. Friaries with more than twenty-four ordained priests were to survive, although a prohibition on reception of novices would assure their eventual demise. The committee's proposal received overwhelming endorsement from the Cortes (107 deputies in favor, 32 against) and became law.[33]

The *ley de monacales* became another source of dissension between the liberal State and most of the ecclesiastical leadership. But the reform of 1820 did not envisage total suppression of the regular clergy. It represented an attempt to rationalize the distribution and numbers of both religious houses and their members. By 1822, 801 monasteries and friaries had been closed. But 860 continued to function. The Cortes, moreover, tried to assure the material survival of religious forced to leave their residences by voting pensions to monks and friars who wished to be "secularized," that is, to become members of the secular clergy. And to a considerable extent the reform went a long way toward resolving the problems it was designed to address. Regions such as Asturias and Galicia, where the numbers of monasteries and friaries were small, lost fewer houses than Andalusia, where one-half of the numerous religious communities suffered closure.[34] But the process was not always logical. Subsequent legislation ordered the suppression of monasteries and friaries in towns with fewer than 400 inhabitants, thereby depriving many small communities of religious and educational services.

The reform of the regulars and other legislation—the abolition of the special judicial exemptions of the clergy, for example—altered the Church's position, but the changes fell within the moderate limits acceptable to the deputies of 1812, who occupied government ministries until March 1821. Their influence, however, declined progressively before the pressure of young, urban radicals, or *exaltados,* who demanded more far-reaching political reform. The growing influence of the radicals was expressed through a vigorous press, political clubs known as "patriotic societies" and, on occasion, mob violence manipulated with considerable skill. All these created a climate of instability that undermined the fragile liberal consensus and made any accommodation with the Church impossible on the basis of the reforms already carried out. Ecclesiastical legislation in the autumn of 1820 left the bishops angry but disoriented and unsure of a course of action. Even the reform of the regulars failed to evoke a massive episcopal reaction, save for a few representations sent to the Cortes, such as that of the archbishop of Valencia, Arias Teijeiro, who was promptly expelled from the kingdom for his temerity. Between a conservative Church resentful of the changes imposed on it and the liberal State suspicious of clerical sincerity an atmosphere of mutual exasperation developed by the end of 1820 that could not be dissipated.

Growing political instability throughout 1821 and early 1822 as well as urban violence encouraged by the exaltados made the new ministry formed in March 1821 ineffective from its beginning. Harassed by radicals and street violence on the left and by the intrigues of the king and his supporters on the right, the second liberal government staggered from crisis to crisis without a sense of direction. It lacked a clear policy with respect to the Church other than to expel prelates it judged subversive—those of Cádiz, Ceuta, and Málaga—and to fill important ecclesiastical positions with liberal clerics. But its nominations of José d'Espiga for Seville, Diego Muñoz Torrero for Guadix, Félix Torres Amat for Barcelona, and Manuel Abad y Queipo for Tortosa—all known for their support of moderate ecclesiastical reform—were refused by Pius VII, although the pope approved one reformer, Antonio Posada Rubín de Celis, for the bishopric of Cartagena. Failing to fill episcopal vacancies with its own men, the State used pressure, including mob violence and the threat of force, to compel cathedral chapters to elect interim diocesan administrators well disposed to the regime. In Orihuela the direct intervention of the city's mayor and council caused the chapter to retract its first choice and elect a canon sympathetic to liberal views. In Oviedo the presence of armed men at the electing chapter was sufficient to persuade the canons to choose a progovernment administrator.

Open resistance by ecclesiastics to the liberal State began in 1821 on a limited scale. Jerónimo Merino, an ex–parish priest in the province of Burgos whose guerrilla exploits against the French in the war of independence had earned him a canonry in Palencia from a grateful Ferdinand VII, took to the hills against the liberals. However, massive clerical participation in armed opposition to the regime did not begin until 1822. The election of a more radical Cortes in that year destroyed whatever possibility remained for an accommodation with the Church.

The declining influence of the reformers who had inspired the ecclesiastical changes of 1820 left initiative on Church matters with a group of exaltado clerics, including Juan Antonio Llorente, an old reformer of the 1790's whose views had become more extreme.[35] The new Cortes decided to take up the question of a sweeping reform of the Church. After forbidding bishops to ordain priests until the question had been resolved, the assembly named a commission with a substantial representation of parish priests to draft a general plan for the clergy. The proposals, presented in January 1823, went far beyond the reform of 1820.[36] They called for radical restructuring of the dioceses to accord with provincial boundaries, reduction of the pope's role in episcopal appointments to that of an adviser, abolition of the tithe, and creation of a special tax to pay the clergy's salaries. The reform plan was never passed by the Cortes, because of opposition to the scheme and perhaps because of a tacit recognition that changes so radical would do the regime little good in what had become a civil war between liberalism and its opponents.

The radical drift of the liberal revolution in 1822 as well as the obvious insincerity of the king, who was doing everything possible to bring down the constitutional system, led to a series of uprisings against the regime from Galicia to Catalonia. The most ambitious, an invasion into northwestern Catalonia financed and encouraged by the conservative government of Louis XVIII of France, began successfully by capturing the city of Urgel in the summer of 1822. The royalists were unable to follow up their initial victory, although sporadic fighting continued in the countryside for a year.

Royalist revolts did not pose an immediate danger to liberal military dominance, but they won extensive support from conservative churchmen, particularly intransigent opponents of the regime living in exile in France, and from disaffected members of the regular clergy angry over their treatment by the liberal State. Two ecclesiastics known for their commitment to absolutism—Juan de Cavia González, bishop of Osma; and Victor Sáez, canon of Toledo and ex-confessor of Ferdinand VII—formed part of the five-member regency council established in Urgel in August 1822 to rule in the name of the king, who was by then a virtual prisoner in Madrid.

The ceremony proclaiming the regency revealed the extent of clerical support for the campaign to restore absolute monarchy. Canons of the Urgel cathedral chapter attended, carrying their ceremonial cross and religious standards, while a large group of friars wearing swords on their clerical dress looked on. Priests, particularly from the regular clergy, did not hesitate to take arms against the liberals in Catalonia; over 100 perished in the royalist assault on the city of Cervera. An ex-Trappist lay brother, Antonio Marañon, terrorized rural districts with a band of unruly troops exhorted into battle with the cry: "Long live the King and Religion! Death to the Constitution!"[37] For every friar who took up arms, many more gave the royalist cause their support through preaching. The Franciscans of Catalonia later boasted that they had pronounced "constant invectives against triumphant impiety" when they preached during the war against liberalism.[38] The active participation of ecclesiastics in the revolts of 1822–1823 revealed how deeply the conservative Church was committed to the restoration of absolutism.

Clerical involvement in royalist rebellions moved the liberal State, increasingly under the influence of its most radical elements, to reprisals. The executions, burnings, and sackings of religious institutions, and the general harassment of the clergy during 1822 and 1823 were not carried out on a massive scale nor did they occur throughout the country. But the attacks on the persons and property of the clergy represented the first example in modern Spanish history of a violent anticlericalism. Liberal exasperation was greatest in Catalonia, where the Church was suspected of conspiring with the royalists of Urgel.

In Barcelona the Franciscans were accused of hiding arms and signaling from their windows to royalist agents. The authorities carried out periodic searches for arms in the order's friaries throughout the region, even opening tombs in Lérida. Between September and November 1822 the friars' position grew more precarious. Not daring to venture onto the streets, they heard cries of "traitor," "enemies of the nation," "death," and "let them die and be drawn and quartered."[39] Individual friars judged most suspect by the authorities were arrested; others fled rather than await whatever fate was in store for them. The friars of Horta thus abandoned their friary on October 16. The buildings, including the church, were set on fire after their departure. The monks of the great monastery of Poblet, one of the few monastic houses allowed to remain open after the 1820 legislation on the regular clergy, left on November 26. Local residents, long resentful of the monks' financial exactions, then invaded the monastery, burned the choir and organ, and carried off everything of value including the locks on the doors.

The campaign against the regular clergy culminated in the suppression on November 25 of all friaries and monasteries in Catalonia. By that time hundreds of religious had already abandoned their houses. Those remaining either adopted the status of secular priests or went into exile. Two boat loads of Franciscans from Barcelona were sent to Málaga and Cartagena; another two, composed of the most recalcitrant friars, were dispatched to Cuba.

The second liberal revolution and its ecclesiastical policies deepened the antagonisms within the Church that had existed since Cádiz. In Lérida the cathedral chapter divided between the priests who avidly supported the constitutional regime and those who continued to place their confidence in absolute monarchy. Among the liberal canons were Antonio Forriol, who was accused in the later royalist reaction of having shouted "Constitution or death!" from the cathedral pulpit, and Martín Laguna, whose ardent defense of the constitution in a local periodical led to his exile in 1824.[40] On the other side stood Canon Domingo Cossio, who was exiled to Ávila by the liberal authorities, and Doctor José Vidal, former administrator of the diocese, who was arrested in February 1823 along with Bishop de Rentería. In Barcelona the liberal cause received support from several ex-members of the religious orders who had taken advantage of the legislation authorizing secularization. Eudaldo Jaumeandreu, an ex-Augustinian, accepted a chair established by the local junta de comercio for the explanation of the constitution; Alberto Pujol, a former Carmelite, published a political catechism "to instruct the Catalans in the rights, privileges and advantages which the Political Constitution of the Spanish Monarchy provides."[41] Apart from a handful of prelates, such as González Vallejo, the liberal cause won little support among the bishops, however. Occasionally, the government could rely on the adherence of lesser diocesan authorities, as in Tarragona where the vicar general of the archdiocese condemned the regency of Urgel as a "criminal insurrection" designed to "change the actual system of government which the entire nation has embraced."[42]

But the situation of ecclesiastics committed to liberalism became untenable with the destruction of Church property and the executions carried out in Catalonia by increasingly undisciplined troops. The execution of more than fifty priests in the diocese of Barcelona—including the bishop of Vich, Raimundo Strauch, who had been arrested for his proabsolutist views—along with wide-spread indiscriminate violence—such as the sacking of the cathedral of Solsona by liberal soldiers in June 1823—deprived priests still loyal to the regime of whatever remained of their credibility. Even Félix Amat, the grand old man of the reforming movement and its leading intellectual exponent for two decades, finally welcomed the return of Ferdinand VII to power as the only way of ending the disorders characteristic of the liberal revolution's later stages.[43]

The conflict between the Church and the liberal State reinforced the bishops' tendency to look to Rome for defense. Although Pius VII had urged moderation on the hierarchy following the revolution of 1820, he vigorously attacked the ecclesiastical legislation of the Cortes. Prelates, such as Pedro de Inguanzo of Zamora, maintained close contacts with the papacy, which was increasingly seen as one of the few bulwarks of a Church under siege.[44] The regalism of the episcopacy during the eighteenth century became a thing of the past. The rancors and jurisdictional disputes that had once inspired an anti-Roman attitude among bishops disappeared before the much graver threat posed by the liberal State.

In April 1823 an invasion mounted by the French with the approval of the European powers put an end to the liberal experiment. The regime, weakened by divisions within its ranks and unable to reestablish its authority in the face of continued mob action and military indiscipline, succumbed virtually without a struggle. The French army moved easily through the kingdom and was welcomed by a population weary of anarchy and violence. The conservative Church, which had resisted the Napoleonic invasion with fervor, looked to the "100,000 sons of St. Louis" as saviors. In Santiago the cathedral chapter, although nearly bankrupt, donated 30,000 reales to help finance the campaign against the liberals; when the French arrived in the city, the canons sent a special delegation to receive the commander with expressions of gratitude. The rapid triumph of the invasion led quickly to the reestablishment of Ferdinand VII's absolute power. The Church again looked to the king to restore its traditional place within Spanish society, but events between 1820 and 1823 had given the Church a shock as shattering as the one it had received during the war of independence.

A Church Besieged, 1820–1823

The economic decline of the Church, only partially halted between 1814 and 1820, accelerated during the period of liberal rule. The Cortes elected in 1820 did not carry out a thorough restructuring of Church financing, although it received petitions from peasant proprietors asking for an end to the "slavery" of the tithe. In 1821 the Cortes ordered the tithe reduced by one-half and set a salary scale for the secular clergy designed to reduce expenditures on the upper levels of the ecclesiastical establishment. The reform was intended to redistribute income from bishops and canons to the parish clergy. It was in accord with liberal exaltation of parish priests as a civic and religious elite engaged in educating a rural population in public and spiritual virtues. Parish priests were "the natural educators of the people," said a liberal periodical in 1820. They would plant "the seeds of virtue" among their flocks by assisting the poor, explaining the law, and teaching the constitution.[45] The reform of 1821 attempted to resolve an obvious problem, and it promised a political return by appealing to the group that had suffered most from the inequalities of the Old Regime Church.

The hopes raised by financial reform and discussion of other projects to improve the status of parish priests were quickly disappointed. The "half-tithe" (*medio diezmo*) did not yield what was necessary to pay clerical salaries. In rural districts the pattern of tithe evasion established during the war of independence continued. Moreover, the 300-ducats-a-year salary established for parish priests still left them badly paid relative to the ecclesiastical elite, and there is evidence that in some dioceses—Palencia and Oviedo, for example—the real income of the parochial clergy declined substantially between 1820 and 1823. Diocesan revenues based on the half-tithe continued their downward spiral. By 1823 the income of Toledo, once the most opulent diocese of the Spanish Church, had fallen by one-half, compared with 1800. The revenues of the cathedral chapter of Ávila declined to their lowest level since 1764.[46] The financial reform of 1821 irritated the ecclesiastical elite of bishops and canons, who saw their incomes reduced and were resentful, in any event, of special levies, such as the 2 million reales demanded by the authorities from the chapter of Santiago in 1820. Nor did the reform satisfy the parish clergy, whose situation was as bad as ever.

In spite of declining revenues the secular clergy at least retained ownership of the rural and urban property on which its survival depended. The regular clergy was less fortunate. The 1820 reform of the regulars provided for the sale of the property of suppressed monasteries and friaries, with the proceeds to relieve the State's desperate finances. The disamortization ordered in 1820 represented the straightforward reaction of a government that saw the wealth of the orders as a convenient remedy to its own fiscal crisis; it also reflected liberal belief in economic individualism as opposed to the collective ownership of land by the traditional corporations of Spanish society. Although the State had auctioned off the property of charitable institutions and religious endowments of certain types during the reign of Charles IV, it had not directly attacked the property of either the secular or regular clergy.

Between 1820 and 1823 the government seized monastic property and began to sell it to individual buyers in a preview of the massive disamortization after 1835. Unfortunately, sale of the regulars' property after 1820 has not been studied extensively, but it is known that the State realized over 700 million reales from public auctions.[47] In 1821 alone the State disposed of the property of forty monasteries, including cloisters, churches, and ancillary buildings. Not all the holdings of the suppressed houses were sold, however. Some monastic buildings were taken over by local and military authorities for use as hospitals, barracks, asylums, and the like. The property of other religious communities—particularly of the mendicants, who depended less on tithes and rental income for financing—was often judged unattractive by prospective buyers, who offered less than the official appraisal values. Difficult economic and political conditions kept the sale of Church property within limits during the liberal regime, but it established the guidelines for a similar policy that later would destroy the economic base sustaining the religious orders.

The origins of the deeply rooted hostility against the clergy and ecclesiastical institutions that has so troubled modern Spain have not been satisfactorily explored. The proverbial anticlericalism characteristic of sectors of Spanish society in the nineteenth and twentieth centuries is difficult to explain as a simple, fixed phenomenon unrelated to political, economic, and social transformations. The term *anticlericalism* itself is a catchall that contributes little to understanding the distinct and changing anticlericalisms of Spain's recent history. At least as far back as the sixteenth century, an anticlericalism of sorts developed from the critique of the regular clergy by literary satirists and from the questioning of certain aspects of the Church's economic role. But criticism of the Church was cautiously expressed and, in any event, confined to a small group of writers and bureaucrats. A popular anticlericalism also occasionally appeared in violent form in rural areas that were dominated by great monastic foundations with extensive jurisdictional and financial rights over the surrounding countryside. Chronic and sometimes extreme tension was common enough between monasteries and local inhabitants during the eighteenth century and left a residue of bitterness in the wake of lawsuits and occasional armed confrontations. The rural anticlericalism of the eighteenth century, limited in geographic extent and episodic, did not pass to the cities, where the charitable, educational, and economic activities of the regular and secular clergy ameliorated the lot of the masses and made the Church a necessary social institution.

During the first quarter of the nineteenth century the prestige and popularity of the Church and the clergy began to wane. The Church's inability to play its traditional social role, as well as the political struggle between absolutists and liberals in which clerics were deeply involved, contributed to this process. But it was not until the second liberal regime that hostility against the Church spread so extensively that it assumed broader significance. The anticlericalisms of the past surfaced again and with a vengeance. A flood of satires, more pointed than their predecessors, ridiculed aspects of ecclesiastical life. One of the most popular, written by a priest, Salvador Miñano Bedoya—*Political Laments for a Poor Little Idler Accustomed to Live at Someone Else's Expense* (1820)—ridiculed priests living off the tithe as freeloaders whose demands were ruining the peasantry. In Miñano's work as in others, monks and friars—"the fat fathers" as one author described them—were subject to particularly intense criticism as parasitic loafers contributing nothing to society.[48] The satires of the liberal period appealed not to a restricted and cultivated elite but to a broader audience of intellectuals, reforming clerics, lawyers, bureaucrats, army of-

ficers, journalists, and others supporting the liberal cause. Miñano's work, for example, went through several editions.

Political circumstances between 1820 and 1823 lay behind the
popularity of these satirical attacks on the Church. Similar works
in the eighteenth century made fun of the foibles and shortcom-
ings of the clergy, but they dared not question the position of an
institution enjoying immense prestige and royal favor. By 1820
the consensus that once protected the Church no longer existed.
The Church had become the focus of political controversy. Liberals resented the support it had given to Ferdinand VII, and
they questioned the retention of its social and economic privileges
in the new society.

It should be stressed, however, that at no point did liberal opinion envisage a campaign against either religion or the idea that
Spain must be a Catholic State. In 1821 a decree of the Cortes
left no doubt on this score. "Anyone who conspires . . . to establish
any other religion in . . . the Spains or that the Spanish nation
should abandon its profession of the Catholic, Roman and Apostolic Religion will be persecuted as a traitor and will suffer the
death penalty."[49] As at Cádiz liberals sought to adapt the Church
to new political and social conditions while leaving intact its position as the official religion of the nation. Even the most radical
liberals, the exaltados who formed the revolutionary patriotic societies, tried "to reconcile religion and the Constitution."[50] Discussion on ecclesiastical reform in the Madrid club, one of the
most active, took an essentially moderate course designed to show,
according to one orator in 1820, "that the liberals are the true
Christians," while the opponents of change are "the enemies of
Jesus Christ."[51]

Both liberal moderates and extremists wished to remodel the
Church in their own image—to create a Church with a public-
spirited clergy, a kind of religious civil service to spread knowledge
and progress to the illiterate masses, a Church to contribute to
economic improvement rather than drain the kingdom of its productive capabilities. The obstinacy of the hierarchy and many
clerics in clinging to their memory of the privileged Church of
the eighteenth century should not have surprised liberal opinion,
and perhaps it did not. But successive liberal governments did
not know how to deal with the Church's refusal to accept this new

role. As a result a political anticlericalism developed, which took the form of rhetorical attacks on the Church in parliamentary debates and a press campaign that grew in intensity as the liberal experiment followed a more radical course. Liberals looked to public opinion to force the Church to mend its recalcitrant ways.

The unrest of local populations, irritated by the financial and jurisdictional demands of monasteries, surfaced again during the period of liberal rule. The sacking of the Cistercian monastery of Poblet in November 1822 and the invasion of the Carthusian house of Santa María de las Cuevas near Seville by a crowd that "profaned" the Church "with irreverent excesses" are examples of the "monastic," rural anticlericalism of the past.[52] Popular reaction to monasteries depended on local conditions and the nature of the exactions they imposed. Smaller foundations with modest resources that performed real services for isolated peasants often won their affection, as in Batuecas, where a small community of fifteen monks, "the principal source of religious information, of spiritual assistance, and of medicinal relief," was so esteemed by the shepherds of the district that they petitioned for the monastery's survival after the 1820 decree of suppression.[53] Hostility directed against the monasteries was still sporadic and uneven in extent, but it was expressed more violently than ever before. Moreover, it reflected the deep antagonism between the corporate property characteristic of Old Regime society and the interests of local peasants.

Between 1820 and 1823 resurgent popular opposition to and violence against monastic foundations represented the settling of decades-, perhaps centuries-old rural scores. The appearance of a distinctly popular urban anticlericalism, however, was new. We know little of its nature, its geographic extent, or the social background of its adherents. There is no study similar to that of George Rudé on the urban masses during the French Revolution. Few areas of research would be more useful for an understanding of the urban lower classes' contribution to Spanish revolutionary politics between 1820 and 1873. It is at least clear that the remarkable docility characteristic of urban populations during the eighteenth century gave way by 1820 to a mood of unrest and agitation in which hostility toward the Church was prominent. The crowds that surged through the inquisitorial prisons of Barcelona and

Madrid in March 1820 scattering papers and freeing inmates, the threats and insults directed against the Jesuits and the regulars in both cities, as well as occasional physical attacks—such as that inflicted on a Franciscan friar in the town of Mora who was dragged through the streets by an enraged mob and hurled into the river Ebro in 1822—reveal how the situation had changed. The cry "Death to the friars!" entered the vocabulary of the urban masses.

The new anticlericalism of the cities, however, was neither universal nor indiscriminate. It was most visible in Madrid, the center of the nation's political life, where the attitudes of liberal politicians could filter down to the streets through pamphlets, broadsheets, and simple word-of-mouth propaganda. But it was also important in Barcelona, where feeling against the Church ran high because of royalist activity in the region.

The specific contours of violent, urban anticlericalism in liberal Spain before 1874 remain to be studied. But it is at least clear that the declining charitable capabilities of the Church, the long and painful crisis of city economies after 1808, and the gradual conquest of the urban masses by liberalism destroyed the social contract that had protected the Church during the eighteenth century. Although it is tempting to see the historic origins of the massive anticlerical outbursts of the twentieth century in the violence of 1820–1823, the assassinations of the regular clergy that took place in Madrid and Barcelona in 1834 and 1835, and the episodic attacks occurring after the revolution of 1868, violent anticlericalism in liberal Spain developed within a narrower context than did its counterpart in the twentieth century. The most serious attacks took place early in the period, during the second liberal revolution and at the beginning of the third (1834–1835), and they focused largely on the regular clergy and its property. Once the issue of the regulars was resolved with the suppression of most of the male orders in 1836, urban violence against the Church declined noticeably. There was little during the government of General Espartero (1840–1843) and even less under the revolutionary government of 1854 to 1856.

Violence against the Church in the cities reflected the state at any given moment of the conflict between liberalism and absolutism. Attacks on the Church generally increased when the struggle was going badly for the liberals and decreased when their

cause was prospering. This may explain the lack of violence between 1854 and 1856, when the Church's threat was not perceived
as serious, and the presence of violence, although with nothing
like the virulence of 1822–1823, following the outbreak of the
Carlist War in 1872. Although the occasional violence against
the Church in the cities reflected the inchoate resentment of the
urban masses against an apparently powerful economic institution, it arose more directly from the political struggle between
liberalism and ecclesiastical interests. In the twentieth century
hostility to the Church in the cities had deeper roots in the reaction of the dispossessed against the excesses of a conservative
social order arising from the development of an industrialized
economy.

Clerics themselves perceived that the Church was losing influence; hence their frequent attacks on the cities as "modern Bab-
ylons." Whether hostility toward the Church indicated the spread
of dechristianization in large urban areas is less clear, although
evidence suggests that this may have been the case, at least in
Madrid, where the desertion of men from religious services was
being noted by observers.[54] The development of popular anticlericalism in the cities between 1820 and 1823 was limited, but
it signaled a significant change in the Church's relationship to
urban populations. The eighteenth-century Church had been urban
in a rural society, but by the 1820's the Church began to turn
slowly away from the cities and large towns toward a more reliable
Catholic countryside. The foundations were already being laid for
the divorce between the Church and the cities, which would be
as significant for the nineteenth-century Church as the isolation
of its eighteenth-century predecessor from the rural world had
been.

By 1823 the reforming movement that had developed in the
Church decades before was a spent force. The moderate clerical
reformers of 1820, nourished in the vital ecclesiastical culture of
the late eighteenth century, were an aging group incapable of
producing a second generation to carry on the struggle. The death
of Félix Amat in 1824 deprived them of their last figure of intellectual significance, and absolutist purges did the rest. A few
reformers lingered on, Pedro González Vallejo and Antonio Posada Rubín de Celis, for example, to reappear after 1835, but the

religious and intellectual atmosphere that had allowed the movement to flourish had dissipated long since.

The reformers of 1820 looked to the liberal State to transform
the Church so that they might realize their lofty, moral vision of
the institution. By the end of 1820 their hopes lay in ruins because
of their own miscalculations about the reform of the regulars, the
growing antagonism between conservative ecclesiastics and the
Cortes, and, not least, the radical direction of the liberal revolution. By 1822 the question for liberal exaltados and the minority
of clerics supporting them was no longer the purification of the
Church so that it might fulfill its spiritual mission more effectively,
but the domestication of an institution refusing to cooperate with
the State. Caught between the recalcitrance of the conservative
Church and the frustration of liberal politicians, the reforming
ideal that had inspired a select and cultivated clerical minority
since the 1780's was doomed.

The declining influence of the ecclesiastical reformers at least
clarified the problem of the Church for both liberals and the
ecclesiastical leadership. By 1823 neither side accepted the idea
of reform that had emerged from within the royal Church of the
late eighteenth century. The alliance between the regalistic policies
of the old monarchy and the liberalism of a new political elite had
obscured, if anything, the problem of a Church intent on preserving its traditional situation in a time of rapid political change.
The ground was clear for a straightforward conflict between a
Church that was increasingly ultramontane in its sympathies and
allied with Ferdinand VII and the diverse currents of liberal
opinion determined to force it into line.

Throne and Altar, 1823–1833

The conservative Church welcomed the restoration of Ferdinand VII to absolute power. As in 1814 the king hastened to
satisfy the Church by annulling liberal ecclesiastical legislation,
allowing the regulars to reoccupy their houses, and appointing
his ex-confessor, Victor Sáez, a clerical ultra of the first order, to
an influential ministry. Sáez quickly commanded that devotions
to the Blessed Sacrament be held throughout the kingdom to
appease divine wrath for the injuries inflicted on the Church dur-

ing liberal rule. He also dispatched missionary friars to preach against what he saw as erroneous and heretical opinions. On the surface the situation appeared similar to that of 1814; in fact, the measures taken to appease the Church did not satisfy a growing body of intransigent clerics. The illusion that once led ecclesiastics to trust Ferdinand to inaugurate a golden age of religion had long since dissipated. Instinctively, churchmen realized that the king had cleverly used them for his own ends; they did not intend allowing him to play the same game again. Moreover, clerical participation in two years of conspiracy and armed revolt against the liberal State gave some ecclesiastics a taste for political intrigue that they did not abandon when their cause triumphed.

The vague, theocratic hopes that had inspired the Church in its crusade against the Cortes of Cádiz gave way to a more straight-forward objective—the eradication of liberalism from Spanish soil. Royalist periodicals under clerical influence demanded that all "apostles of irreligion" should leave the country and that civil and ecclesiastical posts should be held only by the "truly Catholic."[55] The Church set about purging liberal sympathizers from its ranks. Bishops such as González Vallejo and Rubín de Celis were sent packing, and cathedral canons turned on colleagues who had sup-ported liberalism. In Oviedo the canons accused Domingo So-moza, the diocese's administrator during the liberal regime and a prominent exaltado cleric, of being guilty of "perversion"; they stripped him of his canonry and benefices. Miguel de Riego, an-other canon of Oviedo and brother of the hero of 1820, suffered the same fate; in Badajoz the chapter purged one of its members for criticizing the king and displaying "implacable hatred" against the Inquisition. The purge even reached down to the parish clergy; in San Roque in Cádiz the parish priest was ousted simply for having baptized a child with the name "John of the Constitution."[56]

Conservative ecclesiastics and the king shared an aversion for liberalism, hence the campaign of repression carried out by Church and State against dissidents. But the Church, or at least its most ultra representatives, who had learned a thing or two about po-litical pressure and manipulation during the liberal period, were determined to force Ferdinand VII to conform entirely to their demands. Their campaign centered on restoring the Inquisition. Even before the liberal regime's end, the bishops living in exile had petitioned Pius VII for revival of the Holy Tribunal as the "strongest bulwark of the faith."[57] An intransigent royalist press under clerical influence insistently demanded the reestablishment of the Inquisition during the summer and autumn of 1823. The dismissal of Sáez in December and a royal proposal drafted under French pressure for a limited amnesty in 1824 aroused the apprehension of the ultras, who redoubled efforts to force the king into line. A letter the bishop of Urgel sent to Ferdinand in January 1824 reveals how aggressive and independent the conservative Church was becoming. Bishop Bernardo Francés Caballero denounced the monarch for timidity in not having restored the Inquisition and accused the new ministry, composed of more moderate figures than the deposed Sáez, of being masons and Jansenists in disguise.

During 1824 Church opposition to even the slightest concession to the vanquished liberals became more threatening. "Do not forget what Isaiah said," declared the bishop of León, "you should not have union with the impious even in the grave." Secret royalist societies in which ecclesiastics were represented proliferated. Although historians previously doubted the existence of these societies, Tejada has proven through the use of police records that they formed the nucleus of conspiratorial activity designed to bring the government under their control.[58]

Societies in Madrid, Valencia, Murcia, Tortosa, Barcelona, Oviedo, Extremadura, Granada, and Jaén included prominent churchmen. The intendant general of police in Valencia reported to Madrid that the administrator of the archdiocese, José María Pujol, and members of the religious orders—such as Fray Serafino de Penaquilla, a Capuchin known for his preaching abilities— were engaging in conspiratorial activity. In Murcia the cathedral dean, Blas Ostolaza, an ex–traditionalist deputy at Cádiz, was implicated; in Tortosa the bishop and many of the canons were involved. The appearance of these "apostolic juntas" as well as of a group of intriguers in Madrid, who suitably named themselves the Society of the Exterminating Angel, created a climate of agitation and coercion not unlike that with which the liberals had pressured Ferdinand VII between 1820 and 1823.

The activity of these conspiratorial groups did not pose a serious threat to the government, however. Police spies, including some ecclesiastics such as Canon Solera in Madrid, kept the king fully informed of what was transpiring. Suspected clerics, like the general of the Franciscans, Fray Cirilo Alameda, later cardinal and archbishop of Toledo, were closely watched by the authorities. An attempted ultra rising at Manresa in 1825 was easily quashed, as was a more serious revolt, *la guerra de los agraviados,* in rural Catalonia two years later.

The ultra Church, frustrated by the king's refusal to reestablish the Inquisition and deal as severely as possible with dissenters, began to turn in 1825 toward the king's brother and heir to the throne, Charles. The unimaginative and reactionary prince had won clerical approval by voting in the Council of State to reestablish the Inquisition. To what extent Charles was involved in the widespread intrigues of the mid-1820's is not entirely clear, but the authorities suspected that conspirators in Madrid maintained contact with him through Cirilo Alameda using the cover of Franciscan friaries. How much support the clerical ultras had within the Church is also difficult to establish. The papal nuncio, Giustiniani, and Rome counseled Spanish ecclesiastics to follow a policy of moderation, and many did so though they continued to support royal absolutism. In fact, a division took place within the conservative Church between a minority of bishops, canons, and friars who were deeply involved in efforts to impose their will on the king and a "silent" majority who were as docile as ever to governmental authority. The ultras had a following among the parish clergy in certain regions, notably Catalonia, where the memory of liberal attacks on the Church was still fresh, and Cuenca, where a government circular to the bishop urging civil peace was read "through gritted teeth" by local priests according to police reports.[59]

Confronted by aggressive clerics, Ferdinand VII did not have the luxury available to him in 1814 to deal with a Church unequivocally committed to the maintenance of his absolute power. The king, aware of clerical complicity in the risings of 1825 and 1827, mistrusted the ultras and regarded their campaign to reestablish the Inquisition as a threat to the Crown's independence. He could not, however, afford to alienate the segment of the Church most hostile to liberalism by a policy of repression against ecclesiastical extremists. Ferdinand chose instead to follow a dangerous but shrewd course—balancing the respective interest groups supporting his regime. He hemmed and hawed on the Inquisition, occasionally leaning in favor of reestablishment but in the end successfully resisting ultra pressure on the question.

The king was faced with a more difficult problem beginning in 1824, episcopal inquisitions organized without Madrid's approval in Valencia, Tarragona, and Orihuela. These "Juntas of Faith," operating with the sanction of local authorities and eventually with the tacit but grudging approbation of the central government, were designed to secure, according to Simón López, the archbishop of Valencia, "correction, salutary penitences, retractions and the return of a thousand who have repented to the bosom of the Church."[60] The juntas never enjoyed official standing, but they went about their work with inquisitorial thoroughness. The junta of Valencia sentenced a liberal canon to ten years' imprisonment after forcing him to denounce the constitution as "detestable, sacrilegious, [and] contrary to divine and human law."[61]

The independent action of the juntas troubled the king, who unsuccessfully ordered their dissolution in 1825. The junta of Valencia continued and in 1826 secured the execution of a liberal school teacher, Cayetano Ripoll. Although the central government through the minister of justice had no choice but to approve the sentence, Madrid knew very little of the judicial process until it was nearly completed. Moreover, the government's police officials increasingly resented the juntas' autonomy and raised obstacles to their operation. The king, fearing that the juntas could be as dangerous to him as the Inquisition, kept them from spreading, and by 1827 those already established had ceased to function. Their brief existence, however, revealed the delicacy of the political balance in the mid-1820's.

Until his death in 1833 Ferdinand successfully frustrated ultra hopes for the establishment of a totally repressive regime. Although the king occasionally had to recognize their strength, as he did following the attempted liberal rising of 1830, he relied on moderate ministers—such as Francisco de Cea Bermúdez—who, though committed to absolutism, fell within bureaucratic traditions much like those of the Old Regime monarchy. Ferdinand's suspicions of ultra intentions lay behind his moderate direction during his later years. The birth of a daughter, the future

Isabella II, in 1830 to the elderly monarch and his young wife, María Cristina of Naples, reinforced these tendencies. The king's resolve, encouraged by the queen's insistence, to secure the accession of Isabella, setting aside Charles's claims, created an atmosphere of political intrigue at the court. Partisans of Charles and Isabella struggled to influence Ferdinand's decision. The king vacillated under intense ultra pressure, but in the end held to his original intention. The need to broaden the base of support for Isabella's controversial succession led to the beginnings of an uncertain and tentative policy of accommodation, designed to persuade liberal opinion to support a more moderate royal absolutism against Charles's ultra tendencies.

Between 1824 and 1830 the Church experienced a recovery similar to that of 1814–1820. The religious orders repossessed their property from purchasers, who were unceremoniously expelled from their holdings.[62] But there were indications that neither the secular nor the regular clergy could recover their prerevolutionary prosperity. Christian Hermann has noted the catastrophic decline in income suffered by certain episcopal households (Table 4). The continuing crisis of agriculture as well as the destruction of buildings between 1820 and 1823 placed monasteries and convents in economic difficulties from which they never recovered. Wealthy foundations, such as the monastery of Guadalupe, were forced to sell property to survive. The friaries of the mendicants, which depended heavily on pious donations to meet expenses, were caught in even more difficult circumstances. The Minims of Andalusia found themselves so hard-pressed that they refused to accept novices who could not pay for their own food and lodging.

There are indications that some monasteries and friaries reversed the long downward trend in recruitment, but overall the orders' demographic decline continued.[63] Statistics gathered in 1835, before the final dissolution of the regulars, set their number at 30,906, a loss of more than 3,000 since 1820 and of over 18,000 since the census of 1787.[64] Declining numbers, however, did not reverse the deteriorating quality of religious life. Superiors constantly lamented departures from the norms of conventual practice, and the chronic factionalism that had characterized the orders since the eighteenth century continued unabated. Disputes be-

Table 4. Revenues of selected episcopal households, 1813–1827 (in reales).

	Revenues in the year—				
City	1813	1815	1823	1826	1827
Granada	1,786,897	—	834,666	—	528,153
Jaén	1,106,093	—	873,815	535,104	—
Málaga	—	1,404,497	759,819	674,722	—

Source: Christian Hermann, "Les revenus des évêques espagnols au dix-huit-ième siècle (1650–1830)," *Mélanges de la Casa de Velázquez,* 10 (1974), 196.

tween friars and their superiors troubled many convents, as in Almagro, where in 1833 the prior appealed to the civil authorities for assistance in restoring order after discovering one of his novices carrying a pistol under his habit.[65]

Nor did any fundamental changes in the situation of the secular clergy occur. The episcopacy continued to be dominated by a clerical minority of well-educated prelates, but they had less intellectual breadth than their predecessors of the eighteenth century. Pedro de Inguanzo, named archbishop of Toledo and primate of Spain in 1824, was typical of the members of the Fernandine hierarchy. An able canon lawyer and polemicist, Inguanzo devoted himself primarily to defense of the Church's rights and support of Ferdinand VII rather than to the cultural and social projects common under the Caroline bishops.

The clerical elite of cathedral canons and university professors produced few figures to recall the public-spirited and cultivated clergy of the eighteenth century. One of the handful of distinguished intellectual figures in the Church of the 1820's was Félix Torres Amat, nephew of the celebrated Jansenist intellectual. Torres Amat undertook a new translation of the Bible, held membership in the Royal Academy of History and other learned societies, and gathered a fine collection of Catalan books and manuscripts in Barcelona. The fate of his translation of the Bible, however, reveals the intellectual decline of the clergy. Although Torres Amat devoted years to his work, he had to struggle against the opposition of the archbishop of Toledo, Inguanzo, and the papal nuncio, Giustiniani, to the translation's publication. Only the financial assistance of Anglican friends in London allowed the work to appear between 1833 and 1835 after numerous delays.[66]

There was no indication that the condition of the lower clergy had improved as the reign of Ferdinand VII drew to a close. In 1831 the papal nuncio, Francesco Tiberi, reported to Rome that ignorance and moral irregularities were still common among the secular clergy.[67] Moreover, the fundamental problems of the eighteenth-century Church remained—the imbalanced distribution of resources, a large number of beneficed clergy who did no pastoral work, and the reluctance of priests to accept posts in poor rural districts.

In 1824 the Church turned again to traditional pastoral methods to maintain its religious position. The reestablishment of the regulars allowed the missions to resume. Although some missionaries compared favorably with the great figures of the eighteenth century, notably the Franciscan Fray José de Areso, the missionary effort was no longer an effective instrument of popular evangelization. The increasingly political character of preaching as well as the lack of religious vitality and commitment in the orders reduced the missions to formal exercises, which contrasted with the emotional fervor of both priests and congregations during the eighteenth century.

Within the ritual life of the Church, the old chasm between extravagant ceremonial and the practices of "popular" religion persisted. In spite of declining ecclesiastical wealth, cathedrals still held Masses of Baroque splendor. A visitor to Toledo in 1830 thus marveled at the "heavenly" music of the high Mass, sung to the accompaniment of "a variety of bassoons, viols, and violins and a powerful choir of voices." At the shrine of Begoña in the Basque Provinces, the clergy still went to the portico of the church at the beginning of every thunderstorm to sprinkle the sky with holy water.[68] Devotionalism encouraged by the Church—particularly the cult of the Sacred Heart, which began to develop into the nineteenth century's most popular devotion—suffocated the modest efforts of eighteenth-century reformers to create a simpler, more interior faith. The Scriptures, although available in various vernacular editions, were not widely read, even by the clergy.[69] The combination of popular religion and devotions promoted by the Church completely dominated forms of religious expression and would do so well into the twentieth century.

Between 1823 and 1833 the Spanish Church enjoyed for the last time the privileges and power it had accumulated over the centuries, despite their diminution over the preceding four decades. In retrospect, these years can be seen to have formed a brief interlude in the struggle between a Church determined to preserve its institutional position within the State and society and new political forces bent on modifying the Church to conform to their ideology and economic principles. It was in the end an unequal struggle. With its material resources depleted and its intellectual and spiritual vitality sapped, the Church had few inner resources to sustain it in the long conflict with liberalism. Increasingly politicized and factionalized, it continued to place its hopes on the survival of absolute monarchy, whether that of Ferdinand VII or the more extreme version propounded by supporters of Charles. Both would prove incapable of saving the Church from the revolution imposed on it by a triumphant liberalism.

5 / The Destruction of the Old Regime Church, 1833–1843

Upon the death of Ferdinand VII in 1833 the struggle between the Church and liberalism entered its decisive phase. Although Spanish liberals were divided into factions whose commitment to reform ranged from moderate to extreme, they were agreed at least on the necessity of redefining the Church's position within a new political and social order. There was no question of allowing the eighteenth-century Church to transfer its privileges intact into a society with political, economic, and intellectual assumptions so different from those that had characterized absolute monarchy. In the end the conflict between liberalism and the Church was an uneven contest, which the latter could not hope to win. By 1843 the institutional base of the Old Regime Church had been largely dismantled. And in response to the changes imposed by the State, the Church began to acquire a new character that in one form or another would survive until the ferment produced in Spain by the reforms of the Second Vatican Council.

Between the death of Ferdinand VII in September 1833 and the departure into exile in July 1843 of General Espartero, whose radical policies seemed to threaten the survival of the Church, a battered ecclesiastical organization collapsed before a final liberal assault. Institutions, functions, and intellectual assumptions that had long sustained the Church disappeared before a new wave of reforms. For Catholic apologists the events of this decade provided convincing evidence of a "great undertaking to decatholicize Spain."[1] But the struggle between the Church and liberalism was too complex to allow for easy generalizations. The kingdom remained officially Catholic even in the most radical phase of the extended liberal revolution. The Constitution of 1837 proclaimed: "the religion of the Spanish nation is the Catholic and Roman."[2] But in this still confessional State, monks and friars were murdered, priests assaulted, churches and monasteries sacked, and dioceses left without bishops. Yet the faith continued to be practiced, and successive governments accepted financial responsibility for support of the parochial clergy. At the height of legislation seen by many churchmen as a direct attack on Catholicism itself, a provincial governor of Toledo imposed fines and prison sentences on citizens failing to fulfill the Easter Communion obligation, while the bishop of Cádiz secured funds to complete the city's enormous Neoclassic cathedral, which had stood unfinished for forty years.[3]

This apparent confusion arose from a simple fact; the issue between 1833 and 1843 was not Catholicism or anti-Catholicism. No politician suggested the separation of Church and State or advocated a campaign to destroy religion. Longares Alonso, in his recent study of the liberal press in Barcelona during the 1830's, noted that atheistic or openly irreligious sentiments rarely found their way into local newspapers.[4] For Spanish liberals, religion was as important to the progress of the new society as for traditionalists committed to the old social order. Liberalism and Catholicism would remain identified, though admittedly in a difficult relationship, for over a century until the Second Republic disassociated the Church from the State for the first time in the nation's history. Liberal opinion demanded that the Church adjust to the needs of a changing society dominated by an emerging bourgeoisie, a society secular in its concerns and committed to the doctrines of economic individualism and human progress.

Liberalism rejected the theocratic ideology of the Old Regime Church, with its mingling of the sacred and the secular, and resented the Church's economic structure and judicial privileges. Clerical support for absolutism intensified liberal determination to eliminate the Church as a source of political opposition, but this was to be accompanied by an effort "to reduce . . . beliefs . . . to the grave and mysterious simplicity of primitive Christianity, to the contemplation of divine morality and the progressive development of its perfections." The Church, then, was to be confined to a purely spiritual and vaguely philanthropic role in which religion was "pure, peaceful and perfect," a natural complement to a secular society in control of its own destiny.[5] Conflict inevitably arose between these opposing interpretations of the

Church's place within Spanish society. The traditional ecclesiastical order, though deeply scarred by the battles of 1810–1813 and 1820–1823, yearned for a return to the glories, wealth, privileges, and piety of the past.

Gradual Reform and Carlism, 1834–1835

The dynastic preoccupations of Ferdinand VII, who had twice saved the Church from revolution, opened the way to liberalism's triumph. The arrangements for Isabella's orderly succession rested on the ability of the queen regent, María Cristina, and the chief minister, Francisco Cea Bermúdez, to continue the moderate absolutism of Ferdinand's later years. These hopes were quickly frustrated. The monarch's death on September 29, 1833, stimulated reforming demands from within the regime by aristocrats, courtiers, generals, and bureaucrats wishing to broaden the base of the Crown's support to avoid a return to the popular radicalism of the early 1820's. Cea Bermúdez's obstinate refusal to contemplate changes weakened the government, but the decisive blow came from another source, the general rising in diverse parts of the peninsula of those supporting the dynastic claims of the king's brother, Charles. The government's failure to dominate the revolt endangered the fragile succession of Isabella II and forced the queen regent to turn to the moderate liberals of 1812 for the support that would destroy Carlism and save the throne. In January 1834 María Cristina called a former deputy at Cádiz to head the government, Francisco Martínez de la Rosa. The third liberal revolution within a quarter of a century had begun.[6]

With few exceptions, the hierarchy recognized the young princess as heiress to the throne in a long ceremony at the church of the Hieronymites in Madrid in June 1833. The crusty archbishop of Toledo, Pedro de Inguanzo, who had fought many an absolutist battle, refused to attend on the grounds of health, although he later took the oath of loyalty under pressure. The most prominent episcopal absentee, Joaquín de Abarca, bishop of León and a fervent supporter of the pretender, had fled his diocese for the mountains of Galicia. From there he urged his fellow prelates to refuse their loyalty to Isabella in a letter promptly burned by most of the bishops receiving it. Superiors of the religious orders published statements praising the young queen throughout the autumn of 1833.[7]

The adhesion of the clerical establishment to Isabella arose in part from a profoundly conservative mentality, which would allow no questioning of the succession established by a legitimate sovereign. But it also developed from many bishops' sincere conviction that only Isabella's succession could prevent the horrors of civil war. "To recognize, love and obey the Queen," said Pedro Martínez de San Martín, bishop of Barcelona, "was the only way to assure the peace, the unity, the felicity, the mutual love which we owe to one another . . . and so necessary for the prosperity of states, particularly our beloved country which is unfortunately divided into diverse opinions and parties."[8] On the practical side, the continuation of Cea Bermúdez in office soothed a clergy uneasy about the future. But there were early signs of clerical participation in the Carlist rising that began in October. The priestly veteran of two previous campaigns against liberalism, Jerónimo Merino, immediately joined the revolt. He assisted at the ceremony in Aranda that proclaimed the pretender as Charles V, as did several Franciscans from a nearby friary in Aguilera. Even the papal nuncio admitted in December that clerics were participating in the rising.[9] Yet the prevailing tendency among the clergy was to wait uneasily on events.

The government of Martínez de la Rosa (January 1834–June 1835) rested on an alliance between the Crown and the moderate elements of liberalism—the landowners, merchants, prosperous lawyers, and noblemen committed to restoration of a parliamentary regime dominated by an enlightened elite. Its fundamental constitutional document, the *Estatuto Real* of April 1834, provided for a narrow franchise designed to exclude the exaltados who had taken control of the revolution of 1820. But oligarchic liberalism proved unworkable. The proliferation of the exaltado press, allowed by the government itself, and the eventual return to political life of the radicals combined with military failure against the Carlists to undo the settlement of 1834 and move the revolution in a more extreme direction.

The ecclesiastical policy of the oligarchic liberals resembled that of 1820; it emphasized reform of the regular clergy, improvement in the economic condition of parish priests, and elimination of "superstition" from the Church. The most influential advocate of reform, the minister of justice, Nicolás Garelli, believed from his experience as a member of the commission that had drafted the *ley de monacales* in 1820 that the government had erred then by not seeking the Church's cooperation. Having been burned once by clerical reaction to its legislation, the government approached the problem in 1834 with greater caution and, from a tactical point of view, some common sense. In April it appointed a royal commission, the Real Junta Eclesiástica, composed of ten bishops and four laymen to study the question of the regulars.[10] Garelli, however, did not intend to rush headlong into reforms. The commission was instructed to gather statistical information on the orders before drafting a comprehensive plan of reform. The commission went about its work thoroughly and gathered the most accurate statistics on the regulars since the census of 1797.

If political events had not undermined oligarchic liberalism, the government would have reduced the number of religious houses to the same extent as in 1820. Whether the Church would have accepted such a reform is doubtful. The government appointed bishops to the commission known for their "sincere adhesion to legitimacy." They included the handful of liberal prelates who had previously supported reform: the bishop of Sigüenza, Manuel Fraile; the bishop of Astorga, Félix Torres Amat; the bishop of Cartagena expelled by Ferdinand VII, Antonio Posada Rubín de Celis; and Pedro González Vallejo, who had been ousted from the diocese of Mallorca in 1823. Although the commission survived until 1836, the disintegration of the government in 1835 revealed that a limited reform of the regulars would not satisfy either the Church or liberal exaltados. Ecclesiastical change based on reform of the orders was either too much or too little. It satisfied no one.

An ecclesiastical policy based on a cautiously implemented reform might have succeeded in 1820; it was swept aside by events in 1834 and 1835. For the government restraint became difficult beginning in the spring of 1834 as friars and monks joined the Carlist rising. Monasteries and convents in isolated mountain areas of the Basque Provinces, Navarra, Galicia, Toledo, Cuenca, and Andalusia furnished food, supplies, and quarters to passing Carlist bands. The wealthy monastery of Sobrado in Galicia was said to have donated 22,000 reales to local Carlist troops; similar accusations were directed against the Benedictine monastery of Oña in the Burgos Mountains and the Capuchins of Casares in the Ronda hills of Andalusia. The extent of support varied enormously. In some cases religious provided help because they had no choice. "Let those live whom God wishes," said the superior of a Dominican priory in the Santander Mountains when he learned that he had just given supplies to a group of Carlists.[11] Other houses were more deeply implicated. The Franciscans of Bilbao were rumored to have manufactured 2 million cartridges for the Carlist army.

The contribution of the regulars to the rising, however, should not be exaggerated. Although the regions where Carlism enjoyed considerable military success between 1833 and 1839—a long swath running from the Basque Provinces through Navarra and mountainous Aragón to the hills of Catalonia—were known then as now for their Catholicism, there were relatively few monasteries and friaries in these districts of small, peasant proprietors. The urban character of the Old Regime Church came to haunt the regulars, for the cities were firmly under liberal control. Revuelta González in his study of the religious orders has shown that the vast majority of the regulars, though sympathetic to the cause of Carlism, remained passive and fearful as they awaited the fate the liberal State was preparing for them. The secular clergy was also represented in Carlist ranks. At the end of 1834 the governor of Logroño drew up a list of clerical conspirators including twenty-five secular priests as well as fifteen monks and friars. Although only a minority of the regular clergy actively supported Carlism and seculars were as deeply implicated, liberal opinion, which had not forgotten the orders' earlier defense of absolutism, concentrated its hostility against them. In March 1834 Martínez de la Rosa ordered the closing of all religious houses left vacant by the desertion of at least a sixth of their residents to the rebellion. This led to the suppression of fifty, such as the Capuchin house of Pamplona, which the authorities found empty on the morning of August 6 after the friars had carried off sacred vessels, vestments, small statues, and supplies during the night.

The closing of abandoned or subversive monasteries and friaries affected an insignificant number of the kingdom's 1,940 male religious houses, but it irritated clerical opinion. Legislation making novices liable for military service and suspension of appointments to canonries and other benefices without pastoral functions also aroused ecclesiastical tempers. The archbishop of Seville, as early as January 1834, wrote that the new government's policies "presaged a fatal future for the Spanish Church."[12] But during its first six months in office, the ministry of Martínez de la Rosa moved with such caution that no comprehensive plan of Church reform was either drafted or implemented. Measures taken against the rebel clergy were limited in character and imposed by political circumstances as even the papal nuncio, Francesco Tiberi, recognized when he informed Rome that the "perversity and malice" of some priests had moved the "Catholic, pious and just Queen" to take action against some regulars.[13]

The political strategy of the liberal elite controlling the government proved as unworkable as it had been fourteen years earlier. Ecclesiastical reform was postponed because the ministry feared that the Church would desert en masse and contribute to the victory of Carlism. The relationship of the Church to Carlism is a complex topic as yet inadequately studied, but it is clear that while Carlism was identified with the Church, the Church was not exclusively identified with Carlism. Charles V proclaimed his intention to respect the organization and privileges of the Old Regime Church. His propaganda dwelt on the Catholic nature of his monarchy and the persecuting character of the liberal State. Perhaps a decisive majority of the clergy sympathized with the objectives of Carlism, but this did not mean they actively participated in the struggle against liberalism. The Church, with its resources and personnel concentrated in the liberal cities, lacked the freedom of action to contribute in any practical way to the triumph of a movement that failed to establish itself outside its northern, rural strongholds. Relations between the Church and the liberal regime would deteriorate rapidly after 1835, but even then, in spite of clerical rhetoric, the Church could do nothing other than survive as well as possible and await better times. With a sense of the possible, the episcopacy did not rush to identify itself with Carlism even in the most difficult moments. Prelates such as Joaquín de Abarca, later Charles V's chief minister, were unusual; most bishops at odds with the liberal State preferred prudent exile to a journey to the northern mountains of the Carlist domain.

The situation of the Church in absolutist Spain was not as comfortable as Carlist apologists maintained. Charles V might attend Mass and participate in processions giving testimony to his Catholicism, as he did when he visited the Jesuits of Loyola in 1835, but the reality of the Church's position was harsher. The Carlist kingdom of the north desperately required financial resources and did not hesitate to appropriate parish tithes in areas under its control. Nor did the Church escape the violence inevitable in a relatively undisciplined army. The religious press complained about the depredations of Carlist troops as bitterly as it did about liberal exactions: "the advocates of Charles," said a Catholic paper, "did not recognize any limits, any subordination or discipline," as they moved through the rural districts of the archdiocese of Tarragona "trampling upon the unfortunate inhabitants."[14] The ecclesiastical leadership, by avoiding direct support of the Carlist cause, implicitly recognized that, whatever the movement's ideological appeal, it could not guarantee the Church's institutional survival.

The government of 1834 overestimated the extent to which the Church could contribute to a Carlist victory, and it underestimated the strength of a new generation of liberal exaltados. The radicals—drawn from the less affluent sectors of the middle classes, lawyers, journalists, minor government employees, and others—demanded a less restrictive constitution, a total reform of the Church, and economic policies less favorable to an oligarchy dominated by landowners and financial and commercial interests. The exaltados were committed, however, as firmly as their liberal opponents to the principle of private property. But unlike them, they were prepared to use extraparliamentary methods to achieve their political goals. Secret societies, masonic lodges, a forceful and flamboyant press, manipulation of lower class discontent through mob violence, and resort to military intervention—all had a place in the exaltado arsenal. To realize his objective of political stability administered by the liberal elite, Martínez de la Rosa desperately required victories over the Carlists. His generals, foiled by the brilliant tactics of Colonel Zumalacárregui in the north, did

not produce them, and liberal politics entered a turbulent period
of municipal revolution, popular rioting, and exaltado ascendancy.

Hopes for a limited ecclesiastical reform came to an end on a
hot summer day in 1834. On July 17 rioting mobs in Madrid left
seventy-eight Jesuits, Franciscans, Dominicans, and Mercedarians
dead and their residences devastated. Never in Spanish history
had there been such a savage, collective attack on the clergy. For
generations of clerical historians, July 17 was the "day of infamy"
initiating the violent anticlericalism of the nineteenth and twentieth centuries. Whether the attack on the regulars resulted from
a carefully planned conspiracy by the exaltados is unclear to this
day. Martínez de la Rosa believed that his extremist opponents
had fomented the riots through the secret societies, using their
influence in the city's militia. The most recent study of the events
of July 17, by Revuelta González, argues for the idea of a radical
conspiracy instead of "spontaneous combustion." The truth may
lie somewhere between.

Conditions in Madrid on the eve of the rioting formed an explosive mixture ready for ignition. In the oppressive heat of the
summer rising food prices aroused popular resentment; rumors
of impending Carlist attacks heightened tension, and the appearance in the city for the first time of the dreaded disease of the
nineteenth century, cholera, created a mood of terror. To the
high cost of bread, fear of attack, and the pervasive presence of
death must be added an intense atmosphere of political propaganda and intrigue. The fatal link of death and misery with the
regulars took the form of a rumor that monks and friars allied
to Carlism were poisoning the wells, and that this had caused the
epidemic ravaging the city. On the afternoon of July 17, crowds
drawn from the lower classes, but with the significant participation
of urban militiamen, gathered in three of Madrid's squares, the
Plaza Mayor, the Puerta del Sol, and the Plazuela de la Cebada.
At the cry "Poison! poison! Death to the Jesuits! Death to the
friars!" the mobs converged on the Jesuit church of San Isidro
and the adjoining Colegio Imperial.[15]

Scenes of bloodletting and violence followed that no conspiracy
could have planned. The crowd invaded the Jesuit house and
murdered fourteen priests, including several who had escaped to

the streets only to be identified immediately because they wore
hats in the heat to disguise their tonsures. Religious objects were
smashed and the bones of saints kept in reliquaries were ground
into dust as the mob surged through the buildings. After sacking
the Colegio Imperial, the crowd moved to other religious houses.
The same scenes were repeated at the Dominican priory of Santo
Tomás, although most of its friars escaped at news of the earlier
assault. The Franciscans of San Francisco were less fortunate;
forty perished in a ferocious attack that saw some stabbed, some
drowned in the wells, some hanged, and others hurled to their
deaths from the rooftops where they had taken refuge. On the
streets women danced a macabre ballet in stolen religious vestments. The bloody scenes did not end until well into the night.

During the rioting the authorities were less than vigorous. The
captain general of Madrid, present for an extended time in the
Colegio Imperial, failed to take action, and a sizable contingent
of troops outside San Francisco watched the destruction passively.
But a small band of soldiers succeeded in saving the Carmelite
friary from assault. The paralysis of the local military and police
may have reflected simple confusion and indecision rather than
complicity. The government of Martínez de la Rosa condemned
the violence; dismissed the captain general, provincial governor,
and superintendent of police; and took steps to preserve public
order in the days following the rioting. Neither the government
nor the liberal press attached particular importance to the *matanza
de los frailes*. Liberals of both camps saw the rioting as a regrettable
breakdown of law and order and a lapse from the norms of civ-
ilized behavior but as an event somewhat understandable given
the state of popular passions.

The disturbances of July 17 resembled the traditional urban
riot of the eighteenth century rather than later attacks on the
clergy and Church property. Arising from a popular mood of
resentment and fear, the rioting took the form of a brief, violent
outburst, which died down more of its own accord than through
official intervention. The local character of the disturbances, the
absence of any statement of goals, and the terrible savagery of
the assaults make it dubious that July 17 represented a radical
conspiracy to bring about a political revolution at the expense of
the regular clergy, although liberal exaltados were willing to ex-

ploit popular animosities. But these events marked a turning point in the history of the Spanish Church. Although the royal commission charged with drafting a moderate reform of the regulars continued its work, the possibility of implementing such a policy was remote in the face of the indifference or hostility of liberal opinion and the fury of popular feeling against monks and friars. July 17 revealed beyond a shadow of a doubt that the esteem the orders had once enjoyed among the urban lower classes was a thing of the past. It was only a question of time before the final assault would begin against this bulwark of the Old Regime Church.

Between July 1834 and Martínez de la Rosa's departure from office in June 1835, political stability became increasingly difficult to sustain. A limited electoral franchise failed to keep the radicals from winning substantial representation in the Cortes elected under the terms of the *Estatuto Real*. Exaltado criticism of the government in parliament and the press grew more intense in the face of a deteriorating military situation. Popular riots in Zaragoza in April 1835 against Archbishop Francés Caballero, known for his absolutist views, provided a reminder of the continuing danger from the urban crowd. The ministry's inability to control the country and the Cortes became evident in the spring 1835 parliamentary debate over the fate of the property of the regulars that had been sold to private purchasers between 1820 and 1823 and returned to the orders by Ferdinand VII in 1824. The government's project, to compensate the purchasers with state bonds and delay a final decision on the property until the Real Junta Eclesiástica presented its recommendations, initiated furious debate. The issue went beyond the disposition of the property holdings involved in the disamortization of 1820–1823. It signified nothing less than the fate of the orders.

The radicals, assisted by some ex-deputies of 1812, such as Agustín Argüelles, quickly took the offensive. Their attack on the orders was unrelenting. Martínez de la Rosa's argument that reform must come with "firm and measured steps, although they appeared slow," was swept aside by a torrent of criticism.[16] The regulars, said a radical deputy, were only state employees, and the government could dispose of their jobs and property as it wished. Deputies contrasted the "useful citizens" who had purchased clerical property with the idle monks and friars and goaded the ministry with accusations of timidity before the power of the orders accused of rebellion and treason. "The clergy, gentlemen, as a class, is fighting the principles of liberty in every nation, and it is combating them in Spain," said the prominent deputy, Antonio Alcalá Galiano. The regulars were compared to "a robust plant which extends its branches through all Spain," a plant that could not be trimmed but must be deprived of "the water which irrigates and feeds it."[17] The ministry's project suffered a humiliating defeat. The prime minister's days in office were numbered.

The brief ministry of the conde de Toreno (June–September 1835) represented a final, desperate effort to preserve the dominance of the liberal elite. Toreno hoped to win at least the acquiescence of the radicals through a policy of concessions—namely, the restoration of clerical property to the purchasers of 1820–1823, the suppression of the Jesuits, and the appointment of a reputed financial wizard and exaltado sympathizer, Juan Alvárez Mendizábal, to the ministry of finance.[18] Toreno, however, still clung to the basic premises of his predecessor's ecclesiastical policy. The Real Junta Eclesiástica finally produced its long-awaited recommendations, which were a good deal more moderate than the 1820 legislation on the religious orders. The commission recommended the decree, and the queen regent formally assented to it, appropriately enough on July 25, the feast of Saint James, patron of Spain. It suppressed male monasteries and friaries containing fewer than twelve religious and ordered the sale of their property with the proceeds to be used to reduce the national debt. The Junta Eclesiástica envisaged the closing of 892 houses; the remainder would survive. The decree, however, was not worth the paper it was written on. A radical revolution had already begun in the provinces that sealed the fate of both the ministry and its ecclesiastical policy.

The provincial risings of July–August 1835, beginning in Zaragoza and spreading to Catalonia, Valencia, Andalusia, Old Castile, and Galicia, were directed in their initial stages against the regular clergy.[19] The revolutionary movement, resting on an uneasy alliance of urban mobs, militiamen, and local radicals, quickly became an attack on the government itself as Madrid lost control of entire regions. The disturbances in Zaragoza (July 5–6) followed the same course as the *matanza de los frailes* in Madrid a year earlier; three friaries were sacked and burned. From Aragón the antireligious wave swept into Catalonia. The Carmelite house of Riudoms was assaulted on the twenty-third, the celebrated Carthusian monastery of Scala Dei on the twenty-fifth, and Poblet a few days later. Barcelona, with its twenty-six friaries and 800 religious, provided a natural focus for radical and popular discontent. On July 25 the attacks began. The victims were not as numerous as in Madrid during the previous year; friars escaped through sewers, on ropes from the rooftops of their burning residences, or simply disguised as civilians. Confronted with violence, the authorities could do nothing other than take nearly 300 religious under protective custody in the fortress of Montjuich. Throughout Catalonia monasteries and friaries were abandoned either under the pressure of municipal authorities or because the terror-stricken religious themselves sought permission to leave. For all practical purposes the religious houses of men were empty by the first of August.

Although the wave of violence was directed primarily against the regulars, the secular clergy also suffered. Parish priests began to abandon their churches in some towns. The archbishop of Tarragona, fearing for his life as the attacks reached his diocesan seat, fled to a ship in the harbor, although not before a mob threatened to hurl him into the sea and seized trunks containing his episcopal regalia. Having failed to detain the prelate, the rioters contented themselves by parading about the town in his miters and capes. There too the government authorities were impotent before the fury of the revolutionary crowds.

Urban risings elsewhere were less violent but no less damaging to the regulars. The revolutionary juntas formed in many cities by local exaltado politicians after the initial manifestations of popular discontent demanded the expulsion of all religious from their houses. In August the junta of Valencia ordered suppression of all monasteries and friaries in the provinces of Valencia, Alicante, Castellón, Murcia, and Albacete. This pattern was repeated in Málaga, Cádiz, Salamanca, Valladolid, Zamora, and throughout Galicia. Only in a few areas—Burgos, Logroño, Soria, Palencia, León, Asturias, Santander, and Ciudad Real—was the government able to maintain a semblance of authority and proceed with a more limited closing of religious houses under the terms of the

July 25 decree. The policy of moderate ecclesiastical reform was irrelevant. Revolutionary events had closed the vast majority of the kingdom's friaries and monasteries by September, when Toreno recognized political reality and stepped aside for the great hope of the radicals, Mendizábal.

Domestication of the Church, 1835–1840

Juan Alvárez Mendizábal (1790–1853) took power in the midst of revolutionary agitation in the country, a worsening situation in the civil war with the Carlists, and severe fiscal problems that had burdened the nation with enormous debts. He represented the hopes of the exaltados, who demanded a fundamental revision of the *Estatuto Real* in the direction of the Constitution of 1812; reform of taxation, particularly through elimination of the tithe; and profound changes in the administration of justice and the organization of provincial and municipal governments. The program of Mendizábal sought to obliterate the vestiges of Old Regime privilege that Martínez de la Rosa and Toreno had tried to eliminate through a slow legislative process. The political unrest of 1834 and 1835, moreover, had made evolutionary reform from above directed by a narrow political elite chosen by a highly restricted body of voters impossible.

Mendizábal shrewdly saw that the character of liberal politics itself was changing from the struggle of parliamentary factions to a more complex conflict of interest groups at both the local and national levels. The old ideal of liberal unity still found its adherents, however. Martínez de la Rosa indignantly rejected the suggestion that he belonged to any party.[20] In fact, the differences among the liberal factions on such issues as freedom of the press, jury trial, civil rights, and taxation policy, as well as greater political awareness in the country as a whole created the circumstances that favored the appearance of the two great parties of liberal Spain.[21] Mendizábal saw the importance of presenting a comprehensive program of reform that would win the support of parliamentary exaltados and at the same time respond to the intense politicization that had taken place at the local and regional levels. By the end of the decade, according to a history of liberal Spain written shortly afterward, "the militant factions" had taken on "their exclusivistic denominations: the more ardent defenders of the revolution were called *progresistas,* its more moderate and slow [defenders] were given the name of *moderados.*"[22]

Martínez de la Rosa hoped to resolve the problem of the religious orders that had preoccupied liberal opinion since Cádiz with a compromise that would have lowered the number of foundations while reducing the national debt through sale of suppressed monasteries and friaries. Neither the prime minister nor his supporters objected in principle to the sale of the orders' holdings. But the government's solution, embodied in the recommendations of the Real Junta Eclesiástica, continued to rest on a combination of reform of the regulars with partial disamortization. The exaltado press of 1834 and 1835 made clear that it wished to go further. One writer suggested that the dissolution of the regulars would be "very useful and necessary."[23] Another declared that the sale of the orders' property would allow the liberal regime to build up a body of supporters tied to it by self-interest; yet another argued that the vast, unworked lands of the Church raised obstacles to agricultural progress.

It fell to Mendizábal, himself a believer who never doubted that the liberal State should be Catholic, to break the connection between reform and disamortization. A decree of October 11, 1835, suppressed the kingdom's monasteries save for a handful, such as El Escorial and Poblet, which were allowed to remain open temporarily; another of February 19, 1836, ordered the sale at public auction of the property of the suppressed communities to benefit the public treasury. On March 8 the government dealt the final blow to the millennial history of the orders in Spain. In a decree of fifty-seven articles, the State argued from a premise dear to the liberal mind. "The force of civilization is no less irresistible than that of time," the decree declared, as it ordered the suppression of all religious communities of men save for three seminaries in Valladolid, Ocaña, and Monteagudo responsible for training missionaries for Spain's colonies; the houses of the teaching Order of the Pious Schools (Piarists); the hospitalers of the Order of St. John of God; and a small number of friaries providing clergy for Spanish churches in the Holy Land.[24] The orders of women, untouched by liberal legislation between 1820 and 1823, were treated more gently, perhaps because of the assumption that women who had spent their lives cut off from the world in contemplative communities could not adapt easily to a secular life.[25] The State agreed to pay modest pensions to the religious being expelled from their houses, and it took measures to open ecclesiastical appointments to former religious who became members of the secular clergy.

Mendizábal's motives were straightforward, and he established them clearly in the decree of October 11. The monasteries were "useless and unnecessary . . . for the spiritual assistance of the faithful"; their vast property holdings were "prejudicial" to the kingdom; and it would serve "the public convenience . . . to place these in circulation to increase the resources of the State and open new sources of wealth."[26] In the decree of February 19, Mendizábal spelled out the benefits—fiscal, economic, and political— that he expected to flow from the disamortizing legislation. It would open "a most abundant source of public felicity, giving new life to moribund wealth, removing obstacles to the channels of industry and the circulation [of wealth]"; and it would create "a copious family of proprietors . . . whose existence will rest principally on the complete triumph of our actual institutions."[27]

The sale of the regulars' property proceeded slowly at first. Prospective buyers may have feared the fate suffered by the purchasers of 1820–1823 upon the collapse of the liberal regime. But by 1837 such fears had given way to a feverish desire to buy. By the beginning of 1839 more than 15,000 separate parcels had been sold at auction for 792,459,390 reales.[28] The sales of 1836– 1839 formed the first stage of an extensive process that would last until 1860. It would later include the sale of the property of the secular clergy, municipal common lands, and the holdings of charitable institutions.

The massive transfer of wealth away from the Church and other corporations possessing property acquired during the Old Regime profoundly affected the development of both the economy and society. Mendizábal's hopes of creating a body of property owners whose interests were linked to the survival of the liberal State were realized. The removal of property from the "dead hands" of the Church also made possible the more efficient exploitation of land and the later commercialization of agriculture within a modern market economy. The disamortization did not resolve the State's fiscal problems, however, and over the long term it created social problems as serious as those it was designed to solve. Critics of the time noted that the auction process limited purchasers to those with sufficient capital, thereby excluding the peasantry and land-less agricultural workers. The purchase of Church property by the urban middle classes substituted one form of unbalanced land-holding for another. Its social consequences would reach into the twentieth century.

The suppression of the male religious orders and the subse-quent sale of their property undermined one of the fundamental institutions of the Old Regime Church. Although the number of regulars had declined significantly since the late eighteenth cen-tury and the internal problems of the orders had not disappeared, their elimination deprived the Church at a stroke of its most active evangelizers, educators, and propagandists. The vacuum left could not easily be filled by a secular clergy ill prepared to assume ex-panded responsibilities. The disappearance of most of the male orders, moreover, allowed the liberal State to extend its authority over two areas, charity and secondary education, in which the regulars had played a decisive role during the eighteenth cen-tury.[29]

The long-term effects of the suppression and disamortization of 1835–1839 would influence Church-State relations well into the twentieth century. The Church retained a bitterness over de-struction of the orders that would lead to persistent efforts to bring about their restoration. These had limited success during the 1850's and 1860's, when a handful of orders received gov-ernment authorization to reestablish themselves. After 1874 suc-cessive governments allowed the orders to return on a massive scale but in circumstances that made the problem of the regulars as serious in the late nineteenth and early twentieth centuries as it had been during the Old Regime. Post-1874 conservative min-istries refused to recognize any financial obligation to the restored orders, insisting that they should be entirely self-sufficient. This policy, reflecting the residual liberalism of the new Liberal-Conservative party of Cánovas del Castillo, meant that the revival of the regulars depended on massive donations from the urban Catholic upper classes, which saw the orders as a bulwark against social revolution. No study has been done of the financing of the regulars after 1874 by the conservative nobility and bourgeoisie, but there is no doubt that it was extensive enough to recreate, albeit in a slightly different form, the imbalanced distribution of resources between the regulars and the parish clergy that had characterized the Church before 1836.[30] The regulars, moreover, quickly resumed their traditional role as ecclesiastical shock troops combating secularism, liberalism, freemasonry, socialism, republicanism, and Protestantism, thereby reviving the bitter controversy over the orders that had seemed to be resolved once and for all by Mendizábal.

Between 1834 and the successful progresista revolution of September 1840, the two families of Spanish liberalism struggled for dominance in an atmosphere of popular agitation, intense political debate, and military intervention. Political instability during these years arose in part from the failure of the progresista and moderado parties to reach agreement on how far the revolution should go. It also came from the nature of the parties themselves. Each was clear enough about its objectives, at least in relation to those of the opposition. But internal coherence and discipline were missing in both parties. Each represented a parliamentary and electoral alliance of diverse groups that cooperated uneasily in the unstable political maneuvering of the late 1830's.[31] The inability of the parties to reach even a minimal constitutional accord and the factionalization afflicting both moderados and progresistas burdened liberal Spain with a damaging political liability for which it would pay dearly. The political struggle tilted in favor of the moderados in May 1836, only to reverse direction shortly afterward as the progresistas resorted to the tried and true formula of urban disturbance and revolutionary conspiracy to regain power.

Once the problem of the regular clergy had been resolved (even the moderados were unwilling to reverse the sale of the orders' property), the issue of ecclesiastical reform receded before the debate on the nation's political future. Government ecclesiastical policy focused on the domestication of the Church through legislation designed to punish churchmen opposing the regime and create a Church organization subordinate to the State. During the radical Calatrava ministry (August 1836–August 1837), the State deprived bishops absent from their dioceses for political motives of their incomes and ordered that clerics caught opposing the government's military plans be treated as conspirators. Ecclesiastics were forbidden to leave their customary places of residence without the consent of their bishop and the local governor. To reduce the size of the clergy, long a fond aspiration of liberalism, the government reaffirmed legislation suspending the provision of benefices and forbidding bishops from ordaining more priests. A radical reform of the secular clergy presented to parliament in 1837 was, however, rejected by the queen regent and fell by the wayside as the moderados returned to power.

The liberal State did not directly attack the property of the secular clergy, but it established absolute control over its finances through legislation declaring such holdings "national." A decree of July 29, 1837, undermined one of the Church's traditional sources of income by abolishing the tithe, although the government undertook to pay the salaries of the clergy.[32]

Between 1834 and 1840 the organization and direction of the Church were thrown into confusion. The deadlock between the papacy and the liberal State prevented the appointment of new bishops to replace the twenty-five who died during these years. Eleven prelates fled into exile; four others were confined with limited freedom of movement to their dioceses. For all practical purposes only eleven of the kingdom's sixty dioceses were being administered by their bishops as 1840 drew to a close, and all eight of the metropolitan sees were vacant because of the death or exile of their incumbents.[33] In these circumstances the few bishops still governing their sees scarcely knew where to turn. "Observing the furious interference of the revolution, they were usually ignorant of how they could salvage the ship of the Church in the midst of such shocks," said Bishop Romo Gamboa of the Canaries, one of the few prelates to remain in his diocese.[34]

The liberal State sought to win support in the Church by nominating prelates favorable to liberalism. It named Pedro González Vallejo to the primatial see of Toledo, although the pope refused to approve the appointment, and it nominated Antonio Posada Rubín de Celis for the archbishopric of Valencia. The regime was also able to rely on the support of Félix Torres Amat who, curiously, had been named bishop of Astorga by Ferdinand VII shortly before the latter's death. Both Torres Amat and González Vallejo served as members of the Real Junta Eclesiástica in 1834–1835;

the former accepted a seat in the Senate in 1837. The liberal prelates did not necessarily accept all the measures the State imposed to reform the Church, but they represented the vestiges of the old alliance of Constitution and Altar from 1810 and 1820 between liberal politicians and reforming ecclesiastics. The reforming bishops of the 1830's were few in number, however; they were aging figures from an earlier time who were given a nearly impossible task. Torres Amat thus tried to convince Rome that the real state of affairs in the Spanish Church had been obscured "because of the exaltation of dominant passions which blind reason."[35] The bishop of Astorga defended the measures taken against the regulars and attacked the fanaticism, superstition, and ignorance of the Spanish as the causes of the nation's difficulties. But Torres Amat's long identification with attempts to reform the Church with State support rendered him suspect in Rome's eyes as "an instrument of the Government for ecclesiastical innovations."[36]

Blocked by Rome from appointing new bishops for vacant dioceses, the State turned to a device that rekindled the civil war which had ravaged the Church between 1810–1813 and 1820–1823. Cathedral chapters traditionally enjoyed the right to elect diocesan governors until new incumbents had been approved by the State and the papacy. The government instructed chapters to elect as governors those priests whose episcopal nominations were being refused by Rome. "Her Majesty the Queen Regent invites and exhorts . . . the chapter . . . to name as governor of this miter its bishop-elect D.N. . . . and it is the pleasure of H.M. that the chapter should proceed to this election as soon as possible."[37] Although González Vallejo, who benefited from this measure by being elected governor of the archdiocese of Toledo after the death of Inguanzo, defended the procedure, it provoked a storm of protest within the Church. Critics alleged that force was used to compel chapters to elect administrators desired by the government.[38] The revived civil war within the Church also reached the diocesan level. In Astorga, Torres Amat clashed frequently with a cathedral chapter sympathetic to Carlism and expelled a third of his seminary students, who were accused of trying to set the seminary on fire as part of a Carlist plot to seize control of the city.[39]

The rapid dissolution of the orders served the liberals well in a tactical sense, for it removed the possibility, however remote, of any threat from this source. Ex-friars and monks scrambled for a living. Some found employment as parish priests and assistants, but the majority depended on the modest pensions from the State, and these were paid infrequently, like "a bone thrown to a dog" according to a petition sent to the Cortes in 1840.[40]

The parish clergy were only slightly better off. Although the State's financial arrangements for the clergy in 1837 took different forms, none of them was effective; clerical incomes fell drastically. In the diocese of Jaca, the secular clergy—from bishop to parish priests—received only 37 percent of the amount theoretically assigned by the government for their salaries in 1837. The average revenue of a parish priest in the diocese between 1836 and 1839 ranged from nothing to 1,300 reales in a time when a minimum clerical salary was set at 3,000. Over the short term, the misery of the parochial clergy threw the Church into such disarray that no coherent opposition to the State's policies could arise. Nearly half of the parishes of the Tarragona archdiocese lacked priests by 1840. In poor villages of the Toledo archdiocese, some clergy, deprived of any income, abandoned their parishes, leaving the population without religious services. In many dioceses parish priests remained on duty, working at secular occupations while attending to their congregations as best they could.[41]

The Spanish Church had suffered dislocation after 1808 and 1820, but had not lost its militant spirit. In the 1830's it reeled under shocks so disruptive that it thought not of victory but of survival. The Church's disarray prevented a significant movement of opposition to the State's ecclesiastical policies. Few bishops protested the suppression of the Jesuits in 1835. Only the aged archbishop of Seville, Francisco Xavier Cienfuegos, pleaded with the queen regent for the order's survival. The decree suppressing the regulars evoked episcopal protests, but even these representations to the Crown, respectful in tone and legalistic in argument, lacked the fire and theocratic vision of earlier defenses of the orders.

Between 1810–1814 and 1820–1823 the Church struggled vigorously against liberalism. After 1834 it looked not to itself but to Rome for protection. Relations between Pope Gregory XVI (1831–1846) and the liberal State had been tense since Martínez de la Rosa took office. The pope, alleging the necessity of a neutral stance between Isabella II and Charles V, refused to recognize either claimant, thereby irritating the government and creating an impasse over the appointment of bishops to vacant sees.[42] The suppression of the Jesuits led to a strong papal protest, and a further deterioration of relations between Madrid and Rome prompted the withdrawal of the nuncio in August 1835. Liberal ecclesiastical legislation in 1836 produced the final rupture. On February 1 the pope spoke to a secret consistory of cardinals and justified the break in diplomatic relations with a sharp attack on the progresista government. Gregory XVI could do little to protect the Church, but his decisiveness strengthened the bond between Rome and Spanish ecclesiastics that had been developing since 1810. Henceforth, predicted a supporter of the Church, Catholic Spaniards must look to the "Vicar of Christ" who "will comfort the weak and console all, stimulating them to maintain themselves firm in their faith and to defend themselves against the diabolic spirit of the revolutionary government of Madrid."[43] Rome had won another battle in the war for control of the Church.

The Liberal versus the Roman Church, 1840–1843

At the end of the decade pressure on the Church began to ease. The return of the moderados to power and the end of the Carlist War in 1839 produced an uneasy atmosphere of conciliation. The government dealt with the Church in a less heavy-handed manner and reestablished the tithe, primarily to save its own bankrupt finances rather than to pay ecclesiastical expenses. But the moderados succumbed again to revolution in September 1840.

The revolution, the most successful progresista rising until 1868, rested on the old alliance of radical parliamentary and municipal politicians, local militias, and the urban lower classes. But a new force in the turbulent political world of liberal Spain, the military, gave the revolution its backbone and allowed it to survive until 1843. The hero of the final Carlist campaigns, General Baldomero Espartero, an immensely popular figure supported by officers and soldiers of the army that had ended the civil war, seized the initiative—which forced the resignation of the government and the abdication of the queen regent—and eventually installed himself as regent. The revolution was not a simple military coup d'etat, nor was the regency a purely personal dictatorship. The new regime allowed political institutions to function with relative freedom and depended for its survival on the continuing support of radical politicians, the army, and the urban masses.[44] By its very nature the alliance was too unstable and the interests of its constituent groups too diverse to permit permanent consolidation of the revolution.

The regime, although vaguely populist in character, lacked a coherent program of revolutionary action. The regent never contemplated economic or social changes to benefit the urban masses who had supported the September rising. But the State had clear plans for the Church. Between 1841 and 1843 the government attempted to realize the progresista vision of a national Church subordinate to the civil authorities. The movement to create a Church in the service of liberalism reached its logical conclusion.

In May 1841 the minister of grace and justice presented the most ambitious reform project yet advanced. The proposals reflected the long-held liberal view that the organization of the Spanish Church required overhaul. The State called for redrawing of the ecclesiastical map to alter boundaries that had remained unchanged for centuries. Two new archdioceses were created, Madrid (designated as the primatial see) and Barcelona. Toledo, seat of the primate since Visigothic times, was relegated to the status of a simple diocese. Seventeen dioceses located in small and unimportant towns were suppressed in favor of thirteen new sees in larger population centers—including Ciudad Real, Alicante, Soria, Vitoria, La Coruña, and Guadalajara.

All collegiate churches staffed by the secular clergy were to be closed. The State also reduced the size of the clerical elite by eliminating over 3,000 canonries and chaplaincies in cathedral chapters and ordered a parish reorganization that required elimination of at least 4,000 of the kingdom's 19,000 parishes. The number of priests with cure of souls was set at 22,000, all to receive fixed salaries according to a schedule ranging from 2,000 to 8,000 reales for the parochial clergy and 50,000 to 90,000 reales for the hierarchy.[45] A proposal submitted to the Cortes in January 1842 exalted the apostolic mission and authority of the bishops and limited contacts between the Church and Rome to the purely ceremonial. The project stopped short of a complete denial of a link with the papacy, although many churchmen regarded the plan as schismatic. The long tradition of Spanish regalism, once widely supported within the Church itself, had come full circle. The Church was to be reformed not by the alliance of Constitution and Altar that the liberals of 1810 and 1820 had espoused, but by the State alone.

The regency's undertaking to pay decent salaries to the secular clergy according to an equitable and fixed scale promised to remedy the imbalanced distribution of resources characteristic of the Old Regime Church. In return, the government exacted a heavy price. On September 2, 1841, parliament passed a law ordering sale of the secular clergy's holdings, with the proceeds to service the national debt. The liberal State had possessed effective control over Church finances for some time. But the regency's decision to dispose of the seculars' property represented a significant break with the policies of the past. Liberal idealization of the role of parish priests had saved the secular clergy until this time from the fate of the religious orders.

Clerical support for Carlism during the 1830's as well as ecclesiastical resistance to government reform of the Church may have diminished the old enthusiasm for the seculars. But the State left no doubt that it was moved primarily by fiscal considerations. Interest on a large foreign debt had gone unpaid for months. The regency, said the minister of finance, "could not lose a single moment proclaiming to the face of the world that the most sacred as well as the most imperious obligation of the Spanish nation is the payment of interest due or about to fall due. . . . The honor of the entire nation," he declared, was at stake.[46] The disamortizing legislation was passed by the Cortes without extensive discussion. Prospective buyers rushed forward to take advantage of a new round of public auctions. By the end of the year nearly 10,000 parcels had been sold for 320 million reales. Sales continued at a brisk level until the summer of 1844. By the time they were halted, 62 percent of the secular clergy's property had been sold. Although some Church property remained by the mid-1840's, the massive sales, which had yielded more than 3 billion reales, broke the back of the imposing structure of ecclesiastical wealth that had sustained the Church for centuries.[47]

The State also attempted to take firm control of the ecclesiastical administration. Priests aspiring to clerical appointments needed to possess a certificate of loyalty (*atestado*) from the local governor attesting to "their good conduct and adhesion to the legitimate government."[48] Working in cooperation with the ministry of grace and justice, the principal governmental agency responsible for clerical reform, the elite of the liberal Church attempted to purge politically unacceptable priests. González Vallejo, the ex-bishop of Mallorca placed in charge of the Toledo archdiocese in 1836, removed most of the parish priests of the diocesan capital and several officials of its administration for being "little devoted to the actual institutions of the kingdom."[49] In Valencia the administrator of the diocese suspended all priests from hearing confessions who could not produce loyalty certificates, an example imitated by his counterpart in Lugo, where thirty-four churchmen lost their canonical licenses to preach and hear confessions because they lacked the *atestado*.

The government acted vigorously to punish priests whose sermons questioned state policy. Local authorities maintained constant vigilance over preaching, as in León where an ex-Franciscan was arrested after giving a sermon in the cathedral "alarming the consciences of the faithful" and censuring "the conduct of the supreme government of the Regent."[50] Three bishops protesting the ecclesiastical reforms—Juan Díaz Merino of Menorca, Pablo García Abella of Calahorra, the Judás Romo Gamboa of the Canaries—were hauled before the courts. At a local level the activities of the clergy were subject to close scrutiny. The parish priests of Romanones in Guadalajara thus complained that they could not travel the three and a half leagues to the provincial capital's market "because here there is much vigilance."[51]

Between 1841 and 1843 the State—using the instruments of power at its command, supported by a minority of proregime priests, and facing a leaderless clerical opposition—seemed on the verge of completely implementing its ecclesiastical plans. The creation of a national Church, however, was decisively checked by a spontaneous and widespread campaign of civil disobedience among the clergy hostile to the government's program. The sudden recovery of the Church from its mood of fatalistic resignation arose from a grass roots movement among the parochial and cathedral clergy. The hierarchy, decimated by deaths and exile and dominated by a handful of bishops sympathetic to the regime, could not provide leadership. But protests among parish priests were ignited by a discourse of Gregory XVI on the condition of the Spanish Church (March 1, 1841). The pope attacked the course of liberal legislation since 1834, imposed canonical sanctions on those responsible for it, and spoke harshly of the clergy cooperating with the State.[52] The papal speech did not directly incite open resistance, but its publication in the Catholic press evoked a deep, emotional reaction among the mass of the lower clergy, who had hitherto been on the margins of the debate concerning civil authority over the ecclesiastical order.

The battle cry "Rome is our end! Rome is our hope!" swept through the Church.[53] Priests across the length and breadth of the kingdom, in cities and remote country villages, flooded Catholic journals with fervent expressions of support for the papal interpretation of recent events. The parochial clergy, for so long the silent and uncertain element in the struggle to control the kingdom's ecclesiastical organization, spoke forcefully in favor of papal supremacy and a Church in control of its own destiny.[54] The unexpected outpouring of support for Rome and the deep hostility of the majority of the clergy to the progresista design for the Church revealed beyond a doubt that the regalism of the past was dead. The clergy, declared a Catholic review, "prefers poverty, jail, exile, expatriation, every humiliation, before denying its faith, before separating itself from Rome, before consenting to the division of the seamless tunic of Jesus Christ."[55]

The revolt of the clergy focused on resistance to liberal bishops and diocesan administrators. Incidents between the progovernment clergy and the "Roman" opposition multiplied following the papal statement of March 1841. Forty-three priests were arrested in Toledo for refusing to give up their licenses to preach and hear confessions; thirty *curas* of the Alcarría district were taken to court for having supported Gregory XVI's declaration. The ecclesiastical governor of the archdiocese of Zaragoza, Manuel La Rica, engaged in a conflict with his chapter—still loyal to the exiled archbishop—so bitter that he carried the dispute to the courts and secured the exile of all the canons to the Balearics for eight years. Members of the collegiate chapter of Daroca suffered a similar fate for daring to question La Rica's right to his office. Five parish priests of Miranda del Ebro were arrested and accused of having given "subversive counsel to the faithful in the act of sacerdotal confession." In the village of Requejo in Astorga, the *cura* was exiled from his parish and his property confiscated for having read Gregory XVI's address to his congregation.[56] Exile, trial, and imprisonment failed to break clerical resistance. Priests hostile to the liberal Church did not always express their sentiments as dramatically as did those of Toledo and Alcarría, but they often gave silent albeit no less forceful manifestations of opposition. In Málaga, for instance, the newly appointed diocesan administrator arrived at the cathedral for the customary reception by the local clergy only to find it shuttered and empty. Even the lowly bell ringer refused to appear to sound the chimes of welcome.

The resilience of a clergy deprived of episcopal leadership, cast upon its own resources, and subject to intense pressure from the State, marked a significant development in the evolution of the modern Church. It should be remembered that the regency's policies were not directed to the destruction of religion, nor even to the separation of Church and State. The regent, personally devout to the point of superstition, and the ministers of justice most intimately involved with ecclesiastical reform—Alonso and Becerra—stressed the importance of religion in the progresista State. The organization, finances, and social role of the Church were to be different from the ecclesiastical order of the Old Regime, but the regent and his ministers were as fully committed to the continued existence of an official Church as Ferdinand VII had been.

The bishops and priests to whom the regency looked to direct the Church found themselves in a difficult, ultimately impossible position. The liberal clerical elite formed a rump church dominated by a handful of elderly bishops first appointed between 1820 and 1823 and by a group of younger priests—such as Miguel Golfanguer, successor to González Vallejo as governor of the Toledo archdiocese in 1842, and Manuel La Rica, the diocesan administrator of Zaragoza. The liberal bishops were not the ogres their clerical opponents pictured them to be. Although committed to realizing the old ideal of ecclesiastical reform in alliance with the State, they rejected out of hand the accusation often levied against them of advocating a break with Rome. Moreover, their views on public morality and the condition of the kingdom's intellectual life were identical to those of their clerical foes. No bishop, for example, attacked "the prideful impiety" and "the absurd and delerious" rationalism of the times as vigorously as Félix Torres Amat.[57]

The situation of ecclesiastical reformers whose ideas went back to the "Jansenism" of the eighteenth century and the attempts at change undertaken at Cádiz was untenable; it became clear that reform would be brought about not by the alliance of Constitution and Altar but by diplomatic agreement between the State and the papacy. Although bishops such as Torres Amat believed that a concordat with Rome would resolve the problem of the Church in liberal Spain, the hostility they evoked in Rome prevented them from playing a role in the process. Torres Amat's controversial pastoral letter of 1842 defending the "Jansenist" views of his distinguished uncle led to a papal prohibition on its publication and a long campaign of harassment that followed the aged prelate to his deathbed.[58] The rising prestige of Rome among the rank and file of the clergy also undermined the already tenuous position of the liberal clerical elite, as did its failure to persuade the regency to put ecclesiastical finances on a sound basis. The aggressive conduct of diocesan governors appointed under state pressure further alienated the liberal clergy from the mass of their fellow clergymen. The liberal ecclesiastical reformers of 1834–1843, intellectually mediocre with few exceptions, identified too closely with a government seen as repressive by most of the clergy, and unable to bring about any amelioration in the Church's material condition, could not extend their influence over the Church as a whole. Their failure made impossible the creation of a Church intimately allied to the liberal State.

The regency's inability to resolve the chronic problem of Church finances eliminated what little hope remained of winning support among the lower clergy. In return for suppression of the tithe and sale of the secular clergy's property (the "sacking of the patrimony of Jesus Christ," according to ecclesiastical critics),[59] the State undertook to pay clerical salaries. The method of raising and paying the necessary funds varied between 1840 and 1843 but rested on a combination of surplice fees paid by parishioners for marriages, funerals, and baptisms and a national Church tax, the latter amount being set by Madrid but its assessment left in the hands of local authorities. The difficult situation of the national treasury as well as cumbersome bureaucratic procedures slowed transfer of funds to the diocesan commissions charged with paying parish priests. Delays were aggravated by the resistance of provincial and municipal authorities to the tax. In 1842 the provincial government of Barcelona complained to Madrid that the tax was "oppressive and unnecessary" and that only those benefiting personally from the services of the clergy should be expected to pay it.[60] Municipal governments often took matters into their own hands by refusing to levy the tax. Complaints poured into the Catholic press from aggrieved priests throughout the kingdom; one alleged that "all the municipalities of the region are asleep and look with the greatest indifference on the fulfillment of the law on financing the cult and the clergy." A priest in rural Galicia reported the situation had reached such desperate straits in his town that "we do not know, if anyone will even give us a mouthful of bread."[61] Espartero's inability to honor the government's pledge to the clergy deepened cynicism and destroyed what little confidence remained in liberal politicians among parish priests.

The Church recovered from the confusion and uncertainty of the six years preceding 1840 because circumstances forced a fundamental readjustment of its relationship to the political power. Few ecclesiastics believed that Carlism had the capacity to destroy liberalism and restore the old alliance of Throne and Altar. But as long as the rebellion continued, a faint hope lingered that the union of absolutism and religion might sweep to a final, apocalyptic victory. Carlism's defeat in 1839 ended that illusion. Sympathy for the Carlist cause continued among the clergy—particularly in regions such as the Basque Provinces where the interests of the Church were identified with the defense of local traditions—but in general the ecclesiastical commitment to Carlism receded before reality. The liberal State had triumphed and imposed on the nation a new set of institutions.

Between 1840 and 1843 a Church deprived of episcopal leadership and any means of collective expression (the regency even forbade the recently established Society for the Propagation of the Faith, fearing that its ostensible purpose, the support of foreign missions, would allow the clergy to meet together for subversive activities) slowly began to learn the techniques of survival in a world of parliaments, newspapers, political debate, and popular agitation. Realizing that no savior waited in the wings, the Church began to use the weapons of liberalism, which it had for so long feared and attacked, for its own defense. Only in 1840, for example, did a truly effective Catholic press emerge.

The Church had previously used newspapers and journals, as after 1824, but the early press, filled with triumphalist and long-winded tracts against liberalism, served a totally polemical purpose. The new press—*La Revista Católica* of Barcelona, *El Católico* of Madrid, and *La Cruz* of Seville—had a different character. Through publication of the State's ecclesiastical legislation, detailed news of government harassment, and simple letters to the editor, the Catholic press provided an isolated clergy with a sense of unity and purpose. *El Católico* thus defied the government by publishing Gregory XVI's address of March 1841 and launched a distinctly modern campaign to elicit expressions of support from the parish clergy. The torrent of replies from cities, distant towns, and villages illustrated the force of the new journalism. The priests of Puebla de Sanabria in Astorga wrote to the paper, whose very existence had been unknown to them a few weeks before, that it had inspired them to speak out and write an endorsement of the papal statement.[62] The emerging press also produced a breed of tough, aggressive journalists as skilled in the struggle to win public opinion as their liberal counterparts. The Catholic press could not match liberal journals in either numbers or circulation, but more than any other force it inspired resistance to the grand design for a state Church.

The shattering of the Carlist illusion also forced the Church to reassess its traditional identification with absolutism. The dream of a theocratic society resting on the alliance of Throne and Altar never entirely disappeared, but between 1840 and 1843 the Church perceived that its own self-interest was not necessarily that of absolute monarchy. Defense of the faith became the rallying cry of ecclesiastics who realistically assessed the situation of the Church in a liberal State. *El Católico,* in the significant issue of February 26, 1841, published a proposal for formation of a Catholic Association, revealing the new tendency within the Church to secure its position in the existing political order. The association was to have a single purpose: "to defend the Catholic religion which is designated as the religion of the Spains in the fundamental code of the nation," and to do so "by the means authorized by law." The project envisaged a voluntary association of a million members organized through the efforts of the parish clergy and directed by the newspaper's editors. The proposal reflected a shrewd awareness of the transformation of the nation's political life. The Church must see to its own interests by building an organization capable of mobilizing public support to influence government policy.

Although the plan was intelligent in its perception that the Church must struggle as an interest group in the arena of parliament and public opinion, it was ahead of its time. Not for another quarter-century would anything resembling the Catholic Association come into being. But the revolt of the clergy in 1841 and 1842 was an example of the new, realistic tactics. Devoid of any advocacy of Carlism, the clerical reaction to the scheme for a state Church represented in a limited way an ecclesiastical strategy that in one form or another would survive until 1931.

The new realism of the Church during the early 1840's arose not only from a pragmatic reaction to the events of the Espartero regency. One group of clergy came to realize that the wealth and privileges of the past could not be restored. The movement owed a great deal to the most brilliant intellectual figure of the nineteenth-century Church, the young Catalan priest Jaime Balmes (1810–1848). Philosopher, social thinker, journalist, and political essayist, Balmes possessed the historical sense to see that the struggle of liberalism against absolutism in the form of Carlism marked a decisive stage in the nation's history. It was a conflict "between the old society and the new; between the society of beliefs and religious customs . . . and a society of innovation and the development of material interests."[63] Balmes had no use for the progresistas or the moderados; he regarded the former as being moved by destructive passion; the latter he saw as "detestable."[64] Although his proposal for a Catholic-Monarchical party rising above the divisions between Carlists and supporters of Isabella II was impractical given the circumstances of the time, he urged the clergy to remove themselves entirely from partisan politics. And he believed that political controversy focusing on the Church could only be eliminated through a formal agreement between the liberal State and the papacy. The suggestion for a negotiated settlement to establish the place of the Church within a regime that for good or ill dominated the country implied abandonment of historic claims to the ecclesiastical riches and privileges of the past—claims upon which some clerics continued to insist.[65]

The realism of Balmes found a counterpart in the attitude of some members of the hierarchy. Bishop Romo Gamboa of the Canaries declared in 1843: "reason dictates that prescinding from rights which have been swept away forever, and submerged . . . at the bottom of the sea, we should content ourselves with saving those which, floating to the beaches, are still capable of being saved . . . we find ourselves with certain losses which it is impossible to re-establish without new sacrifices." Like Balmes, Romo Gamboa believed that only realistic negotiations between the liberal State and the papacy would be able "to assure the future of the Church."[66]

Such a settlement seemed impossible as long as the Espartero regency survived. But the regency proved no more durable than the governments preceding it; in July 1843 it fell. The revolution began as a general movement of protest against a government increasingly isolated from its own supporters and unpopular because of its economic and fiscal policies. Division within the military and progresista ranks made the success of the rising possible. A series of local disturbances, usually initiated by dissident radicals and some partisans of a republic, were soon dominated by the more conservative liberal bourgeoisie, who for the first time succeeded in turning the provincial revolution to its advantage.

Clerics participated in the revolutionary juntas of Tarragona, Tortosa, Gerona, Valencia, and Teruel. Elsewhere the clergy did nothing "to block the march of the national rising nor lend support to the insolent Regent."[67] Espartero's fall was greeted with ill-disguised enthusiasm by the clergy. In Seville Canon Manuel López Cepero preached a violent sermon exulting in the failure of "the miserable little tyrant, the bastard fungus of fortune."[68] Clerical expectations that a new day had arrived for the Church rose with the measures taken by provincial juntas to reverse the regency's ecclesiastical legislation. In July the juntas of Tarragona, Teruel, Lugo, Santiago, Palencia, Cáceres, and Mallorca abolished the hated certificates of loyalty; others suspended the sale of the secular clergy's property.

During the summer of 1843 the groundwork was laid for the compromise between the Church and a bourgeoisie fearful of social revolution that would give nineteenth-century Spanish Catholicism its distinctive character. For if the Church had become aware of the advantage of working within the liberal State, the latter's more conservative elements began to see the Church as a bulwark of stability and order within a turbulent society. Under the banner "Mother of God, Liberatrix of Spain," the revolutionary junta in Valencia affirmed its loyalty to the Constitution of 1837, the guarantor of "the religion of our ancestors, the throne of our kings and the liberty of our persons."[69] To the cry "Long live religion and liberty!" the junta added an appeal for measures to provide financial support for the clergy and a concordat to end the long estrangement of official Spain from Rome. The circumstances were present for an accommodation between liberalism and the Church. The process of adjustment would take longer than a euphoric clergy expected in 1843, but it had begun.

A New Church, 1834–1843

By 1843 the framework of the eighteenth-century Church had collapsed under the weight of liberal reform. The religious orders of men had disappeared with few exceptions; many dioceses lacked bishops, and the number of cathedral canons fell from 1,738 to 1,079 because of the State's refusal to fill benefices unconnected to pastoral work. The parochial clergy maintained its strength at approximately the eighteenth-century level, with nearly 25,000 priests engaged in the cure of souls.[70] This did not mean that overall the number of clerics increased, for the ex-regulars provided a pool of manpower for the parishes. In addition, 10,000 priests from the suppressed orders survived on government pensions. The effective clerical personnel of the Church composed no more than a third of the number of priests reported in the last censuses of the Old Regime. In this respect the liberal State achieved one of its objectives. The decline in priestly numbers was not, however, accompanied by a more rational distribution of resources and personnel. Southern dioceses continued to be badly understaffed compared with the northern, and the suppression of parishes decreed by the State, though begun in some dioceses— Valladolid, Salamanca, and Toledo—did not lead to the rationalization of parish size and resources the authorities desired.[71] Moreover, the destruction of the orders and the reduced numbers of the clerical elite accentuated the shift from the urban Church of the Old Regime to the rural Church of the nineteenth century. The parish clergy, profoundly conservative, devoted to Rome, and concentrated in an isolated countryside, became the dominant group within clerical ranks. The demographic and organizational transformation of the Church after 1834 contributed to a reorientation of the ecclesiastical mentality that would create serious difficulties in a later period of industrial growth and urbanization.

The destruction of the religious orders, the penury of the secular clergy, and liberal legislation ended the charitable and educational activities vital to the social role of the Old Regime Church. Clerical influence over education rested on the secondary schools maintained by the regulars. On the whole the orders were not as deeply involved in primary teaching. Village schools were numerous in the Old Regime and catechetical instruction obligatory, but the latter was the responsibility of the parish priest, who appeared for perhaps an hour a week to put the pupils through the rudimentary memory questions of the catechism. The schools of the orders catered to local elites, although Ferdinand VII had attempted to direct the regulars into elementary teaching. The quality of these schools varied enormously—from the classical education of the Jesuits and the modern instruction given by the Piarists to that provided in smaller towns, where lay students sat side by side with friars pursuing their clerical studies in arts courses. The general quality of the orders' schools declined during the first third of the nineteenth century, but they continued to educate the small minority dominating intellectual, political, and social life until the disamortization of Mendizábal.

By destroying the orders and reducing the income of the secular clergy, the liberal State also diminished the Church's traditional charitable function. The charity of the Old Regime, widespread and diffuse in character, included a priest's donation of a few reales to passing beggars, the distribution of bread and soup at episcopal gates, and the administration of hospitals, orphanages, and other institutions. Religiously inspired poor relief had not functioned well since at least 1800, but it received the coup de grâce after 1834. Liberal opinion had little use for the apparently chaotic and indiscriminate distribution of alms by ecclesiastics. A royal order (July 1, 1836) established local commissions to assume responsibility for aiding the poor, and charitable institutions, such as hospitals, fell directly under government control as charity became public assistance. For churchmen the change seemed a scandalous departure from the centuries-old norms of a Christian society. In spite of clerical laments, however, removal of ecclesiastical institutions from their decisive place in poor relief was another step in the liberal policy of reducing the Church to an exclusively pastoral function.

To what extent the collapse of the material and social foundations of the Old Regime Church affected levels of religious practice between 1834 and 1843 is difficult to assess because there are few studies of observance. Churchmen compared their situation to that of the persecuted Christians of ancient Rome. "Nero, Tiberius and Domitian could not have been worse," said a Catholic periodical of Espartero.[72] The disintegration of the traditional ecclesiastical organization diminished the Church's ability to provide religious services on an eighteenth-century scale. Monasteries, convents, and their churches were closed and either sold to speculators, who often pulled them down in favor of new residential and commercial construction, or converted them to public use. The urban concentration of the regulars meant that their disappearance inevitably reduced the number of churches open for services in the cities. In Madrid, for example, the number fell from 100 to 70 within five years.

By destroying the orders the State shifted the entire burden of ministering to the population to parish priests. But the geographic distribution of the parochial clergy widened the gap between well-served areas—Old Castile, León, Aragón, the entire Cantabrian coast—and the chronically understaffed dioceses of Andalusia and Extremadura, where traditionally a small body of priests administered large parishes and depended on the religious orders for pastoral assistance. The disappearance of the regulars in Seville, Córdoba and Jaén, where they had once formed at least half the clerical population, placed the secular clergy under pressure that could have been relieved only by creation of new parishes and recruitment of priests to fill them. This was not done, and the imbalances inherent in the southern Church's infrastructure were magnified.

Forms of religious expression central to the life of the Old Regime Church were compromised by both legislation and the clerical establishment's poverty after 1834. The disappearance of the orders—the most important agents of popular evangelization as well as the most avid propagators of devotions, such as the Sacred Heart and the Stations of the Cross—threw the burden of sustaining faith on a secular clergy ill prepared for the task. Moreover, the emergence of a highly individualistic society ensured the decline of the collective manifestations of religious sentiment that had characterized the eighteenth-century Church. The old confraternities, reflections of the traditional social categories of a hierarchical order, were transformed into simple associations of pious individuals. Social changes had already made the *cofradías* superfluous in the old sense, but the State accelerated their decline by ordering the sale of their property in May 1841 along with that of the secular clergy. Thus, the governor of Salamanca suppressed the confraternities of that city in May 1842. The devout continued to pay homage to their patrons, but they did so as private citizens willing to donate the funds necessary for services.

Religious processions, however, did not disappear during the decade of liberal revolution. They survived because the State wished them to. An impoverished Church could no longer afford its taste for religious spectacle. But the progresistas were as committed to the great processions of Holy Week and Corpus Christi as the absolutist monarchs of old. Municipalities willingly donated the necessary funds, as in Cuenca where the authorities gave 20,000 reales in March 1842 for the traditional rites of Holy Week. Espartero presided over the Corpus Christi procession in Madrid in June 1841.[73] This attitude, so different from later anticlerical manias against processions, reflected the government's commitment to the Church it was attempting to create. Religious processions, in which the National Guard and army invariably participated, had been transformed from displays of ecclesiastical wealth and grandeur into manifestations of the unity between Church and State in the new social and political order.

In spite of clerical laments that irreligion was leading society to its ruin, there is no convincing evidence that a massive desertion from the Church occurred between 1834 and 1843. The disruption of the ecclesiastical organization, the effects of the Carlist War in some regions, and the Church's general poverty may have accelerated the slippage of practice in the cities and magnified the weaknesses of the Church in areas where faith rested on uncertain foundations, but no massive drift into dechristianization took place. One of the few statistical studies of religious practice for the period, an analysis of the number of persons fulfilling the Easter Communion obligation in the parish of Santiago El Real in the city of Logroño in La Rioja, shows that the rate of observance changed only marginally between 1828 and 1843. The proportion of nonobservants was uniformly low, ranging between 1.0 percent and 6.0 percent of the parochial population falling under the obligation, with the higher percentages being reached in only two years (1836, 6.0 percent and 1841, 4.5 percent). The Logroño statistics cannot be used to generalize about the kingdom as a whole, but they are significant given the extremely large number of parishioners failing to fulfill the Easter duty during the last third of the nineteenth century (in 1887 the nonobservants formed 58.3 percent of the total). The statistics reveal that dechristianization made rapid progress in the city during the century, but it is clear that this transformation had not yet begun between 1834 and 1843.[74]

The *matanza de los frailes* in 1834 and 1835 combined with the dismantling of the structure of the Old Regime Church led to the myth, assiduously promoted by ecclesiastics, that unbridled anticlericalism fostered by the State was threatening the survival of religion itself. But liberalism, either in its progresista or moderado version, had no such intention, and in fact there was a noticeable decline of anticlerical violence once the question of the religious orders was resolved and the Carlist revolt ended. Between 1840 and 1843, years of revolutionary upheaval and economic unrest, few physical attacks were made on ecclesiastical buildings or the clergy. Incidents did continue to occur which revealed that the Church was still losing ground in the cities. In Tarragona a group of youths invaded the cathedral on Wednesday of Holy Week in 1842; they threw the service into confusion by breaking into "noisy and disorderly sounds"; in Cádiz masked figures attired in liturgical garments appeared on the streets during carnival "to ridicule the august ceremonies of our religion," according to the Catholic press. In Madrid drunken revelers attending the Christmas midnight Mass scandalized the devout with their irreverent singing and general conduct. But if these incidents revealed a lack of respect for religion unthinkable a half-century before, they did not constitute a violent, frontal assault on the Church. Moreover, the progresista authorities intervened energetically to curb such excesses. Even the Catholic press had to praise the intervention of the municipal officials of Tarragona for having "punished severely the disturbers of public tranquility" and caused "the mysteries of our religion to be respected."[75]

As an institution with its roots deep in a noble, agrarian, and absolutist past, the Church fared badly at liberal hands; as a religious body it survived better than ecclesiastical observers believed. Clerics bemoaned the effects of the liberal decade. But by maintaining the link between Church and State—indeed by encouraging religious observance—successive governments, whether moderado or progresista, provided the means for the Church to adapt to changing political and social circumstances with some success. This pattern would survive with one exception until 1931.

Whether a religious revival took place after 1840, as churchmen of the time maintained, is unclear. The Catholic press gloried in publishing reports of massive attendance at services during the regency. The lack of statistical evidence on religious practice makes it impossible to establish the accuracy of these claims. It is clear, however, that the Church, deprived of its traditional educational, charitable, and seigneurial functions, began to redefine the significance of observance. Eighteenth-century practice, the collective manifestation of the pious sentiments of a hierarchical society, gave way to a religion of testimony, to individual professions of faith promoted by a Church believing itself the victim of persecution. The faithful no longer attended services or participated in the processions of Holy Week as members of artisan guilds or noble confraternities, but as individuals testifying to belief in a Church under siege: "What a victory against unbelief! What a

triumph for religion!" said the correspondent of *La Cruz* of massive attendance at services in the town of Vinaroz.[76] The liberal
ideal of a Church reduced largely to the spiritual and pastoral
had triumphed. But it also destroyed any possibility of a Church
in the service of liberalism, for in religious observance the Church
found an effective weapon against the regime's ecclesiastical reforms.

Having learned the rules of the new politics and preserved a
sense of identity by developing a defensive mentality, the Church
could not adapt as easily to the emergence of a society with new
norms of economic behavior and sociability. The liberal revolution
of 1834–1843 was primarily political in character. Although the
old society of orders, hierarchical and seigneurial, was effectively
dismantled, the social base of liberal Spain rested on a landowning
oligarchy of aristocrats and a conservative urban bourgeoisie eager
to lay its hands on the spoils of Church property. To them must
be added a sprinkling of Catalan industrialists, prospering from
the growing cotton textile industry of Barcelona, and Madrid financiers and speculators. The oligarchy was more open than the
noble society of the past. Aristocrats, generals, bankers, merchants, and manufacturers mingled in salon, parliament, literary
society, and business in a fashion unthinkable a few years before.
The new social order was as profoundly conservative as the one
it replaced, but its undisguised acquisitiveness, its penchant for
ostentatious display, and its secular cultural tastes clashed with an
ecclesiastical mentality deeply rooted in the quasi-medieval, scholastic interpretation of social organization that had long dominated clerical thinking.

For churchmen imbued with an ideal of society organized around
the subordination of individual interest to the collective good and
the pervasive influence of religion in every aspect of life, forms
of liberal sociability seemed shocking departures from standards
of Christian civilization. Even Balmes, the most perceptive observer of what was happening to the Church in the early 1840's,
lamented the disappearance of an idealized Catholic Spain where
"religion, piety, faith, and hope . . . filled the streets, squares, and
byways" of the kingdom in favor of a society "occupied with its
industrial progress, its mercantile circulation, its hunger for gold,
its thirst for pleasure, its ostentatious luxury, its dissipation, its

scientific and literary vanity, its political delirium and its refined egoism."[77] For clerics still attached to the anticapitalist and corporatist social preoccupations of the Old Regime Church, the sale of ecclesiastical property, the destruction of traditional charity, and the emphasis on economic development were signs of a society in the midst of dissolution. Thus, a Catholic periodical complained: "What license! In the capital of Spain we constantly see in the press these announcements: Money to Loan. Money lent at moderate interest." Another lamented that "in Madrid, the capital of Catholic Spain, . . . commerce continues on its daily course even on Sundays and feast days" in the name of "utility and progress," thus delivering the nation to "the most ferocious customs" calculated to make Spaniards "as barbarous and slavish as the English."[78]

For the Church the sale of the regular and secular clergy's property provided the supreme example of a society dominated by acquisitive passion, hence the frequent denunciations of the purchasers as "infamous egoists" who built "colossal fortunes" at ecclesiastical expense.[79] In fact, the infrastructure of the national economy had not changed dramatically by 1843. Still agrarian save for a developing Catalonia and a handful of manufacturing towns scattered across the kingdom, Spain maintained its preindustrial character. The most significant change was the sale of ecclesiastical property, which left a legacy of resentment that would survive through generations of churchmen. Moreover, the connection between the sale and the freewheeling economic activities of the liberal State reinforced clerical hostility toward a developing capitalist society.

Nor did the Church contemplate the proliferation of newspapers, literary reviews, theaters, and other cultural institutions of the new society with anything less than horror. Although the State retained the power of censorship, it deprived the bishops of the authority to impose legal sanctions on offending works other than through purely canonical means. The relatively free expression of ideas after 1834 led to what many churchmen considered a wave of antireligious and indecent publications. Reports from local correspondents poured into the Catholic press alleging that the nation was being swept by a wave of libertinism that "attacks religion and is opposed to good customs." In Santiago the clergy called the construction of a theater in the town "most prejudicial to the decorum of the religion which the Spanish profess." There is no evidence that the nation was being submerged by the depravity clerics believed they saw about them. What they were lamenting was the collapse of the controls used for centuries by Throne and Altar to preserve the purity of faith. Obsessed since the middle of the eighteenth century with the danger of "libertinism"—the wanton expression of individual tastes and pleasures beyond clerically defined moral standards—the Church saw in liberal social and intellectual expression "a rebellion against God and against human society."[80]

Political circumstances forced the Church into a pragmatic reassessment of its role in the liberal State; ecclesiastical perceptions of economic and social changes after 1834, however, strengthened its traditional foreboding view of what was happening to Spanish society. Church leaders had no choice but to yield the theocratic ambitions that had dominated clerical thinking since at least 1808. But clerics had not abandoned the moral and philosophical principles that provided the rationale for earlier attempts to convert absolute monarchy into an instrument for creating the kingdom of God on earth. A new political order had come into being, and the Church proposed to use it to realize its aspirations. To do so in new economic, social, and intellectual conditions would be no easier than before. Indeed, the process would create problems and controversies that have survived to this day.

6 / The Conservative Church, 1844–1868

With the collapse of the Espartero regency in 1843 the liberal balance of power shifted from the progresistas to the moderados, who monopolized the government until 1868 save for the interlude between 1854 and 1856. Although committed to maintaining the political, economic, and social gains made at the expense of the hierarchical order of the past, the moderado program reflected the basic conservatism of its supporters. Fearful of the popular radicalism exploited by the progresistas, the moderados wished to slow the pace of change and consolidate a regime to be dominated by a small elite chosen by a restricted body of electors. Above all, the moderados wished to enjoy the economic benefits of possessing power and to avoid a revolution demanding wider participation in the political process and redress of popular grievances. The progresistas were no less terrified of social revolution, but their willingness to use lower-class unrest to further their objectives made them suspect in moderado eyes.

Moderado dominance of government between 1844 and 1868 provided the Church with an opportunity to recover from the shocks it had suffered since 1834. The moderados saw the Church as a useful ally in the struggle against radicalism and possible revolution; ecclesiastics, abandoning their commitment to absolutism, saw the possibility of employing the conservative-liberal State to recoup their losses. But the accommodation between the moderados and the Church was essentially a marriage of convenience. A tense and difficult union in the best of times, it did not resolve the fundamental problem of the Church's relationship to the new political and social order.

Recovery and Resentment, 1844–1854

The failure of progresista ambitions to create a liberal clergy as well as moderado fears of revolution produced an accommodation between Church and State that would endure save for brief periods until the proclamation of the Second Republic in 1931. The successful uprising against Espartero in July 1843 heightened Catholic expectations for "a new era, one of hope and consolation for the Spanish Church."[1] These aspirations were not immediately fulfilled. The provisional government, representing an uneasy coalition of moderados and progresistas disenchanted with the regency, dared not alienate its supporters on the delicate issue of halting the sale of the secular clergy's property. The suspension of auctions by some local juntas during the summer so threatened the government's stability that on August 7 the prime minister, J. M. López, ordered that the sales should continue. The State's action irritated clerical opinion, which had expected an immediate transformation of the Church's position in the new political circumstances. The government's unwillingness to take decisive action led the Catholic press to pose the question: "will the moderado party have enough nerve . . . to repair the infinite evils which the Church has suffered in ten years . . . of revolution and upheaval?"

Political developments rather than strong nerves finally made possible the easing of tensions between Church and State. The disintegration of the coalition of 1843 and the emergence of an exclusively moderado government in 1844 opened a long period of conservative rule. The new order suffered from serious weaknesses: the exclusion of the opposition from acquiring power through parliamentary means, a narrow electoral franchise denying the vast majority of the population any voice in the political process, an imperfectly developed party system encouraging factionalism even within moderado ranks, and a monarch, Isabella II ("she has a great deal of willfulness, but no will of her own," said a contemporary observer), with both the constitutional prerogative and the disposition to be drawn into the intrigues generated by a turbulent political system.[2] The moderados preserved their hegemony by creating the strongly centralized State that in one form or another would survive until the 1970's and by resorting to force to repress dissent. Provincial radicalism and lowerclass unrest were held in check; political life was controlled through the manipulation of elections and restrictive press laws. Successive moderado governments, however, carried out certain important reforms, such as codification of the criminal law and creation of a relatively efficient tax system. In the end, the inflexible political character of the regime and the narrow social base on which it rested caused its collapse, but for more than two decades it was strong enough to impose its model of government on the kingdom.

For the moderados, intent on excluding the progresistas from power and determined to preserve the gains made from destruction of the old social order, an accommodation with the Church seemed tactically sound. The failure of the regency's ecclesiastical policy and the prestige of the papacy among Spanish clerics revealed that a unilateral settlement of the problems between Church and State was out of the question. Moreover, the moderados, who had profited handsomely from the sale of ecclesiastical property and continued this policy for fully a year after the 1843 revolution, could contemplate halting the process because the best holdings had been auctioned to private purchasers.[3] An arrangement with the Church also promised clerical support for the regime and an undermining of Carlism in regions where it enjoyed popularity. For the Church the necessity of a settlement was even more obvious. In 1846 twenty-nine of the kingdom's sixty-one dioceses lacked bishops because of the impasse between the State and Rome over episcopal nominations; the number of capitular clergy had fallen drastically, and the irregular support provided by successive governments for the priests and the maintenance of church fabrics had left an impoverished clergy and deteriorating ecclesiastical buildings.

In early 1844 the State embarked on a deliberate policy of improving civil-ecclesiastical relations. A royal order of January 19, designed "to bury . . . all the quarrels, aggravations and recriminations which might serve as obstacles to a new era of beneficence and reparation," authorized the return from exile of two aged prelates once known for their intransigent defense of absolutism—Cardinal Cienfuegos of Seville and Archbishop Vélez of Santiago.[4] Subsequent decrees allowed other exiles to resume the administration of their dioceses. In March Cardinal Cienfuegos and the bishops of Calahorra and Plasencia were invited to visit the queen at the royal palace. The bishops knelt and kissed the royal hand in a traditional ceremony symbolizing the hierarchy's acceptance of Isabella II. Other measures—the abolition of the controversial certificates of loyalty, government affirmations of its commitment to pay clerical salaries, and the reestablishment of the ecclesiastical marriage tribunal, the Rota—also created a climate of opinion favorable to more substantial changes.

The accession to power in May 1844 of the strong man of moderado politics, General Ramón Narváez, opened the way for more concessions to the Church. Narváez, a "daring, energetic, obstinate and iron-nerved soldier of fortune,"[5] by no means enjoyed the total support of the moderado political factions. But his toughness and determination together with his prestige among conservative generals allowed the government to implement a vigorous policy along a broad front including the Church.[6] In spite of progresista hostility and some grumbling among moderado politicians, the State suspended the sale of the secular clergy's property that summer. As the government consolidated its position, it acted more decisively. In April 1845 it ordered the return of all property as yet unsold. And a new constitution in 1845, going beyond the terms of the charter of 1837, affirmed that "the religion of the Spanish nation is the Apostolic Roman Catholic religion. The State binds itself to maintain the cult and its ministers."[7] Such measures were welcomed by clerical opinion, but the State did not give all its cards away. Until a definitive settlement with Rome, the government continued to apply the restrictions imposed during the 1830's on ordinations and parish appointments. Nor was it prepared to oust the proregency diocesan administrators who had taken office under Espartero, although some resigned their posts voluntarily.

Both moderado and clerical opinion recognized that only a formal agreement with the papacy could end the deadlock between the liberal State and the Church. Less than a month after taking office, the Narváez government sent a diplomatic agent to Rome to negotiate with Gregory XVI on the following basis: (1) papal recognition of Isabella II as the kingdom's legitimate sovereign; (2) suspension of sale of the property of the secular clergy and the female orders; and (3) recognition of the pope's role in episcopal appointments subject to the traditional right of royal patronage stipulated in the Concordat of 1753.[8] The anxiety of both sides to reach agreement led to the rapid conclusion of negotiations. By January 1845 the *convenio* worked out between the

papal secretary of state and the Spanish representative in Rome
was being discussed in Madrid. Although the agreement met the
State's original terms, a new provision authorizing the reestablishment of the male religious orders at an "opportune" time aroused
controversy in the cabinet. Further, rumors of the *convenio*, which
had been negotiated secretly without reference to parliament, provoked the ire of both moderado and progresista newspapers, as
well as that of moderados resentful of the government's heavy-
handed tactics and covert diplomacy. Although the ministry might
have forced acceptance of the agreement, parliamentary and press
uproar following publication of the *convenio*'s text in *The Times* of
London revealed that the government underestimated the extent
of opposition, even among its own supporters, to a definitive settlement with the Church. Faced with open hostility to other aspects
of its policy, particularly in the area of tax reform, the Narváez
ministry elected prudence by refusing to sanction the *convenio*.[9]

The government's unwillingness to ratify the *convenio* of 1845
irritated Catholic opinion, but it did not end the modus vivendi
worked out between the secular and ecclesiastical authorities. The
election of a new pope in 1846 again raised hopes for a settlement.
Pius IX, whose moderately liberal views were regarded with sympathy by the government in Madrid, showed his good intentions
by recognizing Isabella as queen of Spain in 1848 and by agreeing
to cooperate in filling episcopal vacancies. Negotiations for the
long-awaited concordat were finally resumed, as before in secrecy
so extreme that a Catholic paper complained that "neither the
clergy nor even the illustrious prelates of the Church . . . know
what it will contain."[10] The complex and at times difficult negotiations were finally concluded during the ministry of Juan Bravo
Murillo on March 16, 1851. Rome and Madrid had reached an
agreement that would determine the place of the Church within
Spanish society for generations.

The concordat's terms were received with open hostility by the
progresistas, discreet reserve by the moderados who always feared
being tarred with the brush of ultramontanism by the opposition,
and quiet acquiescence by clerics.[11] Few were enthusiastic in their
support of a document that offered neither startling innovations
nor the prospect of a certain end to the difficulties between the
civil and ecclesiastical authorities. The settlement of 1851 was a

practical arrangement designed to regularize the position of the Church within the liberal State. At first glance it offered concessions to both sides. Pius IX accepted the sale of Church property carried out until that time, confirmed the traditional rights of the Crown in episcopal appointments, endorsed the principle of parish reorganization, and authorized a modest revision of diocesan boundaries.[12] The State formally accepted responsibility for sustenance of the secular clergy and church fabrics, recognized the right of the bishops to exercise their pastoral functions independently, committed itself to the support of seminaries, authorized the Church to hold property, and consented to a limited reestablishment of religious orders of men in an ambiguous clause soon to arouse controversy.[13] Article 1 affirmed that Catholicism "to the exclusion of any other cult continues being the only religion of the Spanish nation," and that it was to enjoy "all the rights and prerogatives" corresponding to it "according to the law of God and the sacred canons." Article 2 declared that teaching at all educational levels must conform to the "purity of the faith's doctrine."[14]

In spite of the rhetoric of Article 1 and progresista outrage at certain provisions of the concordat—particularly those involving religious orders and education—the moderado State played a shrewd hand in its dealings with the papacy. The concessions made to the Church were neither substantial nor costly. The Catholic press pointed out that the affirmations of Articles 1 and 2 were illusory, because they were not accompanied by specific recommendations for implementation.[15] Moreover, the government's declaration of its willingness to support the Church financially was only a restatement of intentions made by every liberal ministry since 1834. The terms of the financial settlement (an annual budget for culto y clero of approximately 153 million reales), although more generous than the expenditures of Espartero on the Church, fell short of the 265 million reales clerics thought necessary to meet the cost of ecclesiastical salaries and the upkeep of churches.[16] In addition, papal recognition of the traditional patronage rights of the Crown gave the State significant leverage in its relations with the Church. Rome also accepted a reduction in the number of capitular clergy and a limited degree of internal reorganization—reforms demanded by liberal reformers since the Cortes of

Cádiz. Finally, papal acceptance of the sale of Church property put to rest the fears of liberal supporters who had acquired ecclesiastical holdings since 1834.

The settlement of 1851 did not allow the moderados to fulfill the old hope of a Church in the service of liberalism. Internal reform of the Church was to take place with the cooperation of the ecclesiastical authorities, hence the dilatory pace of parish reorganization and the creation of new dioceses. And opposition to the liberal political order by no means disappeared among the clergy and those committed to Carlism. The moderados, however, could count on a hierarchy loyal to Isabella II with few exceptions, and they maintained control over the mechanisms of finance and patronage necessary to keep the Church in line.

Certain provisions of the concordat, particularly those recognizing the right of ecclesiastical institutions to own property, brought immediate advantages to the Church. But the principal benefit of the settlement rested less on specific concessions than on the creation of a legal framework allowing the Church to function normally for the first time since 1834. The clergy was not happy with an agreement worked out secretly between Rome and Madrid. Objections were soon voiced to its financial terms, particularly those establishing low salaries for the rural clergy.[17] Such reservations were justified. In spite of a rhetorical campaign carried on by figures such as Donoso Cortes—a conservative Catholic thinker, writer, and orator—that advocated the alliance between Church and State against the danger of revolution, both sides expected different consequences to flow from the agreement of 1851.[18] Fear of revolutionary agitation provided a weak ideological glue incapable of binding the secular and ecclesiastical authorities to a specific program of action.

If the official Church accepted Isabella II as queen and the liberal regime as the established political order, it also believed that the affirmation of Spain's Catholicism in the concordat demanded that the State take initiatives in the fields of religious dissent, education, social customs, and censorship that would restore the nation to a new age of piety and morality. The Church expected as much from the liberal State as it had demanded of Ferdinand VII. The ecclesiastical and secular authorities were to function as supreme moral censors to purge a society regarded as fundamentally corrupt. The objectives of the moderado State were more practical. The moderados were willing to placate the Church within limits as one of the many interest groups supporting the regime, but they had no intention of allowing the Church to dictate public policy. The Concordat of 1851 ameliorated the tense relations between Church and State prevailing before 1844, but it laid the groundwork for a continuing struggle over the Church's determination to install its vision of the kingdom of God on earth in a secular and economically changing society.

The moderado accommodation with the Church diminished a possible threat to the survival of the regime, but it moved the clergy into more immediate involvement in the turbulent world of liberal politics. Churchmen no longer worried about survival as they had done during the decade of revolution between 1834 and 1843. The Concordat of 1851 recognized the Church as an official interest group along with the landowners, industrialists, bankers, and generals already forming the backbone of the moderado State. Within the framework of unstable and factionalized party struggles, a strong and meddlesome royal power, and the give and take of the struggle to influence public opinion through the press, the Church was ready to advance its fortunes through the mechanisms of the new political order.

The Concordat of 1851 accelerated the institutional recuperation that had begun in 1844. The Catholic press observed with satisfaction what it believed to be signs of a religious revival. From Pontevedra in Galicia came a report of a notable increase in "religious enthusiasm," and a correspondent in Córdoba noted "the marvelous turn of events" that had seen "indifference" turn to "fervor, devotion and care for the cult."[19] At the level of ecclesiastical organization, the normalization of relations between Church and State allowed vacancies to be filled in both parishes and cathedral chapters, the latter still decimated on the eve of the concordat's signing. The government's decision in 1852 to authorize a Jesuit seminary to train missionaries for the colonies in the old Jesuit college at Loyola permitted the order to resume its activities in Spain. The order staffed several diocesan seminaries at the invitation of local bishops and provided the vanguard for a new campaign of domestic missions.[20] Jesuit missionaries moved through Catalonia, Andalusia, and the Basque Provinces during the early

1850's in the most ambitious effort at popular evangelization since the late eighteenth century.

The concordat did not bring about a massive reintroduction of the male religious orders, whose members numbered only 1,683 in 1860. But the State permitted the selective reestablishment of certain houses, such as that of the Hieronymites in the monastery of El Escorial in the spring of 1854. More substantial was the development of orders of women engaged in charitable and educational work. The moderado State deliberately encouraged female orders engaged in charity and teaching, perhaps in tacit recognition of its own inadequate efforts in the realm of public assistance. The Sisters of Charity, though present in Spain since the late eighteenth century, expanded their activities at midcentury; they were often invited by municipal and provincial authorities to staff local hospitals, asylums, and orphanages. Between 1844 and 1854 several new orders of women were established— the educational orders of the Sacred Heart (1846) and Jesus and Mary (1850)—while other congregations engaged in active work expanded. The feminine branch of the Order of Pious Schools (Piarists), particularly active in Catalonia, increased its convents from two in 1843 to seven, with new houses being established in Sabadell (1846), Igualada (1849), Vendrell (1850), Masnou (1852), and Gerona (1853).[21] The recovery of the Church was also evident in the revival of the liturgical ceremonial, last seen in its glory during the days of absolutism. Services held in Seville during the spring of 1854 to mark the beatification of three Jesuits would have satisfied the most demanding eighteenth-century partisan of Baroque liturgy as processions, sermons, illuminations, and fireworks succeeded one another in a dazzling display.[22]

In spite of the regularization of the Church's position between 1844 and 1854 and obvious signs of institutional recuperation, the ecclesiastical leadership and the confessional press were anything but content. It became evident that the religious and moral transformation that clerical opinion expected from the alliance with the moderado State was not to be realized. The moderados made their gestures toward the unbending theocratic demands of the clergy (the penal code of 1848 called for jail terms and fines on those daring "to mock the mysteries or sacraments of the Church"), but they had too many troubles from divisions within their own ranks to yield to ecclesiastical pressure except in a haphazard way. During the early 1850's churchmen poured out a stream of articles and pastoral letters railing against the continued existence of Spain's tiny Protestant minority, the corruption of social customs, and the unwillingness or inability of the civil authorities to curb the opposition press from questioning the theocratic ideology vigorously promoted by the episcopacy. In a circular to the clergy of the archdiocese of Toledo dated March 1, 1854, the vicar general lamented "the excesses . . . and the frightening relaxation of customs spreading through all classes . . . like gangrene" and expressed disappointment at government inaction, because the State alone had the "coercive force" to compel "the rebels" to fulfill their obligations toward Church and society.[23]

Ecclesiastical resentment exploded in the winter of 1853–54 during the last stages of the first period of moderado government, following announcement of the publication of a literary series under the title "The Library of the Free Man." It included works by Rousseau, Lamennais, and others the Church condemned. José Domingo Costa y Borrás, the bishop of Barcelona, took the lead in promoting an aggressive campaign against the series and the progresista press, which published excerpts of some of the offending works in spite of ecclesiastical authorities' censure. A strident public controversy, embarrassing to a semiauthoritarian government beset by internal divisions, followed. Although the State tried to restrain clerical intemperance by summoning Costa y Borrás to Madrid and forbidding the publication of ecclesiastical condemnations of the books to prevent the conflict from fueling the fires of opposition discontent, controversy continued.

The dispute was more than a debate over a specific issue; it provoked a clerical indictment of society and, by implication, of the moderado State's refusal to heed ecclesiastical demands for the creation of a rigid Catholic culture and standards of conduct reminiscent of the Old Regime. In the midst of the struggle, Costa y Borrás issued a pastoral letter, perhaps the most long-winded in the history of the Spanish Church, that won the endorsement of the Catalan bishops.[24] The prelates of Catalonia fulminated against Protestantism, secular culture, religious toleration, liberty of expression, and "theatres, dances, cafes," and sundry other evils. The sentiments expressed by the Catalan episcopacy were not immediately political. The bishops vehemently denied the accusation of Carlism hurled against them by the opposition press. The controversy revealed, however, the still ambiguous nature of the relationship between the Church and the moderado State. And it showed that the Church intended to push its case aggressively. "Catholic Spain is passing through a religious crisis more serious than . . . in previous years" claimed *La Cruz*. Costa y Borrás called on Catholics to embark upon a "holy crusade, peaceful and inoffensive, in favor of virtue and religious truth."[25] The battle lines for a long struggle were falling into place.

Revolution to Revolution, 1854–1868

The clerical ambitions so vociferously expressed during the spring of 1854 were curbed by a summer revolution that eventually restored Espartero to power.[26] Moderado political dominance collapsed because of the severe internal divisions that had developed among its supporters since 1851. Isabella's taste for power, encouraged by her mother and a camarilla of the most conservative politicians, produced a succession of ministries governing in semiauthoritarian fashion in defiance of parliament and the broad currents of moderado opinion. Discontented moderado politicians and generals, of whom the most prominent was Leopoldo O'Donnell, allied with cooperative progresistas to topple this thinly disguised royal dictatorship through a confusing series of military encounters of no great consequence combined with popular agitation in Madrid and Barcelona. In spite of the participation of the lower classes of the kingdom's two largest cities, the revolution soon lost its popular character. The new regime, though committed to a modest expansion of the electoral franchise and a less authoritarian constitution, rested still on a narrow liberal elite, whose main concerns were protection of private property, promotion of economic development, and avoidance of social revolution.

The revolution of 1854 was primarily a political upheaval carried to a successful conclusion without massive violence. In Madrid, the site of the most serious disorders, four days of popular rioting culminated in the sacking and burning of the queen mother's palace and the houses of several ministers. Churches and ecclesiastical buildings escaped untouched. There was no recurrence of the popular anticlericalism that had set monasteries to the torch in 1834 and 1835.[27]

But the Church would not emerge unscathed from the hands of the new government. In the midst of the revolutionary events of July 1854, provincial juntas took action anticipating the policy of the Constituent Cortes to be elected in the autumn. The junta of Burgos, after accusing the Jesuits of "fanaticizing spirits," ordered them to leave the city within two days; the junta of Seville demanded that the archbishop dismiss officials of the diocesan administration who had shown themselves "opposed to the national rising."[28] Other measures followed from the provisional government, in which a veteran of the ecclesiastical wars of the early 1840's, José Alonso, sat as minister of grace and justice. The government expelled the Hieronymites from the monastery of El Escorial in September, only a few months after they had unpacked their bags, and ordered that no parish vacancies should be filled until the parochial reorganization so long demanded by liberal reformers was carried out. The fundamental question of the place of the Church within the new regime, however, awaited the election of a new parliament in October.

In these circumstances there was little possibility of the Church conserving the advantages bestowed by its accommodation with the moderados. La Cruz suggested that a Catholic Electoral Union should be formed to contest the elections on a program of "defending the Catholic religion and sustaining the dispositions of the last Concordat."[29] This suggestion for the creation of a political party committed to the defense of the Church's interests, a dream of clerical apologists well into the twentieth century, did not prosper then, nor would it later, because of the antagonism between Catholics who accepted the liberal State and those who did not. Moreover, the terms of the electoral franchise worked against the election of deputies favoring the ecclesiastical status quo. The electorate of approximately 700,000, though significantly larger than the minority allowed to vote before the revolution, was too small to permit the election of pro-Church deputies in regions known for their religious observance—the Basque Provinces, Navarra, and Old Castile—where a vastly enlarged electorate would have benefited proclerical candidacies. Some progresistas and the small party of Democrats toyed with the idea of universal suffrage, but set their theories aside fearing a Carlist electoral success. A few deputies ready to defend the Church were elected, notably Tomás Jaén from Navarra and the sharp-tongued Candido Nocedal, a moderado from Pontevedra. But the new assembly was dominated by the progresistas allied to a sprinkling of reform moderados led by O'Donnell, who became minister of war.

The revolutionary coalition proved as unstable as any government before it. It was not without accomplishment during the two years of its existence, particularly in economic policy, but its grander projects, such as the implementation of a new constitution, were never realized as internal factionalism, the poor quality of leadership, and the watchfulness of an intriguing queen finally led to the disintegration of the progresista government.

The policies of the new regime had a familiar ring. The Jesuits were as usual the first to suffer. The State closed the missionary college in Loyola in the heart of the Carlist domain and removed the order to Mallorca, where presumably it could be kept from mischief. Bishops were instructed to proceed with the task of reorganizing parishes in accord with population size (one of the terms of the 1851 concordat), and convents with fewer than twelve nuns were ordered closed. In December 1854 the authorities, stung by clerical criticism of their ecclesiastical policies, felt their regalist oats by forbidding the publication of Pius IX's bull proclaiming the dogma of the Immaculate Conception, an order immediately defied by El Católico of Madrid, which published the document in the midst of acrimonious controversy with the progovernment press. The State struck early against episcopal censorship by ordering bishops to refrain from publishing censures until their requests had received government approval. This, too, was defied; the archbishop of Santiago, for example, condemned as "impious" a book by Francisco Pi y Margall, a future leader of Spanish republicanism.[30]

These conflicts were minor compared with the furor generated by the clauses on religion in the proposed constitution. There was no question either in the commission charged with drafting the constitutional project or in parliament of separating Church and State. The progresistas and their allies were as loathe as the moderados to let the Church escape from their vigilance. The constitutional text reaffirmed the Catholicism of the State, albeit by the back door: "The nation is obliged to maintain and protect the cult and the ministers of the Catholic religion which the Spanish profess." The following sentence, however, provoked controversy: "But neither Spaniards nor foreigners can be persecuted for their opinions or beliefs as long as these are not manifested by public acts contrary to religion."[31] Although there was considerable sympathy for a firm statement of religious toleration among progresistas and Democrats (an amendment establishing liberty of conscience and full toleration was defeated by only 138 to 72 votes), the majority elected the path of discretion. The deputies feared that anything more substantial would encourage a revival of Carlism and political machinations by the queen, who had expressed firm opposition to breaking the Church's religious monopoly on the day before the constitutional debate opened.[32]

For clerical opinion, obsessed with the danger of Protestantism since its appearance in Spain in the 1830's under the influence of the English Bible societies, any suggestion of concessions was a red flag certain to arouse a vitriolic reaction. Thirty-three bishops sent representations to the Cortes asking that "Catholic unity" be preserved; the confessional press lamented parliamentary action as a violation of the concordat and a betrayal of the nation's heritage. One conservative and proclerical paper predicted that Protestants "would form numbers superior to those of the Catholics and that Catholicism would be ruined legally in Spain" as a result of the legislation.[33] In fact, recognition of the right to hold private religious beliefs was a modest concession giving formal sanction to what had been practiced under moderado and progresista governments for two decades. Moreover, passage of the controversial text did not lead the authorities to turn a blind eye to Protestant evangelization; in Seville, for example, the governor issued "the most severe orders to repress with a strong hand" the sale of books by religious dissenters.[34]

The passions aroused by the constitutional discussions had scarcely cooled when debate opened in March on a proposed law to resume sale of the remnants of the secular clergy's property. The progresistas, determined "to finish the work undertaken by don Juan Alvárez Mendizábal of glorious memory," easily passed the law of May 1, 1855. It was the most ambitious disamortization of the nineteenth century, which included not only religious holdings but the property of educational and charitable institutions as well as municipal common lands.[35] Ecclesiastical property composed only about a third of the holdings made available for public auction. Although the law exempted the residences and adjoining gardens of bishops and parish clergy in addition to the property of the Piarists, whose work in education had won progresista esteem, it led to the sale of most of the Church's remaining property, nearly 25,000 separate plots, which brought the treasury over 300 million reales. Clerical reactions to another disamortization were vigorous. The bishop of Osma wrote directly to the Cortes and defended "the right of the Church . . . to possess property" and cited the "anathemas hurled by canon law against those who try to disturb it in its possessions or to seize its goods violently."[36] Other bishops passively resisted by refusing to cooperate with government officials examining ecclesiastical land titles before the public auctions.[37]

A deterioration in relations between Church and State followed the legislation of early 1855. In July the papal chargé d'affaires left Madrid for Rome, although not until he had said Mass in the chapel of El Escorial before Isabella II and the court. He prayed for the victims of the cholera epidemic then ravaging the country and, appropriately, for the clergy who had perished in 1834 under the assault of "popular fanaticism."[38] The government followed with a note to Spanish embassies abroad for distribution to the states to which they were accredited affirming that "the Government of the Queen, who is honored with the title of Catholic, has not ceased being Catholic for a single instant, nor has it given the least offense to the dogmas of religion and the most sacred doctrines of the Church" and throwing the blame for the crisis on the papacy. Pius IX, who had long since abandoned his liberal sympathies, riposted by claiming that Spain had violated the concordat and given "new injuries to the Church and its rights."[39] The conflict with Rome led the State to close the ecclesiastical marriage tribunal and to press its reforming demands, such as parish reorganization, more aggressively; the authorities began to enforce the order to suspend priestly ordinations until such reforms were carried out. In Oviedo government officers entered the cathedral after an ordination ceremony, marched the new priests off in a body, and seized the certificates attesting to their new status.[40]

Progresista ecclesiastical legislation and the break with Rome signaled the beginning of another wave of persecution for Catholic opinion. But the Church suffered less between 1854 and 1856 than during the revolution of 1834–1843. The State continued to finance the Church, although the 124 million reales appropriated for 1855 was less generous than the subvention provided by the moderados in 1851.[41] The progresista government sold clerical property and denied ecclesiastical institutions the right to own land and buildings in the future, but it allowed the Church to receive gifts and bequests as long as these were converted into interest-bearing treasury notes. The Church, however, saw the exile imposed on the bishops of Barcelona and Osma and a royal order of May 1855, occasioned by a flurry of Carlist agitation in the north, that commanded the removal from their parishes of priests "designated as dangerous by the civil authorities," as a return to the harassment of the early 1840's.[42]

These measures were exceptional, however. The State had the sense to see that the Church did not pose a threat to its survival. Most bishops either kept silent or affirmed their loyalty to Isabella II. In a circular to his diocese the bishop of Badajoz protested that his criticism of government policy was not moved by lack of respect for the constituted authorities nor by a spirit contrary "to obedience of the law and the loyalty and love which all display to Her Majesty the Queen."[43] The civil authorities did not repeat the regency purges of clergy unsympathetic to their aims. Churchmen smarted under constant barrages from the progresista press, vigorously expressed criticism that showed the continuing strength of anticlericalism among the politically aware. But the sentiments expressed in newspapers and often in parliamentary sessions did not translate into a revival of the popular and violent anticlericalism that had led to physical attacks on Church property and priests during the mid-1830's. Agitation among the industrial working class of Barcelona, though frequent during the two years of progresista rule, was not directed against the Church but against a regime with economic and financial policies plainly opposed to workers' interests. The Catholic press lamented displays of what it saw as government-inspired anticlericalism—the prohibition of religious processions in Seville and Lebrija, for example—but on other occasions the authorities cooperated with the Church. The governor of Huelva thus took action against residents of the mountain town of Jabugo who had refused to remove their hats as a procession passed through the streets. Although the Church was affected adversely by the sale of its remaining property holdings and by measures against the religious orders, its position within both State and society was not fundamentally altered. The progresistas undertook no new or spectacular initiatives in ecclesiastical reform.

The events of 1854–1856 were perceived in a different light by churchmen and Catholic apologists. The State's legislation was seen as another example of the rising sea of corruption, materialism, and rationalism threatening to engulf the nation. "The days of danger have arrived, the black flag of persecution has been raised; war has been declared against God, against Christ and against His mother. The hour of the Lord's battle has arrived," declared La Cruz.[44] The Church of the 1830's struggled to survive, that of the early 1840's to defend itself; the Church of the 1850's saw itself called to combat. "Today," said the bishop of Ávila, "it is not possible to be silent knowing what the apostles of impiety are doing to extend their prejudicial works."[45] In a mood reminiscent of the messianic prophetism that had swept through the Church following the French Revolution and the Napoleonic intervention, clerics preached their harsh message convinced, like José Domingo Costa y Borrás, that religion "is the only thing capable of bowing the necks of men who have generally forgotten or are ignorant of their duties."[46]

The most conservative members of the hierarchy, such as Costa y Borrás and Horcos Sanmartín of Osma, gave the pastoral letter a new dimension. Their admonitions moved from theocratic generalities to denunciations of specific newspapers questioning episcopal pronouncements on censorship and moral standards. Catholic journals, such as La Cruz and El Católico, gloried in defying the government. Both were hauled into court for publishing statements the authorities regarded as provocative. Not all bishops were as forthright as the prelates of Barcelona and Osma, but many inundated the civil authorities with requests for state action against those who had offended the Church through their statements or conduct. The new spirit of combat reached down to the lower clergy. In the province of Lérida the governor began judicial proceedings against parish priests refusing baptism to the children of parents who had not fulfilled their Easter Communion obligation.[47] The principal legacy of the *bienio progresista* for the Church—one that would make its presence felt until the mid-twentieth century—was the deepened conviction that the clergy must enter into a new struggle, exerting pressure on the State to meet clerical demands and engaging in what was regarded as a necessary and heroic effort to defeat the enemy through polemical combat.

Internal divisions, particularly the disaffection of O'Donnell and the centrist moderados who had supported the revolution of 1854, brought the period of revolution to an end. Between this change in July 1856 and the "Glorious" Revolution of September 1868, a measure of political stability was achieved. A short-lived moderado government was followed by a ministry of Liberal Union (1858–1863) led by O'Donnell, who attempted to create a broadly based coalition. Although this "long" ministry governed with a spirit of political tolerance and pragmatism, it had come into being because of the failure of both moderados and progresistas to create a constitutional regime based on effective party politics. The Liberal Union was itself an amalgam of factions engaged in constant struggle for influence. As time passed the inevitable tensions within the coalition grew stronger and ensured its collapse. O'Donnell saw clearly enough that the union had not resolved the fundamental dilemma of liberal politics—its inability to devise a mechanism for the peaceful transfer of power from government to opposition. His suggestion for a way out of the impasse—his resignation and the formation of a progresista government while he led a party of loyal opposition—foundered on the implacable hostility of the queen toward a progresista ministry.[48]

The resignation of O'Donnell in 1863 opened a new period of instability marked by the return of Narváez to power (1864–1865), a final and desperate attempt to create a workable Liberal Union (1865), and, finally, the installation of a semidictatorial regime (1866–1868) with Narváez serving as prime minister until his death in the spring of 1868. The ministerial shifts of the mid-1860's arose from the glaring weaknesses of moderado politics: a queen who increasingly showed that she was her father's daughter in the desire for personal power; the lack of an effective party system, which created an opposition hostile to the monarch and the political order; and the continuing importance of praetorian politicians such as O'Donnell and Narváez. In the end all led to the breakdown of the moderado State.

In spite of ministerial changes the Church prospered between 1856 and 1868. The ecclesiastical legislation of the progresistas was undone by the Narváez ministry between 1856 and 1857. The government halted the sale of Church lands and passed a law on public instruction (the Moyano Law) in 1857 recognizing the importance of religion in education at all levels. The accession of O'Donnell in 1858 aroused clerical apprehensions, but the new ministry reached a settlement with the papacy on the sale of ecclesiastical property in 1859, and its imperialist adventures in Indochina and Morocco evoked enthusiasm among churchmen, who regarded these expeditions as new crusades. (The joint French-Spanish campaign in Cochin China in 1858 was described as "a war of religion" designed "to conquer the holy liberty of preaching the gospel.")[49]

The Church's ability to function within the kaleidoscope of liberal politics during the final decade of the moderado State benefited directly from clerical ascendancy over Isabella II. The queen, whose private life alternated between illicit amours and religious devotion, regarded the Church as one of the bulwarks of her personal power. The appointment in 1857 of the archbishop of Santiago (Cuba), Antonio Claret, as royal confessor brought close to the throne a shrewd and intelligent cleric, the supreme example of the theocratic apoliticization characteristic of the mid-nineteenth- and early twentieth-century Spanish Church.[50] Claret, a former domestic missionary and religious propagandist who had revolutionized popular evangelization techniques, accepted a post at court believing that providence had called him to a charge from which he could advance the welfare of the Church. Although progresistas, Democrats, and Republicans saw Claret as a sinister gray eminence, the confessor's influence was circumscribed by political reality. He could not, for instance, prevent recognition of the kingdom of Italy in 1865, a move that threatened the remnants of Pius IX's temporal power. But his position at court gave him considerable influence over episcopal appointments and the authorization of new religious orders.

Claret, though personally loyal to Isabella and hostile to Carlist adventurism, believed himself above partisan politics ("I have never involved myself in factions nor political parties, but have occupied myself with my ministry"), but his deep disdain for political life was itself a form of politics.[51] "Spain is like a gamblers' table," he once remarked, "the gamblers are the two parties; . . . the moving force of all politics is nothing more than ambition, pride and greed." Claret saw that the moderado State could be used to aid the Church in its mission, which he conceived in theocratic terms worthy of the Middle Ages, but in the end he expected little from the moderados. "Spanish politics is to be compared to an elephant hunt in which the hunters first dig a hole; others cover it so that the elephant will not see it . . . and when it has fallen into the trap, others arrive and give it a good whack; finally, the last to arrive on the scene pull it from the hole and lead it with ropes where they wish, . . . since the elephant always recognizes those who have done it a favor. This last is what is being done to Religion in Spain by the political parties, if we except the Catholic [those committed to a narrow defense of ecclesiastical interests]. The Republican party is the one which digs the hole; the liberal [progresista] covers it and prepares the trap, then whacks the Church while, finally, the conservative [moderado] . . . ties it with deceitful ropes."

The ecclesiastical elephant stepped more adroitly than Claret believed. Between 1856 and 1868 the institutional recovery interrupted by the revolution of 1854 resumed. The Jesuits, as resilient as ever, possessed twenty-five houses by 1863. The moderado State, although willing to authorize new religious foundations, continued to limit the introduction of male religious orders. But the Redemptorists, later prominent in the great missionary campaigns of the early twentieth century, established their first Spanish house at Huete in 1864; the Order of Saint John of God, well known for its work in hospitals during the eighteenth century, began its modern history at Barcelona in 1867. The Benedictines, expelled from their monasteries during the 1830's, were allowed to reoccupy the famous Marian shrine of Montserrat in Catalonia, which was raised to the status of a full abbey in 1862. The growth of female orders engaged in charitable and social work continued. Established congregations, such as the Piarists in Catalonia, opened more convents, and new orders, often of local origin—such as the Dominicans of the Annunciation (Vich, 1858) and the Daughters of Our Lady of Sorrows and Saint Philip Neri (Seville, 1859)— spread throughout the kingdom.

The Church also pursued its evangelizing work with renewed determination through the publication and distribution of thousands of catechisms and aggressive missionary campaigns. Moreover, the ecclesiastical authorities, assisted by a combative Catholic press, urged the State to take firm action against Spain's Protestants. Between 1860 and 1863 provincial governors in Andalusia, the center of Spanish Protestantism in the nineteenth century as it had been in the sixteenth, subjected dissenters to a persecution recalling the rigors of the Inquisition. One of the victims, Manuel Matamoros, became a hero to Protestant Europe when he was sentenced to eight years of hard labor for having opened a church in Granada.[52]

In spite of the benefits secured by the Church from the moderado State, particularly after 1865, Catholic opinion became increasingly resentful of a society refusing to fit into a theocratic mold. Bishops and Catholic laymen committed to the realization of old dreams rushed onto the battlefield of polemic prepared to strike their enemies with words and harass them with deeds. The ranks of Catholic apologists included figures, such as the deeply conservative Candido Nocedal and the Carlist Antonio Aparisi, whose ability at polemic in parliament and the press made them effective rhetorical champions in the bruising propaganda wars carried on without respite between defenders of narrowly conceived ecclesiastical interests and advocates of new intellectual currents.

Controversy followed controversy. In 1857 the inaugural lecture given in the Universidad Central of Madrid by the philosopher Julián Sanz del Río, advocating a secular and scientific system of education, provoked a bitter public dispute.[53] The degree of ecclesiastical influence over education remained a sore point for ecclesiastics in spite of the Moyano Law and Article 3 of the concordat, both of which churchmen considered to be virtually ignored. In 1863 the bishops began a public campaign for "the greater christianization of public teaching and the direct, preventive and continuous intervention of the Spanish episcopacy in plans of study, textbooks and . . . with respect to any books . . . which could offend Religion and the traditional customs of the country."[54] In 1865 the Catholic press, led by the pro-Carlist *El Pensamiento Español*, began a successful campaign for the dismissal of university professors who had not directly questioned religious dogma but whose commitment to the free expression of ideas shocked the theocratic sensibilities of conservative Catholic thinkers derisively labeled "neocatholics" by their opponents.

Episcopal censures of books judged "immoral, dissolute and incompatible with all social order" multiplied. The bishops of the metropolitan province of Valencia believed that such publications were being "introduced in a fabulous way even into the smallest towns." In 1863 state authorization of Victor Hugo's *Les misérables* aroused episcopal resentment both for its contents, thought hostile to religion, and because the government had dealt "a serious blow to the essential rights of the episcopacy" by refusing to heed clerical censures.[55] Ecclesiastical frustration with the moderado State deepened with the publication of Pius IX's celebrated indictment of secularism and liberalism, the *Syllabus of Errors,* in 1864 (even Narváez initially refused to allow its publication). Although Cardinal Primate Alameda and other bishops were reluctant to defy the government by publishing the *Syllabus* in Spain, they eventually did so under the pressure of a determined episcopal faction led by the archbishop of Burgos, Fernando de la Puente y Primo de Rivera. The hesitant bishops at least succeeded in limiting publication to a Latin version printed in diocesan bulletins.[56] The recognition of the kingdom of Italy by the last government of Liberal Union in 1865 further antagonized Catholic opinion and led to disenchantment with Isabella II, who was suspected, not without justification, of agreeing to the recognition to save her shaky throne.[57]

The Church chose to nibble at the moderado hand feeding it just at the moment when the survival of the regime itself came into doubt. The hierarchy knew enough not to break with Isabella II, although segments of Catholic opinion sympathetic to Carlism—increasingly vociferous during the 1860's—were prepared to consume the dynasty and the liberal State at a single sitting. As the regime plunged deeper into political impasse from 1865 on, the Church was incapable of forming a united front to maintain the gains won since 1844. In the midst of resentments and frustrations, the ecclesiastical leadership continued to place its hopes on the willingness of a discredited monarch and a widely disliked semiauthoritarian government to realize the old clerical dream of a pious, Catholic Spain. The Carlists, divided into several factions, were agreed on the necessity of restoring an absolutist and theocratic state; Catholics belonging to the political groups opposed to the small clique of moderados governing the nation between 1866 and 1868 resented clerical support for the existing government. Divisions within Catholic ranks reduced the Church to being a bystander as the moderado State entered its death throes, although loud clerical and Carlist rhetoric might lead to the opposite conclusion. The dictatorial ministry of Narváez rested on little save a small circle of extremely conservative politicians and a queen desperate to keep her throne. Under the impact of economic depression, intense political opposition, and military intervention, the regime finally succumbed in September 1868. The "Glorious" Revolution opened a six-year period of upheaval that soon led the Church to regard the years between 1856 and 1868 as a regretted silver age.

7 / Church and Society, 1844–1868

The definitive triumph of Spanish liberalism over royal absolutism after 1833 not only transformed the political organization of the kingdom, it also ensured the demise or decline of institutions that had been essential to the hierarchical order of the eighteenth century. The Church faced the task of adapting both to a new political reality and to a society hostile to the traditional role of religious institutions under the absolute monarchy. The response to this challenge—whether in the form of the reaction to social problems in town and country, the intellectual defenses mounted against the progress of secular culture, or the elaboration of new pastoral techniques to solidify belief in a time of change— created an institution very different from the Church of the Old Regime.

The Organization of the Church, 1844–1868

In spite of the transformation of the Church's relationship to the State after 1834, the ecclesiastical organization varied little from that of the Old Regime. Although the Concordat of 1851 envisaged a limited rationalization of diocesan boundaries, only three new dioceses were created—Vitoria (1861), Ciudad Real (1875), and Madrid (1885). A stipulation that dioceses in small provincial towns should be amalgamated with sees in larger cities was only partially fulfilled, although successive governments tried to move a reluctant Church to action. As late as 1902 a proposal to suppress the diocese of Tortosa provoked a popular demonstration after placards appeared urging the local inhabitants to protest this threat to municipal pride. The reluctance of the archbishops of Toledo to lose Madrid delayed the creation of a diocese there for more than a quarter of a century.[1]

The liberal State, even in periods of moderado rule, continued

209

to insist on a reduction in the number of parishes. The authorities were less concerned with devising a rational parochial organization than with the financial savings anticipated from parish reform. According to the Concordat of 1851 the number of parishes in a given town had to correspond to population size. Thus, Salamanca's twenty-four parishes in a city with 15,000 inhabitants were to be reduced to three according to the formula set out in a royal directive of 1854. Reductions in the number of parishes were begun in many dioceses, but local bishops resisted through effective foot-dragging techniques. In Salamanca, for example, the diocesan authorities spun out negotiations through successive governments in an effort to strike a better deal. Only in 1868 was agreement reached with the ministry of Narváez, which consented with great reluctance to a compromise establishing the number of parishes in the city at six. The reform was not carried out, in fact, until the 1880's.[2]

The concordat also met liberal demands to the extent that the extreme differences of wealth among the bishops disappeared in favor of a salary scale established according to the importance and size of dioceses. The archbishop of Toledo, as incumbent of the primatial see, received the largest salary, 120,000 reales; the archbishops of Seville and Valencia received 100,000; the income of the remaining prelates ranged from 70,000 to 90,000 reales.[3] A reduction in the number of cathedral canons satisfied a long-held liberal aspiration to diminish the size of a clerical elite whose contribution to pastoral work seemed questionable. Although reduced in size, the capitular clergy continued to exist as a class apart within the ecclesiastical establishment through eligibility requirements that excluded the vast majority of the parish clergy. Successive governments well into the twentieth century believed that the Church had not gone far enough with internal reform. But by abandoning any pretension to state-inspired reorganization, a price the moderados willingly paid in 1851, the authorities had to depend on the goodwill of both Rome and the bishops to carry out changes neither wished to implement, laying the groundwork for later controversy.

Between a demographic low point during the Espartero regency and the revolution of 1868, the ecclesiastical population grew moderately. The census of 1860 reported a secular clergy of 42,765 (approximately 4,000 more than in the early 1840's). The increase was reflected in seminary enrollments, which rose from 16,077 in 1853 to 24,376 in 1862. The functional role of the seculars, moreover, differed from the eighteenth-century pattern, in which only a minority of priests were engaged in the cure of souls. A decline in the size of the capitular clergy and in the number of priests holding benefices (the effect of liberal legislation and the loss of Church property) created a clerical population devoted in the vast majority to parish work. In spite of the overall reduction in priestly numbers during the first decades of the nineteenth century, then, the ratio of clergy with pastoral responsibilities to the general population improved dramatically. There was one priest for every 1,745 persons in the archdiocese of Seville in 1768, but only a minority of the clergy were engaged in the cure of souls; by 1859 there was one clergyman active in pastoral work for every 428. This proportion was repeated for other dioceses, although in some cases the change was less spectacular.[4] Churchmen would have been loathe to admit it, but the liberal revolution forced a reorientation of clerical activities in a pastoral direction.

Other problems, however, remained. Disparities in parish size from one region to another continued. Average parochial populations in Andalusia (7,493 in Cádiz; 2,594 in Seville; 3,090 in Córdoba) contrasted with those of the smaller parishes of the north (458 in Oviedo, 618 in Santiago, 488 in Salamanca).[5] The State's financial commitment to support the parish clergy did not allow for the support of all ordained priests. In 1860 only two-thirds were eligible for government salaries, continuing the centuries-old problem of a floating population of clerics whose conduct often gave rise to scandal. As late as 1885 the first bishop of Madrid tried to curb the activities of unsalaried clergy moving from church to church in quest of Mass stipends, a reform that so enraged one unemployed and unstable cleric that he assassinated the prelate on Palm Sunday in 1886.[6]

In spite of ecclesiastical pressure for a general restoration of the male religious orders, the liberal State, whether in moderado or progresista hands, refused to authorize expansion beyond a handful of orders including the Piarists, an educational order surviving the suppression of the 1830's; the Oratorians and Vincentians, authorized by the Concordat of 1851; and the Franciscans, Jesuits, Augustinians, and Dominicans, who were allowed to establish a small number of houses to train priests for Cuba, Puerto Rico, and the Philippines. Even the progresistas set aside their customary hostility to the orders on the assumption that they contributed to the maintenance of Spanish rule in the remnants of the colonial empire. By 1860 male religious numbered only 1,683, distributed in sixty-two houses. The orders, aside from the Jesuits whose domestic missions contributed to renewed efforts at popular evangelization, did not play an important part in the mid-nineteenth-century Church's recovery. The expansion of the orders after 1874 in more favorable conditions from an ecclesiastical point of view (by 1923 the male orders contained 17,210 members) would make the regular clergy as burning an issue in the twentieth century as in the nineteenth.[7]

Of all groups within the Church none survived better than the religious orders of women. The 1860 census reported a total of 18,817 nuns, compared with 22,000–25,000 estimated for the later years of Ferdinand VII's reign. Although the majority of nuns belonged to cloistered communities devoted to prayer and contemplation—activities regarded as socially useless by the secular reformers who destroyed the male orders on these grounds— the liberal State, even during periods of progresista rule, treated nuns more gently than male religious. To force women from convents where they had passed their lives isolated from the world offended the humanitarian sentiments of the liberals, who at their most radical did little more than close smaller houses and restrict the admission of novices in the hope that such measures would bring about the eventual disappearance of the female orders.

The moderados encouraged communities such as the Sisters of Charity, whose services were required to staff hospitals, asylums, orphanages, and old-age homes falling under state administration after the poor relief reform of the 1830's. Between 1854 and 1868 the order expanded from 887 members to 1,657.[8] The development of the Sisters of Charity, along with the appearance of other active communities—such as the Little Sisters of the Poor, introduced into Spain for the first time at Barcelona in 1863—was not, however, extensive enough to alter the traditional monastic character of the female orders.

The Church emerging from the ordeal of liberal revolution

also differed from its eighteenth-century predecessor in the extent and nature of its material resources. Abolition of the tithe and sale of the regular and secular clergy's property undermined the twin pillars that had supported the finances of the Old Regime Church. Although ecclesiastics regarded disamortization as a fatal blow, the Church may not have suffered as catastrophically as clerical lamentations would suggest, at least as far as the secular clergy were concerned, leaving aside the fluctuations in income caused by political instability. By assuming responsibility for salaries and the maintenance of church fabrics, the liberal State might well have saved the Church from the consequences of the long deterioration in traditional sources of income evident since the 1790's.

The Church of 1860 was poorer than the Church of 1760 but not so badly off compared with the Church of 1830 given the shrinking of the ecclesiastical establishment after 1834. Between 1829 and 1833 the annual income of the secular clergy averaged 253 million reales. The budget of *culto y clero* in 1851 provided 153 million reales, which rose to nearly 180 million on the eve of the revolution of 1868.[9] Although the decline in revenue was substantial, it must be placed in the context of the Old Regime Church's heavy expenditures on building and decoration as well as on charitable activities later administered by the State. With its range of activity constricted largely to the religious sphere after 1834, the Church did not require such enormous resources, however much churchmen lamented their passing. And there were advantages to state financing. The Church could rely with some assurance during periods of stability on regular payments from the treasury in contrast to the extreme fluctuations of income inherent in the old system's dependence on levels of agricultural production.

Ecclesiastics resented the refusal of the liberal State, always watchful of its purse strings under both moderado and progresista governments, to subsidize nonpastoral activities. To supplement their income they turned to private donations, a development that later would have serious consequences through the identification of clerical and middle-class interests. How extensively the prosperous contributed to the Church before 1868 is difficult to establish. But the process was clearly under way by the 1860's.

Collection of "Peter's Pence," an annual donation sent to the pope, in the diocese of Vitoria rose from 8,788 reales in 1862 to 864,392 in 1868; a fund-raising campaign for the cathedral of Zaragoza produced 7 million reales between 1863 and 1872.[10] Although a complete study of ecclesiastical wealth following the liberal reforms is yet to be made, there is some evidence that by 1868 the Spanish Church had weathered its fiscal storms.

Along with changes in the configuration of the religious population and ecclesiastical wealth, other transformations made the Church a very different institution from its eighteenth-century predecessor. The disappearance of traditional sources of wealth, as well as the complementary relationship between Crown and episcopacy characteristic of the royal Church of the eighteenth century, forced the hierarchy to descend from the "high lookout point" described by Charles III's archbishop of Toledo to a more limited field of action. Bishops no longer enjoyed the autonomous revenues that had allowed them to build bridges, establish vocational schools, and indulge in other secular benefactions. The liberal State was officially Catholic, but its financial arrangements for the Church as well as its unwillingness, even in periods of moderado rule, to accept the corpus of theocratic assumptions promoted by the bishops left the latter constantly restless and frustrated, dreaming always of return to an idealized Catholic Spain of the past. Chronic dissatisfaction with liberal policies converted the episcopacy into an ecclesiastical lobby using the pressure tactics common to any politicized society to persuade the government to accept its vision of Spain's future.

The bishops found their role circumscribed from the ample episcopal responsibilities of an earlier age, but they saw their authority within the Church considerably expanded. And they did not shrink from declaring their determination to exercise their powers to the full. "Place the Cross of Jesus Christ at the gate of the sacred field of the Church," declared Bishop Costa y Borrás of Barcelona, "the bishops shall guard it without ever letting anyone penetrate it save those who come, whatever their situation, to humble themselves before an offended God . . . If any audacity of word or deed is found within, it shall be excluded with supreme and unanimous authority."[11] The disappearance of most of the male religious orders eliminated the exempt jurisdictions enjoyed by monasteries and convents during the Old Regime as well as the difficulties of exercising episcopal control over a large population of friars. The Concordat of 1851, moreover, represented a limited victory for the bishops, for the moderado State, while keeping ecclesiastical finances and patronage in its hands, abandoned the regalist tradition of interfering in the internal life of the Church. After 1860 the government permitted the convocation of diocesan synods for the first time in decades to allow bishops to remedy "abuses . . . and the corruption of customs" introduced into ecclesiastical discipline.[12]

The reinforcement of episcopal authority brought advantages to the liberal State. Both moderados and progresistas relied on the hierarchy to restrain the Carlists and the closely related neocatholics from using the Church to challenge the very existence of the regime. Bishops, Carlists, and neos often joined in denunciations of government policy, but in the end the hierarchy maintained its loyalty to the Isabelline monarchy, whatever its misgivings.

The decimation of the episcopacy between 1834 and 1843 permitted the creation of a new hierarchy beginning in 1847. The appointment process, based on procedures outlined in the Concordat of 1753, rested on royal nomination of three candidates to the pope, who selected one. But as Cuenca Toribio has shown, being chosen a bishop was far from simple. Political circumstances and the influence of ministers, deputies, the papal nuncio, and others entered into the complex game of selection before the ministry of grace and justice produced a list of names for royal consideration. After 1857, under the influence of Antonio Claret, Isabella II assumed greater responsibility for the final choice, as "she listened to the interior inspiration which she asks from God in order to know whom she should choose."[13]

The queen's selections were far from inspired. Episcopal appointments fell generally to churchmen whose principal qualifications were loyalty to the sovereign or who were perceived as not being openly hostile to the liberal State. There were occasional exceptions. Fray Cirilo de Alameda, a Franciscan and old absolutist conspirator of the 1820's, was named to the archbishopric of Toledo in 1857; a handful of Carlist prelates filtered through the screen, such as José M. Caixal, later episcopal chaplain to the rebel forces during the second Carlist war.[14] Bishops known for their opposition to the regime were relegated to unimportant sees—Caixal to Urgel, Pedro Lagüera to Burgo de Osma, Cosme Marrodán to Tarazona, and Pedro Casas Souto to Plasencia—and were denied promotion to larger dioceses. Although the moderados abandoned the progresista tactic of trying to create a pro-liberal hierarchy by force, they preferred candidates known for their support of the regime. But the disintegration of the liberal Church left few suitable candidates; one was Miguel Salvá, a man of letters and historian, named bishop of Mallorca in 1851.[15] The range of choice was limited, therefore, to those candidates, often of deeply conservative views, who accepted the liberal State as the established political order. Episcopal appointments thus reflected the ambiguities of the Church's position in Isabelline Spain.

The mid-nineteenth-century hierarchy resembled the episcopacy of the eighteenth century, but more in its vices than its virtues. The bishop continued to live in a world apart from that of his parochial clergy. Although episcopal revenues had declined, a prelate enjoyed an income twenty times that of the urban priest, forty times that of the rural *cura*. For all practical purposes parish priests stood little chance of penetrating the barriers of education and influence that excluded them from episcopal nominations. Social class, namely noble status, was no longer an important consideration in recruitment, largely because of the disappearance of the lesser nobility, which had furnished the majority of the episcopacy during the Old Regime. There were some bishops of aristocratic birth, but the proportion of prelates drawn from the *clases modestas* increased substantially according to the recent analysis of recruitment carried out by Cuenca Toribio.[16] In spite of the hierarchy's more open character, excessive educational qualifications reminiscent of those prevailing during the eighteenth century favored candidates with advanced degrees in theology and canon law. Membership in a cathedral chapter or, increasingly, in diocesan administration formed the *cursus honorum* indispensable for fulfillment of episcopal ambitions.[17]

The bishops were as highly educated, at least in a formal sense, as their Old Regime counterparts, but, having been trained in the conservative setting of the Fernandine university, they lacked the intellectual vitality of the episcopacy of the Caroline Church. Bishop

Salvá of Mallorca—fluent in English, French, and Italian, active in the royal economic society of the island, and responsible along with Martín Fernández de Navarrete for the publication of a fundamental collection of texts (*Colección de documentos inéditos para la historia de España*) still used by historians—was an isolated survivor of the broader ecclesiastical culture of a vanished era.

The career of one of the new bishops of the Isabelline Church, Antolín Monescillo (1811–1897), reveals how far the episcopacy had drifted from the eighteenth-century model. Ordained at the height of the liberal revolution, in 1836, Monescillo went successively to the bishoprics of Calahorra (1861), Jaén (1865), Valencia (1877), and Toledo (1892). His career in the Church came about because of the liberal social changes, which made it possible, through the disappearance of the lesser nobility, for the son of poor peasants to attain the episcopacy. Monescillo's ascent was also a result of his abilities as an ecclesiastical politician who knew how to profit from the uncertainties of the Church's situation under liberalism. He appreciated the importance of journalism and its effect on public opinion from the beginning of his career. He first came to prominence as a young priest for his editorial crusades in Toledo against Miguel Golfanguer, the diocesan administrator appointed during the Espartero regency.[18] Forced into exile because of his involvement in the campaign against Golfanguer, Monescillo returned to Spain when Narváez took power and began his rise in the Church with canonries in Granada and Toledo while continuing his journalistic efforts, particularly as a contributor to *La Cruz*, which his longtime friend and Carlist supporter León Carbonero y Sol edited and published.

In spite of his association with *La Cruz*, which was openly Carlist in its sympathies, Monescillo remained a firm supporter of Isabella II, whom he repeatedly praised in pastoral letters, journalistic articles, and official representations during his years as bishop of Calahorra and Jaén. Along with loyalty to the queen, Monescillo's ideology rested on hostility to government interference in Church affairs even during periods of moderado rule, absolute devotion to the Holy See, and intransigent opposition to religious toleration as well as to the secular intellectual trends of the day. Thus, he participated in the episcopal campaign against Victor Hugo's *Les misérables* in 1863 and defied the Narváez government by publishing the text of the *Syllabus of Errors* in his diocesan bulletin.[19] Yet in the midst of the polemics in which he was constantly involved, Monescillo remained a nimble politician. He had no particular enthusiasm for the government of Liberal Union (1858–1863), which he believed had not gone far enough in recognizing the Church's claim to be the nation's supreme moral censor, but he behaved respectfully toward it. He felt more at home with the moderado ministry of Narváez, although he was by no means completely satisfied with it.[20] As a bishop Monescillo was conscientious enough, but his real interests lay elsewhere—as a polemicist, publicist, and lobbyist seeking to defend and advance the fortunes of the Church within the liberal political order. In him were combined the pragmatism and ideological intransigence characteristic of the Church's position in Isabelline Spain.

The majority of bishops at midcentury were graduates of the ecclesiastical faculties of the universities, but they supported one of the most significant changes in the Isabelline Church—the shift of priestly education from universities to diocesan seminaries. During the eighteenth century the kingdom's clerical elite flocked to the universities rather than to seminaries, which they regarded as second-rate institutions reserved for a socially inferior lower clergy. During the decade of liberal revolution, students began to abandon the universities for seminaries. After discovering that theological students in the former numbered only 300, with nearly as many professors, in 1845 the moderados ordered suppression of the faculties of Barcelona, Granada, Salamanca, Santiago, and Valencia, leaving open only Madrid, Oviedo, Seville, Valladolid, and Zaragoza. The Concordat of 1851, by assuring state support for seminaries, sealed the fate of a centuries-old tradition of theological education in the universities. In 1852 the government ordered the closing of faculties surviving the 1845 suppression.[21] Few changes were more enthusiastically welcomed by the bishops, who saw the universities as centers of moral and intellectual decadence threatening to impressionable clerical students. The Church must begin sacerdotal education, said the rector of the seminary of Seville, "by separating the young from the corruption of the world."[22]

The triumph of the seminary served another purpose; it reinforced the authority of the bishops over their clergy. By bestowing complete authority over seminaries on the hierarchy, the concordat gave the bishops a measure of control over their priests they had never enjoyed before. Bishops imposed regulations for the governance of seminaries that reached draconian proportions. The bishop of Cuenca, for example, forbade parents from visiting their sons save in the presence of a seminary official. Nor would the episcopacy tolerate opposition to its administration. In 1858, when the seminarians of Segovia rebelled against a harsh regimen, the bishop expelled sixty-three, leaving behind a corporal's guard of only seven students.[23]

The physical separation of seminarians from the world about them accentuated the clergy's intellectual isolation. Although an 1852 reform of clerical education introduced the sciences into the curriculum, the course of study, taught in Latin, was narrowly ecclesiastical in focus.[24] If students were made aware of the existence of a secular culture apart from the theocratic preoccupations of the Church, it was only as a dangerous threat to the survival of the faith. The seminary revolution of the mid–nineteenth century resolved one of the problems of the Old Regime Church by providing a standardized education for all candidates for holy orders. But even this advantage was compromised by the introduction of the *carrera breve,* an abbreviated course of study designed to produce as many priests as possible within a short time. The *carrera breve* occasionally produced capable priests, such as Cardinal Sancha, the archbishop of Toledo at the end of the century, but more often it graduated poorly educated clerics doomed to spend their lives in rural parishes and abandon any hope of advancement.[25]

Nor did the reform eliminate the social distinctions characteristic of the eighteenth-century clergy. The distinction became simpler and more brutal—between students who could pay tuition fees and those who could not. The latter, known as *sopistas* or *fámulos,* earned their keep by serving as janitors and waiters in the seminaries; they developed, understandably, a keen sense of social inferiority. In the end the seminary reform of the Isabelline Church created as many problems as it solved. Culturally narrow and weak on pastoral training (as late as 1913 seminarians in Madrid received scarcely any instruction in preaching techniques),[26] the seminary produced generations of priests facing the challenges of changing social, political, and economic conditions with inadequate preparation.

Parish priests, perennial victims of the unequal distribution of resources within the Church, found that their position at the bottom of the ecclesiastical ladder had changed scarcely at all as a result of the Concordat of 1851. They had heard, said a group of rural clergymen from Galicia, "a mysterious voice telling them continuously: your ills will end; a new concordat will drag you from the abjection to which Providence has submitted you to prove your virtue and constancy."[27] But there was no mystery in the financial arrangements worked out between Madrid and Rome. Parish salaries ranged from a minimum of 2,200 reales for rural *curas* to a maximum of 10,000 for the highest paid urban clergy. In an age when the average yearly income of an industrial worker was estimated at 2,827 reales and the minimum thought necessary for a modest clerical style of life was 4,300 a year, the vast majority of the clergy did not prosper. Of the 19,820 priests eligible to receive government salaries in 1851, over 11,000 received under 3,500 reales; 3,706 reached the watershed figure of 4,300; 2,042 exceeded 5,500; and only 1,268 attained incomes of 7,000 reales.[28]

For the parochial clergy, the Concordat of 1851 was a deception leading to bitter protests, such as that sent to the papal nuncio by a group of priests from Santiago de Compostela, and criticism in the Catholic press. The papacy's failure to insist on more equitable treatment of parish priests in comparison with the generous terms meted out to the clerical elite perpetuated the social evils not uncommon among the clergy of the eighteenth century—the constant pressure on resentful parishioners to pay stipends for services such as baptisms, marriages, and funerals as well as the temptation to engage in business activities—which inevitably aroused local hostility. And the continuation of the eighteenth-century system of competitive examinations to fill parish vacancies (*concursos de curatos*) contributed at worst, according to one clerical critic, to spreading "envy, avarice, ambition, detraction and denunciation" among priests and at best to a constant drain of the most qualified clergy from poorer to richer parishes.[29]

Financial disadvantages aside, the prospect of a priestly career appealed to well-off peasant families in certain dioceses—León, Burgos, Pamplona, Solsona, Barcelona, Valencia, and Orihuela—

with the best record of seminary recruitment in the mid–nineteenth century. The opportunity to secure an education in a world lacking decent rural schools and to enter an occupation endowed with modest social prestige made a clerical career seem attractive to a conservative peasantry. Moreover, it was not a difficult goal to attain. An analysis of seminary registrations revealed that virtually all students who began their studies survived to ordination, a commentary in itself on the lack of intellectual selectivity in recruitment.[30]

In spite of the increasing importance of the rural clergy in the nineteenth-century Church, little is known of the mentality and personal circumstances of parish priests. Until studies of their role and influence were undertaken with particular reference to regional differences, it is possible to assess their position only in general terms. It is clear that the life of the rural *cura* was far from comfortable. Poorly paid in relation to his superiors, an outsider in a closely knit community, a representative of distant civil and ecclesiastical authorities, an educated man in the midst of an often illiterate peasantry, the parish priest faced the difficult task of establishing himself as an effective force.

A manual written by Father Juan Planas on the organization and administration of parishes at midcentury provides some clues to the problems and pitfalls facing the *cura*. The parish priest was first of all to confine himself to the spiritual direction of his congregation, "for the material interests of the parishioners have not been entrusted to you by God." Yet the *cura* depended of necessity on the support of the local notables raised up by decades of liberal social and economic change to carry out his pastoral mission. He was to treat rich and poor alike, but he was bound to cooperate with the powerful and influential in his village: "the parish priest should live in good intelligence and harmony with the most notable personalities of the town," for "to repress scandal . . . a slight sign from the mayor or some other proprietor serves better at times than all the efforts . . . of the *cura*." The priest specifically required the support of local notables represented on the junta of studies controlling primary education. According to law the parish priest sat ex officio on the junta. He was urged to use his influence to persuade his fellow board members to choose "the most moral and religious" for appointment to teaching posts, even at the cost of naming teachers who were "inferior to the other candidates in literary attainments."[31]

The *cura* also needed the cooperation of the local authorities to carry out one of his most important functions, that of "pastoral vigilance." The *cura vigilante* was encouraged to move "continually through all the parish . . . examining everything well, houses, taverns, shops, schools, dance halls, etc., attempting to ascertain what is being said in such places, what is being done or not done, sure in the conviction that in all he will find abuses to correct and scandals to reprove." As the supreme moral censor of his parish, the priest was urged to do everything within his power to remove occasions of temptation for his congregation. He should forbid dancing completely if possible; if not, he should at least eliminate those dances that "carried the greatest danger of perversion." He must act to prevent flirting among youth, "the greatest danger which can be presented to human weakness," and he must attack at every turn "the impurity which has come to be the ordinary sauce of conversations" among the young.[32] The *cura* was also expected to fulfill a variety of pastoral responsibilities—teaching the catechism, conducting religious services with decorum, preaching with care and thoughtfulness, visiting the sick, and assisting the poor.

The negative aspects of the parish priest's life were treated with circumspection by Father Planas. Yet his veiled warnings to his clerical readers rested on his observations of actual problems. The *cura* was warned that "he could not abandon his parish without abandoning the most sacred of his duties," a reference to priests who absented themselves from their congregations for personal gain and comfort or to seek advancement. Planas admonished churchmen who became involved in political controversy or the personal quarrels of their parishioners, the former almost certainly directed against clerical involvement in the constant and bruising polemic between Carlists and the supporters of liberalism. He also emphasized the necessity of upright moral conduct. The *cura* must not support relatives in his residence, "for parishioners do not look favorably upon this, . . . because they think, and at times they are right, that these are rewarded with the goods of the Church." "Gossip becomes general, and discontent reaches its height," Planas maintained, when the *cura* spends much of his time advancing the fortunes of his relatives. The priest was warned to exercise special care in the selection of a housekeeper. He required a woman who was "religious and discreet" both to avoid scandal and to avoid interference in parish administration, "for nothing is more of an affront for an ecclesiastic than to allow himself to be dominated by a woman."[33]

The ideal parish priest necessarily stood aloof from the community to which he was assigned. He was to take every precaution to avoid the gossip and innuendos endemic to the isolated rural village. The *cura* was to fulfill a lofty spiritual mission, yet he required the support of the politically and socially influential. It was a difficult life, one "of dangerous loneliness" in which there were times when "not even the devil will call at his door," as a later authority on the parish clergy expressed it.[34] Personal isolation made boredom an ever-present risk for priests whose narrow education deprived them of intellectual support in the midst of an often unlettered peasantry. It led also to the cases, cited with vehemence by anticlerical writers, of priests maintaining liaisons with women. How extensive this problem was is impossible to say, but the problem existed, as it had for centuries. Thus, Father Juan Villada, the parish priest of Cardeñadijo in Burgos in the late 1880's, declared that he had been living with his housekeeper for twenty-six years and that the situation was not uncommon among the rural clergy of his day.[35] Given the dearth of knowledge on the parish clergy of the mid–nineteenth century, it is impossible to provide a detailed profile of its role within the Church. There were certainly regional differences between, for example, Andalusia with a religiously indifferent population and the more devout countryside of the north. It is at least clear that the lot of the parish priest was anything but easy.

The Church and the New Society

Liberal ecclesiastical policies after 1834 made it impossible for the Church to play the pervasive social and cultural role it had had in the eighteenth century. The sale of clerical property, the near disappearance of the male orders, and the assumption by the State of activities once the preserve of religious institutions set the midcentury Church adrift. The economic developments churchmen deplored during the 1840's followed an even more expansive course beginning in 1854. Between 1855 and 1868, 5,000 kilometers of track were laid down in a frenetic railway boom equal to the capitalist excesses of more advanced countries. Banks, trading companies, and factories flourished in a heady atmosphere of uncontrolled speculation. The transfer of agricultural lands from the Church and municipalities, whatever its social consequences for peasants without the resources to participate in the disamortization, pushed agriculture in a more capitalist direction. More land was placed under cultivation to meet the demands of an expanding population and international markets. Spain's midcentury economic revolution was, however, incomplete. The kingdom remained agrarian in character; industrial development was confined largely to Catalonia and the Basque Provinces; agriculture was only imperfectly modernized.

But economic changes further transformed society. The new elite of bankers, financiers, industrialists, generals, and large landowners consolidated its position during the 1850's and 1860's. Flamboyant and extravagant, the new rich did not shrink from displaying their wealth with as much bravado as any eighteenth-century aristocrat. But if the alliance of capitalism and liberalism made fortunes, it also created paupers. The sale of Church and common lands to those with money to buy them reduced the vast landless population of Andalusia and Extremadura to even greater misery, for the new proprietors managed their holdings with ruthless efficiency compared with religious institutions. Even in regions of peasant ownership, a lack of capital spread the ubiquitous curse of moneylending at exorbitant rates of interest. In the cities, particularly Madrid and Barcelona, population growth and the decline of traditional artisan trades created a new class of poor. But the condition of workers in industrial centers, such as Barcelona (over 100,000 were employed there in the textile industry in 1861), was no better. Working-class discontent exploded in Catalonia in serious form for the first time between 1854 and 1856, and thereafter it became a constant feature of social life. Resentment among the landless of the south, already manifested in a series of local revolts in 1840, became more intense after 1855.[36] Risings in the province of Seville in 1857 and at Loja in

1861 revealed the full extent of the rural poor's hostility to the society liberalism had created.

The pragmatism with which the Church adjusted to political reality vanished when it confronted an expansive capitalism and secular culture existing beyond the reach of clerical supervision. In the eyes of churchmen, liberalism had created a society out of control in which individual passions were allowed to run riot at the expense of morality and religion. Whether moderados or progresistas governed the country made no difference. In a sermon preached in the cathedral of Valladolid in 1847 with the moderado ministry of Narváez in power, Canon García Mazo began with a Latin text from Saint Paul, "dies mali sunt," as he painted a picture of unrelieved moral corruption in Spanish society. "Faith nearly extinguished, charity frozen or deadened offers nothing more to our eyes than Christians without souls and without life. The times are obscured by clouds of vice and the dark mists of error."[37] Antonio Claret expressed the same sentiments more directly in 1857: "the world is evil, very evil."[38]

The pervasive sense of being surrounded by corruption lay behind the chronic tensions that characterized interactions between the Church and the liberal State beyond the level of simple civil-ecclesiastical relations. Ecclesiastics were exasperated by what they perceived to be the moderado State's refusal to take the steps necessary "to save the nation from a sure and inevitable ruin."[39] Bishop Costa y Borrás' frequent clashes with both moderado and progresista governments during the 1850's over liberty of expression and public morality provide the most spectacular examples of the struggle between this theocratic vision and the realities of the new society. A polemicist of the first order, the bishop of Barcelona provoked official wrath in a series of incidents in which he gave "the voice of alert . . . against the torrent of evil doctrines emerging from the press, against evil books, obscene pictures, immoral theatrical presentations and dances."[40] The bishop took the extreme step on one occasion of having an episcopal order forbidding a certain play posted on the church doors of Barcelona. The provincial governor responded promptly by sending the local police to cut the posters down with their swords.

During the late 1840's and 1850's, few aspects of liberal society moved the clergy to more rhetorical paroxysms than the economic changes that had produced wealth in abundance for the kingdom's elite. Clerical hostility to the economic order through the 1850's reflected in part the sour-grapes resentment of the Church against liberals, whether moderados or progresistas, who had profited from the sale of ecclesiastical property. But it went deeper. The Church continued to adhere to an organic view of human society derived from a centuries-old scholastic tradition. Such a philosophy demanded that the individual curb his natural acquisitive passions for the common good. It required that the rich restrain their taste for luxurious living in order to help the poor through charity. What churchmen saw about them was a consumer society, admittedly confined to a minority, which defied this traditional view of social organization.

Antolín Monescillo expressed the prevailing sentiments of churchmen concerning the profound changes taking place before their eyes: "Mathematics, the natural sciences, discoveries, machines, the invention of steam and its application to every kind of industry serve only to enrich entrepreneurs to the prejudice of the working classes, to encourage tyrannical egoism, . . . to form a feudalized aristocracy enemy of the poor when religion does not enter into progress."[41]

Another clergyman stressed the corrosive effects of acquisitiveness on the population as a whole: "There is not only avarice among the great but also among the rich, not only among the rich but also among the poor who, deprived of temporal goods, burn with desire to have them; there is avarice among those who have jobs, among merchants and artisans . . . There is no estate in which in one form or another the avaricious cannot be found."[42]

The ingrained hostility of the Church to the burgeoning capitalism of the mid–nineteenth century contributed to the chronic tension between it and the liberal State, even when the latter was controlled by its more conservative elements. The alliance between ecclesiastical interests and liberalism could never develop into anything more than a tactical arrangement until the Church was willing to accept the social transformation brought about by economic change. It never did so completely, but by the 1860's a process of uneasy accommodation with the new economic system was under way that would develop still further after the revolutionary period between 1868 and 1874.

In one sense the Church's stubborn adherence to its traditional interpretation of society allowed the clergy to see the destructive social effects of economic change with some clarity. Already in 1840 Jaime Balmes had warned of the dangers that would flow from a disamortization excluding the peasantry. Balmes also saw that relations between workers and employers in his native Catalonia were changing in a fundamental way as traditional artisan enterprises gave way to a factory system in the first stages of Spain's industrial revolution. Balmes himself witnessed the earliest conflicts between capital and labor during the Espartero regency, developments "most alarming to the eyes of every thinking man." Balmes concluded that one of the causes "of this evil" was that men had discovered "the means of producing and increasing this production indefinitely, without at the same time having found the art of distributing its products in a convenient way, and without having established a system capable of confronting the pressing necessities which the excessive multiplication [of production] has brought with it."[43] The triumph of industrial capitalism and the impoverishment of a working class forced to work long hours under iron discipline scarcely spread beyond the borders of Catalonia during the 1840's and 1850's, but there the Church first confronted the social problem that would be crucial to its later history.

The moderado ministries ruling the country since 1844 repressed the Catalan industrial workers' attempts to come together in associations designed to protect their interests. The progresista revolution in 1854 gave the workers an opportunity to organize in support of their demands, although, in fact, the progresistas were no better disposed toward the workers than the moderados. Indeed, the revolutionary government quickly repented of its early tolerance of working-class associations. The spread of labor unrest in the early months of 1855 evoked a harsh reaction from Madrid, which suspended the workers' associations and confiscated their funds. This led, in turn, to the first general strike in Spanish history, which took place in the industrial towns of Catalonia on July 2.

In the absence of Bishop Costa y Borrás of Barcelona, who had been summoned to Madrid by an irritated progresista government, it fell to the bishop of Vich, Antonio Palau, to publish a pastoral letter, widely reproduced in the press, that expressed the Church's position on the course of events. Palau refused to enter into an analysis of the causes of the conflict; he urged the workers to "return to work . . . to your factories where with the honored work of your hands you can gain sustenance for your families. If in spite of all you cannot satisfy all your necessities; . . . religion will console you promising the most abundant felicities in the life to come."[44] Whether Palau was simply naive or urged resignation on the workers because he feared social revolution is unclear. But by 1858, when he had succeeded to the see of Barcelona, he sang a different tune. He told the rich of his diocese: "Your pride will cause the disbelieving masses to rise up; your banquets will irritate the appetite of the naked and hungry crowds, and neither laws, courts, gallows nor armies will be sufficient to contain the outburst of the unbridled multitude."[45]

Confronted with social conflicts of unfamiliar intensity and character, the Church was unsure what course it should follow. Clerical dislike of the capitalist extravagance and arrogance of the new society was sincere enough. But churchmen were even more frightened by the prospect of a social revolution directed against private property. As early as 1840 the Catholic press vigorously attacked the utopian socialist doctrines making their way into Spain.[46] These denunciations were repeated with increasing insistence during the 1850's and 1860's. Antonio Palau, along with his warning to the rich, also admonished the workers of Barcelona against "the golden dreams of modern utopians," who pretended to establish "a perfect equality of fortunes among all men."[47]

If at one level the clergy perceived the serious social problem created by economic change, at another it failed to see that growing class consciousness among industrial workers alienated from the institutions of the liberal State contained dangerous implications for the Church itself. Having allied itself to the new political order, however reluctantly, and operating with an ingrained respect for authority, the Church in the end came down on the side of law and order against possible revolution. The ecclesiastical response to social unrest was little more than the worn-out formula of charity, although Balmes had seen the necessity of some kind of mutual benefit associations for workers. Thus, Costa y Borrás told the faithful of Barcelona in 1852: "the sacred books recommend and prescribe almsgiving, and this . . . can only be practiced if there are rich and poor to a greater or lesser degree."[48]

The Church at midcentury dwelt on the importance of charity as fully as its eighteenth-century predecessor. Clerics reproached the liberal State for having "beheaded charity" by depriving the Church of the wealth that had once allowed it to help the poor.[49] In spite of the ink poured from clerical pens on this issue, the Church lacked the resources to furnish significant assistance to the victims of economic change. The charitable activities of religious groups, such as the Sisters of Charity and the Society of Saint Vincent de Paul, introduced to Spain in 1849, could not equal the massive and diffuse charity of the Old Regime. The Church failed to see that the problem itself had changed. Charity appeared meaningless in a society in which economic grievances were keenly felt and class consciousness was rising. It might be argued that the nature and rapidity of the social transformation of Catalonia between 1840 and the late 1850's was such that no clerical initiative in the realm of social policy would have succeeded.[50] In any event, no such initiatives were undertaken. In the end the Church was puzzled by a society in ferment. As a result, it fell between two stools. Its dream of a return to the charity of the past was impractical; its horror of radical social forces made it a defender of private property and the existing social order in an economic system the clergy fundamentally disliked.

The triumph of liberalism also transformed the role of the Church in education. The nearly complete destruction of the male religious orders during the 1830's swept away the vast majority of the regulars' schools save those of the Piarists, whose progressive methods won the admiration of even liberal reformers. And the decline of the ecclesiastical faculties in the universities, particularly those of theology and canon law (the latter were abolished in 1842) considerably diminished the once formidable religious character of higher education.

Although liberal educational legislation was not especially coherent and changed in accord with political circumstances, the three fundamental laws governing education before 1868—the

Law on Primary Education (1838), and the Laws on Public Instruction (1845 and 1857)—did not seek to eliminate religion from state schools.[51] All three laws, reflecting moderado concern with the importance of religious teaching as a foundation of civic and moral conduct, included religion as a mandatory subject at every level. Primary school students received instruction in the catechism and religious history and marched in a body, at least in theory, to attend Sunday Mass under the watchful eye of the local schoolmaster. Secondary school students in the state *institutos* of 1850 were obliged to take a course in "Religion and Morality" in four of their five years of instruction. Moreover, the Church enjoyed a limited supervisory role over state schools. Parish priests served as members of local school boards under the terms of the 1838 law, and teachers hoping for appointments had to produce certificates of good conduct signed by their *curas*. After 1845 the State tolerated a modest expansion of private Church schools staffed by the religious orders. After 1851 moderado governments recognized diocesan seminaries as secondary schools qualified to prepare students for university entrance.

The Church did not fare badly at liberal hands in education, particularly during periods of moderado rule. The Concordat of 1851 and the Moyano Law of 1857 recognized the Church's general right of supervision over education, although both were vague about how this was to be exercised. Between 1857 and the revolution of 1868 the Church waged a persistent and ultimately successful campaign to exert greater control over instruction. Changes introduced just before the collapse of the moderado State in 1868 gave the Church a greater role in the authorization of school texts and more substantial representation on provincial and local school boards.[52] Clerical objectives were straightforward. The Church wished absolute freedom to establish schools of its own, and it demanded the right to supervise curricula and teacher recruitment in the state schools. Although the liberal State made substantial concessions to the Church in education, ecclesiastical interests were never satisfied with these arrangements.

Clerical discontent arose from the State's insistence, whether it was in moderado or progresista hands, on its right to control education at every level, from university to primary school. The University Law of 1845, passed when the moderado government of Narváez was in full flood, established the highly centralized university system that in one form or another survived through the 1970's. In spite of concessions made to the Church in particular aspects of educational policy, clerical interests resented a system in which their plans for a rigidly Catholic instruction depended ultimately on the suffrance of the civil authorities.

Hostility to the state monopoly of education was closely linked to clerical fears that schools would be used to propagate secularizing ideas opposed to the Church's still essentially theocratic vision of the organization and purpose of human society. Julián Sanz del Río's inaugural lecture in the Universidad Central in 1857 confirmed the worst fears of Church defenders. Sanz del Río, an intellectual of little originality who had taken up the views of the minor German philosopher Karl Krause, expounded the philosophy of his mentor, a "curious blend of subjective mysticism and vague modernism," from his university chair.[53] Although Sanz del Río tried to avoid an open confrontation with the Church, his views were immediately attacked as "pantheistic" by a chorus of Catholic detractors. That a university professor taught such a philosophy from an official post in a centralized state university system outraged the Church. The Catholic apologist Ortí y Lara warned his readers that unless steps were taken to put an end to the "freedom of the chair" in universities the Church stood to lose future generations for the faith. The philosophy of Sanz del Río, he maintained, was "the fountain from which the future teachers of Spanish youth would have to drink. What more powerful enemy is being prepared against the Catholic faith!"[54] The polemic initiated in 1857 raged on for a decade, until the purge of university professors undertaken by Narváez in 1867. The conflict revealed again the fundamental ambiguity of the Church's position within the secular State liberalism had created.

Was Spain Catholic?

Whether a religious revival took place after 1843 is unclear in spite of the obvious signs of the Church's institutional recovery. Until socioreligious studies of the incidence and quality of observance are available, a definitive assessment of the extent of a "spiritual" recovery cannot be made. But the Church produced a successful amalgam of religious devotions and evangelization techniques that appealed to broad sections of the population, from the peasantry to the urban bourgeoisie. On the surface religious life at midcentury appeared similar to that of the Old Regime. The folkloric customs of "popular" religion—placatory in nature and connected to the fears and preoccupations of an uneducated peasantry—continued in the forms of local shrines, pilgrimages, and rites designed to evoke intercession to remedy specific ills. The nineteenth-century traveler could still describe folk beliefs depicted by visitors to the peninsula a century before: the Murcian peasant who believed "that no disease can affect him or his cattle if he touches them with the cross of Caravaca, which angels brought from heaven," the hermit of Manresa who showed tourists the cave in which Saint Ignatius Loyola did penance and sold them the dust "of its pulverized stones" to cure a variety of infirmities, and those who went to the shrine of Santa Engracia in Zaragoza hoping to be cured of scrofula by the smoke of its holy lamps.[55]

During the eighteenth century the practices of "popular" religion evoked the disapproval of bishops and Inquisition alike. For the clerical elite of the Caroline Church, the excesses of "popular" religion appeared an obstacle to their ideal of a simple, interior Christianity. With a certain intuitive brilliance the nineteenth-century Church realized that the appeal of primitive beliefs had deep roots that could be turned to advantage. "Popular" religion, once rejected or at best tolerated as a necessary evil, entered fully into the life of the Church. Extraordinary claims of miraculous happenings that once would have led to inquiries by the Inquisition were given credence in clerical circles. In 1853 the official bulletin of the Toledo archdiocese referred approvingly to the excited crowds flocking to the funeral of a pious woman in Antequera, "the little saint," whose fame was such that the congregation, believing in her miraculous powers, struggled to touch the body with their handkerchiefs. Six months later the bulletin reported with similar confidence on the appearance of a dead uncle to his nephew in the small town of Villanueva de Alcolea in Tortosa.[56]

Although the ecclesiastical authorities followed the usual procedure of canonical inquiry in these cases, they were more disposed to accept claims than their eighteenth-century predecessors, and for a straightforward reason. Years of liberal criticism of the "superstitious" character of Iberian Catholicism elicited the opposite reaction from churchmen, who saw in these occurrences a divine confirmation of the Church's mission. Thus, a report from Valencia in 1854 of a miraculous cholera cure in a man who had drunk water from a well at the house of Saint Vincent Ferrer provoked a controversy between the local liberal press and the clergy. A priest challenged the miracle's journalistic detractors to drink part of a glass of water from the well while he drank the rest, assuring his foes that they would die from an attack of the disease and he would escape unharmed.[57] "Popular" religion had become acceptable testimony to faith.

The triumphal sweep of devotionalism in religious practice also extended the appeal of the midcentury Church. Cults associated with the divine in various manifestations were as old as Christianity itself, but the appearance in the seventeenth and eighteenth centuries of devotions emphasizing the personal and sentimental aspects of petitioning for divine intercession differed from the corporate, community-oriented devotions of earlier periods. These "new" devotions, directed and spread by the Church largely through the religious orders, had already attained popularity in Spain, but they suffered a setback with the extinction of the regular clergy.[58] Yet the liberals also created the conditions necessary for the devotions' recovery by destroying the hierarchical society around which Old Regime religious life revolved. *Cofradías* continued to exist, but they lacked social meaning. The great processions of Holy Week and Corpus Christi did not disappear, but they were no longer miniature collective expressions of an entire society. Many had become popular spectacles designed, said one critic in 1858, "to satisfy curiosity . . . and to serve for recreation and distraction."[59]

The official liturgy of the Church offered little competition to devotionalism. Cathedral services were as grandiose as ever and were often conducted with full orchestras and operatic singing that paid little attention to religious significance. The parish liturgy was in an even more dismal state. The official ecclesiastical bulletin of Toledo published a series of articles describing each and every gesture the priest should make during Mass, an indication that some clerics lacked even this basic knowledge. In 1858 the bishop of Guadix threatened to suspend priests saying "hasty Masses lacking in devotion," that is, Masses said in less than twenty minutes.[60] The problem had scarcely changed four decades later. Ramón Sarabía a well-known Redemptorist missionary of the early twentieth century, recalled the impoverished parish life of the small Asturian town where he had grown up in the early 1880's. Sunday after Sunday passed without anyone receiving Communion. Sermons were preached only twice a year, on Corpus Christi and the feast of Saint Martin, the village patron.[61] Revived devotionalism thus filled a liturgical vacuum and marked the character of the Spanish Church for generations.

By 1868 an immense range of devotions appealed to every religious taste. Older cults, such as those of the Sacred Heart and the Eucharistic Forty Hours, took on new life, as did that of the rosary, largely through the efforts of Antonio Claret, who promoted it with great enthusiasm. By 1860 it was not uncommon to find entire congregations telling their beads during Mass.[62] Proclamation of the dogma of the Immaculate Conception by Pius IX in 1854 reinvigorated the Marian devotion that had been part of the Spanish Church's tradition for centuries. Pious groups committed to the cult of the Virgin multiplied; the Devotion to the Heart of Mary organized by Claret and the Court of Mary founded by Ramón García Leal with over 50,000 members by 1865 are two examples. In addition, specific religious celebrations—the "Flowers of Mary" held during May and ceremonies marking Saturday as the day of the Virgin—attained great popularity. Marian devotions from abroad, such as the Virgin of Lourdes, quickly made their way into Spain and attracted the attention of the devout.[63] Devotions to individual saints also flourished in the new atmosphere.

A pious visitor to Madrid on a single day (September 7, 1851) could satisfy his religious needs by choosing from a bewildering array of devotions: the Forty Hours in the parish of Santa María; the novena of Jesús Nazareno in the church of the same name; a service in honor of the Sacred Heart in the church of the Salesian nuns with full orchestra; or novenas to the Most Pure Heart of Mary (San Cayetano), Our Lady of Mercy (San Sebastián), and the Virgin of Guadalupe (San Millán). At San Sebastián the novena began with solemn Mass at ten in the morning followed by the

Stations of the Cross and the rosary at 4:45 with sermon. The day ended with a solemn service in which the Salve Regina was celebrated with full musical accompaniment. Devotional associations, such as the Archconfraternity of Our Lady of Grace and Our Lady of Carmen, held special ceremonies for their members. On the following day, a novena to Our Lady of Zarza began in the chapel of the convent of San Pascual, and another service to the Sacred Heart opened in the oratory of the Santísimo Sacramento.[64]

The mid-nineteenth-century revival of piety was encouraged by the Church. Scruples that led some eighteenth-century bishops to restrain cults were set aside in favor of an effort to spread them like seeds thrown upon the fields. The devotionalist resurgence has not been adequately studied, but it may explain the Church's ability to survive as a popular institution during this period. To the peasantry, for whom religion warded off disaster and secured good fortune, the intercessionary aspects of devotion complemented rituals of traditional "popular" religion, which often had little to do with formal belief. Moreover, the character of these devotions, individual acts of piety directed toward a specific purpose and requiring little intellectual effort, made them easy to understand. And their individualist emphasis may have appealed even to the educated middle classes of moderado persuasion. Devotionalism's concern with the relation of the individual rather than the collectivity to the divine provided a convenient means for the man who had bought Church property to prove his religious worth with ease of conscience and to overcome Catholic social thought and its medieval, corporate preoccupations with personal acts of piety. Revived devotionalism may have been one of the bridges leading the more conservative elements of liberalism not back to the Church, because they had never left it, but toward more emotional forms of religious practice. The growth of personal devotions owed something to the individualistic character of the new society, as liberalism and Catholicism came together again in curious alliance.

The increasing acceptance of "popular" religion by the official Church, the revival of devotionalism, and the reintroduction of the missions traditionally used by the ecclesiastical authorities to preserve faith among the population, contributed to the devel-

opment of religiosity in the liberal era. The destruction of the
regular clergy during the 1830's ended for the time being the
Church's long missionary history, although much of the fire and
brimstone of popular evangelization had vanished before the death
of Ferdinand VII. Without the front-line troops provided by the
orders and preoccupied with the struggle to survive, the Church
could do little to marshal its evangelistic forces.

In 1841 Antonio Claret, still a young and unknown secular
priest in rural Catalonia, received the title of apostolic missionary
from Rome and began to preach in Catalan throughout the countryside. Although Claret followed the time-honored techniques of
generations of missionaries, using processions, sermons, and pious
devotions, he believed that traditional methods, though they aroused
temporary religious enthusiasm, were insufficient to conquer the
masses "in a more efficacious and lasting way."[65] For Claret, missions must form part of a more comprehensive program of evangelization involving permanent catechetical instruction, parochial
schools, parish libraries, and charitable associations, such as the
Saint Vincent de Paul Society.

In Claret's eyes, the more sophisticated purpose of the modern
mission required a team approach involving a high degree of
coordination and functional distribution of responsibilities. Claret
applied his ideas on popular evangelization through the formation
during the late 1840's of an effective team with himself as director
of missions; Francisco Coll, another indefatigable missionary, as
director of spiritual exercises; and José Caixal.[66] Caixal's title, director of propaganda, revealed how much Claret had learned
about the necessity of abandoning the messianic preaching of the
traditional mission in favor of modern methods of influencing
opinion. From Caixal came the idea of distributing massive quan-
tities of religious books, simply written and cheaply produced.
Claret welcomed the suggestion, believing that only such a large-
scale effort could counter the effect "of the evil and pestilential
books" distributed by the "impious."[67] Between 1848 and 1866
the publishing house Claret established printed 2,811,100 books;
1,509,600 pamphlets; and nearly 5,000,000 posters and broadsheets. Claret's adaptation of the mission and his appreciation of
the importance of religious propaganda within the new society of
liberal Spain provided the Church with an instrument of popular

evangelization that to some extent compensated for the near disappearance of the proselytizing religious orders.

The resurgence of the missions, particularly after 1851, arose from the determination of the Isabelline bishops to deal with "immorality and indifference" through direct combat.[68] The episcopacy could rely on the members of the restored male orders, who threw themselves into the work of popular evangelization with an enthusiasm that made up for their limited numbers. The missionaries, of whom the Jesuits were the most important, made a point of living austerely. The Jesuits active in Seville in 1858 took pains to move on foot from parish to parish, rejecting offers to ride in carriages, and they tailored their activities to the social situations of their congregations. Services in the parish of San Bernardo—with a population of agricultural workers, bullfighters, and employees of the famous Seville tobacco factory—began at five in the morning rather than the usual eight so that "without ignoring their material occupations, the residents could devote themselves to the care of their souls."[69]

The missions still followed the traditional formula. They usually opened with a procession of children intoning the hymn "The Mission Calls You" in an effort to touch adult sensibilities. Missions generally lasted for two weeks; included Masses, sermons, devotions such as the rosary, and confessions; and ended with a general Communion. Preachers were not above using sensationalism in the old flamboyant style. An earthquake in Seville in October 1858 in the midst of a round of missions was seen as a divine admonition against "the faults and crimes of which this society, today more corrupt than ever, is filled." The clergy used the natural disaster to warn the inhabitants to repent. But missionaries in this period paid more attention to catechetical instruction than their predecessors had. In the little town of Mairena del Alcor near Seville, for example, the Jesuits preaching the mission enlisted thirty laymen to teach catechism to both children and adults; a house in each street was set aside for this purpose. Wherever they went missionaries also distributed "little books" on the truths of religion written "in language which even the most rude and ignorant can understand."

The Church believed that the missions provided the best means of realizing "a complete moral and religious restoration" that would "bring morality to the people, and extinguish the hatreds . . . which the passions of parties and families sustain and propagate." They would thus lead to "that good faith, those Christian and gentlemanly customs which have been the characteristics of our nationality."[70] At least over the short term, the missions enjoyed some success. In 1851 the clergy of Catalonia congratulated itself on the "happy results" of the missionary campaign just concluded in the region; in 1858 more than 20,000 received Communion during the missions of Seville. And in 1866 Jesuit preachers carried off one of their most impressive evangelical triumphs with a series of missions in the Basque Provinces. Reports from parish priests of small towns and villages recorded nearly universal participation in the services; in Zaldivia, for example, 2,500 people received Communion, while only 6 residents did not.[71]

The success of the missions arose in part from the support they received from moderado notables, the prosperous men of property dominating local governments. At a mission in Organa in Lérida, the preachers were received by a delegation of "clergy, municipal councillors and the most select part of the population," and this pattern was repeated elsewhere.[72] There were solid reasons for moderado support of the missions. The absolutist tirades that had been a stock in trade for the missionaries of the 1820's and early 1830's yielded to sermons teaching respect for the government and warning against social unrest. The missions of Seville, declared La Cruz in 1858, "had destroyed in their foundation the antisocial ideas that had spread in Andalusia. Charity was inculcated in the rich, resignation in the poor. All were led to the faithful observance of the Commandments, to love of God . . . and respect for the clergy and submission to the constituted authorities."[73] Bishop Costa y Borrás similarly praised missions, "because only the salutory influence of religion can make the Catalan character docile and governable and avoid insurrections."[74] For the moderados, obsessed with the danger of social revolution, the preaching of submission from missionary pulpits offered a soothing remedy. At Éibar in the Basque Provinces, factory owners allowed their workers to attend a mission without loss of pay; Isabella II, upon being urged to dispatch more troops to repress the peasant rising at Loja in 1861, was said to have remarked:

"you are mistaken. Soldiers are not required in Loja. Missions are."[75]

Claret's dream of broadening the base of popular evangelization was partially realized by 1868. A revived interest in religious instruction led to the publication of new catechisms to replace the texts used for centuries. García Mazo's *Catecismo explicado* (1837), Claret's work of the same title (1848), and Costa y Borrás' *Catecismo de la doctrin cristiana* (1858) replaced the rote memorization of questions and answers with clear and simple exposition. Claret, for example, abandoned the traditional technique of organizing a catechism around the Ten Commandments in favor of one revolving around the themes of faith, hope, charity, and good works.[76] Each section was preceded by an engraving to illustrate the brief explanation following. The new catechisms were easy to comprehend and for the first time attached importance to the explanation of doctrine. Claret also recognized the necessity of making catechisms available to non-Castilian readers. His own text in its Catalan version was already into its third printing by 1850.

In addition, a new devotional literature, which differed substantially from that produced during the eighteenth century, flourished. The excessively detailed texts of the Old Regime, larded with scriptural citations, were replaced by short and straightforward works with an almost exclusive emphasis on private devotions. García Mazo's *Diario de la piedad* (1839) stressed the importance of individual acts of piety, the rosary, confession, Communion, visits to altars, and the Blessed Sacrament.[77] Concern with the collective expression of religious sentiment so important to the earlier literature had virtually disappeared. Claret's contribution, the *Camino recto y seguro para llegar al cielo* (1843), was an instant success; it would become the most widely published work of its kind in the history of Spanish devotional writing. Claret, too, emphasized the quest for salvation as an individual affair. The sense of mutual obligation, albeit within the framework of a hierarchical society, typical of similar works in the eighteenth century found no place in the *Camino recto*. Claret's advice to workers must have been welcomed by the new liberal society: "Do not waste time"; "Do not cause expenses or damage to your employers"; "Work with all diligence and exactitude."[78] The emphasis of the

new devotional literature on specific acts of piety as well as the
publishing success of works such as the *Camino recto* reveal again
that the Church was able to adapt its propaganda techniques to
the individualistic society created by liberalism.

The individualistic emphasis of devotionalism found its counterpart in the proliferation of voluntaristic religious associations
very different from those of the Old Regime. During the eighteenth century lay participation in the life of the Church had been
channeled through corporate groups reflecting the divisions of a
hierarchical society. The voluntaristic associations spreading through
the Spanish Church after 1840 were open in theory to all with a
sincere commitment to religion and good works. These societies
covered a wide range of charitable and educational activity. The
Society of Saint Vincent de Paul devoted its attention to assisting
the impoverished; the Confraternity of Christian Doctrine, founded
at Madrid in 1842, provided religious instruction in hospitals,
prisons, and orphanages. The new voluntarism also made it possible for women to take a much more active role. In 1858 a group
of women, drawn largely from the ranks of the nobility, founded
the capital's first Sunday schools and thereby began one of the
most successful catechetical initiatives of the nineteenth-century
Church. *Escuelas dominicales* were established in large numbers
throughout the country.[79]

In addition, countless devotional associations were founded.
Thus, Francisco Coll, the celebrated missionary of the 1840's,
established throughout rural Catalonia a number of such associations—the Congregation of Minerva, devoted to the cult of the
Blessed Sacrament; the Congregation of the Unworthy Slaves of
Jesus in the Sacrament; the Confraternity of the Most Holy Rosary; and the Congregation of the Virgin of Sorrows.[80] The proliferation of voluntaristic groups within the Church arose in part
from the institution's recovery from its paralysis of the 1830's.
But it also developed from the widespread appeal of associations
stressing individual works of piety and charity. Such an emphasis
fit neatly into the mentality of the politically liberal but socially
conservative elite dominating Spanish society during the middle
years of the century.

Popular religion, devotionalism, improved evangelization techniques, and the increasing importance of voluntaristic associations

allowed the Church to adapt to the configuration of liberal society with surprising ease, clerical laments about the corruption of the times notwithstanding. But how successful was the Church in maintaining its religious influence? The question is no easier to answer for the mid–nineteenth century than for the eighteenth. Studies of religious practice are, if anything, more difficult to find for the later period. It is at least clear that sometime between 1850 and 1900 a process of accelerated dechristianization left Spanish Catholicism with a highly regional character. There were abundant signs of losses in the south by the 1880's. Visiting the town of Villanueva del Rosario in February 1886, the bishop of Málaga found a population in which "indifference and even apostasy" had made deep inroads.[81] The missions of the "Apostle of Andalusia," Francisco Tarín, in 1889 revealed as gloomy a picture. In the parish of San Roque in Seville, with 16,000 inhabitants, only 30 appeared for the first service of the mission. In Andújar, Tarín found "estrangement from the Church"; in the mining town of Linares, a "focal point of corruption and perversion," the missionary was chased along the streets by young boys who shouted curses and threw stones.[82]

There is similar impressionistic evidence for the decline of religious observance in cities with a growing working class. The Catalan priest Josep Gatell, recalling the religious state of Barcelona around 1850, believed it was still "a Christian town" in which "factories closed a half-hour before the celebration of the last Mass during which our churches were filled with men in their workers' shirts." But for Gatell, "the day arrived when this people, who until then appeared Catholic, abandoned religious practices little by little."[83] The dechristianizing aspects of the modern city, so frequently observed by religious sociologists, were already being noted by Bishop Palau of Barcelona in 1858: "Who can doubt that people from all parts of the world, of all religions . . . flow to the great centers of manufacturing and commerce, and communicate . . . their religious indifference." Of his own diocese, Palau remarked: "the faith has grown languid, charity has gone cold [and] religious sentiment has grown weak."[84]

In spite of the lack of serious study on nineteenth-century dechristianization in Spain, there are some partial indications of the religious state of the kingdom. In 1869 opponents of religious toleration organized an ambitious and highly successful campaign for a protest petition to be presented to parliament. Although the provincial and local authorities who had come to power with the revolution of 1868 did their best to discourage the collection of signatures, the results were impressive given the organizational problems involved; 2,837,144 people signed the petition. Analysis of the geographic distribution of the signatures reveals that in 1869 the regional character of Spanish Catholicism was already in place (see Map 2). There are, to be sure, anomalies in the 1869 results, and it should be remembered that the number of signatures gathered in a given province depended on the efficiency of local organizers. The cartography of the petition campaign, however, shows the lowest levels of support in Andalusia, Extremadura, and La Mancha. The two provinces standing at the very bottom of the list, Albacete and Málaga, were both located in the south. The greatest levels of support were in Old Castile—Salamanca, Ávila, Valladolid, Zamora, Burgos—Santander; León; the Basque Provinces, particularly Vizcaya; Navarra; Aragón; and the Balearic Islands. The Mediterranean littoral produced mixed results, with a strong showing in Alicante (perhaps because of the Catholic hinterland around Orihuela) and Valencia. The Catalan provinces did less well but were by no means among those with the lowest level of response. The support provided by the province of Madrid, seat of the national capital, placed it near the bottom of the list.

The cartography of the 1869 campaign shows an interesting and surprising resemblance to the map of religious practice drawn in 1972.[85] In spite of the massive demographic and economic changes after 1950, the latter shows a clear line of division running approximately through the center of the Iberian Peninsula along the Guadarrama Mountains. Regions below the line—New Castile, Extremadura, La Mancha, Andalusia, and the Mediterranean littoral save for rural Valencia and Orihuela—record the lowest levels of observance. Areas above the line—Old Castile, León, the Basque Provinces, and Aragón—show a high level of practice. The correspondence between the 1869 and 1972 maps is not exact. Catalonia, for example, had clearly slipped over the course of the century, save for the high rate of practice observed in the dioceses of Solsona and Vich. But the rough north-south division

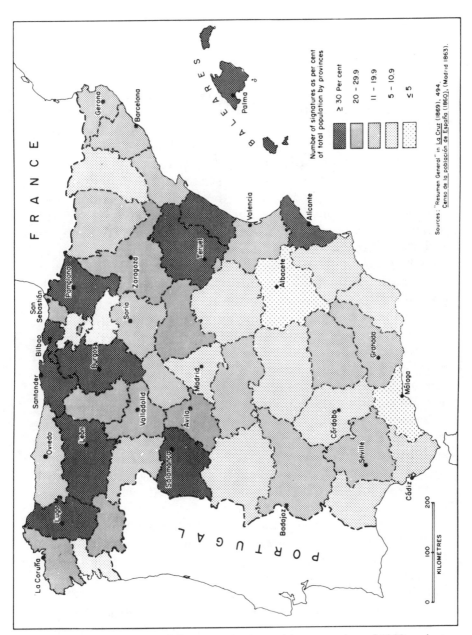

2. Geographic distribution of signatures in the petition campaign of 1869 against religious liberty.

evident in 1869 was still clearly visible more than a century later. The Church was strongest in areas of large peasant populations who had reasonable security of land tenure and lived in numerous small villages with a strong sense of communal life. It was weakest in the great latifundia lands of Extremadura, La Mancha, and Andalusia, where a rural proletariat lived in desperate economic circumstances. And already by 1869 the weakness of the Church in metropolitan centers was becoming evident.

The results of the 1869 petition campaign provide a general overview of the strength of the Church in the kingdom as a whole. They do not provide guidance on the equally important question of differences within regions. Such local variations were certainly important, between, for example, an industrialized Barcelona and the more Catholic Catalan hinterland. Until detailed regional studies of religious practice are undertaken, no adequate cartography of nineteenth-century Catholicism can be drawn. The limited study of observance in the province of Logroño carried out for the period illustrates the importance and necessity of research in this field. It reveals that by the end of the century dechristianization had made rapid progress among the poorly paid workers in the expanding vineyards that engaged in a market-oriented wine trade; among railway workers along the Zaragoza and Bilbao line, which opened for traffic in 1861; and among industrial workers in small industrial towns such as Munilla, Enciso, and Haro.[86] The regions of the province where traditional agriculture conducted by a secure peasantry persisted—the districts adjacent to Álava and Navarra—were untouched by the drift away from the Church. The statistics gathered by Sáez de Ocariz for the parish of Santiago el Real in Logroño suggest that the critical period for the spread of declining observance occurred between 1867 and 1875.[87] The percentage of those who did not fulfill the Easter Communion obligation, which hovered between 5 percent and 10 percent during the early 1860's, rose dramatically beginning in 1867. (Table 5)

The limited example of a single parish cannot be applied to the kingdom as a whole. The chronology and pace of dechristianization certainly varied depending on social and economic circumstances, the degree of industrialization and urban growth, changes in agriculture, the condition of rural workers, and other

Table 5. Nonobservants of the Easter Communion obligation in the parish of Santiago el Real, 1860–1890.

Year	Nonobservants (percent)
1860	6.68
1867	15.50
1868	17.70
1869	29.90
1870	28.30
1871	21.80
1872	28.10
1873	41.00
1874	45.00
1875	54.80
1880	45.00
1890	57.80

Source: M. Sáez de Ocariz y Ruiz de Azua, "El cumplimiento pascual en la ciudad de Logroño a lo largo del siglo XIX," *Berceo*, no. 76 (1965), 275–279.

factors. There may have been historic conditions in certain regions to account, at least in part, for the religious crisis evident by the end of the century. The inadequate parochial structure of Andalusia and the imperfect evangelization efforts of past centuries may have contributed to the nearly universal alienation of the south's rural, landless population.

The Church's failure to hold its own in the growing urban centers during the second half of the century arose in part from its inability to increase the number of parishes in the face of massive population growth. The State's unwillingness to finance new urban parishes beyond a bare minimum created serious pastoral problems. The bishop of Madrid asked the government to create forty new parishes in the mid-1880's but received funding for only thirty. In succeeding years the number of parishes increased only marginally while the population doubled. The districts most badly served in the capital were the working-class suburbs, where impoverished and understaffed parishes were the rule. Father Herranz Establés, parish priest of San Sebastián in Carabanchel Bajo during the early twentieth century, served a parish of 16,000 with one assistant. From one end to the other the parish extended six kilometers and embraced an unstable population employed "in the least dignified occupations." Ministering to those "atomized socially, without any civil, social or religious structure," absorbed "by the struggle for life" presented the parish clergy with insuperable problems.[88] Nearly all parishioners died without the last sacraments. By the eve of the civil war in 1936 the failure of the Church in the working-class parishes of the Madrid suburbs had reached catastrophic proportions. In the parish of San Ramón in Vallecas, with 80,000 residents, 10 percent of the terminally ill died without receiving the sacraments, 20 percent of the marriages were civil, 40 percent of those about to be married in the parish did not know the Our Father, and 90 percent of the children educated in the parochial school "neither confessed nor went to Communion" once they had left.[89] Statistics for other Madrid parishes were equally grim.

Historic conditions and organizational weaknesses may have contributed to dechristianization in certain regions and urban centers. It is unlikely, however, that these were the decisive causes. Ecclesiastics in the mid and late nineteenth century insisted that Spain was resolutely Catholic. Even the pessimistic Antonio Claret declared: "the people are bad generally speaking; but their evil is superficial; they still have faith."[90] In fact, the commitment to Catholicism as an ideology faced a serious challenge with the appearance of radical social doctrines. The revolutionary period between 1868 and 1873 allowed anarchist and socialist ideas to spread unrestrained, in spite of bitter clerical complaints. It was not yet completely evident that the new doctrines would emerge triumphant among industrial workers and the landless of the south, but it is clear that the Church had not the slightest idea of how to proceed other than to lament: "the popular classes are deaf to religion."[91] Indeed, the increasingly individualistic character of Spanish Catholicism as it developed under liberalism left the Church particularly unprepared to deal with the collectivist aspirations that were already exercising great appeal by 1870. In the end, the Church would pay a heavy price for its tenuous alliance with the liberal State and the society that government had created.

The institutional recovery of the mid-nineteenth-century Church as well as its ability to adapt its devotional and pastoral norms to the new society allowed the Church to hold its own in the peasant regions of the north and to enlist the support of the more conservative elements of liberalism in the cities. But the Church's inability to perceive, much less face, the serious social problems created in town and country foretold the massive losses that were not far off. Clerical responses to religious indifference and unbelief did not differ substantially from those made to the dislocating effects of the French Revolution and the work of the Cortes of Cádiz. Ecclesiastical energies were not directed to reforming the Church from within but to blaming an array of external forces for attempting to "decatholicize" Spain—the liberal State for having sold Church property, politicians for disregarding the Church's theocratic admonitions, and intellectuals for advocating cultural innovation.

The Church's failure to perceive the necessity of changes deeper than those provided by devotionalism, "popular" religion, and new forms of religious propaganda would prove costly in the long run. Between 1843 and 1868 the Church enjoyed a breathing space created by its accommodation with the liberal State and the inchoateness of radical social forces. Anticlericalism, although already a stock-in-trade of some politicians and intellectuals, had not yet been translated into the popular violence of a later period. (The bloody events of 1834 and 1835 were not repeated.) But, unable to take advantage of the respite, the Church entered the revolutionary period beginning in 1868 ill prepared to encounter the most secular and radical of Spain's nineteenth-century political and social upheavals.

8 / From Revolution to Restoration, 1868–1874

Between the revolution of 1868 and the restoration of the Bourbon monarchy in 1874 the Church faced the most serious threat to its privileged situation since the 1840's. Clerical identification with the discredited moderado State exposed the Church to a revival of the more extreme ecclesiastical policies associated with the progresistas and later to a project (under the First Republic) to separate Church and State for the first time in the nation's history. The Church's difficulties were magnified by the outbreak of another Carlist revolt in 1872 and by chronic social disorders in town and country. In spite of organizational disruption and some anticlerical violence, the Church survived this new onslaught in better condition than ecclesiastical laments of the time would suggest. Moreover, for the first time some clerics, whether from the conservative or revived liberal Church, began to question the wisdom of maintaining constitutional ties to the State. In the end, the establishment of a reformed version of moderado government, which promised a restoration of some, though by no means all, ecclesiastical privileges, swept aside clerical reservations. The Church entered again into an alliance with the civil authorities that would last, at least in terms of ecclesiastical policy, until the Second Republic disestablished this historic union.

Revolution and the Church, 1868–1869

At a ceremony held in the royal palace early in 1868 Isabella II received from the papal nuncio the Golden Rose, traditionally bestowed by popes on monarchs contributing to the progress of the faith. Conferral of the papal decoration symbolized the comfortable relationship between Rome and Madrid as the era of the semiauthoritarian moderado State drew to a close. The glitter of ritual, however, could not disguise the growing unpopularity of the sovereign and her ministers before rising public criticism and conspiratorial activity. The forces opposing Isabella, a disparate grouping of Liberal Unionists, progresistas, and Democrats encouraged by Carlists and Republicans, finally coalesced in September to launch the military revolt and popular local risings that sealed the queen's fate. After the defeat of loyal government troops at Alcolea on September 28, Isabella abandoned her summer residence in the Basque Provinces to take refuge in France; she was followed by the architect of her ecclesiastical policy, Antonio Claret.

The revolution of 1868 was launched by the coalition of liberal generals and urban radicals responsible for Spain's major political upheavals since 1834. But the contribution of local revolutionary juntas to the success of the 1868 rising led the provisional government, whose dominant personalities were Generals Francisco Serrano of the Liberal Union and Juan Prim of the progresistas, to accede to demands for a broad democratic program including universal suffrage, freedom of the press, and freedom of association. The troublesome question of who, if anyone, should occupy the democratic throne was left aside for the moment, but those in power were determined that it should not be given to a Bourbon. From its inception the new regime was beset by severe internal difficulties, which in the end caused its collapse and paved the way for proclamation of the First Republic in February 1873. Tension among the partners in the governmental coalition constantly threatened its stability. Only the forceful and determined leadership of Prim, a popular and astute politician, warded off disintegration. Prim's assassination on a Madrid street in December 1870 just days before the arrival of the new king, Amadeo of Savoy, stimulated the divisive tendencies of the coalition parties and began the process of political fragmentation that made a republic possible.

The regime also had to contend with a deep economic crisis, made all the worse by the strain of efforts to break the colonial revolt that had broken out in Cuba in 1868. And from the beginning the new government faced opposition from the Carlists, confident at last that their hour was near. Carlist armed agitation began in isolated fashion in 1869 and developed into a full-scale revolt in 1872. The Republicans were no less restive. Resentful of the promonarchist provisional government, they directed steady fire against it while zealots in Cádiz and Málaga revolted even before the Cortes elected by universal suffrage met in early 1869. In addition, the revolution opened a Pandora's box of social agitation in the industrial cities and the southern countryside. Unrest was too sporadic to threaten social revolution, but it contributed to the climate of instability, sometimes verging on anarchy, that characterized the democratic monarchy during its short existence.

The rapidity with which the September revolution was accomplished (only ten days separated the initial rising and the battle of Alcolea) prevented any large-scale assault on a Church identified closely with the Isabelline monarchy. But the action of local revolutionary juntas showed that the Church was not forgotten. The Jesuits, perennial first victims of revolution, were ousted from their residences in several towns. In Oviedo the junta closed the diocesan seminary; in Vich the authorities expelled priests belonging to an order founded by the now vilified Claret. Local measures against the Church, however, varied according to the strength of urban radicalism. The junta of Seville, one of the most extreme, closed six of the city's churches and assigned some to revolutionary groups for political purposes. The sight of the republican flag hanging from the high altar of the church of the Minims left the local clergy fuming. But in other cities—Cartagena, Murcia, and Lorca, for example—the juntas acted with moderation toward the Church.

The autumn of 1868 also saw the resurgence of the popular anticlericalism previously held in check by the moderado State. Although the Catholic press dwelt on "sacrileges and attacks" directed against the Church in the weeks following the revolution, the incidents reported did not reveal massive violence against either the clergy or ecclesiastical buildings. Occasional acts of violence did occur, such as the assassination of a Claretian priest in La Selva in Tarragona early in October, but this was an isolated event. More common were flamboyant manifestations of defiance designed to provoke clerical anger. In some towns revolutionaries fired their guns at religious statues; in others groups of radicals invaded church services and intimidated the faithful by shouting political slogans. In Salamanca a small band wearing the red hats of revolution entered a church and scandalized those present by smoking cigars and proclaiming "vivas" to liberty.[1] Although not a serious threat, popular anticlericalism, always emotional and easy to arouse, showed that the issue of the Church could still provoke a reaction among the urban lower classes.

The first measures taken by the provisional government against the Church in October 1868 seemed familiar manifestations of the vigorous regalism associated with the radical elements of liberalism since 1820. Successive decrees suppressed religious communities introduced since 1837, forbade the legally authorized orders from owning property, and announced a reduction in the number of convents by one-half save those belonging to the Sisters of Charity and other congregations engaged in teaching and hospital work. As usual the Jesuits received special treatment. A decree of October 12 ordered them to leave their residences within three days and expropriated their wealth for the benefit of the State. The government declared that it was acting to punish the Church for its intimate ties with the Isabelline monarchy. Religious communities, a decree asserted, "formed an integral and principal part of the shameful and oppressive regime which the nation has just overthrown with so much glory." It was, therefore, "necessary and urgent" to deal with them "to consolidate . . . the revolution and construct new institutions."[2] The reaction of the hierarchy to these attacks was surprisingly moderate, although some prelates, notably Bishop Monescillo of Jaén, complained of "a cabinet filled with a malign fever and suspicious of the Church." But Manuel García Gil, archbishop of Zaragoza, considered events with more equanimity and urged his clergy not to become disturbed or discouraged. He counseled his priests to avoid political activity, because it "contributed nothing to piety," and to devote their attention "to conciliate, attract, win and save souls."[3]

The provisional government faced the task of elaborating a long-term ecclesiastical policy. Opinion on what ought to be done with the Church varied among and within the parties of the ruling coalition. Republican demands for an outright separation of Church and State received little support. The coalition partners continued to adhere to the liberal tradition that the State should maintain official ties with the Church, but they also nourished the hope that the ecclesiastical establishment could be persuaded to abandon its theocratic preoccupations and its willingness to support semiauthoritarian governments disposed to uphold its privileges. The Church, said Eugenio Montero Ríos, a devout Catholic and, as minister of grace and justice in 1870, the author of a plan of ecclesiastical reform, might have a brilliant future but this would depend "on the acceptance on its part of the great principles and political rights which form the patrimony of free peoples."[4]

The patrimony to which the Church was expected to subscribe was considerably larger than the one it attacked so vehemently in 1854. On October 25 the provisional government issued a manifesto to the nation affirming rights, such as freedom of the press and association, unpalatable to the ecclesiastical elite. But the government struck a harsher blow by declaring its intention to introduce religious liberty. Although the manifesto asserted that the proposal would improve the Church by encouraging it to attend to its pastoral responsibilities, it left no doubt that the project arose from "a protest against the theocratic spirit introduced with such insidious persistence in the essence of our institutions by the previous regime."[5] Acceptance of the principle of religious liberty represented a significant departure from the identification of political reform with the maintenance of "Catholic unity" since the Cortes of Cádiz a half-century before.

The willingness of the ruling coalition to abandon a basic tenet of Spanish liberalism arose primarily from the leftward drift of the progresista party since the revolution of 1854. The progresistas, who had then turned aside proposals for religious liberty, took a harder line on the issue of the Church, because they resented its support for the semidictatorial moderado State of the 1860's and because they feared the danger on the left from the Democrat and Republican parties, both committed to the creation of a purely secular State. The conversion of the great progresista parliamentarian Salustiano de Olózaga to the cause of religious liberty after having opposed it in 1854, ensured its acceptance. The October manifesto proposed a second change certain to arouse clerical opposition: "freedom of education is another of the cardinal reforms which the revolution has demanded" to counter "the unbridled and blind reaction against spontaneous manifestations of human understanding" taking place before 1868.

Clerical protests against the October manifesto soon appeared in print, although the intensity of episcopal sentiment was not uniform. Miguel García Cuesta, the archbishop of Santiago, re-stated in restrained language the traditional case against religious liberty while accepting the use of universal suffrage in the coming elections and declaring that he did not intend "to condemn any form of government."[6] Bishop Lagüera of Osma, a prelate known for his Carlist sympathies, fired a rhetorical shot reminiscent of an earlier era when he accused the provisional government of wishing "to undermine the unity of religion by introducing false religions and laying the foundations of temples which will not be dedicated to the true God." Manuel García Gil of Zaragoza showed the same common sense he had displayed in an earlier pastoral letter. Although he lamented the government's actions, he saw no point in levying accusations against the authorities. Deprived of the support of the State, the Church must depend on its own inner resources to survive. The Church "lives and will live its own life . . . although all governments abandon it." He urged his clergy to concentrate their efforts on evangelization to remedy "the great ignorance of religion [existing] among a great part of the population."

The Church's place in the new order would not be determined by episcopal protests to the authorities. On December 6 the provisional government called elections in mid-January to choose deputies for a Constituent Cortes. It was symbolic of the changes that had taken place since 1843 that defense of the pre-1868 ecclesiastical settlement fell primarily to laymen. In December a group of Catholic notables linked to the conservative moderados and the Carlists established the Association of Catholics in Spain "to propagate and defend the doctrines, institutions and social influence of the Church, particularly its liberty and the Catholic unity of Spain . . . through peaceful means and under the protection of the law."[7] The association, modeled on similar bodies in Belgium and Germany, won episcopal and papal approval and spread to twenty-eight cities, including Barcelona, Seville, Segovia, Santiago, Salamanca, and Palma de Mallorca. Local associations were invariably dominated by men of substance holding deeply conservative political views. In Palma, for example, a wealthy landowner, Fausto Morell, served as president; other notables, such as merchants, manufacturers, and landowners, filled the remaining offices.

From the beginning the association declared that it had no other purpose than to defend the interests of the Church. This theoretical neutrality, although regarded as desirable by the pope and the bishops, really arose from the divisions within the organization among moderados, the more extreme neocatholics, and the Carlists, who wished "to see Charles VII sit on the throne of his ancestors."[8] At a meeting in early January the junta superior of the association prudently declared that it would not propose candidates for the coming elections. Local associations, however, did not always follow these instructions. Over a thousand members filled a hall in Toledo and nominated Antolín Monescillo, bishop of Jaén, the fierce neocatholic Candido Nocedal, and the conde de Cedillo to stand for the province. Where the directives of the association were observed, ad hoc Catholic-Monarchist associations were formed to present candidates. The avowedly political character of the latter, as well as the obvious hostility of the Association of Catholics to the revolutionary government, soon led to clashes with supporters of the regime. In Tortosa a crowd of Liberal Unionists and progresistas surrounded a meeting of Catholic-Monarchist electors and forced them to desist from nominating candidates; conservative defenders of the Church awoke in the morning to find gallows painted on their doors.[9]

Incidents between defenders of the ecclesiastical status quo and supporters of the government multiplied with the approach of the elections. The shouts and whistles of proregime sympathizers disrupted a Catholic-Monarchist meeting in Barcelona; a group of liberals armed with sticks invaded a similar meeting in Toledo. To the cries of "Long live liberty!" and "Long live Charles VII!" the two bands waged a pitched battle in the hall. During the days set aside for the elections further clashes took place. In Palencia Catholic opponents of the regime ran a gauntlet of progresistas and Republicans uttering threats and shouting "neos, priests and sacristans do not have voting rights" before they could reach the polling station.[10] Harassment of Catholic-Monarchist candidates and voters was bitterly attacked by the Catholic press, but it contributed little to the overwhelming victory of the government parties. Neither the Association of Catholics nor the ad hoc Catholic-Monarchist groups possessed the organization and resources that would have allowed them to struggle on equal terms with their opponents.

The electoral results further inflamed relations between the government and defenders of the pre-1868 Church. The junta superior of the Association of Catholics issued an intemperate statement declaring its intention "to struggle in hand to hand combat against the impious revolution" and accusing advocates of religious liberty of being "renegades" who were not truly Spanish.[11] A more violent reaction took place in Burgos on January 25. A Carlist mob invaded the cathedral cloister and assassinated the provincial governor to the cry of "Long live religion and Charles VII!" After stabbing the governor innumerable times, the crowd dragged the bloody and half-naked body down the church steps and abandoned it in the cathedral square. The authorities arrested the dean and several other canons on suspicion of complicity, although they were later released for lack of evidence. News of the Burgos assassination set off anticlerical demonstrations. In Madrid a crowd proclaiming "priests have murdered the governor of Burgos," rushed to the residence of the papal nuncio and toppled the pontifical crest on its facade, and the government press attacked the Church with particular ferocity. The brutal violence of the event in Burgos, however, checked the rising passions of proclerical forces. The Catholic press, taken aback by the savagery of the murder, condemned it, and the archbishop of Burgos issued an emotional appeal for calm and respect for the authorities.[12]

Church, State, and Secularization, 1869–1873

With the opening of the Cortes on February 11, 1869, public attention shifted to parliamentary discussion of a new constitution. The poor electoral showing of advocates of the 1851 ecclesiastical settlement left the resolution of the Church question in the hands of the government parties, faced by a vigorous Republican opposition. Defense of clerical interests fell to three churchmen who had won election: the polemical bishop of Jaén, Antolín Monescillo; the more moderate archbishop of Santiago, Miguel García Cuesta; and an intransigent canon of Vitoria, Vicente de Manterola. The ecclesiastical deputies presented their case as best they could in a chamber that was not about to heed their arguments in any case. The tone of debate was remarkably civil; there were few savage anticlerical onslaughts save for the speech of the Republican deputy Suñer y Capdevila, who shocked the Cortes and provoked services of reparation in the churches by calling the doctrine of the Trinity nothing more than a "gabble."

From the beginning the Republicans pressed for the formula "a free Church in a free State," meaning the separation of the civil and ecclesiastical orders, the end of government financing of the Church, and the corresponding termination of the State's traditional regalian rights. Although the Republican leaders, Francisco Pi y Margall and Emilio Castelar, argued forcefully for the separation of Church and State, the coalition parties were not yet ready to break with liberal tradition. After considerable discussion they agreed on a constitutional provision similar to that in the draft constitution of 1856. The text avoided an explicit statement of the confessionality of the State but committed the government to pay clerical salaries and provide for the maintenance of churches.[13]

With the preservation of its official relationship with the State, the Church had little cause for complaint. Indeed, it fared better than might have been expected in the days following the September revolution. But this modest gain was forgotten in the midst of the emotional reaction aroused by parliamentary discussion of the principle of religious liberty. In spite of the insignificant size of Spain's Protestant minority, churchmen saw the prospect of toleration as certain to destroy Catholicism, endanger society, corrupt families, and lead to a host of other ills. Defenders of the ecclesiastical status quo were unable to organize satisfactorily to contest the elections, but they galvanized themselves to prevent the Cortes from accepting religious liberty. The Association of Catholics launched a massive petition campaign on the grounds that deputies would be moved "not by faith, religion nor by the fear of God but only by the fear of public opinion."[14] The faithful were urged to sign because the petition deliberately did not refer to "a republic or a monarchy, nor to this or that person; it speaks only of religion." By divorcing the lobbying effort from the divisive issue of the Carlist pretender, the association assured that its campaign would appeal to the different currents of Catholic opinion united only by their commitment to uphold the Church's privileged situation. The success of the petition (2,837,144 signatures) in the face of considerable opposition testified to the strength of proclerical forces in certain regions. In one Old Castilian town municipal councillors adhering to the government parties privately threatened members of the local Association of Catholics but dared not ban the gathering of signatures lest "they appear as Jews to the people."[15]

The petition, suitably bound and tied with ribbons, was ostentatiously carried to the Cortes in carriages, but it failed to affect the outcome of the parliamentary debate. Republican support for the constitutional provision establishing toleration enlarged the already substantial support for the measure among the coalition partners. Castelar's emotional and eloquent speech on April 12 in defense of religious liberty ("Great is the religion of power, but the religion of love is greater; great is the religion of implacable justice, but the religion of merciful pardon is greater") evoked thunderous applause from the chamber, which overwhelmingly approved the constitutional text on May 5.[16]

Parliamentary action in favor of toleration was a foregone conclusion, but news of the final vote provoked an outpouring of resentment among ecclesiastics and defenders of religious unity. The pro-Carlist, Catholic newspaper *El Pensamiento Español,* made the announcement on a front page bordered in black; bishops ordered services of atonement in the churches. These ceremonies (over a thousand were conducted by mid-June) became militant testimonies to faith and a form of protest against the government. At a service attended by hundreds of Madrid's notables in the church of the Carmen, the patriarch of the Indies asked the congregation to take an oath: "Do you swear by God and these Holy Gospels to believe, observe and sustain the profession of faith which you have heard?" The congregation replied with "a unanimous cry, 'Yes, yes, until death!' "[17] The authorities regarded these services as provocations; in some cities they prevented them from being held. In Madrid they ordered the arrest of a noted preacher whose fiery sermons led aroused congregations to cry: "Let the heretics die who voted for the liberty of cults!"[18] Religious ceremonies of reparation against toleration led inevitably to counterdemonstrations by supporters of the government; in Oviedo youths invaded a procession and shouted "indecent" slogans at the bishop, whom they struck before being restrained.

The introduction of religious toleration led to a marked deterioration in relations between the civil and ecclesiastical authorities. In Soria the governor could not find a single priest to sing a Te Deum upon the proclamation of the constitution. A government order in 1870 commanding bishops and priests to take an oath of loyalty to the constitution met a hostile reception. The parish clergy of Barcelona refused the oath on the grounds that they could not give their "adherence to the undermining of our Church"; only 24 of the 189 parish priests of the diocese of Almería swore the oath, although eleven of the cathedral's thirty-eight canons did so.[19]

The higher proportion of capitular clergy supporting the constitution arose from the modest revival of the liberal Church after three decades of silence. Priests openly favoring the government were few in number, perhaps only 2,000 of the kingdom's more than 40,000 clergy.[20] They included at least one bishop, Andrés Rosales of Almería, who refused to imitate many of his episcopal colleagues in their hostility toward the constitutional oath. In a pastoral letter Rosales justified his moderation by declaring that he did not wish "to throw more wood on the fires of discord burning in this unfortunate country." He criticized his episcopal brethren for encouraging "resentment and great confusion" by refusing to take the oath. The duty of the bishops, he maintained, did not involve "taking on the very grave responsibility of fomenting the disobedience of their subjects toward the existing powers."[21] Most of the bishops, however, remained firm in their rejection of the constitutional oath.[22]

The majority of liberal priests were drawn from the ranks of clergy in cathedral chapters and parishes. Through their journal, appropriately named *The Harmony of Catholicism and Liberty (La Armonía)*, they defended the Cortes for its action in favor of religious liberty: "the Spanish Cortes have not committed a heresy . . . but have rather consecrated an eminently Christian principle"; they argued that the defense of Catholic Spain could be achieved only if the clergy would "confirm our brothers in faith through instruction and example."[23] By defending toleration as a positive good and endorsing democratic institutions, liberal priests anticipated the stand taken by progressive groups within the Spanish Church nearly a century later following the Second Vatican Council.

The prospect of reestablishing the liberal Church as an effective force was remote. Clerics taking the oath to the constitution were reviled by their colleagues. Two canons in Córdoba (where the chapter refused to celebrate an anniversary Mass for the dead of the battle of Alcolea) were totally ostracized by their fellows and subjected to sarcastic comments even from the choirboys. But the greatest obstacle to reform from within the Church was the indifference of the government. With a few exceptions, the State did not attempt to repeat the tactic of forcing appointment of bishops and canons sympathetic to its aims, nor did it listen to the pleas of liberal priests for improvements in the career opportunities and financial situation of the lower clergy. Parish priests, declared *La Armonía,* hoped for "a more open horizon"—by which it meant access to canonries, bishoprics, and other positions still monopolized by a small elite—lest their "knowledge be buried in a small village and their expectations of life murdered."[24] But the government paid no heed. A reform project presented by the minister of grace and justice, Montero Ríos, in March 1870 passed over the institutional discrimination still as much a part of the Church as during the eighteenth century. Moreover, the government, by reducing the budget for *culto y clero* and by falling into arrears in its payments to the lower clergy, repeated the mistake of the 1830's and early 1840's by alienating the one group within the Church that might have become a natural ally.

No one within the Church was more disillusioned than the liberal clergy. The State, they held, was in a position "to fulfill the promises which it had made over fifty years ago with priests who . . . continued being loyal to the flag of progress." But with what result? "Has the importance of cathedral chapters been reduced?" "Has [the State] attempted to increase their [the clergy's] salaries?" To these questions posed by *La Armonía* came the reply: the government has not responded "in any way to the necessities of this suffering and working clergy."[25]

Resentment among conservative priests unhappy with the direction of the government grew with the introduction of an extensive body of secularizing legislation. In this respect post-1868 governments went beyond the initiatives of previous revolutionary regimes. Abolition of the ecclesiastical *fuero* (the right of priests to be tried in Church rather than state courts) and creation of civil registers to record births, deaths, and marriages—a function previously exercised by the clergy—irritated ecclesiastical opinion. But these measures were pinpricks compared to 1870 legislation establishing civil marriage and assigning the administration of cemeteries to the State. Although churchmen reproached the national government for replacing canonical marriage as the only legal form with "public concubinage," the initiative for breaking the Church's monopoly frequently came from municipalities.[26] Already in the autumn of 1869 radical town councils were allowing civil marriages; in a village of Almería, for example, a couple knelt before the mayor and received his "benediction" according to an enraged Catholic press.

The spread of civil marriage from 1870 onward and the attempt of the authorities to control cemeteries provoked attacks from the hierarchy and resistance from the parish clergy, as incidents multiplied that added a new dimension to popular anticlericalism. Priests refused to allow those married civilly to stand as godparents at baptisms or to receive Christian burial. The clerical argument that civil marriage removed those who had entered it from the ranks of the faithful was not appreciated in small towns and villages where baptisms and funerals were ritualistic rites of passage for the entire community. In one town after the *cura* refused to baptize a child because the godparents had been married civilly, an indignant crowd invaded the parish house and threatened to murder the priest if he did not carry out the ceremony. In another town a cleric would not baptize a child whose parents declared they wished General Prim to be the godfather. In Huelva a parish priest provoked controversy by declaring that "he could not admit into his church the body of a man who during his life never entered it" and who had married civilly. An angry family appealed to the municipal authorities, who seized the keys to the cemetery and then "took the body with great ceremony and solemnity" through the streets to the burial place.[27] The multiplication of such conflicts embittered the clergy against the regime and led to increased tension between priests and residents of local communities.

Religious liberty and the secularizing tendencies of the government created a climate of ecclesiastical opinion hostile to a workable accommodation with the State. The Constitution of 1869 had left the task of elaborating the specific terms of the relationship between the civil and ecclesiastical orders to the ordinary parliamentary process. A reform project presented to the Cortes in March 1870 by the minister of grace and justice, Montero Ríos, offered the Church an arrangement not unreasonable given the political circumstances. In return for modest internal reforms, such as parish participation in the nomination of *curas* and the integration of the territory of the old military orders into existing dioceses, the State offered to abandon its traditional right to intervene in the Church's internal affairs except for the right of patronage over appointments financed by the government. The project provided for the ownership of property by the Church subject to expropriation only in cases of "public utility" through the courts and with proper indemnization. It also offered an annual budget of approximately 130 million reales for clerical salaries and church maintenance. Although these terms were not ideal from an ecclesiastical point of view (the budget of *culto y clero* was 50 million reales less than in 1868), they partially satisfied clerical ambitions for freedom from government interference and preserved the State's commitment to finance the Church, albeit in reduced form. The bishops, however, objected to the proposals. Cardinal García Cuesta of Santiago complained of the financial terms and the planned participation of parishioners in the selection of their priests; the bishop of Osma called the provisions "execrable . . . pernicious and lamentable."[28] The scheme was also opposed by the Republicans and the more radical elements of the governmental coalition, and it came to nothing.

Tension affecting relations between Church and State after the revolution of 1868 did not lead to the nearly complete break that had occurred during the 1830's and early 1840's. With the papacy embroiled in the final stages of its struggle with the kingdom of Italy and in the work of the First Vatican Council, there was little Pius IX could do to help the Spanish Church. Relations between

Rome and Madrid were not easy, but they at least survived at a minimal level.[29] Moreover, it was far from clear to the ecclesiastical leadership what course should be taken to reassert the Church's position. By nature cautious, the hierarchy avoided committing itself to the Carlist cause after sporadic outbreaks of rebellion in 1869. A majority of the bishops responded favorably to a government order of March 1869 requiring them to take action against priests who were "preaching a war without truce" against the State.[30] The minister of grace and justice, Manuel Ruíz Zorilla, a radical progresista known for his anticlerical views, even congratulated the prelates who "had responded worthily and satisfactorily" to the State's order, although he initiated judicial proceedings against García Cuesta of Santiago and two openly Carlist bishops, Caixal of Urgel and Lagüera of Osma, for their defiant replies.[31] Given the extreme division of opinion among Catholics willing to defend the pre-1868 status of the Church on the issue of the Carlist pretender, the hierarchy could not afford to compromise its position by supporting Charles VII. The government continued to support the Church financially, although it fell into arrears paying the clergy, and it seemed the only force capable of restraining the outbreaks of disorder that appeared to threaten social revolution.

During the final year and a half of the democratic monarchy (July 1871–February 1873), relations between the civil and ecclesiastical authorities became more difficult. With the collapse of the governmental coalition in the summer of 1871, power alternated between the progresista faction headed by Ruíz Zorilla and that led by Práxedes Sagasta. In general, progresista ministries adopted a harsher attitude on ecclesiastical resistance than had previous governments. In January 1872 the State attempted to break clerical hostility toward civil marriage by declaring that children born to couples married only in a religious ceremony would be regarded as legally illegitimate; in March the minister of grace and justice announced the reimposition of the *exequatur,* the right of the State to approve all papal bulls and briefs before their publication in Spain. And the transformation of what had been an ineffective Carlist revolt into dangerous rebellion in April 1872 increased government suspicions against the clergy in mountainous zones of the Basque Provinces, Navarra, and Catalonia.

The Church expected little from the government. "Let us not entertain illusions," said a clerical journal, "the civil power is no longer Catholic."[32] Ecclesiastical rhetoric notwithstanding, the State had not lost its Catholic character. The Supreme Court, for example, upheld a judgment imposing a two-and-one-half-year prison sentence on a godfather for shouting: "In the name of the Father, Son, Holy Spirit and the Federal Republic," as a priest attempted to pronounce the customary words of the baptismal ritual.[33] And amicable relations between the Church and local officials were sometimes possible. Bishop Joaquín Lluch of Salamanca conducted the affairs of his diocese so skillfully that not a single religious building was closed during the stormy years of revolution.[34] Nor did the difficult relationship between Church and State prevent a pilgrimage in October 1872 to the shrine of Our Lady of the Pillar in Zaragoza attended by more than 60,000. The old association of liberalism with the Church survived, though in battered form.

The Republic and the Church, 1873–1874

The disintegration of the coalition of 1868, the unpopularity of King Amadeo, the failure to break the Carlist rebellion, as well as social and economic difficulties combined to end the democratic monarchy. In 1872 ministry succeeded ministry as fragmentation of the parties made stable government impossible. By February 1873 the king, recognizing that he was personally unpopular and had lost the confidence of the politicians, decided to abdicate. On February 11 he did so, leaving the Cortes responsible for deciding any change in the form of the State. The deputies, having tried one constitutional experiment and lacking enthusiasm for a Bourbon restoration, turned to a republic as the only solution to their dilemma.

Proclamation of the First Republic on February 11 was greeted with an indifferent shrug by much of the clergy and the Catholic press. Even the prospect of separating Church and State evoked little more than ritualistic protests. "How can anyone speak of separation?" asked a clerical periodical, when "it is already an accomplished fact."[35] The bishops contemplated the republic with a suspicious neutrality best expressed by Archbishop Monzón Martín of Granada: "the Church does not reject in principle any of the known forms of government including the republican," although he added the proviso, as long as "the laws of God and the Church" are respected.[36] Among some defenders of the old ecclesiastical order, there was a curious uncertainty over the meaning of the republic. In Medina Sidonia, for example, a proclerical city council, upon receiving the news sent "an attentive letter" to the clergy of the town inviting them "to the proclamation of the Catholic, Roman and Apostolic Republic."[37]

Successive republican ministries, although committed to the separation of Church and State, felt no scruples about using the same regalist tools employed by preceding governments in their relations with the ecclesiastical authorities. The unilateral abolition of the medieval military orders with their network of parishes outside the control of local bishops provoked an early conflict with the Church. An order of the ministry of grace and justice on May 23 instructing provincial governors to assess the value of churches led to widespread clerical protests. Although the State claimed the measure was designed only to provide information necessary for financial negotiations with the Church, this was insufficient to calm a rising wave of extraordinary rumors: that the government intended to sell the churches in a new disamortization; that Catholics would be forced to ransom their parish churches or else see them demolished; that the State intended to use the churches as collateral for a loan to be floated in Germany.[38]

In spite of the tension produced by these conflicts, the Church was less central to republican concerns than to those of previous governments. Republicans believed that they had a simple and direct solution at hand, the separation of Church and State. And they had enough troubles of their own to be unduly preoccupied by the ecclesiastical question. Severe internal disagreements on the exact nature of the republic's constitutional structure (how federal should it be?) prevented the formation of stable ministries. In less than a year the republic had four presidents. The outbreak of a revolt in the summer of 1873 designed to establish virtually independent republican city-states (cantons) and a succession of Carlist military victories made surviving more important to the central government than resolving the problem of the Church.

The Church and the republic shared an uneasy common ground

of self-interest before the pressures for autonomy generated by extremist partisans of federalism, who were also regarded as rabid anticlericals, although not always with justification. The federal principle won general acceptance from Spanish Republicans, but the question of how it was to be applied provoked disagreement.[39] Local politicians, drawn generally from the ranks of the lesser urban bourgeoisie, wished a degree of independence that would have reduced the national government to a figurehead. Even before the outbreak of the cantonalist revolt in July 1873, churchmen contemplated the actions of certain municipalities and signs of republican anticlericalism with deep unease. In Seville youths dropped red dye into the holy water fonts of the churches so the faithful would emerge with brows tinted the color of revolution; in Cádiz a musical band irritated Catholic opinion by striking up the march of Garibaldi outside a chapel where a solemn benediction was taking place. The republican municipality of Cádiz, one of the most anticlerical, ordered the demolition of the Candelaria convent to provide work for the unemployed and changed traditional religious street names to those of the republican litany— Voltaire, Fourier, Garibaldi, Mazzini, Juárez, and Lincoln.[40]

As long as the apostle of federalism Francisco Pi y Margall continued as president of the republic, the restless forces of local autonomy were partially restrained. But Pi's departure from office in mid-July because of the factionalization of republican politics was followed by declarations of virtual independence by cities and towns from Salamanca to Cádiz. The emergence of the cantons threatened the already weak authority of the central government, under the presidency of Nicolás Salmerón, and led to outbursts of anticlericalism in Cádiz, Málaga, Sanlúcar de Barrameda, Jérez, and Córdoba. In Cádiz the cantonal government, formed into a committee of public safety in imitation of the French Revolution, prohibited the teaching of religion in the schools in favor of "universal morality," abolished religious orders in the city "since celibacy is a state contrary to nature," proclaimed the immediate separation of Church and State, and took possession of churches and parish archives.[41] Gold and silver objects from the churches, particularly the great monstrance of the cathedral, were put up for sale at public auction. At Sanlúcar the revolutionaries expelled the Piarists and closed parish churches; in Málaga the canton suppressed convents and ordered the bishop to vacate his palace.

News of these events was reported with horror by a Catholic press that saw the cantonal movement as nothing less than irreligious Jacobinism bent on the destruction of the Church. In fact, anticlericalism was not synonymous with cantonalism. In Salamanca the authorities maintained good relations with the Church; in Cartagena, the canton to survive longest, priests were able to walk the streets in clerical dress even during the siege of the city maintained by the central government. In Granada the committee of public safety released the archbishop from jail, where he had been placed by an overzealous militiaman, with effusive apologies.[42] Even in the radical cantons there was little direct physical violence against the clergy.[43] The central government had no sympathy for the anticlerical excesses of some cantons, perhaps because it wished to avoid giving Carlism another propaganda stick with which to beat the regime. The minister of grace and justice during the presidency of Pi y Margall assured the bishop of Málaga: "the government of the Republic is completely divorced from the measures taken by the municipality; it understands and laments the trouble to which you have been put."[44]

If Church and State agreed on the necessity of ending the cantonalist rebellion, they concurred no less in their hostility toward the social disorders sweeping the southern countryside. The seizure and distribution of land by a dispossessed peasantry seemed to herald the terrible day of revolution so long predicted by churchmen and just as feared by republican politicians in Madrid. With the rising of the textile workers of Alcoy on July 9, clerical fears of impending disaster deepened.[45] The Catholic press was filled with tales of violence in Alcoy and what was seen as the wanton seizure of property by peasants in the southern provinces. Although there was a dose of anticlericalism present in the disturbances, they were not directed primarily against the Church. It possessed little agricultural property and the economic situation of the clergy, many of whom had not received salaries in three years, made the Church less attractive as an object of popular resentment than the monasteries had been during the 1830's.

Agitation focused more on the liberal bourgeoisie, who had profited from the acquisition of ecclesiastical lands. In at least one town, Morera in Badajoz, peasants seizing property from landowners insisted that the parish priest bless the redistribution in a formal ceremony. Even in Alcoy, where revolutionaries inspired by the First International put the houses of prominent residents to the torch and assassinated others, the parish priest of Santa María, Manuel Benlloch, remained in the city at the height of the disturbances assisting the victims without ever being troubled.[46] In the end there was no danger that either the cantonalist revolt or social unrest would lead to revolution. But the Church welcomed the suppression of both by the central government. This did not mean reconciliation with the republic, but churchmen were not ungrateful for its protection of the existing social order.

The most serious physical attacks on the Church during 1873 did not take place in Andalusia and the Levante, where social and political revolution threatened, but in the battle zones of the north. Carlist military victories in the Basque Provinces, Navarra, and Catalonia provoked the same violent reaction among troops and supporters of the government that had characterized the war of the 1830's. The second great Carlist rebellion, feeding on peasant resentment at the centralizing policies of successive governments in Madrid and on the disgust created by the religious legislation of the democratic monarchy, broke out in 1872 under the personal direction of the young and dashing pretender Charles VII. Defense of religion again formed one of the cornerstones of Carlist propaganda. The pretender's brother told the troops under his command: "in you is represented the glorious traditions of Catholic Spain," when "the religion of our fathers is oppressed."[47] Carlist soldiers, often without regular uniforms, entered battle with a badge of the Sacred Heart on their chests bearing the words: "Halt enemy, the Heart of Jesus is with me."[48]

The identification of Carlism with militant Catholicism won the revolt support among the parish clergy of the north. Several *curas* joined the rebellion at its beginning. The most feared, Manuel de Santa Cruz, the parish priest of Hernialde, gained an unfavorable reputation even among his compatriots with his guerrilla exploits and cold-blooded tactics. Although assiduous in the daily reading of his breviary, Santa Cruz felt no scruples at having twenty prisoners shot without benefit of confession.[49] Only a minority of the clergy, of course, took arms, but priests in the north sympathized with the rebellion and contributed what they could to its success.

When Charles VII visited the sacred town of the Basques, Guernica, in August 1873, he was received by the local clergy in ceremonial splendor and led into the church for the singing of a Te Deum; a well-known Capuchin preacher, Esteban de Adoáin, interrupted the mission he was giving in Lastaola to exhort Carlist troops demoralized by a surprise attack.[50]

The hierarchy maintained its usual caution before the rebellion. Some bishops, such as Landeira of Cartagena, hoped for the triumph of Charles VII, but few lent the rising active support save for Caixal of Urgel, who became chaplain general to the pretender's armies. Events would reveal the prudence of episcopal circumspection. The second rebellion stood little more chance of success than the first, and for similar reasons. Although Carlist outbreaks occurred in other regions—near Cuenca, Orihuela, in the southern hills, and in Galicia—the movement rested still on the narrow base of the northern peasant provinces, which had a strong sense of grievance against Madrid. It was no more successful in breaking the hold of the central government over the cities than four decades before. It suffered, too, from serious internal divisions, including the opposition of a significant body of Carlist opinion to armed insurrection itself.

Successive Carlist victories in the spring and summer of 1873 exasperated opponents of an absolutist restoration and deepened hostility toward the clergy in regions where military operations were being carried on. At Elgueta in Guipúzcoa the authorities arrested all the town's parish priests who were suspected of conspiring with the enemy.[51] Anticlerical passions rose most fiercely in Catalonia because of the character of the war there. The Carlists failed to take the large cities—Barcelona, Tarragona, Gerona—but they operated with considerable success in the countryside and against the smaller valley towns of the interior from bases in the Catalan hills.[52] Both sides moved over the same terrain and took, lost, and recaptured towns in an atmosphere conducive to mutual reprisals.

Political conflict within anti-Carlist ranks added more fuel to the fires of popular resentment against the clergy. Extremist federal Republicans and revolutionaries of the First International challenged the authority of the national government in Barcelona and seemed on the verge of establishing an independent canton with a distinctly radical character. During a series of disturbances between March and July, the partisans of revolution invaded religious services shouting anticlerical slogans and occupied some churches.[53] A number of priests abandoned their parishes and sought protection on ships lying in the city's harbor. The Catholic press believed that the disorders would lead to even worse excesses, assassinations, church burnings, and the like, but forces loyal to the national government were able to maintain control of the situation and prevent widespread physical attacks on the clergy and on ecclesiastical buildings. There was no repetition of the bloody events of 1835.

At Reus the republican authorities acted with similar vigor and took possession of the town's churches upon hearing that a mob was about to seize them. At Graus a revolutionary crowd set one church ablaze, but even there the republican city council, dominated by moderates, earned the praise of the Catholic press for bringing the disturbances to an end.[54] Restraint was less evident among the soldiers, the "Volunteers of the Republic," actively engaged in armed conflict with Carlist forces. In the districts near Igualada, the plains of Molins de Rey and Vendrell, troops assassinated three priests and harassed others with frequent searches of churches and parish houses. By midsummer many clergy had abandoned their posts and taken refuge in France.[55] Although anticlerical violence in Catalonia led to clerical denunciations, moderate Republicans had no interest in encouraging a massive wave of attacks on the Church, because such a campaign might well get out of hand, given the revolutionary exaltation of extremists, and redound to the benefit of Carlism. The ecclesiastical leadership in Catalonia realized that a break with the republic in favor of Charles VII would expose the Church to even greater danger. Neither the Church nor moderate Republicans could afford the luxury of completely antagonizing each other.

The turbulent events of the summer of 1873 did not prevent the introduction of the long-awaited proposal for separating Church and State. While Pi y Margall still held office, the government presented its project for a new constitution providing for separation (Article 35). On August 1 (under the presidency of Salmerón), the minister of grace and justice brought forward a draft law spelling out the State's intentions in greater detail. The republic's plan for ending the historic union between the civil and ecclesiastical orders was not the radical, anticlerical document that critics perceived it to be. The State renounced its powers over ecclesiastical patronage and the other regalian privileges Spanish governments had enjoyed for centuries in ecclesiastical matters. It recognized the right of the Church to conduct its affairs "with complete independence" and to hold property subject to the general laws of the nation; it agreed to continue the pensions paid to nuns under the terms of the Concordat of 1851 and to honor legal contracts already made for the repair of churches. Although Article 37 of the proposed constitution forbade any state financial support for the Church, the draft law was ambiguous on this point, perhaps deliberately, declaring simply that further legislation would be introduced. The Church was also assured that all buildings being used for religious purposes would continue to be so employed, although those declared artistic monuments were to fall under the supervision of the government.[56]

The announcement of legislation proposing separation provoked an immediate reaction from clerics, who called it a plan "to erect persecution of the Church into a system of government."[57] But the Church stood to gain something from separation—freedom from the state interference under which ecclesiastics had chafed for generations. The prospect of losing financial support was disturbing, but the irregularity of payments since 1868 had already forced the Church to rely on its own fund-raising efforts.

Clerical opinion attacked the proposed law on separation, but for the first time in the history of the Spanish Church it also began to question the utility of the traditional connection with the State. The exhortation of Archbishop García Gil of Zaragoza in 1868 for the Church to rely on its own resources and devote its energies to pastoral work in a time of revolutionary upheaval was received with greater sympathy by ecclesiastics disenchanted with the slim benefits the Church had derived from its ties to the government. A conservative and anti-Carlist periodical widely read by the parish clergy declared: "the faith has lost much ground among us. To reconquer it, we do not need the civil power in any way . . . Society needs apostles, and apostles are sent by God not by governments." Even an avowedly pro-Carlist newspaper in

Madrid asserted: "we Catholics must have nothing to do with the government; we must conduct ourselves only by the laws of the Church, and we ourselves must carry out the separation of Church and State."[58]

This flirtation with reality created by the possibility of "a free Church in a free State" did not develop into a serious affair. Improved relations with the fourth and last president of the republic, Emilio Castelar, removed any temptation for the Church to venture on its own. The sudden twists and turns of factionalized republican politics brought Castelar to power in September 1873. His eloquent defense of religious liberty in April 1869 had not endeared him to Catholic opinion. But he was the least anticlerical of the republic's presidents, and his determination to break the last remnants of the cantonalist revolt as well as to crush social agitation calmed a Church uneasy about the danger of revolution. There were points of strong tension between the civil and ecclesiastical authorities, but the draft law on separation remained unpassed as Church and State stayed united during the republic's short history.

Castelar hoped to win support for the regime by opening negotiations with the papacy to fill the numerous episcopal vacancies that had occurred since 1868. The successful outcome allowed the president of the republic to do what King Amadeo had never been able to do. Both the Catholic and opposition press expressed irritation at the unlikely sight of a president engaged in the business of negotiating episcopal appointments with Rome. "Castelar has turned himself into a sacristan," complained one newspaper.[59] Castelar's suggestions included some of the ablest figures of the late-nineteenth-century episcopacy: Victoriano Guisasola, later as archbishop of Toledo one of the few Spanish bishops to appreciate the extent of the working class's alienation from the Church; Ceferino González, a Dominican intellectual responsible for reviving the study of the philosophy of Saint Thomas Aquinas; and Joaquín Lluch, recommended for the diocese of Barcelona, who had shown as bishop of Salamanca that it was possible for the Church to conduct itself with moderation in a time of political change. Even a hostile Catholic press had to admit that Castelar had suggested priests "worthy for their virtue and orthodoxy."[60]

Castelar's attempt to create a conservative republic acceptable

in some measure to the Church and to the classes fearful of revolution foundered, however, on the divisions within republican
ranks as well as on the failure to end the Carlist rebellion and the
Cuban war. When a political crisis forced the president's resignation on January 3, 1874, the captain general of Madrid, Pavía,
executed a mini–coup d'etat, ending the republican experiment.
As a result of this upheaval, a government of national union
emerged, still nominally republican and supported by many partisans of the discredited democratic monarchy. The new regime
continued efforts to conciliate the Church. It issued a statement
declaring that the "State . . . cannot ignore nor offend the Church."[61]
The undisguised conservative nature of the new government,
however, could not save it from its own constitutional uncertainties
(should it be a unitary republic or again attempt a monarchical
solution?) nor from growing sympathy within the army for a Bourbon restoration in the person of Isabella's son, Alfonso. Political
support for a restoration in a nation exhausted by six years of revolution and war was also forming through the astute efforts of a
centrist moderado, Antonio Cánovas del Castillo (1828–1897).
Although Cánovas was opposed to installing Alfonso through yet
another military intervention, the rising on December 29, 1874,
by a young general, Martínez Campos, in the name of Alfonso
XII forced the issue. The interim republic, to which its own supporters were not committed, collapsed easily. A Bourbon sat again
on the Spanish throne.

The Church suffered disruption between 1868 and 1874. The
number of vocations declined, sixteen dioceses lacked bishops by
1873, and ecclesiastical finances had fallen into disarray because
of the near bankruptcy of successive governments. Yet clerical
laments about the devastating effects of "revolution" must be taken
with a grain of salt. When the clergy spoke of "persecution," they
were referring as much to the impact of secularizing legislation
as to actual interference with the Church's religious mission. No
government between 1868 and 1874 endorsed a national policy
of antireligious harassment and violence. Physical attacks on ecclesiastical buildings and priests did occur in local settings but
were not universal. Religious services were conducted normally

in most dioceses throughout the period; few bishops were exiled from their sees. There are even examples of new religious houses being established, particularly by the orders of women engaged in charitable work. The Little Sisters of the Poor founded two convents (Huesca and Salamanca) in 1872; the Sisters of Charity opened a house in Valladolid during the republic.[62] And in spite of the collapse of state financial support, the Church was able to compensate partially for the loss of income through direct contributions of the faithful.[63] The Church fared less well than during the 1854–1856 revolution but far better than in the decade 1833–1843.

Toward New Conflicts

The political system designed by the constitutional architect of the Bourbon restoration, Cánovas del Castillo, would endure until it was overthrown by General Primo de Rivera in 1923. Its ecclesiastical policy would survive until 1931, when the Second Republic separated Church and State for the first time in Spanish history. Cánovas created what was essentially a more open and flexible version of the moderado State in its less authoritarian moments. The ability of the monarch to interfere in politics was minimized; a mechanism was found to guarantee the opposition a chance to hold power, thus denying the army the leverage that had made it a political force. Moreover, the regime respected within certain limits traditional liberal rights, such as freedom of the press, and avoided on the whole the excesses committed against intellectual dissent characteristic of its pre-1868 predecessor. Although the restoration settlement suffered from internal weaknesses that eventually would cause its disintegration, it offered a workable system to a nation exhausted by six years of war and constitutional experimentation.

The success of the restoration over the short term rested on its ability to attract support from those opposed to republicanism, Carlism, and social agitation. Cánovas saw the necessity of reaching an accommodation with the Church to undercut the appeal of the Carlists and to strengthen the forces of order and stability on which the regime depended. The Church appeared to profit handsomely from the State's policy of conciliation. The Consti-

tution of 1876 affirmed the confessionality of the State and reduced religious toleration to narrow limits; the government
undertook to honor the financial commitment made in the Concordat of 1851 for support of the clergy, and it freed the Church
from the restrictions imposed after 1868 on establishment of new
schools. The restored monarchy also sought papal support by
improving diplomatic relations with Rome in 1875.[64]

But Cánovas had no intention of yielding to clerical pressure
for full recovery of the privileges the Church had enjoyed before
1868. Although the Church had official status and the new constitution provided for nineteen episcopal seats in the Senate, Cánovas sought to reduce the clergy's direct political influence by
excluding them from the more influential Congress of Deputies.
The State retained its traditional powers over ecclesiastical finance
and patronage and generally resisted demands for the persecution
of Spain's tiny Protestant minority. Moreover, the restoration political settlement permitted the emergence of a two-party system,
which made a policy of wholesale concessions to the Church impossible. The two parties, eventually known as Liberal and Liberal-
Conservative, lacked the internal unity and political honesty necessary for long-term stability, but they were agreed at least on
preserving the principal gains nineteenth-century liberalism had
made at the expense of the old absolutist order. Cánovas mistrusted the more democratic program of the Liberals but remained committed to the idea of a constitutional, parliamentary
regime. And he recognized the necessity of winning Liberal support to guarantee its survival. As the political heirs of the progresistas, the Liberal party, under its brilliant and opportunistic
leader Práxedes Sagasta (1827–1903), viewed the Church with
considerable suspicion. But both parties followed similar ecclesiastical policies based on the need to conciliate the Church within
the limits of a constitutional and parliamentary state based on
nineteenth-century liberal principles. Successive restoration governments pursued a delicate policy designed to balance ecclesiastical demands for greater privileges against the political realities
of the new regime.

The attempt of Cánovas to neutralize the Church as a political
force and to win its support for a socially conservative but polit-

ically liberal government was only partially successful. Clergy and laity attached to Carlism or to the neoabsolutist Integralism of Ramón Nocedal remained firmly opposed to the restored constitutional monarchy. As the architect of the new system, Cánovas was mercilessly pilloried by the Carlist and Integralist press until his assassination in 1897. The enormously successful pamphlet (over sixty editions had appeared by 1960) *Is Liberalism a Sin?* published in 1884 by a Catalan priest, Sardá y Salvany, symbolized the hostility of the most traditional elements of Spanish Catholicism toward the restoration State.[65]

The ecclesiastical leadership, however, had long since learned the necessity of compromise. With few exceptions the hierarchy supported the regime. The bishops welcomed the restoration of the male religious orders, state financial support, and a political system that appeared to offer protection against the danger of social revolution. Yet the attitude of the official Church remained as ambiguous as it had been toward the moderado State of the 1840's and 1850's. The Church resented the refusal of successive restoration ministries to increase substantially the budget for *culto y clero;* it complained bitterly of the government's failure, even when Cánovas was in office, to enforce strictly the constitutional provisions against public manifestations of Protestantism, and it regarded the State's unwillingness to repress intellectual dissent in favor of religious orthodoxy as either betrayal or weakness.[66]

In spite of the hierarchy's support for the constitutional monarchy, the Church was as determined as ever to bring about a new golden age of religion and morality. It viewed the advantages secured from the restoration State as insufficient and pressed relentlessly for more concessions in the realms of education, finance, censorship, and public morality. Although the ecclesiastical leadership recognized the benefits obtained from the State, it did not fully appreciate how closely the survival of its privileged situation was linked to the delicate political balance of the restoration. The deaths of Cánovas and Sagasta stimulated the inherent factionalism of the two governing parties. And the rise of Catalan regional sentiment coupled with the growing strength of Republicans and Socialists after 1900 undermined still further the fragile consensus that had allowed the constitutional monarchy to function as an effective political system. The progressive disintegration of the restoration State demanded caution from the Church. Instead, the Church moved aggressively to preserve its position, while vigorously attacking the new social and political movements that appeared to threaten revolution. The neutralization of the Church as a political force that Cánovas expected thus only partially materialized. The disintegration of the restoration settlement in the first two decades of the twentieth century exposed the Church as a powerful lobby committed to the maintenance of its own privileges and the survival of a conservative social order. The searing anticlerical battles of the early twentieth century were signs of even greater struggles ahead.

In spite of an outward appearance of strength, the Church was ill prepared for a new round of struggles over its place within the State and society. Its privileged situation as a state church could not disguise glaring internal and moral weaknesses: the mediocrity of ecclesiastical intellectual life, the inability to adapt to an increasingly urban and secular society, the corresponding incapacity to appeal to the economically dispossessed, and the dominance of a sugary devotionalism without deep spiritual roots. Perceptive clerics came to see that the Church, outside its bastions in the northern Catholic countryside, had failed to realize its fond dreams for the recreation of Catholic Spain. Writing in 1909, Father Perales y Gutiérrez lamented the religious indifference of the south: "the masses who labor in the fields of Andalusia and Extremadura are not in general indoctrinated in the mysteries of the faith. They live in nearly complete paganism." And he noted the catastrophic failure of the Church among the workers: "today there are great concentrations of workers who do not practice a religious life; in fact, they hate it."[67] In 1914 the Augustinian Bruno Ibeas complained that even among churchgoers the practice of faith was nothing more than "the mingling of ritualistic and routine devotion and unconscious incredulity . . . Our Christian society," he maintained, is "a pagan society covered by the appearances of Christianity."[68]

This spirit of self-criticism was not shared, however, by the vast majority of bishops and priests. Frustrated by the Church's ob-

vious failures and by the increasing virulence of anticlerical attacks, they blamed their misfortunes on the impious conspiracy
that had obsessed the ecclesiastical mind since the 1790's. In the
end, the Spanish Church began to look for another Ferdinand
VII, another "Desired One," who would lead it to a new religious
promised land. In 1936 it found such a figure in Francisco Franco.

Notes

1. The Organization of the Church, 1750–1790

1. For a more detailed discussion of the eighteenth-century reforming monarchy, see Jean Sarrailh, *L'Espagne éclairée de la seconde moitié du XVIIIe siècle* (Paris, 1954); Richard Herr, *The Eighteenth-Century Revolution in Spain* (Princeton, 1958); and Antonio Domínguez Ortiz, *Sociedad y Estado en el siglo XVIII español* (Madrid, 1976).

2. Isidoro Martín, "En el segundo centenario del concordato español de 1753," *Revista Española de Derecho Canónico*, 8 (1953), 754–755.

3. C. C. Noël, "Opposition to Enlightened Reform in Spain: Campomanes and the Clergy, 1765–1775," *Societas*, 3, no. 1 (1973), 30–32.

4. Francesc Tort Mitjans, *El Obispo de Barcelona: Josep Climent i Avinent, 1706–1781* (Barcelona, 1978), 362–367.

5. Alfredo Martínez Albiach, *Ética socio-religiosa de la España del siglo XVIII* (Burgos, 1960), 16.

6. Pedro de Valdés, *El padre de su pueblo o medios para hacer temporalmente felices a los pueblos con el auxilio de los señores párrocos*, 2nd ed. (Barcelona, 1806), 73.

7. Ibid., 14. On the attempt to direct the clergy into broader social and economic concerns, see C. C. Noël's excellent Princeton University dissertation, regrettably unpublished, "Campomanes and the Church."

8. For a discussion of the imbalanced ecclesiastical structure of the eighteenth-century Church, see Antonio Domínguez Ortiz, *La sociedad española en el siglo XVIII* (Madrid, 1955), 133–134.

9. Antonio López Ferreiro, *Historia de la Santa A. M. Iglesia de Santiago de Compostela*, 11 vols. (Santiago, 1898–1909), X, 28–29.

10. Joseph Townsend, *A Journey through Spain in the Years 1786 and 1787*, 3 vols. (London, 1791), III, 326.

11. Alexandre Laborde, *A View of Spain*, 5 vols. (London, 1809), V, 14.

12. "Demografía eclesiástica," in *Diccionario de historia eclesiástica de España*, 4 vols. (Madrid, 1972–1975), II, 733. The kingdom of Naples thus had nearly 50,000 secular priests in a population of approximately 5 million. Mario Rosa, "The Italian Churches," in *Church and Society in Catholic Europe of the Eighteenth Century*, ed. W. J. Callahan and D. C. Higgs (Cambridge, 1979), 69.

13. *Censo de la población de España de el año de 1797* (Madrid, 1801).

14. Juan Sáez Marín, *Datos sobre la Iglesia española contemporánea, 1768–1868* (Madrid, 1975), 294.

15. Expediente sobre aumento de dotación del Curato de Cavañas de la Dormilla y Cubillinos (1800), Archivo Histórico Nacional (hereafter AHN), Consejos, leg. 15578, exp. 8.

16. Sáez Marín, *Datos sobre la Iglesia*, 298–299.

17. Representation of the bishop of Cádiz to the *Cámara* of Castile, February 15, 1788, AHN, Consejos, leg. 15647, exp. 4.

18. Quoted by Noël in "Campomanes and the Church," 47.

19. Ibid., 43.

20. Townsend, *A Journey through Spain*, II, 150–151.

21. Laborde, *A View of Spain*, V, 34. This view, however, was not universal. A midcentury critic, Gregorio Mayáns, attacked the bishops of his time as "very ignorant men who had obtained miters through ambitious solicitude and perhaps worse means." Antonio Mestre Sanchis, *Ilustración y reforma de la Iglesia: Pensamiento político-religioso de Don Gregorio Mayáns y Siscar, 1699–1781* (Valencia, 1968), 220.

22. There is an excellent recent biography of the early life of Lorenzana: Luis Sierra Nava-Lasa, *El Cardenal Lorenzana y la Ilustración* (Madrid, 1975).

23. Townsend described the *oposiciones* he attended in Seville and noted the extraordinary importance of these examinations for the candidates: "Vehemence, on such occasions, is not only sanctioned by custom, but is certainly excusable in men who are contending, not merely for fame, but bread." *A Journey through Spain*, II, 315.

24. *Historia eclesiástica de la ciudad y obispado de Badajoz*, 2 vols. (Badajoz, 1945), II, 89.

25. Jean François Bourgoing, *Tableau de l'Espagne moderne*, 3 vols. (Paris, 1797), III, 4–5; Antonio Rodríguez Mas. *El arzobispo urbanista: D. Joaquín de Santiyán y Valdivielso, 1779–1783* (Tarragona, 1956), 55.

26. Townsend, *A Journey through Spain*, III, 56.

27. For a detailed institutional study of a cathedral chapter, see Juan Ramón López-Arévalo, *Un cabildo catedral de la Vieja Castilla: Ávila* (Madrid, 1966).

28. Sebastián Padrón Acosta, "El Dean Don Jerónimo de Róo," *Revista de Historia*, 16, nos. 90–91 (1950), 179–198.

29. Escrito sobre los párrocos, ms., n.d., n.p., Fundación Universitaria, leg. 17/16; Maximiliano Barrio Gozalo, *Estudio socio-económico de la Iglesia de Segovia en el siglo XVIII* (Segovia, 1982), 128. Another study of Segovia assigns a somewhat lower portion of the tithe (24 percent) to the parish clergy. Angel García Sanz, *Desarrollo y crisis del antiguo régimen en Castilla la Vieja: Economía y sociedad en tierras de Segovia, 1500–1814* (Madrid, 1977), 312.

30. Juan Pérez, *Directorio de sacerdotes* (Madrid, 1733), 45.

31. Joaquín Lorenzo Villanueva, *De la obligación de decir Misa con circunspección y pausa* (Madrid, 1790), prologue.

32. Father Pedro de Calatayud, *Juizio de los sacerdotes: Doctrina práctica y anatomía de sus conciencias* (Valencia, 1736), 10, 62, 87. The Capuchin Father Juan de Zamora, author of a manual for the guidance of the parish clergy, also believed that the problem of parish priests engaged in business activities had reached serious proportions. Such a priest, he held, was worse than "the most greedy farmer of the place" where he served as *cura*. *El eclesiástico perfecto* (Madrid, 1781), 398–399.

33. Leandro Higueruela del Pino, *El clero de Toledo desde 1800 a 1823* (Madrid, 1979), 43.

34. Ibid., 54.

35. Ibid., 72.

36. There is an excellent monograph on eighteenth-century seminaries: Francisco Martín Hernandez and José Martín Hernández, *Los seminarios españoles en la época de la Ilustración* (Madrid, 1973).

37. Higueruela del Pino, *El clero de Toledo*, 45.

38. *Método que se observa en el arzobispado de Toledo para la celebración de los concursos de curatos* (n.p., n.d.). The examinations were to be held every two years.

In Toledo this meant the appointment of fifty new parish priests and the promotion of sixty more, a good indication of the constant movement within the ranks of the parish clergy.

39. Representation of the bishop of Osma to Charles IV, July 15, 1790, AHN, Consejos, leg. 15980, exp. 1.

40. Leandro Higueruela del Pino, *El clero de la diócesis de Toledo durante el pontificado del Cardenal Borbón* (Madrid, 1973), 14–15.

41. Tort Mitjans, *El Obispo de Barcelona*, 216 n. 7.

42. Miguel Segarra Roca, "Un párroco modelo," *Boletín de la Sociedad Castellonense de Cultura*, 23 (1947), 5–16. See, for example, the account of an active parish clergy in Cardona: J. Serra Vilaró, *Historia de Cardona*, 4 vols. (Tarragona, 1962), IV, 275–309.

43. Barrio Gozalo in his study of ecclesiastical finances in the diocese of Segovia notes that the 4,168 reales of annual income received by the parish priests of the vicarate of Riaza in the early 1770's compared favorably with the salaries of royal administrators in the district. He also notes, however, that tithe income varied substantially from one parish to another over the diocese as a whole. Between 1771 and 1775, 22.5 percent of the parishes received more than 5,000 reales a year in tithe income; 38.79 percent received less than 2,000 a year; and 46.03 percent received between 2,000 and 5,000. Only 6 of the diocese's 219 parishes attained a handsome annual income from the tithe (exceeding 10,000 reales), in contrast to 20 parishes that received less than 500 a year. *Estudio socio-económico de la Iglesia de Segovia*, 153, 438–439, 402–403.

44. L. de Amorós, "Estadística de los conventos y religiosos de las provincias franciscanas de España en el año de 1768," *Archivo Ibero-Americano*, 16, no. 64 (1956), 424.

45. *Historia del Real Monasterio de Poblet*, 6 vols. (Barcelona, 1947–1955), VI, 32.

46. Ibid., VI, 68–69.

47. B. Cuartero y Huerta, *Historia de la Cartuja de Santa María de las Cuevas de Sevilla*, 2 vols. (Madrid, 1950–1954), II, 359.

48. E. Corredera, "Caresmar y Barcelona," *Analecta Sacra Tarraconensia*, 37 (1964), 111; M. Férotin, *Histoire de l'abbaye de Silos* (Paris, 1897), 249–250.

49. Proyecto para hacer los establecimientos de los religiosos más perfectos, ms., n.p., n.d., Fundación Universitaria, leg. 15/20.

50. Amorós, "Estadística de los conventos y religiosos," 432.

51. M. R. Pazos. "Provinciales Compostelanos," *Archivo Ibero-Americano*, 28, no. 112 (1968), 270–271.

52. Francisco Aragonés, *Los frailes franciscos de Cataluña*, 2 vols. (Barcelona, 1891), I, 143.

53. M. R. Pazos, "Provinciales Compostelanos," *Archivo Ibero-Americano*, 31, nos. 122–123 (1968), 405.

54. Rafael García, "Recuerdos y presencia de los Agustinos en Agreda," *Archivo Agustiniano*, no. 172 (1964), 53–85.

55. Libro en que se escriben los decretos y preceptos . . . de esta provincia de Andalucía (1735–1779), AHN, Clero, libro 3749.

56. Fray Melchor de Pobladura, *Seminarios de misioneros y conventos de perfecta vida común* (Rome, 1963), 36–37, 89. Life in the reformed Capuchin convents was to be carried on with the "complete practice of evangelical poverty."

57. Libro en que se prosiguen sentando los decretos . . . de el Oratorio de

Granada, 1761–1804, AHN, Clero, libro 3835; J. Mesenguer Fernández, "El P. Antonio José Salinas, Comisario General de los Franciscanos y Obispo de Tortosa, 1732–1815," *Archivo Ibero-Americano*, 6, no. 21 (1946), 64–65; A. Barrado Manzano, "División bipartita de la provincia de San Miguel en Extremadura," *Archivo Ibero-Americano*, 19, no. 75 (1959), 340.

58. Proyecto para hacer los establecimientos de los religiosos más perfectos.

59. Antonio Astraín, *Historia de la Compañia de Jesús en la asistencia de España*, 8 vols. (Madrid, 1902–1925), VIII, 48.

60. For discussion of the struggle between the Jesuits and the Augustinians, see Herr, *The Eighteenth-Century Revolution in Spain*, 15–18.

61. Quoted in José Navarro Latorre, *Hace doscientos años: Estado actual de los problemas históricos del Motín de Esquilache* (Madrid, 1966), 28. For a pro-Jesuit interpretation of these events, see C. Eguía Ruiz, *Los Jesuitas y el motín de Esquilache* (Madrid, 1947). There is a summary of the recent bibliography on the *motín* in Domínguez Ortiz, *Sociedad y Estado en el siglo XVIII español*, 308.

62. Bartolomé Bennassar et al., *L'Inquisition espagnole, XVe–XIXe siècle* (Paris, 1979), 33–39.

63. See the fine study of Gustav Hennigsen, *The Witches Advocate: Basque Witchcraft and the Spanish Inquisition* (Reno, 1980).

64. Bennassar et al., *L'Inquisition espagnole*, 21.

65. Ibid., 31–32.

66. Marcelin Defourneaux, *L'Inquisition espagnole et les livres français au XVIIIe siècle* (Paris, 1963), 62.

67. Joël Saugnieux, *Les jansénistes et le renouveau de la predication dans l'Espagne de la seconde moitié du XVIIIe siècle* (Lyon, 1976), 200–202.

68. Townsend, *A Journey through Spain*, III, 336.

69. Marcelin Defourneaux, *Pablo de Olavide ou l'Afrancesado, 1725–1803* (Paris, 1959), 293.

70. Saugnieux, *Les jansénistes*, 201. Saugnieux suggests that Bertrán was incapable of resisting the pressure of his fellow inquisitors in the Olavide case. He succeeded, however, in having the sentence reduced to a less severe penalty than that demanded by his colleagues. Alvárez de Morales argues that the case should not be seen as a single, spectacular blow designed to restore the Inquisition to its old authority. He contends that the Olavide case was one of many launched by the Holy Tribunal against leading reformers, but that it was the only one to have progressed to the stage of formal prosecution. In this context the sentencing of Olavide was a minor triumph that could not hide the overall weakness of the Inquisition in the struggle against reforming tendencies in the highest circles of government. Antonio Alvárez de Morales, *Inquisición e Ilustración, 1700–1834* (Madrid, 1982), 130–132.

71. Defourneaux, *L'Inquisition espagnole et les livres français au XVIIIe siècle*, 73.

72. Ibid.

2. Prosperity and Religion, 1750–1790

1. Information on the cadastral register of Ensenada is drawn from Antonio Matilla Tascón, *La única contribución y el Catastro de Ensenada* (Madrid 1947), 92–95, 535–543.

2. Gonzalo Anes, *Las crisis agrarias en la España moderna* (Madrid, 1970), 292.

3. Alfonso Lazo Díaz, *La desamortización de las tierras de la Iglesia en la provincia de Sevilla, 1835–1845* (Seville, 1970), 50; José Mariá Mutiloa Poza, *La desamortización eclesiástica en Navarra* (Pamplona, 1972), 156–157; and Barrio Gozalo, *Estudio socio-económico de la Iglesia de Segovia*, 82.

4. Laborde, *A View of Spain*, II, 271.

5. Juan José de la Inmaculada, *El desierto de la provincia de San Joaquín* (Vitoria, 1956), 118.

6. Lazo Díaz, *La desamortización . . . en Sevilla*, 65.

7. Julio Porres Martín-Cleto, *La desamortización del siglo XIX en Toledo* (Toledo, 1966), 82–83.

8. Ibid., 103.

9. The Hermandad del Refugio of Madrid spent an average 25 percent of the income received in rents on repairs to its urban property. Archivo de la Hermandad, leg. 148.

10. Christian Hermann, "Les revenus des évêques espagnols au dix-huitième siècle (1650–1830)," *Mélanges de la Casa de Velázquez*, 10 (1974), 189; Antonio Domínguez Ortiz, "Las rentas episcopales de la corona de Aragón en el siglo XVIII," in *Agricultura, comercio colonial y crecimiento económico en la España contemporánea*, ed. J. Nadal and G. Tortella (Barcelona, 1974), 20.

11. Sierra Nava-Lasa, *El Cardenal Lorenzana y la Ilustración*, 91.

12. Jacques Soubeyroux, *Pauperisme et rapports sociaux a Madrid au XVIIIème siècle*, 2 vols. (Lille, 1978), I, 135. Townsend, *A Journey through Spain*, III, 16–17, 183.

13. Francisco Bocanegra, *Sermones*, 2 vols. (Madrid, 1773), I, 190.

14. W. J. Callahan, "The Problem of Confinement: An Aspect of Poor Relief in Eighteenth-Century Spain," *Hispanic American Historical Review*, no. 1 (1971), 2.

15. Income increased from 784,076 reales in the decade 1710–1719 to 4,347,750 between 1790 and 1800. Archivo de la Hermandad, Cuentas Generales, 1700–1800.

16. Townsend, *A Journey through Spain*, III, 57.

17. A. Meijide Pardo, "El hambre en Galicia y la obra asistencial del estamento eclesiástico compostelano," *Compestellanum*, 10 (1965), X, 222–238.

18. W. J. Callahan, *La Santa y Real Hermandad del Refugio y Piedad de Madrid, 1618–1832* (Madrid, 1980), 22–23, 106.

19. Mariano Peset and José Luis Peset, *La universidad española: Despotismo ilustrado y revolución liberal* (Madrid, 1974), 566.

20. Sarrailh, *L'Espagne éclairée*, 45–46.

21. Ibid., 186.

22. Thus, the Dominicans of Alicante rushed forward to take control of secondary teaching in the town after the expulsion of the Jesuits to prevent laymen from filling the educational vacuum. The order's College of the Rosary then dominated secondary teaching for the rest of the century. M. Mateos Carretero, *La enseñanza en Alicante en el siglo XVIII* (Alicante, 1967), 158–161.

23. Jean Dedieu, "Christianisation en Nouvelle Castille: Catéchisme, communion et confirmation dans l'archevêche de Toledo, 1540–1650," *Mélanges de la Casa de Velázquez*, 15 (1979), 277–293.

24. Mercedes Mauleón Isla, *La población de Bilbao en el siglo XVIII* (Valla-

dolid, 1961), 166; Angel Bergadà i Escrivà, *Vimbodí: Estudi històric, sociologic i religiós* (Vimbodí, 1978), 192; José Goñi Gaztambide, "El cumplimiento pascual en la diócesis de Pamplona en 1801," *Hispania Sacra,* 26 (1973), 367; Gabriel Llompart, "La catequesis en Mallorca en 1747," *Hispania Sacra,* 25 (1972), 439.

25. Townsend, *A Journey through Spain,* II, 149.

26. José Bermejo y Carballo, *Glorias religiosas de Sevilla o noticia histórico-descriptiva de todas las cofradías de penitencia, sangre y luz* (Seville, 1882), 78, 84, 99.

27. Luis Batlle Prats, "El marianismo en las asociaciones gremiales gerundenses," *Analecta Sacra Tarraconensia,* 30 (1957), 323.

28. *Segundo Congreso de misiones parroquiales (1958)* (Madrid, 1961), 201.

29. Townsend, *A Journey through Spain,* II, 318–319.

30. Ibid., I, 107–109.

31. Laborde, *A View of Spain,* III, 238.

32. Farid Abbad, "La confrérie condamnée ou une spontanéité festive confisquée," *Mélanges de la Casa de Velázquez,* 13 (1977), 366.

33. Defourneaux, *Pablo de Olavide,* 269. Confraternities and brotherhoods also existed in rural villages, but they played a somewhat different social role given the narrower range of class differences in the countryside. For a discussion of the rural association, see Jean-Luc Jamard, "Confréries religieuses et dichotomie sociale," *Mélanges de la Casa de Velázquez,* 8 (1972), 474–488.

34. Farid, "La confrérie condamnée," 369.

35. Tort Mitjans, *El Obispo de Barcelona,* 217 n. 11.

36. Calatayud, *Juizio de los sacerdotes,* 87; Higueruela del Pino, *El clero de Toledo,* 182.

37. Pastoral Letter, February 19, 1765, in *Colección de las cartas pastorales y edictos del Exmo. Señor Don Felipe Bertrán,* 2 vols. (Madrid, 1783), I, 31.

38. Higueruela del Pino, *El clero de Toledo,* 183.

39. For the introduction of this devotion into Spain, see José Eugenio Uriarte, *Principios del reinado del Corazón de Jesús en España* (Madrid, 1880).

40. G. Seguí, "La devoción a los Sagrados Corazones de Jesús y María en Mallorca," *Boletín de la Sociedad Arqueológica Luliana,* 21 (1955–56), 286–291; F. Martí, "Nota histórica acerca de las devociones más populares en Menorca," *Analecta Sacra Tarraconensia,* 28 (1955), 273–278.

41. J. I. Tellechea Idigoras, "La Congregación del Sagrado Corazón de Jesús de Deva," *Boletín de la Real Sociedad Vascongada de los Amigos del País,* 19, no. 2 (1963), 133–146.

42. Antonio Arbiol, *La familia regulada con doctrina de la Sagrada Escritura* (Barcelona, 1746); Francisco Larraga, *Promptuario de la theología moral* (Madrid, 1780).

43. Larraga, *Promptuario,* 507.

44. Arbiol, *La familia regulada,* 66.

45. Larraga, *Promptuario,* 508.

46. For a general discussion of the missions in Europe as a whole, see Jean Delumeau, *Le Catholicisme entre Luther et Voltaire* (Paris, 1971), 274–279.

47. Astraín, *Historia de la Compañia de Jesús,* VIII, 90.

48. Fray Serafín de Ardales, *El misionero capuchino: Compendio histórico de la vida del . . . M.R.P. Fr. Diego Josef de Cádiz* (Cádiz, 1811), 36.

49. Fray Buenaventura de Carrocera, *La provincia de Frailes Menores Capuchinos de Castilla, 1701–1836* (Madrid, 1973), 193–194.

50. Ardales, *El misionero capuchino,* 11.

51. In 1800 the Capuchin was investigated by the Inquisition for several sermons in which he questioned governmental interference in ecclesiastical affairs. *Expediente formado en el Consejo sobre los sermones de Fray Diego de Cádiz.* AHN, Inquisición, leg. 4449, exp. 1.

52. The Council of Castile ruled in favor of the *consulado* and placed a ban on the circulation of Calatayud's published works in the Basque Provinces. The Jesuit, however, remained convinced that he had spoken "with equity and reason according to God and the truth." *Respuesta a una consulta que me hace un comerciante de Bilbao sobre la compra de lanas,* 1764. Biblioteca Nacional, ms. 5809.

53. William Christian, *Local Religion in Sixteenth-Century Spain* (Princeton, 1981), 23–33.

54. Justino Matute y Gaviria, *Anales eclesiásticos y seculares de la Muy Noble y Muy Leal Ciudad de Sevilla, 1701–1800,* 3 vols. (Seville, 1887), II, 123–124.

55. Townsend, *A Journey through Spain,* II, 21.

56. Laborde, *A View of Spain,* 238.

57. Ibid.

58. Higueruela del Pino, *El clero de Toledo,* 186.

59. *Colección de las cartas pastorales . . . del . . . Felipe Bertrán,* I, 56.

60. Ibid.

61. For the intense efforts of Climent against what he saw as superstition, see Tort Mitjans, *El Obispo de Barcelona,* 275–278.

62. Ibid., 275 n. 18.

63. There are two general surveys of the reforming movement: Émile Appolis, *Les jansénistes espagnols* (Bordeaux, 1966); and María Giovanna Tomisch, *El jansenismo en España* (Madrid, 1972).

64. Joël Saugnieux, *Un prélat éclairé: Don Antonio Tavira y Almazán, 1737–1807* (Toulouse, 1970), 52–53.

65. In 1771, for example, the king ordered the removal from the former churches of the Jesuits of all statues and pictures of the Sacred Heart. José Eugenio Uriarte, "La fiesta del Corazón de Jesús y la Corte de España el año de 1765," *Razón y Fe,* 33 (1912), 174.

66. The diocesan Synod of Pistoia was called by Bishop Ricci at the order of Grand Duke Leopold, the brother of Joseph II of Austria. The synod sought to strengthen episcopal authority at the expense of the papacy, purify the liturgy, and restrain the growth of the religious orders. Rome's opposition to these reforming efforts produced bitter controversy within the Church.

67. Joaquín Lorenzo Villanueva, *De la lección de la Sagrada Escritura en lenguas vulgares* (Valencia, 1791), prologue.

3. The First Shocks, 1790–1814

1. José Manuel Cuenca Toribio, *Sociología de una elite de poder de España e Hispanoamérica contemporáneas: La jerarquía eclesiástica, 1789–1965* (Córdoba, 1976), 91. Thus, José Díaz, named vicar general of the Dominicans in 1805, secured the appointment through influence at court in spite of opposition from within the order. J. Cuervo, *Historiadores del convento de San Esteban de Salamanca* (Salamanca, 1914–1916), 678.

2. Consulta hecha por la Rl. Cámara de Castilla sobre la causa hecha contra

el Exmo. Illmo. y Revmo. Sr. Dn. Francisco Fabián y Fuero, Arzobispo que fue de Valencia, 1795. Biblioteca Nacional, ms. 18110.

3. For an account of the ministerial change of 1797, see Herr, *The Eighteenth-Century Revolution in Spain*, 398–400.

4. Luis Sierra Nava, *La reacción del episcopado español ante los decretos de matrimonios del ministro Urquijo de 1799 a 1813* (Bilbao, 1964), 1–2.

5. A study of the income of the Catalan monastery of Poblet between 1783 and 1799 notes that the rising prices of agricultural products contributed to the institution's prosperity during these years. Josep Recasens i Comes, "Les rendes del Mestir de Poblet a l'arqubisbat de Tarragona a finals del segle XVIII," *I Colloqui d'Història del Monaquisme Català* (Santes Creus, 1967), 307.

6. For a discussion of the State's fiscal crisis, see Richard Herr, "Hacia el derrumbe del antiguo régimen: Crisis fiscal y desamortización fiscal bajo Carlos IV," *Moneda y Crédito*, no. 118 (1971), 37–100.

7. López Ferreiro, *Historia de la . . . Iglesia de Santiago*, XI, 97–99.

8. Juan Marichal, "From Pistoia to Cádiz: A Generation's Itinerary, 1786–1812," in *The Ibero-American Enlightenment*, ed. A. Owen Aldridge (Urbana, 1971), 102–103.

9. Alfredo Martínez Albiach, *Religiosidad hispana y sociedad borbónica* (Burgos, 1969).

10. A 1751 sermon of a prominent preacher, Nicolás Gallo, began the late-eighteenth-century obsession with "libertinism," described as a spirit of "dissolution corrupting the morality and customs of the entire nation." Ibid., 156.

11. Ibid., 24.

12. Ibid., 21.

13. Tomisch, *El jansenismo en España*, 86–88. For a more detailed discussion of the civil war within the Church, see W. J. Callahan, "Two Spains and Two Churches, 1760–1835," *Historical Reflections*, 2, no. 2 (1975), 158–181.

14. Javier Herrero, *Los orígenes del pensamiento reaccionario español* (Madrid, 1971), 86–87.

15. García Sanz, *Desarrollo y crisis del antiguo régimen en Castilla la Vieja*, 451. The worsening financial situation of the parish clergy in this period is also noted by Barrio Gozalo, *Estudio socio-económico de la Iglesia de Segovia*, 439–440.

16. How extensive this increase was is difficult to establish given the absence of a census after 1797. There are indications of an increase even in the monastic orders, where an earlier decline had been substantial. Entrants in the Cistercian monastery of Sobrado, for example, increased by a third between 1800 and 1808 over the preceding decade. Similar increases occurred among the male Carmelites of Ávila and the male Mercedarians of Granada. The number of new members in the Dominican house of Santo Tomás in Madrid, which had averaged eleven to thirteen per decade between 1760 and 1789, rose to an average of twenty per decade between 1790 and 1808. AHN, Clero, libros 479, 3052, 3797; Antonio Martínez Escudero, *Historia del convento de Santo Tomás de Madrid* (Madrid, 1900), 84–101.

17. AHN, leg. 4025, exp. 79. The picture of extreme internal tensions in the religious orders is confirmed by later historians. In his history of the Capuchins, Fray Buenaventura de Carrocera observed that the period 1793–1808 was characterized by the "insubordination" of the order's members in Castile. *La provincia de Frailes Menores Capuchinos, 1701–1836*, 299.

18. Martínez Albiach, *Religiosidad hispana*, 59.

19. Isidoro de Villapadierna, "El episcopado español y las Cortes de Cádiz," *Hispania Sacra*, 8 (1955), 276.

20. Sierra Nava, *La reacción del episcopado*, 226–235.

21. Aragonés, *Los frailes franciscos*, I, 42–44, 35. Juan R. Legísima, *Héroes y mártires gallegos: Los Franciscanos de Galicia en la guerra de la Independencia* (Santiago de Compostela, 1912), 207–208.

22. The superior, Fray Rienda, operated around the city of Jaén with thirty-four guerrillas who killed 58 of the 450 French soldiers pursuing them. Juan R. Legísima, "Las ordenes religiosas en la guerra de la Independencia," *Archivo Ibero-Americano*, 22, no. 118 (1935), 204.

23. Mariano Raís and Luis Navarro, *Historia de la Provincia de Aragón, Orden de Predicadores, desde el año 1808 hasta el de 1818* (Zaragoza, 1819), 15.

24. Aragonés, *Los frailes franciscos*, I, 49–50.

25. Legísima, "Las ordenes religiosas," 197.

26. Ibid., 202.

27. Martínez Albiach, *Religiosidad hispana*, 138.

28. Sierra Nava, *La reacción del episcopado*, 86.

29. Martínez Albiach, *Religiosidad hispana*, 61.

30. This quotation and those in the next paragraph are from ibid., 32, 145.

31. *Informe* of Antonio Cebrián y Valdés, October 3, 1809, in *Cortes de Cádiz: Informes oficiales sobres Cortes: Valencia y Aragón* (Pamplona, 1968), 100.

32. Ibid., 87.

33. Raís and Navarro, *Historia de la Provincia de Aragón*, 34.

34. José Manuel Cuenca Toribio, *D. Pedro de Inguanzo y Rivero, 1764–1836: Último prelado del antiguo régimen* (Pamplona, 1965), 112–113.

35. Raul Morodo and Elías Díaz, "Tendencias y grupos políticos en las Cortes de Cádiz y en las de 1820," *Cuadernos Hispanoamericanos*, 201 (1966), 644.

36. Ramón Solís, *El Cádiz de las Cortes* (Madrid, 1969), 267.

37. Ibid.

38. Ibid., 269.

39. Marichal, "From Pistoia to Cádiz," 104.

40. Villapadierna, "El episcopado español," 305.

41. Aragonés, *Los frailes franciscos*, I, 263.

42. Villapadierna, "El episcopado español," 309–311.

43. Ibid. The impact of this work by Bartolomé José Gallardo has been studied by C. Torra, "Bartolomé José Gallardo y el *Diccionario Crítico Burlesco*," in *Estudios sobre Cortes de Cádiz* (Pamplona, 1967), 209–272.

44. Miguel Artola, *Los orígenes de la España contemporánea*, 2 vols. (Madrid, 1959), I, 452.

45. *Actas de las Cortes de Cádiz*, 2 vols. (Madrid, 1964), II, 1058, 1067.

46. Francisco Martí Gilabert, *La abolición de la Inquisición en España* (Pamplona, 1975), 153.

47. Morodo and Díaz, "Tendencias y grupos políticos," 645.

48. Artola, *Los orígenes de la España contemporánea*, I, 530.

49. Ibid., 531.

50. Ibid., 534.

51. Joan Brines Blasco, *La desamortización eclesiástica en el País Valenciano durante el trienio constitucional* (Valencia, 1978), 17; Cayetano Barraquer y Rovi-

ralta, *Los religiosos en Cataluña durante la primera mitad del siglo XIX,* 4 vols. (Barcelona, 1915–1917), I, 54.

52. Artola, *Los origenes de la España contemporánea,* I, 507.

53. Ibid., 598, 603.

54. Martínez Albiach, *Religiosidad hispana,* 184.

55. Ibid., 192.

56. Manuel Garzón Pareja, *Diezmos y tributos del clero de Granada* (Granada, 1974), 43.

57. There were important regional variations in the level of destruction. In Catalonia it was substantial, although a certain number of religious houses escaped, but in Guadalajara, close to the capital and the main supply route to Aragón and Catalonia, it was almost universal. Thus, the richest convent of the city, Santa Clara, was converted into a barracks for French troops; the chapel was made a storehouse. Most of the convent's statues and religious objects were lost or destroyed, and the fabric was damaged by the numerous fires soldiers lit inside to keep warm in the chill Castilian winter. Francisco Layna Serrano, *Los conventos antiguos de Guadalajara* (Madrid, 1943), 104–105.

58. Cuenca Toribio, *D. Pedro de Inguanzo,* 181; Raís and Navarro, *Historia de la Provincia de Aragón,* 64; J. Mesenguer Fernández, "Notas para la historia de la Provincia de Cartagena," *Archivo Ibero-Americano,* 11, no. 43 (1951), 288.

59. *Libro en el qual se escriven las elecciones que se hacen en este convento de N. Sra. del Carmen de la Ciudad de Orihuela (1683–1833),* AHN, Clero, libro 355.

60. Cuenca Toribio, *D. Pedro de Inguanzo,* 180.

61. Higueruela del Pino, *El clero de Toledo,* 193.

62. José Manuel Cuenca Toribio, "Arias Teijeiro ante la restauración religiosa," *Príncipe de Viana,* 26 (1965), 349.

63. AHN, Inquisición, legs. 4490–4491.

64. Villapadierna, "El episcopado español," 315–316.

65. Martínez Albiach, *Religiosidad hispana,* 185.

66. José Manuel Cuenca Toribio, "La Iglesia sevillana en la primera época constitucional, 1812–1814" *Hispania Sacra,* 15 (1962), 155–156.

4. The Struggle Intensifies, 1814–1833

1. Martínez Albiach, *Religiosidad hispana,* 577, 610.

2. For an excellent general study of this period, see Josep Fontana, *La quiebra de la monarquía absoluta, 1814–1820* (Barcelona, 1971).

3. Manuel Revuelta González, *Política religiosa de los liberales del siglo XIX: Trienio constitucional* (Madrid, 1973), 4. Ironically, the Jesuits expelled from Spain by royal absolutism in 1767 had supported the Cortes of Cádiz, hoping that the constitutional regime would allow them to return. Revuelta González, "La supresión de la Compañia de Jesús en España en 1820." *Razón y Fe,* 182, nos. 170–171 (1970), 104.

4. Cuenca Toribio, "Arias Teijeiro ante la restauración religiosa," 344.

5. Aragonés, *Los frailes franciscos,* II, 319.

6. López Ferreiro, *Historia de la . . . Iglesia de Santiago,* XI, 283.

7. Revuelta González, *Política religiosa,* 10.

8. Martínez Albiach, *Religiosidad hispana,* 464–468.

9. Ignacio Lasa, "Las confesiones de Joaquín Lorenzo Villanueva," *Scriptorium Victoriense*, 17 (1970), 320.

10. Within the royal administration bureaucrats imbued with the regalist ideals of the past continued to press for extensive state control over the Church. Thus, the proposal to reestablish the Jesuits received an unenthusiastic response from two of the three Crown attorneys responsible for recommending a policy to the Council of Castile. The third advocated the order's return with an argument that surely must have appealed to the king: "since the destruction of the Company the unfortunate era began which has weakened the empire of religion, authority and knowledge of Catholic dogmas; unbelief and heresy have made terrible progress." Francisco Gutiérrez de la Huerta, *Dictamen del Fiscal Don . . . presentado y leído en el Consejo de Castilla sobre el restablecimiento de los Jesuitas* (Madrid, 1845), 288.

11. Pedro Antonio Perlado, *Los obispos españoles ante la amnistía de 1817* (Pamplona, 1970), 49; Revuelta González, *Política religiosa*, 15.

12. Cuenca Toribio, *Sociología de una elite de poder*, 67.

13. G. Lemeunier, "La part de Dieu: Recherches sur la levée des dîmes au Diocèse de Cartagène-Murcie," *Mélanges de la Casa de Velázquez*, 12 (1976), 379–380.

14. Hermann, "Les revenus des évêques espagnols," 196; Revuelta González, *Política religiosa*, 31–32.

15. *Historia del Real Monasterio de Poblet*, VI, 107.

16. Fontana, *La quiebra de la monarquía*, 202–210.

17. Aragonés, *Los frailes franciscos*, I, 319–321.

18. Cristóbal Pérez Biala, bishop of Jaén, to the King, July 17, 1816. AHN, Consejos, leg. 15884, exp. 1; Manuel Revuelta González, "Clero viejo y clero nuevo en el siglo XIX," in *Estudios históricos sobre la Iglesia española contemporánea*, ed. J. Andrés Gallego et al. (El Escorial, 1979), 162–163.

19. "Exposición del Señor Obispo de Pamplona" (1820), in *Colección eclesiástica española*, 14 vols. (Madrid, 1823), III, 173.

20. Francisco Xavier Tapia, "Las relaciones Iglesia-Estado durante el primer experimento liberal en España, 1820–1823," *Revista de Estudios Políticos*, no. 173 (1970), 69.

21. José Manuel Cuenca Toribio, "La Iglesia española en el trienio constitucional, 1820–1823," *Hispania Sacra*, 18 (1965), 338.

22. Morodo and Díaz, "Tendencias y grupos políticos," 655.

23. Revuelta González, *Política religiosa*, 130–131.

24. Juan Mercader Riba, "Orígenes del anticlericalismo español," *Hispania*, 123 (1973), 109.

25. Aragonés, *Los frailes franciscos*, II, 30, 47.

26. Manuel Revuelta González, "Los planes de reforma eclesiástica durante el trienio constitucional," *Miscelánea Comillas*, nos. 56–57 (1972), 13–15.

27. *Dictamen de la Comisión Eclesiástica sobre el nuevo plan de Iglesias metropolitanas y catedrales de la Monarquía española* (Madrid, 1821), 4.

28. Ibid., 85.

29. *Proyecto de decreto acerca de nueva demarcación de parroquías y dotación de párrocos* (Madrid, 1821), 115–122.

30. Francesc de Colldeforns, *Les parròquies Barcelonines en el segle XIX* (Barcelona, 1936), 47.

31. Only 500 Spanish Jesuits had survived from the expulsion of 1767, but the order quickly won new recruits between 1814 and 1820 in spite of the general decline of vocations among the regular clergy. L. Frías, *Historia de la*

Compañia de Jesús en su asistencia moderna de España, 2 vols. (Madrid, 1923), I, 103; Revuelta González, "La supresión de la Compañia de Jesús," 110.

32. Ibid., 108. The return of the Jesuits was by no means welcomed by all the clergy. The canons of the collegiate church of San Isidro, a capitular community created by Charles III to occupy the former Jesuit church of San Isidro, the city's largest, resented the order's return. So did other groups of priests, secular and regular, forced to move from quarters repossessed by the Jesuits.

33. Morodo and Díaz, "Tendencias y grupos políticos," 659.

34. Thus, Asturias retained all 6 of its religious houses; Galicia lost only 7 of 48. Moreover, the orders suffered in different proportions. The Calced Mercedarians lost 61 of their 80 houses, the Dominicans 133 of 220, the Capuchins 76 of 114. But the Franciscans as a whole lost only 143 of 454 friaries. Revuelta González, *Política religiosa,* 246. There were also differences in the geographic distribution of monastic closings within regions. In Valencia, for example, closings were extensive in some districts, but none took place in Alcoy during the entire period of liberal rule. There, as in certain other jurisdictions, local magistrates and officials with responsibility for implementing the government's decrees refused to act and got away with it. Brines Blasco, *La desamortización eclesiástica en el País Valenciano,* 99, 101.

35. Juan Antonio Llorente (1756–1823) had been active among ecclesiastical reformers since the 1780's. He enthusiastically supported the suppression of the regulars and the Inquisition by Joseph Napoleon and published a celebrated critical history of the Inquisition, *Histoire critique de l'Inquisition d'Espagne,* 4 vols. (Paris, 1817–1818). A list of 355 ecclesiastics accused of being addicted to the exaltado Church drawn up in 1823 and forwarded to Rome is dominated by clerics occupying posts in cathedral chapters and by parish priests. Vicente Cárcel Ortí, "Masones eclesiásticos españoles durante el trienio liberal, 1820–1823," *Archivum Historiaé Pontificae,* 9 (1971), 269–277.

36. Revuelta González, "Los planes de reforma," 40–45.

37. *Historia del Real Monasterio de Poblet,* VI, 107.

38. Aragonés, *Los frailes franciscos,* II, 76.

39. Ibid., 54–55.

40. Ramiro Viola González, "Incidencias religiosas durante el período constitucional (1820–1823) en la diócesis de Lérida," *Anthologica Annua,* 20 (1973), 756, 778–781.

41. Vicente Conejero Martínez, "El clero liberal y secularizado de Barcelona (1820–1823)," *Revista Internacional de Sociología,* no. 34 (1976), 32–35.

42. *Historia del Real Monasterio de Poblet,* VI, 128.

43. Félix Torres Amat, *Vida del Ilmo, Señor Félix Amat, Arzobispo de Palmyra* (Madrid, 1835), 368; Gaspar Feliu i Montfort, *La clerecia catalana durant el trienni liberal* (Barcelona, 1972), 176.

44. Cuenca Toribio, *D. Pedro de Inguanzo,* 222.

45. Revuelta González, *Política religiosa,* 103.

46. Higueruela del Pino, *El clero de la diócesis de Toledo,* 11; López-Arévalo, *Un cabildo catedral de la Vieja Castilla,* 201.

47. Revuelta González, *Política religiosa,* 283. One of the few good studies on the disamortization of 1820–1823 is that of Brines Blasco, *La desamortización eclesiástica en el País Valenciano.*

48. Revuelta González, *Política religiosa,* 60–74.

49. Barraquer y Roviralta, *Religiosos en Cataluña,* I, 602–603.

50. Alberto Gil Novales, *Las sociedades patrióticas, 1820–1823,* 2 vols. (Madrid, 1975), I, 43.

51. Ibid.

52. Cuartero y Huerta, *Historia de la Cartuja de Santa María,* 512.

53. Michael J. Quin, *A Visit to Spain* (London, 1824), 94.

54. Writing in 1830, that is seven years after the restoration of absolutism and clerical influence, an English visitor remarked on the predominance of women at church services in Madrid's largest church, San Isidro: "I do not believe there were 300 listeners to the discourse, and of these at least five-sixths were women." He noted, however, that although in Madrid "there is little attention paid to the ceremonials of religion"; in Valencia by contrast he had never observed "so great a number of persons at devotion." H. D. Inglis, *Spain in 1830,* 2 vols. (London, 1831), I, 167, 159; II, 329.

55. Luis Alonso Tejada, *Ocaso de la Inquisición en los ultimos años del reinado de Fernando VII* (Madrid, 1969), 88. Upon his return to power in 1823, Ferdinand VII launched a campaign of persecution against freemasonry. Since 1814 the king had seen the sinister hand of the masons behind the conspiracies directed against him. The king's intense preoccupation with freemasonry as an instrument of revolution and irreligion began that obsessive identification of masonry and liberalism by conservative forces that would contribute to ideological warfare in Spain well into the twentieth century. José A. Ferrer Benimeli, who has studied the origins of Spanish freemasonry, argued, however, that Ferdinand vastly overestimated the masons' role in the revolutionary politics of the time. *Masonería española contemporánea,* 2 vols. (Madrid, 1980), I, 134–141.

56. The indictment against Somoza, one of the members of the commission that proposed radical reform of the Church to the Cortes in 1823, charged him with having been a leading member of the "partido de exaltación"; Riego was accused of being the "general agent" of the constitutionalists in Oviedo. The parish priest of San Roque, Manuel Villalba, was said to have been one of the individuals of "greatest exaltation and scandal" in the town as well as being "head of the liberals." AHN, Consejos, legs. 16036, exps. 1, 2; 15600, exp. 1; 15649, exp. 3.

57. Tejada, *Ocaso de la Inquisición,* 50.

58. Ibid., 96, 116–123.

59. Ibid., 140–141.

60. Ibid., 150.

61. Ibid., 151.

62. A visitor in Catalonia recalled the process of repossession: "Those who had paid for the land were dispossessed with little ceremony, and the materials which they had been collecting to erect stores were now fastened upon by the returning fugitives [Capuchins] to renew the demolished combination of church and cell, and cloister." A. S. MacKenzie, *A Year in Spain,* 2 vols. (London, 1831), I, 38.

63. Individual religious houses did succeed in recruiting new members, such as the Franciscan nuns of Cosentaynal, who received twelve recruits between 1824 and 1833 compared with four between 1814 and 1820. But the male Franciscans were less fortunate. Membership in the province of Cartagena fell from 530 in 1820 to 469 in 1834; a similar decline took place in the province of San Gabriel in Extremadura. AHN, Clero, libro 283; J. Mesenguer Fernández, "Notas para la historia de la Provincia de Cartagena," 288; A. Barrado, "La

provincia descalza de San Gabriel y sus libros de patentes, 1824–1835," in *Archivo Ibero-Americano*, 28, nos. 109–110 (1968), 149.

64. Sáez Marín, *Datos sobre la Iglesia española*, 200.

65. Although Manuel Revuelta González in his recent work, *La exclaustración, 1833–1840* (Madrid, 1976), 69–79, points out that many religious observed a respectable standard in their convents and monasteries, there had in fact been no serious reform of the problems troubling the orders since the eighteenth century.

66. Julián Barrio Barrio, *Félix Torres Amat, 1772–1847: Un obispo reformador* (Rome, 1976), 67, 82, 102–106.

67. Vicente Cárcel Ortí, *Política eclesial de los gobiernos liberales españoles, 1830–1840* (Pamplona, 1975), 85–86.

68. MacKenzie, *Year in Spain*, II, 32; Inglis, *Spain in 1830*, I, 30.

69. Baldomero Jiménez Duque, *La espiritualidad en el siglo XIX español* (Madrid, 1974), 140–143.

5. The Destruction of the Old Regime Church, 1833–1843

1. *La Revista Católica* (1842), 141.

2. Diego Sevilla Andrés, *El derecho de libertad religiosa en el constitucionalismo español hasta 1936* (Valencia, 1972), 5.

3. *La Voz de la Religión* (1837), 167; (1838), 180.

4. Jesús Longares Alonso, *Política y religión en Barcelona, 1833–1843* (Madrid, 1976), 182.

5. Ibid., 207.

6. For discussion of the political history of this period, see Carlos Marichal, *Spain, 1834–1844* (London, 1977); and Raymond Carr, *Spain, 1808–1939* (Oxford, 1966), chaps. 5, 6.

7. Revuelta González, *La exclaustración*, 99.

8. José Manuel Cuenca Toribio, *Iglesia y burguesía en la España liberal* (Jaén, 1979), 91–92 n. 4.

9. Cárcel Ortí, *Política eclesial*, 111–112, 215; Revuelta González, *La exclaustración*, 93.

10. Revuelta González in *La exclaustración*, 180–190, provides the most detailed treatment of the work of the junta. The government's caution was reflected in the slow pace of change in other areas of ecclesiastical policy. Its initiatives in 1834 were few and far between—the formal suppression of the Inquisition, which had last functioned in 1819, and a decree of March 9 suspending the filling of vacant benefices unconnected to the cure of souls. Income from the canonries, chaplaincies left vacant, was used to reduce the national debt.

11. Revuelta González, *La exclaustración*, 140.

12. AHN, Consejos, leg. 3951, exp. 6.

13. Cárcel Ortí, *Política eclesial*, 238.

14. "Actual estado del arzobispado de Tarragona," *El Católico*, no. 139 (1840), 377.

15. Revuelta González, *La exclaustración*, 208. This work provides the most detailed modern account of the events of July 17 along with the older work of L. Frías, *Historia de la Compañia de Jesús*, I, 610–650. There is not, however, a good study of the social aspects of the *matanza*. A British visitor present in the city during the disturbances noted the role of the militiamen, the *Urbanos*, in

the violence. When they reached the scene, "many of them joined the assassins, instead of helping to deliver them into the hands of justice." *Madrid in 1835: Sketches of the Metropolis of Spain and Its Inhabitants*, 2 vols. (London, 1836), II, 365.

16. Revuelta González, *La exclaustración*, 265.

17. Ibid., 276–277.

18. José Manuel Cuenca Toribio, *La Iglesia española ante la revolución liberal* (Madrid, 1971), 28–30.

19. The following section on the suppression of the regular clergy is drawn from Revuelta González, *La exclaustración*, 361–372.

20. Peter Janke, *Mendizábal y la instauración de la monarquía constitucional en España, 1790–1853* (Madrid, 1974), 274.

21. Antonio Colomer Viadel, "El enfrentamiento de intereses en la división del movimiento liberal, 1833–1836," *Revista de Estudios Políticos*, no. 186 (1972), 109–142.

22. *Cristina: Historia contemporánea escrita por los primeros literatos de la Corte*, 2 vols. (Madrid, 1844–1845), I, 252.

23. Janke, *Mendizábal*, 237.

24. Francisco Simón Segura, *La desamortización española del siglo XIX* (Madrid, 1973), 87.

25. Convents with more than twenty nuns were allowed to remain open, although they were forbidden to receive novices. Nuns actively engaged in charitable work, such as the Sisters of Charity, were permitted to continue their activity in hospitals, old age homes, and orphanages, but only as private citizens engaged by local governments.

26. Segura, *La desamortización*, 85.

27. Ibid.

28. Ibid., 110.

29. See pp. 229–231.

30. In the restoration and expansion of the male orders after 1874, the contributions of private donors were indispensable. Thus, the Jesuit expansion in the order's province of Toledo after 1880 was largely funded by aristocratic donations. The property of their novitiate in Granada was given by a distinguished family, the Pérez de Pulgar, and the cost of the chapel was borne by the marquesa de Blanco Hermoso. The Jesuit college of Chamartín in Madrid, opened at the request of the aristocracy, was located on land donated by the duque de Pastrana, whose wife later sold a Rubens painting to Baron Rothschild to finance the cost of construction. Manuel Cadenas, *La provincia de Toledo de la Compañia de Jesús, 1880–1914* (Madrid, 1916), 16, 38.

31. Manuel Tuñón de Lara, *Estudios sobre el siglo XIX español* (Madrid, 1972), 56–58.

32. The State quickly realized that its financial difficulties would prevent paying the clergy from general revenues. On an annual basis, therefore, collection of the tithe was authorized for 1837, 1838, 1839, and 1840, although continued evasion and the appropriation of some tithe income by the government meant that the Church received only a portion of the revenue generated.

33. Cárcel Ortí, *Política eclesial*, 416–417.

34. Judás José Romo Gamboa, *Independencia constante de la Iglesia hispana y necesidad de un nuevo concordato* (Madrid, 1843), 341.

35. Cárcel Ortí, *Política eclesial*, 415.

36. Barrio, *Félix Torres Amat*, 127.

37. Pedro González de Vallejo, *Discurso canónico-legal sobre los nombramientos de gobernadores hechos por los cabildos en los presentados por S.M. para obispos de sus iglesias* (Madrid, 1839), 89.

38. Severo Andriani y Escofet, bishop of Pamplona, *Juicio analítico sobre el discurso canónico-legal que dió a luz el Exmo. Senor D. Pedro González Vallejo* (Madrid, 1839), xiii.

39. Barrio, *Félix Torres Amat*, 137.

40. *El Católico*, no. 52 (1840), 412.

41. Ibid., no. 54 (1840), 429; no. 30 (1840), 235–236; no. 63 (1840), 501–502.

42. Nancy Rosenblatt, "The Spanish *Moderados* and the Church," *Catholic Historical Review*, 57, no. 3 (1971), 409.

43. Cárcel Ortí, *Política eclesial*, 303.

44. Marichal, *Spain, 1834–1844*, 151–153.

45. The text of the proposed law reorganizing the Church, derisively called "Project to enslave and make Protestant the Spanish Church," was reproduced in *El Católico* in its issue of June 21, 1841, no. 478, 649–652.

46. Segura, *La desamortización*, 116.

47. Ibid., 163, 152.

48. "Circular sobre atestados o certificados de adhesión," December 14, 1841, reproduced in *La Revista Católica* (1842), 29–31.

49. *La Cruz* (1842), 26.

50. Ibid. (1842), 518.

51. Ibid. (1842), 26.

52. In spite of a government prohibition, the papal discourse was reproduced in the Catholic press, see "Alocución de Nuestro Santísimo Padre Gregorio XVI habida en el consistorio secreto de 1 de Marzo de 1841," in *El Católico*, no. 385 (1841), 631–635.

53. *La Cruz* (1842), 98.

54. Under the heading "Catholic Sentiments of the Spanish Clergy," *El Católico* in successive issues of the spring and summer 1841 published letters of support for the pope and against the government's ecclesiastical policies. Thus, a letter of the clergy of Medina del Campo, published on July 19, declared: "we protest . . . that we are united . . . with the chair of St. Peter who speaks through Gregory" and announced that the writers wished to join the priests "gloriously fighting the battles of the Lord" against the danger to the Church posed by liberal reforms.

55. *La Revista Católica* (1842), 141.

56. *El Católico*, no. 469 (1841), 577.

57. Barrio, *Félix Torres Amat*, 189.

58. Ibid., 165.

59. *La Revista Católica* (1842), 126.

60. Ibid., 575–577.

61. *El Católico*, no. 644 (1841), 513; *La Cruz* (1842), 182. Thus, in Astudillo and Ciudad Real, the municipal governments refused to assess the Church tax on local residents, thereby leaving the clergy without income of any kind.

62. *El Católico*, no. 494 (1841), 49–51.

63. Antoni Jutglar, *Ideologías y clases en la España contemporánea*, 2 vols. (Madrid, 1968), I, 105.

64. Ignasi Casanovas, *Balmes: La seva vida, el seu temps, les seves obres*, 3 vols. (Barcelona, 1932), II, 473.

65. Ibid., 368.

66. Romo Gamboa, *Independencia constante de la Iglesia hispana*, 329, 336.

67. *La Revista Católica* (1844), 11, 13.

68. Manuel López Cepero, *Sermón improvisado en la Santa Iglesia Catedral de Sevilla, el dia 30 de julio de 1843* (Seville, 1843), 20.

69. "Manifiesto y exposición de la Junta de Salvación de Valencia al Gobierno de la Nación," July 30, 1843, in *La Revista Católica* (1844), 331–335.

70. Accurate statistics for this period are difficult to find. Sáez Marín estimates the number of priests with cure of souls at 19,206, beneficed clergy at 6,013, and cathedral clergy at 1,815; Sáez Marín, *Datos sobre la Iglesia española*, 327–333. The total of 27,034 compares in approximate terms with the 28,009 reported in the *Boletín del clero español en 1848* (Madrid, 1849), 150.

71. The suppression of parishes, another issue of contention between the government and churchmen opposed to its plans, was carried out on a limited scale—as, for example, in the diocese of Salamanca, where the bishop agreed to the suppression of four of the six parishes in the town of Ledesma—but more often as the result of unilateral action by the civil authorities. In Valladolid the municipal government planned closure of seven of the city's fourteen parishes. The rationalization of parish structures progressed furthest in Old Castile, where for historic reasons the number of churches often exceeded minimal pastoral necessities. The reform, however, did not bring about any substantial reduction in the overall number of parishes.

72. *La Revista Católica* (1842), 130.

73. *La Cruz* (1842), 266, 78; *El Católico*, no. 468 (1841), 569.

74. M. Sáez de Ocariz y Ruiz de Azua, "El cumplimiento pascual en la ciudad de Logroño a lo largo del siglo XIX," *Berceo*, no. 76 (1965), 275–279.

75. *La Cruz* (1842), 170.

76. Ibid. (1842), 178.

77. J. Balmes, "La religión en Barcelona," April 1, 1843, in *La Sociedad*, 4th ed. (Barcelona, 1873), 153.

78. *La Voz de la Religión* (1837), 179; *El Católico*, no. 620 (1841), 321. José Antonio Portero has noted the difficulty the midcentury Church experienced in adapting its moral code to the needs of the bourgeoisie. *Púlpito e ideología en la España del siglo XIX* (Zaragoza, 1978), 193–214.

79. *La Revista Católica* (1843), 31.

80. *El Católico*, no. 125 (1840), 168; no. 307 (1841), 7; no. 159 (1841), 537–539.

6. The Conservative Church, 1844–1868

1. This and the following quotation are drawn from *La Revista Católica* (1844), 109, 102–103.

2. Terence McMahon Hughes, *Revelations of Spain in 1845*, 2 vols. (London, 1845), I, 106.

3. Manuel González Ruíz, "Vicisitudes de la propiedad eclesiástica en España durante el siglo XIX," *Revista Española de Derecho Canónico*, 1 (1946), 403. Royal decrees of July 26 and August 8, 1844, suspended the sales of the property of secular clergy and convents of nuns. *La Revista Católica* complained bitterly of the frenetic pace of the sales in the months immediately preceding the sus-

pension, even after the ministry of Narváez, firmly committed to an accommodation with the Church, took office in May 1844. *La Revista Católica* (1844), 108.

4. *La Revista Católica* (1844), 17–21.

5. Hughes, *Revelations of Spain*, I, 120.

6. For a discussion of the political history of this period, see Carr, *Spain*, 227–246.

7. Nancy Rosenblatt, "Church and State in Spain: A Study of Moderate Liberal Politics in 1845," *Catholic Historical Review*, 62, no. 4 (1976), 591.

8. Federico Suárez, "Génesis del Concordato de 1851," *Ius Canonicum*, 3 (1963), 98–99.

9. Rosenblatt, "Church and State," 594–598.

10. *El Católico*, no. 3672 (1851). For a general discussion of the political significance of the 1851 settlement, see Nancy Rosenblatt, "The Concordat of 1851 and Its Relation to Moderate Liberalism in Spain," *Iberian Studies*, no. 1 (1978), 30–39.

11. José Luis Comellas, *Los moderados en el poder, 1844–1854* (Madrid, 1970), 298.

12. The concordat provided for the creation of three new dioceses—Ciudad Real, Madrid, and Vitoria—and the union of several dioceses with small populations to larger ones—Albarracín to Teruel, Barbastro to Huesca, Ceuta to Cádiz, Ciudad Rodrigo to Salamanca, Ibiza to Mallorca, Solsona to Vich, Tenerife to Canarias, and Tudela to Pamplona. Article 5 of the concordat, reproduced in Suárez, "Génesis del Concordato," 234.

13. The question, still unresolved when the Second Republic was proclaimed in 1931, arose from the interpretation of Article 29: "In order that in the entire peninsula there should be sufficient number of ministers and evangelical workers whom Prelates may use to conduct missions in the towns of their dioceses, to aid parish priests, to assist the sick, and for other works of charity and public utility, the Government of Her Majesty . . . will soon take convenient measures in order to establish where necessary, having heard the diocesan prelates, religious houses and congregations of the orders of St. Vincent de Paul, St. Philip Neri and *another order approved by the Holy See*." (my italics). Whether the phrase "another order" meant simply that one additional order for the entire country would be added to the two already authorized or that each bishop might invite whatever order he deemed necessary to work in his diocese provoked dispute from the moment of its publication. The Church, of course, accepted the second interpretation; opponents of the orders, the first. Ibid., 243.

14. Ibid., 233–234.

15. In its issue of May 13, 1851, no. 3726, *El Católico* remarked: "it should not be regarded as strange that there should be lively fears that . . . what appears favorable to the Church in this Concordat will not be fulfilled, . . . and even that what is favorable to the Church will be turned to its disadvantage."

16. Jaime Balmes believed that 125 million reales was the minimum necessary for the salaries of the parish clergy and that the expenditures on *culto y clero* in the years preceding his calculation (made for 1840) could not satisfy "even the most urgent necessities." He believed that his estimate of 265 million reales was barely adequate. *Observaciones sociales, políticas y económicas sobre los bienes del clero* (Vich, 1840), 83. The State budgeted 75,784,806 reales for the parish clergy in 1851. *El Católico*, no. 3659 (1851).

17. *El Católico*, no. 3726 (1851).

18. For a detailed study of the thought of Cortes, see John T. Graham, *Donoso Cortes* (Columbia, Missouri, 1974).

19. *El Católico*, nos. 3658, 3710 (1851).

20. L. Frías, *La Provincia de España en la Compañia de Jesús, 1815–1863* (Madrid, 1914), 120–121.

21. C. Rabaza, *Historia de las Escuelas Pías en España*, 4 vols. (Valencia, 1917), IV; A. M. Alonso Fernández, *Historia documental de la Congregación de las Hermanas Carmelitas de la Caridad* (Madrid, 1968), 393.

22. *La Cruz* (1854), 737–738.

23. *Boletín Eclesiástico del Arzobispado de Toledo*, March 4, 1854.

24. The entire pastoral letter (April 5, 1854) was printed in *La Cruz* (1854), 516–604.

25. Ibid., 266, 545.

26. The best study of the revolution of 1854 is V. G. Kiernan, *The Revolution of 1854 in Spanish History* (Oxford, 1966).

27. *La Cruz* observed with a certain grim satisfaction: "The thirst for destruction . . . which sacked and burned the luxurious residences of some ministers, not only respected buildings devoted to the cult but also the residences of prelates and priests. Most of the towns where the insurrection spread conducted themselves in the same manner; and although it is no great merit to destroy churches and burn rectories and religious houses, such is the ordinary nature of revolutions that it is necessary to take into account the excesses that are not committed" (1854), 414.

28. Ibid., 416.

29. Ibid., 404.

30. The work in question was *La Reacción y la Revolución*. *La Cruz* (1855), 101.

31. This and the preceding quotation are from the constitutional text reproduced in *La Revista Católica* (1855), 361.

32. Kiernan, *Revolution of 1854*, 126–128. According to *La Revista Católica*, Isabella II called O'Donnell and the minister of war, Luzuriaga, to the palace on February 7 and declared "her explicit desire that in the religious section of the new Constitution the religious unity of Spaniards should be preserved" (1854), 195.

33. Ibid., 197; *La Estrella*, July 16, 1855.

34. *La Cruz* (1855), 114.

35. Segura, *La desamortización*, 175 n. 97.

36. *La Cruz* (1855), 410.

37. Thus, the bishop of Plasencia instructed his clergy that "they should not resist the orders of the government; but they should refuse absolutely to take direct or indirect part in the sale of ecclesiastical property." *La Revista Católica* (1855), 173.

38. Ibid. (1855), 177.

39. "Despacho dirigido al Ministro Plenipotenciario de S. M. cerca de la Santa Sede y circulado a todos los Representantes de España en el extranjero," June 21, 1855, in ibid., 225; "Alocución de nuestro Santo Padre Pío IX, . . . pronunciada en el consistorio secreto del dia 26 de Julio de 1855" in *La Cruz* (1855), 249.

40. Ibid., 474. A government circular to the bishops (April 12, 1855) com-

plained that only six prelates had submitted plans for the restructuring of parishes. *La Revista Católica* (1855), 430.

41. "Presupuesto general eclesiástico, aprobado por las Cortes en 20 de junio último," in ibid., 46–48.

42. "Real orden circular, sobre separación de curas párrocos y ecónomos por circunstancias políticas," May 27, 1855, in ibid., 45.

43. "Circular al venerable clero de la diócesis de Badajoz," June 11, 1855, ibid., 98–99.

44. *La Cruz* (1855), 199.

45. Pastoral Letter of Fray Gregorio Sánchez Rubio, February 2, 1854, *La Cruz* (1854), 67.

46. Pastoral Letter, April 5, 1854, in ibid., 530–531.

47. *La Revista Católica* (1855), 175.

48. Nelson Duran, *La Unión Liberal y la modernización de la España isabelina: Una convivencia frustrada, 1854–1868* (Madrid, 1979), 130–131.

49. *La Cruz* (1858), 592–593; José Manuel Cuenca Toribio, *Estudios sobre la Iglesia española del XIX* (Madrid, 1973), 78. Extravagant rhetoric comparing the campaigns abroad to the great battles of the Spanish past such as Las Navas and Lepanto passed far beyond the practical implications of the modest military victories achieved.

50. Antonio Claret (1807–1870), the son of a Catalan textile manufacturer, was ordained in 1835. After serving as a parish assistant, he began a successful career as a missionary in Catalonia during the 1840's. His success as an evangelist as well as his initiatives in religious propaganda, catechesis, and the foundation of new orders made him one of the most prominent clerics in the Spanish Church. He served in Cuba as archbishop of Santiago before becoming royal confessor, a post he held until the fall of Isabella II in 1868. He died in exile in France in 1870. The standard biography of Claret is Cristóbal Fernández, *San Antonio María Claret* (Madrid, 1950).

51. This quotation and the following are drawn from the perceptive study of José María Vigil Gallego, "San Antonio María Claret: La política de un apoliticismo," in *La política de la Iglesia apolítica* (Valencia, 1975), 88–89.

52. The case reached the British House of Commons, where it was the subject of parliamentary debate. Sir Robert Peel even visited the victim in a Spanish jail. Bonifas Aimé, *Matamoros: L'Aube de la seconde réforme en Espagne* (Pau, 1967), 29. In spite of the Church's obsession with the Protestant threat, the number of religious dissenters was still insignificant by 1870—2,500 formal church members, 8,000 who attended services. C. J. Bartlett, "Religious Toleration in Spain in the Nineteenth Century," *Journal of Ecclesiastical History,* 8 (1956–57), 210.

53. Alberto Jiménez, *Ocaso y restauración: Ensayo sobre la universidad española moderna* (Mexico, 1948), 132.

54. *La Cruz* (1863), 167.

55. "Esposición dirigida a S. M. por el . . . Sr. Arzobispo de Valencia en unión de sus sufragáneos," August 19, 1863, in ibid., 200.

56. José Manuel Cuenca Toribio and S. Miranda García, "Notas para el pontificado burgalés de Fernando de la Puente y Primo de Rivera (1858–1867)," in *Estudios históricos sobre la Iglesia española contemporánea,* 294–296.

57. J. M. Goñi Galarraga, "El reconocimiento de Italia y monseñor Claret," *Anthologica Annua,* 17 (1970), 379–380.

7. *Church and Society, 1844–1868*

1. *La Cruz* (1902), 570.

2. Angel Riesco Terrero, *Evolución histórica de las parroquías en Salamanca* (Salamanca, 1966), 44–54.

3. *El Católico,* no. 3659 (1851), 361.

4. *Censo de la población de España, 1860* (Madrid, 1863), 756–759; Sáez Marín, *Datos sobre la Iglesia española,* 291, 356. The seminary figures, however, include many students who did not intend to pursue a clerical career but were simply obtaining an education.

5. Ibid., 143.

6. A. García Figar, *Vida del Exmo. e Ilmo. Sr. Doctor Don Narciso Martínez Izquierdo* (Madrid, 1960), 156–157, 163.

7. *Estadística de las communidades religiosas existentes en España el 1 de abril de 1923* (Madrid, 1923), xxiii.

8. Sáez Marín, *Datos sobre la Iglesia española,* 286.

9. "Datos estadísticos relativos al personal y a la dotación del clero y del culto," *La Cruz* (1870), 400–402.

10. F. Rodríguez de Coro, *El obispado de Vitoria durante el sexenio revolucionario* (Vitoria, 1976), 315–323; *El Consultor de los Párrocos,* no. 25 (1872), 195–196.

11. *La Cruz* (1854), 569.

12. Ibid. (1863), 44.

13. Cuenca Toribio, *Sociología de una elite de poder,* 165.

14. J. M. de Nadal, *El Obispo Caixal* (Barcelona, 1959), 72.

15. Salvá was a native of Mallorca who had supported the liberal cause in 1810 and 1820. In 1820 he willingly took the required oath to the constitution and supported the proliberal bishop of the diocese, González Vallejo. The restoration of Ferdinand VII to absolute power in 1823 forced Salvá into exile in France, from where he returned in the 1830's. His brother was elected a progresista senator in 1846. A. Ramos Pérez, *El Obispo Salvá: Un capítulo en la historia de Mallorca del s. XIX* (Palma de Mallorca, 1968), 35–53.

16. José Manuel Cuenca Toribio, *El episcopado español en el pontificado de Pío IX* (Valencia, 1974), 26. Of the sixty-eight prelates for whom information on social status is available, sixteen were noblemen, nine were from wealthy families, eleven from the middle classes, and thirty-two from the lower classes, including many of peasant origin.

17. Differences of wealth and prestige among the dioceses of the Spanish Church, although less glaring than in the eighteenth century, were still strong enough to encourage the movement of bishops from lesser to more important sees. The career ambitions of many bishops affected diocesan government adversely in the opinion of Cuenca Toribio. Ibid., 66.

18. Rafael María Sanz de Diego, *Medio siglo de relaciones Iglesia-Estado: El Cardenal Antolín Monescillo y Viso, 1811–1897* (Madrid, 1979), 11.

19. Ibid., 182–183.

20. Monescillo objected, for example, to the arrangement reached between the Narváez government and the papacy without any episcopal consultation to reduce the number of holy days of obligation. He also complained of a government order in 1866 imposing a reduction in clerical salaries, which he declared was "contrary to the desire of the Church to conserve good harmony with the civil power." Ibid., 181.

21. Vicente Cárcel Ortí, *Segunda época del Seminario Conciliar de Valencia, 1845–1896* (Castellón de la Plana, 1967), 8–9; A. Martín, "La supresión de las facultades de Teología en las universidades españolas (1852)," *Anthologica Annua,* 18 (1971), 609–615. In 1854 the progresistas restored these faculties. They survived until 1868, but played a minor role in clerical education.

22. José Manuel Cuenca Toribio, *Notas para el estudio de los seminarios españoles en el pontificado de Pío IX* (Valencia, 1973), 67.

23. *La Cruz* (1858), 265.

24. José Manuel Cuenca Toribio, "Notas para el estudio de los seminarios españoles en el pontificado de Pío IX," *Saitabi* (1973), 61–62.

25. I. García Herrera, *El Cardenal Sancha, 1833–1909* (Madrid, 1969), 47.

26. Kodasver (pseud.), *Medio siglo de vida diocesana matritense, 1913–1963* (Madrid, 1967), 34.

27. *El Católico,* no. 3832 (1851), 610.

28. Miguel Izard, *Industrialización y obrerismo* (Barcelona, 1973), 87; *La Cruz* (1870), 409; *El Católico,* no. 3659 (1851), 361.

29. Juan Villada, *El matrimonio del clero* (Valladolid, 1896), 38. Villada, a parish priest in the diocese of Burgos, provides one of the few highly critical though biased accounts of the condition of the lower clergy in the nineteenth century. Villada's advocacy of marriage for the clergy and his own avowal that he had been living with his housekeeper for many years led the ecclesiastical authorities to expel him from his parish.

30. J. Vicens Vives, *Historia de España y América,* 5 vols. (Barcelona, 1961), IV², 150; Cuenca Toribio, "Los seminarios españoles en el pontificado de Pío IX," 70.

31. Juan Planas, *Arte pastoral o método para governar bien una parroquía,* 2nd ed., 3 vols. (Barcelona, 1860), I, 55, 11, 174.

32. Ibid., 54, 163–167.

33. Ibid., 57, 59, 33, 27.

34. Hilario Herranz Establés, *El párroco y la parroquía en los tiempos presentes* (Barcelona, 1923), 44, 47.

35. Villada, *El matrimonio del clero,* 21, 24.

36. Antonio Calero, *Movimientos sociales en Andalucía, 1820–1936* (Madrid, 1976), 14–17.

37. Santiago José Garciá Mazo, "Sermón sobre la corrupción de costumbres," in *Sermones* (Valladolid, 1847), 97.

38. Antonio María Claret, *Epistolario,* ed. J. M. Gil, 3 vols. (Madrid, 1970), I, 1389–91.

39. José Domingo Costa y Borrás, *Obras,* ed. R. de Ezenarro, 6 vols. (Barcelona, 1865), editor's introduction, I, 33.

40. Ibid., 24.

41. Antolín Monescillo, *Manual de seminarista* (Madrid, 1848), 19.

42. Portero, *Púlpito e ideología,* 215.

43. Casimir Martí, "Datos sobre la sensibilidad social de la Iglesia durante los primeros 30 años del movimiento obrero en España," in *Aproximación a la historia social de la Iglesia española,* ed. M. Andrés et al., 128.

44. Ibid., 133–134.

45. Pastoral Letter, January 30, 1858, in *La Revista Católica* (1858), 401–402.

46. *El Católico,* no. 213 (1840), 225.

47. *La Revista Católica* (1858), 401.

48. Josep Benet and Casimir Martí, *Barcelona a mitjan segle XIX: El moviment obrer durante el Bienni Progresista, 1854–1856,* 2 vols. (Barcelona, 1976), I, 205–206.

49. *La Cruz* (1856), 83.

50. There was one apparent exception to the lack of ecclesiastical imagination before the problem of working-class discontent. In 1851 a former Carmelite friar, Francisco Palau, founded in Barcelona the School of Virtue (Escuela de Virtud) in the church of San Agustín. The school provided instruction on social questions to the workers. During its three-year history it attracted numerous students. In 1854 the progresistas accused Palau of fomenting unrest. The government closed the school and arrested its director. There is, however, no evidence that the School of Virtue was a source of working-class agitation. H. J. Pastor Miralles, "La obra socio-religiosa del P. Francisco Palau en Barcelona, 1851–1854," in *Una figura carismática del siglo XIX: El P. Francisco Palau y Quer, O.C.D., Apostol y Fundador* (Burgos, 1973), 507–512.

51. Peset, *La universidad española,* 461–479, 557–566.

52. Ibid., 577–578.

53. Carr, *Spain,* 303.

54. A. Ollero Tassara, *Universidad y política: Tradición y secularización en el siglo XIX* (Madrid, 1972), 85.

55. Richard Ford, *A Handbook for Travellers in Spain,* 2 vols. (London, 1845), II, 158–159.

56. *Boletín Eclesiástico del Arzobispado de Toledo,* no. 22 (1853), 143; no. 48 (1853), 335–336.

57. *La Cruz* (1854), 644–645.

58. William Christian has noted the connection of religious shrines in northern Spain with monasteries and friaries and the corresponding decline in specific devotions following the suppression of the regulars during the 1830's. *Person and God in a Spanish Valley* (New York, 1972), 53, 55.

59. *La Cruz* (1858), 383–384.

60. "Circular del Señor Obispo de Guadix sobre la dignidad con que ha de celebrarse la Santa Misa," *La Cruz* (1858), 162.

61. Pedro R. Santidrián, *El Padre Sarabía escribe su historia, 1875–1958* (Madrid, 1963), 31.

62. *La Cruz* (1858), 298.

63. Jiménez Duque, *La espiritualidad en el siglo XIX español,* 146–160.

64. "Gacetilla devota de la Corte," *El Católico,* no. 3819 (1851), 475.

65. Fernández, *San Antonio María Claret,* 58, 121.

66. José María Garganta, *Francisco Coll: Fundador de las Dominicanas de la Anunciata* (Valencia, 1976), 155.

67. Claret, *Epistolario,* I, 175–178.

68. *El Católico,* no. 3710 (1851), 163.

69. *La Cruz* (1858), 876. The material following is drawn from an extensive report on the Seville missions in ibid., 870–888.

70. Ibid., 7–8, 88.

71. *El Católico,* no. 3642 (1851), 201; *La Cruz* (1858), 886; Rodríguez de Coro, *El obispado de Vitoria durante el sexenio revolucionario,* 102–103.

72. *El Católico,* no. 3661 (1851), 379.

73. *La Cruz* (1858), 887.

74. Costa y Borrás, *Obras*, I, 25.

75. *La Cruz* (1863), 252. The hostility of the progresistas to the missions confirms their identification with the moderados. The Jesuit missions in San Sebastián in 1854 provoked a war of opinion between their supporters, known as "Russians," and their opponents, called "Turks"—labels drawn, of course, from the contending parties in the Crimean War, which had just begun. Ibid. (1854), 707–708.

76. Antonio María Claret, *Catecisme de la doctina cristiana*, 2nd ed. (Barcelona, 1850).

77. Santiago José García Mazo, *Diario de la piedad o breve reglamento espiritual dirigido a una alma deseosa de su salvación* (Valladolid, 1839).

78. Antonio María Claret, *Camino recto y seguro para llegar al cielo*, 181st ed. (Madrid, 1955), 81.

79. *La Cruz* (1858), 459.

80. Garganta, *Francisco Coll*, 137.

81. *Boletín Oficial Eclesiástico del Obispado de Málaga* (Malaga, 1887), 42.

82. Pedro María Ayala, *Vida documentada del Siervo de Dios, P. Francisco de Paula Tarín de la Compañia de Jesús* (Seville, 1951), 217, 292.

83. Benet and Martí, *Barcelona a mitjan segle XIX*, 203–204.

84. *La Revista Católica* (1858), 393, 397.

85. R. Duocastella, "El mapa religioso de España," in *Cambio social y religión en España* (Barcelona, 1975), 137.

86. Eliseo Sainz Ripa, "La religiosidad en La Rioja durante el siglo XIX," *Berceo*, no. 83 (1972), 165, 181.

87. Sáez de Ocariz, "El cumplimiento pascual en la ciudad de Logroño," 277–279.

88. Herranz Establés, *El párroco y la parroquía*, 315.

89. Francisco Peiró, *El problema religioso-social de España*, 2nd ed. (Madrid, 1936), 14–15.

90. Claret, *Epistolario*, I, 691.

91. *Revista Popular*, no. 109 (1873), 37.

8. From Revolution to Restoration, 1868–1874

1. P. Méndez Mori, *El Emmo. Sr. Cardenal Sanz y Forés, Obispo de Oviedo, 1868–1882* (Oviedo, 1928), 40–41; *La Cruz* (1869), 124–129; Juan Bautista Vilar, *El obispado de Cartagena durante el sexenio revolucionario* (Murcia, 1973), 22.

2. "Decreto del Gobierno Provisional," October 12, 1868, in *La Cruz* (1868), 347.

3. "Esposición de el Obispo de Jaén al Exmo. Señor Ministro de Gracia y Justicia." October 25, 1868; "Carta circular del Arzobispo de Zaragoza al venerable clero de esta diócesis sobre la revolución," October 16, 1868, in *La Cruz* (1868), 372, 365.

4. Santiago Petschen, *Iglesia-Estado: Un cambio polítco: Las Constituyentes de 1869* (Madrid, 1974), 208.

5. "Manifiesto del Gobierno Provisional a la nación," October 25, 1868, in *La Cruz* (1868), 357–358.

6. The quotations in this paragraph are drawn from ibid., 457, 464–469, 500.

7. Ibid., 504. The first president of the association was the marqués de Viluma, a moderado and supporter of Isabella II. Of the two vice-presidents,

one, the conde de Vigo, was a moderado; the other, the conde de Orgaz, was a Carlist. José Andrés Gallego, *La política religiosa en España, 1889–1913* (Madrid, 1975), 1.

8. *El Pensamiento Español,* January 15, 1869.

9. Ibid., January 12, 16, 1869.

10. Ibid., January 11, 19, 1869.

11. *La Cruzada,* February 6, 1869.

12. *La Cruz* (1869), 270–278.

13. The debates in the Cortes are extensively analyzed in Petschen, *Iglesia-Estado.*

14. *El Pensamiento Español,* February 4, 1869.

15. Ibid., January 22, 1869.

16. Carmen Llorca, *Emilio Castelar: Precursor de la Democracia Cristiana* (Madrid, 1966), 142. Article 20 of the proposed constitutional text, "the Nation is obliged to maintain the cult and the ministers of the Catholic Religion," was approved by a vote of 178 to 75; Article 21 establishing toleration was approved 164 to 40. Vicente Cárcel Ortí, *Iglesia y revolución en España, 1868–1874* (Pamplona, 1979), 197.

17. *La Cruz* (1869), 690–694.

18. *El Pensamiento Español,* May 12, 1869.

19. *La Cruz* (1869), 706–710, 141. The resistance of the bishops to the oath has been treated in detail by Cárcel Ortí, *Iglesia y revolución,* 412–437. In the end, a face-saving formula was approved by the papacy to end the impasse with the State over the oath for churchmen.

20. This estimate was made by the journal of liberal clerics, *La Armonía del Catolicismo y Libertad,* April 11, 1871. It may well have been an exaggeration.

21. "Pastoral del Sr. Obispo de Almería sobre el juramento" June 15, 1870, in *La Cruz* (1870), 140–141.

22. "Esposición de los Prelados españoles residentes en Roma," April 26, 1870, in ibid., 465–467.

23. *La Armonía,* December 17, 1870.

24. Ibid., November 15, 1870.

25. Ibid., October 19, 1871. *La Armonía* complained bitterly of the favors the government dispensed toward clergy whose views were "anathema to liberty," while loyal priests were ignored. In the issue of November 19, 1870, the journal published a pathetic letter from the parish priest of a village of eighty residents. A *cura* for more than thirty years, he had not received the salary promised by the State in a year even though he had sworn the oath to the constitution. "And I have taken the oath so that I and my parish can die of hunger?" he asked rhetorically.

26. José Antonio Ortiz Urruela, *La Iglesia católica y la revolución de septiembre* (Madrid, 1869), 27; "Esposición del metropolitano y sufragáneos de Tarragona a las Cortes Constituyentes contra el matrimonio civil," June 19, 1869, in *La Cruz* (1869), 183–187.

27. *El Consultor de los Párrocos,* September 12, May 16, 1872. This journal for the guidance of the parish clergy was explicit in its denunciation of civil marriage. "The person married civilly, since he rejects the benediction of the Church, is nothing more than a heretic and guilty of public concubinage." Ibid., June 6, 1872. Similar conflicts took place between parish priests and local authorities over the ringing of church bells, which the latter claimed could be used

in nonreligious situations, as, of course, they traditionally had been in many villages.

28. The text is reproduced in *La Cruz* (1870), 380; "Esposiciones de los Señores Obispos sobre los proyectos de ley de 22 de marzo 1870," in ibid., 471–479. Pressure to reduce the ecclesiastical budget had been constant since 1869 but was not initially successful. In the waning months of the democratic monarchy, Montero Ríos, again serving as minister of grace and justice, proposed legislation, eventually passed by parliament, that reduced the budget for *culto y clero* substantially. By this time, however, the issue was academic given the desperate fiscal plight of the government, which had long since fallen behind in its financial support of the Church. The terms of the law of December 26, 1872, on ecclesiastical finances are discussed by Cárcel Ortí, *Iglesia y revolución*, 282–290.

29. The delicate negotiations in 1870 over the candidacy of the duke of Aosta for the Spanish throne further complicated relations between the Vatican and Madrid. The government, however, urged Pius IX not to abandon Rome upon its occupation by the kingdom of Italy. Jesús Pabón, *España y la cuestión romana* (Madrid, 1972), 101. News of the occupation produced fervent expressions of support for the pope among Spanish Catholics. The Association of Catholics appealed "for a collective manifestation of sorrow" because of the "unjust despoliation" suffered by the pope when he lost his temporal power. *La Cruz* (1870), 664. For a general discussion of relations between the papacy and the Spanish government during this period, see Jerónimo Becker, *Relaciones diplomáticas entre España y la Santa Sede* (Madrid, 1908), chap. 15.

30. Decree, August 4, 1869, in *La Cruz* (1869), 225.

31. Ibid., 378. Thus, Bishop Uriz, who presided over the diocese of Pamplona in the heart of a region sympathetic to Carlism, preached on the "necessity of peace and the horrors of civil war," in effect repudiating the Carlist cause as a reasonable political option for the Church. José Manuel Cuenca Toribio, *Sociedad y clero en la España del XIX* (Córdoba, 1980), 166–171.

32. *El Consultor de los Párrocos,* October 16, 1872.

33. *La Cruz* (1872), 485.

34. M. T. Aubach Guiu, "El Instituto catalán de artesanos y obreros: Obra del Obispo Lluch y Garriga," *Salamanticensis*, 22, no. 1 (1975), 124.

35. *El Consultor de los Párrocos,* February 20, 1873.

36. "Contestación del Señor Arzobispo de Granada al Gobernador Civil sobre el establecimiento de la República," February 12, 1873, in *La Cruz* (1873), 296.

37. *Revista Popular,* March 8, 1873, 114.

38. *El Consultor de los Párrocos,* June 19, 1873.

39. The best study on the Republic is C. A. M. Hennessy, *The Federal Republic in Spain: Pi y Margall and the Federal Republican Movement, 1868–1874* (Oxford, 1962).

40. *El Pensamiento Español,* April 5, 21, 1873.

41. The program of the Committee of Public Safety in Cádiz is reproduced in ibid., July 19, 1873.

42. *La Cruz* (1873), 246.

43. The bishop of Cádiz, Félix María de Arrieta y Llano, remained in the city during the height of the anticlerical campaign of the canton. He protested against the measures being taken, but with moderation. After the short-lived

republican rising of December 1868, he opened a subscription to aid those wounded during the struggle and petitioned the head of the provisional government, General Serrano, to grant clemency to Republicans placed under arrest upon the rebellion's suppression. Carmen Llorca, *Cádiz y la Primera República* (Cádiz, 1973), 25. Another reason for the lack of violence against the clergy may have been the opposition of the cantonalists, save for those in Sanlúcar, to social revolution. The "political" character of the cantonalist movement in Andalusia has been noted by Temma Kaplan, *Anarchists of Andalusia, 1868–1903* (Princeton, 1977), 108.

44. The minister further assured the bishop that he would take the necessary action so that "the legitimate rights of the Church might be safe-guarded." Minister of Grace and Justice to Bishop Pérez Fernández, July 7, 1873, in *La Cruz* (1873), 242.

45. See the article "Los horrores de Alcoy" in ibid., 242–244.

46. *El Pensamiento Español*, March 17, July 15, 1873.

47. Ibid., suplemento, February 6, 1873.

48. Ibid., September 6, 1873.

49. E. Carro Celada, *Curas guerrilleros en España* (Madrid, 1971), 218, 224.

50. Ildefonso de Ciáurriz, *Vida del Siervo de Dios P. Fr. Esteban de Adoáin, capuchino* (Barcelona, 1913), 356.

51. *El Pensamiento Español*, April 17, 1873.

52. Jaime Vicens Vives, *Cataluña en el siglo XIX* (Madrid, 1961), 419–421; Román Oyarzun, *Historia del Carlismo* (Madrid, 1969), 375–396.

53. The congregation leaving the Carmelite church in Barcelona after services marking the feast of the Sacred Heart found a hostile crowd shouting accusations against the preacher for having "acclaimed Charles VII from the pulpit." *El Pensamiento Español*, July 10, 1873.

54. *El Pensamiento Español* (April 15, 1873) declared: "the city government, which is Republican, has conducted itself honorably. We acknowledge this with great pleasure, since we have good friends in that body."

55. Ibid., April 24, 1873.

56. From the text of the draft law reproduced in *Semana Católica* (1873), 510–511.

57. *El Consultor de los Párrocos*, July 31, 1873. Episcopal protests, however, were less vitriolic. The bishops of the ecclesiastical province of Valladolid wrote to the Cortes and argued that separation was another step on the road to moral dissolution and social revolution. They also stressed the identification of Spain's past glories with the Church: "Spain cannot live separated from the Church. Formed by Catholicism, it owes to the Church whatever it has accomplished in the development of its civilization." "Protesta de los Sres. Prelados de la provincia eclesiástica de Valladolid a las Cortes," August 1, 1873, in *La Cruz* (1873), 234–238.

58. *El Consultor de los Párrocos*, February 27, 1873; *El Pensamiento Español*, August 5, 1873.

59. *El Pensamiento Español*, December 22, 1873. Castelar, however, did not exercise the traditional regalian rights of the State over ecclesiastical patronage. The list of episcopal appointments was worked out through careful and courteous negotiations with the papacy. Becker, *Relaciones diplomáticas*, 264.

60. Ibid.

61. *El Consultor de los Párrocos*, February 8, 1874; "Decreto de la República

restableciendo las ordenes militares," April 11, 1874, in *La Cruz* (1874), 636–640.

62. J. M. Amenos, "El fomento de vocaciones eclesiásticas en España durante la segunda mitad del siglo XIX," *Seminarios*, 1 (1955), 61; *La España Católica*, April 20, 1875; *El Pensamiento Español*, November 11, 1873.

63. Fund-raising efforts often followed the model devised by the bishop of the Canaries, Bernardo Martínez. Parish juntas formed by the *cura* and four laymen sought long-term subscriptions payable on a monthly basis from the faithful. "Obra para el sostenimiento del culto y clero, creada por el Sr. Obispo de Canarias," May 4, 1873, in *La Cruz* (1873), 677–683. The success of these efforts varied from region to region. In Jaén, located in the dechristianized south, they produced so little that the diocesan authorities believed they would have to close the cathedral; but in Toledo the results of a subscription campaign based on the Canaries model "completely fulfilled expectations"; some parishes contributed more than was necessary. *El Pensamiento Español*, October 10, 1874; *El Consultor de los Párrocos*, October 1, 1873.

64. The process of adjusting Church-State relations, however, was not without difficulties, which have been described in detail in the recent study of María F. Núñez, *La Iglesia y la restauración, 1875–1881* (Santa Cruz de Tenerife, 1976); and by G. Barberini, "El articulo 11 de la Constitución de 1876: La controversia diplomática entre España y la Santa Sede," *Anthologica Annua*, 9 (1961), 279–412.

65. Félix Sardá y Salvany, *El liberalismo es pecado?* 2nd ed. (Barcelona, 1884).

66. See, for example, the complaints about inadequate state financing from two bishops of the early-twentieth-century Church, Antolín López Peláez, archbishop of Tarragona, *El presupuesto del clero* (Madrid, 1910); and Enrique Reig y Casanova, archbishop of Toledo, *Presente y porvenir económico de la Iglesia en España* (Madrid, 1908).

67. José de los Perales y Gutiérrez, *El problema religioso en España* (Madrid, 1909), 97.

68. Bruno Ibeas, "Nuestro Cristianismo," *España y América*, 12, no. 3 (1914), 514.

Bibliographic Essay

The literature dealing with the Spanish Church from the eighteenth century to the present is extensive. On the whole the history of the Church has been written by clergymen or laymen sympathetic to its religious mission. Histories of dioceses and religious orders, episcopal biographies, and works on the state of civil-ecclesiastical relations dominate traditional writing on the subject. Its quality varies from simple hagiographies or polemics to documented institutional studies, such as López Ferreiro's fine history of the diocese of Santiago de Compostela. The quality of historical writing from within the Church has improved dramatically in the past two decades with the emergence of a new generation of ecclesiastical historians. Their publications are characterized by solid archival work and a new spirit of self-criticism made possible, perhaps, by the liberating effects of the Second Vatican Council. The books of Antonio Mestre Sanchis, José Manuel Cuenca Toribio, Vicente Cárcel Ortí, Manuel Revuelta González, and others quickly come to mind. The study of the Church has also benefited from attention by social and economic historians, who are less interested in it as a religious institution than as an essential part of the broader society and economy. The work of Gonzalo Anes on the eighteenth-century economy, Pablo Fernández Albaladejo on Guipúzcoa, Angel García Sanz on Segovia, and a number of scholars who have studied the disamortization process of the nineteenth century has made possible a more complete analysis of the Church's economic role within Spanish society.

In spite of the progress these studies represent, this division of research has left important gaps in our knowledge. Research originating within the Church, whether done by clerics or laymen, still tends to follow the path of traditional ecclesiastical history, with heavy emphases on the relations between Church and State, episcopal biographies, and the development of institutions. The study of popular religion—which Catholic sociologists of religion have developed successfully in France, Italy, and Poland—has scarcely appeared in Spain, apart from several studies of contemporary religious practice and William Christian's fine examination of popular beliefs in a region of northern Spain. Little has been done on the social history of the lower clergy in spite of their

obvious importance, although a recent study on the priests of Toledo
in the early nineteenth century by Leandro Higueruela del Pino partially
remedied this deficiency. Nor is there an adequate general study of the
Church's role in education. And work on the charitable function of the
Church, so crucial to its position within Old Regime society, is just beginning.

The contribution of social and economic historians, who are indifferent to the religious aspects of the Church's history, has been useful. But
their work has focused largely on the period before the sale of ecclesiastical lands beginning in 1836. The question of Church wealth after
that, so controversial in the great anticlerical battles of the twentieth
century, has been generally ignored. Historians of pronounced secular
views tend to be uninterested in the Church save in a limited economic
and social context that is frequently Marxist. But it is unlikely that any
convincing study of nineteenth-century anticlericalism can be written
without the contribution of historians of popular movements willing to
explore the radicalization of the urban masses that was clearly taking
place during the first four decades of the century. The history of the
Spanish Church, then, offers abundant opportunities for further work
to historians of different outlooks—whether of the right, left, or center.

The following is a brief, select bibliography designed to call attention
primarily to recent literature on the Spanish Church.

Bibliography and General

Two standard bibliographies, B. Sánchez Alonso, *Fuentes de la historia
española e hispanoamericana,* 3rd ed., 3 vols. (Madrid, 1952) and the bibliographic periodical *Indice Histórico Español* (1953–1976), continue to be
useful, although the historian interested in the Church will find more
manageable bibliographic information following each entry in the *Diccionario de historia eclesiástica de España,* 4 vols. (Madrid, 1972–1975) as
well as the bibliographic essay in Vicente Cárcel Ortí, ed., *La Iglesia en
la España contemporánea, 1808–1975* (Madrid, 1979), xxv–xxxvii. José
Manuel Cuenca Toribio and Jesús Longares Alonso have surveyed recent
periodical literature in *Bibliografía de historia de la Iglesia* (Valencia and
Córdoba, 1976).

There are few good general histories of the Spanish Church. Of several nineteenth-century attempts the best is Vicente de la Fuente, *Historia
eclesiástica de España,* 6 vols. (Madrid, 1873–1875). An attempt to remedy
this deficiency has been undertaken by the Biblioteca de Autores Cris-
tianos under the direction of R. García Villoslada. Volume 5 of this
general history (Cárcel Ortí, ed., cited above) contains essays on the
Church since 1808 by several authors. Inevitably in a collective work the

emphasis varies from piece to piece, but in general the essays concentrate on the political struggle between the Church and liberalism in the nineteenth century and on the great social and political conflicts of the twentieth century. Two studies on more precise themes, Juan Sáez Marín, *Datos sobre la Iglesia española contemporánea, 1768–1868* (Madrid, 1975) and José Manuel Cuenca Toribio, *Sociología de una elite de poder de España e Hispanoamérica contemporáneas: La jerarquía eclesiástica, 1789–1965* (Córdoba, 1976), provide overviews of ecclesiastical demography and the hierarchy respectively.

The Old Regime Church

The best general descriptions of the organizational, social, and economic structure of the eighteenth-century Church are to be found in Antonio Domínguez Ortiz, *La sociedad española en el siglo XVIII* (Madrid, 1955) and *Sociedad y Estado en el siglo XVIII español* (Madrid, 1976). A survey of the eighteenth-century Church is W. J. Callahan, "The Spanish Church," in *Church and Society in Catholic Europe of the Eighteenth Century*, ed. W. J. Callahan and D. C. Higgs (Cambridge, 1979), 34–50. Both Richard Herr, *The Eighteenth-Century Revolution in Spain* (Princeton, 1958), and Jean Sarrailh, *L'Espagne éclairée de la seconde moitié du XVIIIe siècle* (Paris, 1954), devote considerable attention to the relationship of the Church to the Spanish Enlightenment. C. C. Noël focuses on the opposition within the Church to the reforming tendencies of the Bourbon State in two fine articles: "Opposition to Enlightened Reform in Spain: Campomanes and the Clergy, 1765–1775," *Societas*, 3, no. 1 (1973), 21–43; and "The Clerical Confrontation with the Enlightenment in Spain," *European Studies Review*, 5, no. 2 (1975), 103–122. The struggle between the Bourbons and Rome for control of the Spanish Church has been considered in detail by Rafael Olaechea, *Las relaciones hispano-romanas en la segunda mitad del siglo XVIII*, 2 vols. (Zaragoza 1965).

The reforming movement in the late-eighteenth-century Church has produced an abundant literature. Émile Appolis, *Les jansénistes espagnols* (Bordeaux, 1966), provides a general treatment of the so-called Jansenist movement within the framework of a reforming spirit in eighteenth-century Catholicism. In a short but interesting study María Giovanna Tomisch, *El jansenismo en España* (Madrid, 1972), analyzes the doctrinal and philosophical content of Spanish Jansenism. This theme is treated in greater detail by Joël Saugnieux, *Le jansénisme espagnol du XVIII siècle: Ses composantes et ses sources* (Oviedo, 1976). The same author's biography of a leading Jansenist reformer, *Un prelat éclairé: Don Antonio Tavira y Almazán, 1737–1807* (Toulouse, 1970), offers a case study of reform in action at the diocesan level. Saugnieux has also studied the reform of sacred oratory to which the Jansenists attached great importance: *Les jansénistes et le renouveau de la prédication dans l'Espagne de la seconde moitié du XVIIIe siècle* (Lyon, 1976). Antonio Mestre Sanchis has studied an earlier reformer in *Ilustración y reforma de la Iglesia: Pensamiento político-religioso de Don Gregorio Mayáns y Siscar, 1699–1781* (Valencia, 1968). The controversy over the Jesuits, so closely connected to the issues of regalism and ecclesiastical reform, has produced an extensive literature, of which there is a general review in the perceptive introduction of Jorge Cejudo and Teofanes Egido to Pedro Rodríguez de Campomanes, *Dictamen fiscal de expulsión de los Jesuitas de España, 1766–1767* (Madrid, 1977).

In spite of an abundance of literature on ecclesiastical institutions during the eighteenth century, much remains to be done. There are few good diocesan histories. Antonio López Ferreiro's massive history of the archdiocese of Santiago, *Historia de la Santa A. M. Iglesia de Santiago de Compostela*, 11 vols. (Santiago, 1898–1909), still has few competitors for completeness and faithfulness to documentary sources. Episcopal biographies are slightly more numerous, but on the whole not satisfactory save for the recent study of Cardinal Lorenzana, one of the key figures in the Caroline Church, by Luis Sierra Nava-Lasa, *El Cardenal Lorenzana y la Ilustración* (Madrid, 1975), and the biography of Bishop Tavira by Saugnieux (cited above). The recent biography of José Climent, one of the leading reformers of the reign of Charles III, is based on solid research although rather uncritical of its subject: Francesc Tort Mitjans, *El Obispo de Barcelona: Josep Climent i Avinent, 1706–1781* (Barcelona, 1978).

The important topic of episcopal recruitment has been largely neglected save for the brief treatments of Domínguez Ortiz and Cuenca Toribio (cited above), although C. C. Noël's forthcoming study on the subject should remedy this deficiency. Recent work on the capitular clergy has produced a more complete view of the role of cathedral canons in the eighteenth-century Church. Juan Ramón López-Arévalo's *Un cabildo catedral de la Vieja Castilla: Ávila* (Madrid, 1966) provides a detailed account of an Old Regime chapter. There is a good general history of eighteenth-century seminaries: Francisco Martín Hernández and José Martín Hernández, *Los seminarios españoles en la época de la Ilustración* (Madrid, 1973). The condition of the secular clergy below the level of the ecclesiastical elite has been largely ignored. Leandro Higueruela del Pino's short pamphlet summarizing his doctoral thesis, *El clero de la diócesis de Toledo durante el pontificado del Cardenal Borbón* (Madrid, 1973), provides one of the few glimpses of the social and cultural condition of the parish clergy. A more complete view is given in the same author's monograph on the subject: *El clero de Toledo desde 1800 a 1823* (Madrid, 1979).

There is an enormous literature on the history of the religious orders, but much of it is narrowly institutional in focus and neglects the broader social and economic role of the regulars. Among the better institutional histories are *Historia del Real Monasterio de Poblet,* 6 vols. (Barcelona, 1947–1955); and Antonio Astraín, *Historia de la Compañia de Jesús en la asistencia de España,* 8 vols. (Madrid, 1902–1925). Two more recent works on the Franciscans are more successful in relating the history of the order and its branches to cultural and social conditions: Fray Melchor de Pobladura, *Seminarios de misioneros y conventos de perfecta vida común* (Rome, 1963); and Fray Buenaventura de Carrocera, *La provincia de Frailes Menores Capuchinos de Castilla, 1701–1836* (Madrid, 1973).

There is an extensive bibliography on the Inquisition. Henry Kamen provides a brief overview of its role in the eighteenth century in *The Spanish Inquisition* (London and Bloomington, 1965), and Marcelin Defourneaux has described its ambiguous relationship to the Spanish Enlightenment in his excellent biography *Pablo de Olavide ou l'Afrancesado, 1725–1803* (Paris, 1959) and in *L'Inquisition espagnole et les livres français au XVIIIe siècle* (Paris, 1963). A collaborative work by Bartolomé Bennassar and others analyzes the Inquisition in the light of recent research: *L'Inquisition espagnole, XVe–XIXe siècle* (Paris, 1979). Although Antonio Alvárez de Morales gives too much attention to the juridical procedures of the eighteenth-century Inquisition, he provides one of the few useful studies devoted to the institution in its period of decline: *Inquisición e Ilustración, 1700–1834* (Madrid, 1982).

There is as yet no general study of ecclesiastical finances and the impact of the Church on the economy, but a number of well-researched studies in the past ten years have substantially enlarged knowledge of the topic. The best overview of Church wealth is in Gonzalo Anes, *Las crisis agrarias en la España moderna* (Madrid, 1970). The revenues of individual bishoprics have been studied for Castile and Aragón respectively by Christian Hermann, "Les revenus des évêques espagnols au dix-huitième siècle, 1650–1830," *Mélanges de la Casa de Velázquez,* 10 (1974), 169–201; and Antonio Domínguez Ortiz, "Las rentas episcopales de la corona de Aragón en el siglo XVIII," in *Agricultura, comercio colonial y crecimiento económico en la España contemporánea,* ed. J. Nadal and G. Tortella (Barcelona, 1974), 13–43. The best and most complete study of ecclesiastical finances in the Old Regime, although limited to a single diocese, is Maximiliano Barrio Gozalo, *Estudio socio-económico de la Iglesia de Segovia en el siglo XVIII* (Segovia, 1982). Several regional studies have ably illuminated the impact of the Church on local economies. Pablo Fernández Albaladejo, *La crisis del antiguo régimen en Guipúzcoa, 1766–1833* (Madrid, 1975); Angel García Sanz, *Desarrollo y crisis del antiguo régimen en Castilla la Vieja: Economía y sociedad en tierras de Segovia, 1500–1814* (Madrid, 1977); and Jaime García Lombardero, *La agricultura y el estancamiento económico de Galicia en la España del antiguo régimen* (Madrid, 1973) are among the best.

Study of the Church's role within the context of Spanish society is only beginning. Save for the occasional article, popular religion has been largely ignored in spite of its obvious importance. There is nothing comparable to Julio Caro Baroja's study of the sixteenth and seventeenth centuries: *Las formas complejas de la vida religiosa: Religión, sociedad y caracter en España de los siglos XVI y XVII* (Madrid, 1978). Although only marginally concerned with the eighteenth century, William Christian's *Local Religion in Sixteenth-Century Spain* (Princeton, 1981) provides an interesting interpretation and a wealth of information on this important but relatively unstudied theme.

There is no single study of the crisis of the Church during the two decades preceding the events of 1808. The impact of the French Revolution has been studied by Francisco Martí Gilabert, *La Iglesia en España durante la revolución francesa* (Pamplona, 1971), although more remains to be done for the period from a broader perspective. There are two interesting studies of the increasingly conservative nature of the Church through the early nineteenth century. Fundamental in spite of its dense quality is Alfredo Martínez Albiach, *Religiosidad hispana y sociedad borbónica* (Burgos, 1969). Also useful is Javier Herrero, *Los origenes del pensamiento reaccionario español* (Madrid, 1971). Luis Sierra Nava-hasa discusses the regalist conflicts of the late 1790's in *La reacción del episcopado español ante los decretos de matrimonios del ministro Urquijo de 1799 a 1813* (Bilbao, 1964). The tensions within the Church over the issue of internal reform are considered in W. J. Callahan, "Two Spains and Two Churches, 1760–1835," *Historical Reflections*, 2, no. 2 (1975), 158–181. Richard Herr's analysis of the first disamortization, which had serious implications for the Church, illuminates a hitherto obscure area of financial and economic history at the end of the Old Regime: "Hacia el derrumbe del antiguo régimen: Crisis fiscal y desamortización fiscal bajo Carlos IV," *Moneda y Crédito*, no. 118 (1971), 37–100.

The Conflict with Liberalism, 1808–1833

For general background the work of Miguel Artola on the period 1808–1814 is valuable: *Los origenes de la España contemporánea*, 2 vols. (Madrid, 1959). Juan Marichal describes the debt of the reformers of Cádiz to the ideas advanced at the Synod of Pistoia in "From Pistoia to Cádiz: A Generation's Itinerary, 1786–1812," in *The Ibero-American Enlightenment*, ed. A. Owen Aldridge (Urbana, 1971), 97–110. The effect on the Church of the long crisis that began in 1793 is discussed in W. J. Callahan, "The Origins of the Conservative Church in Spain, 1793–1823," *European Studies Review*, 10 (1980), 199–223. The hostility of the hierarchy toward the ecclesiastical policies of the Cortes has been described from the Church's point of view by Isidoro de Villapadierna, "El episcopado español y las Cortes de Cádiz," *Hispania Sacra*, 8, no. 16 (1955), 275–335. The struggle at Cádiz over the fate of the Inquisition has been studied in detail by Francisco Martí Gilabert, *La abolición de la Inquisición en España* (Pamplona, 1975).

Also useful for clerical opposition to reform is the work of Martínez Albiach (cited above). José Manuel Cuenca Toribio's biography of one of the leading defenders of the Old Regime Church until the early 1830's is one of the few studies of this kind for the period: *D. Pedro de Inguanzo y Rivero, 1764–1836: Último prelado del antiguo régimen* (Pamplona, 1965). For the conflict between the Church and liberalism during the revolutionary period 1820–1823, the fundamental work is Manuel Revuelta González, *Política religiosa de los liberales del siglo XIX: Trienio constitucional* (Madrid, 1973). Three articles treating the same theme are also useful: José Manuel Cuenca Toribio, "La Iglesia española en el trienio constitucional, 1820–1823," *Hispania Sacra*, 18, no. 36 (1965), 333–362; Francisco Xavier Tapía, "Las relaciones Iglesia-Estado durante el primer experimento liberal en España, 1820–1823," *Revista de Estudios Políticos*, no. 173 (1970), 69–89; and Juan Mercader Riba, "Los origenes del anticlericalismo español," *Hispania*, 123 (1973), 101–123. Of particular value is a regional study of the impact of the revolution of 1820 on the clergy of Catalonia: Gaspar Feliu i Montfort, *La clerecia catalana durant el trienni liberal* (Barcelona, 1972). A well-researched study of the disamortization of 1820–1823, although regional in emphasis, is Joan Brines Blasco, *La desamortización en el País Valenciano durante el trienio constitucional* (Valencia, 1978).

The final period of Ferdinand VII's absolute rule has been less studied. But Luis Alonso Tejada describes the conflict over the Inquisition among supporters of absolute monarchy and its impact on the conservative direction of the Church during the late 1820's and early 1830's in *Ocaso de la Inquisición en los últimos años del reinado de Fernando VII* (Madrid, 1969). There is very little on the financial, social, and economic role of the Church, although it is clear that the institution experienced changes during this period that were fundamentally important for its later condition under liberalism. Studies of declining Church wealth, clerical demography and recruitment, the erosion of ecclesiastical charity, and changes in evangelization methods are needed, perhaps for this period more than any other.

The Conflict with Liberalism, 1834–1874

The period after the death of Ferdinand VII has received more extensive study. There are several good books on general background. Raymond Carr provides an interpretive overview of the complexities of liberal politics in *Spain, 1808–1939* (Oxford, 1966). Excellent studies of specific periods are Carlos Marichal, *Spain, 1834–1844* (London, 1977); V. G. Kiernan, *The Revolution of 1854 in Spanish History* (Oxford, 1966); and C. A. M. Hennessy, *The Federal Republic in Spain: Pi y Margall and the Federal Republican Movement, 1868–1874* (Oxford, 1962). Several collections of essays provide useful information about the nineteenth-century Church: José Manuel Cuenca Toribio, *La Iglesia española ante la revolución liberal* (Madrid, 1971); *Iglesia y burguesía en la España liberal* (Jaén, 1979); *Estudios sobre la Iglesia andaluza moderna y contemporánea* (Córdoba, 1980); *Sociedad y clero en la España del XIX* (Córdoba, 1980); and J. Andrés Gallego et al., *Estudios históricos sobre la Iglesia española contemporánea* (El Escorial, 1979) and *Aproximación a la historia social de la Iglesia española contemporánea* (El Escorial, 1978).

The struggle between the Church and the liberal State of the 1830's has received considerable attention in a number of well-researched works written from a proecclesiastical perspective. Manuel Revuelta González' study of the nearly complete extinction of the regular clergy, *La exclaustración, 1833–1840* (Madrid, 1976), is impressive, although it does not sufficiently emphasize the weaknesses of the Old Regime religious orders. Vicente Cárcel Ortí describes in detail the condition of civil-ecclesiastical relations during the 1830's in *Política eclesial de los gobiernos liberales españoles, 1830–1840* (Pamplona, 1975). Jesús Longares Alonso considers the impact of liberalism in a local setting in *Política y religión en Barcelona, 1833–1843* (Madrid, 1976). The same author has written an interesting, though sketchy, general essay on liberal ideas on the Church: *La ideología religiosa del liberalismo español, 1808–1843* (Córdoba, 1979). José Antonio Portero applied the techniques of Martínez Albiach to analyze the Church's difficult adaptation to the new bourgeois society created by liberalism in *Púlpito e ideología en la España del siglo XIX* (Zaragoza, 1978). Nancy Rosenblatt studied the politics of accommodation worked out between the Church and the moderate elements of liberalism in three articles: "The Spanish *Moderados* and the Church," *Catholic Historical Review*, 57, no. 3 (1971), 401–420; "Church and State in Spain: A Study of Moderate Liberal Politics in 1845," *Catholic Historical Review*, 62, no. 4 (1976), 589–603; and "The Concordat of 1851 and Its Relation to Moderate Liberalism in Spain," *Iberian Studies*, no. 1 (1978), 30–39. Jerónimo Becker's older work on Spanish-Vatican relations is still useful for this topic: *Relaciones diplomáticas entre España y la Santa Sede* (Madrid, 1908). Regrettably, there is no good study of the relationship between Carlism and the Church.

The situation of the Church during the revolutionary period 1868–1874 has been studied by Vicente Cárcel Ortí with particular emphasis on relations between the State and Rome and civil-ecclesiastical relations within Spain in *Iglesia y revolución en España, 1868–1874* (Pamplona, 1979). Santiago Petschen has analyzed debates on the Church and the question of religious liberty in the revolutionary Cortes of 1869 in *Iglesia-Estado: Un cambio político: Las Constituyentes de 1869* (Madrid, 1974). Jesús Pabón's *España y la cuestión romana* (Madrid, 1972) deals with the impact of the occupation of Rome by Victor Emmanuel and its effect on Spanish politics. María F. Núñez describes the initial stages of the Church's adaptation to the new political circumstances of the restoration in *La Iglesia y la restauración, 1875–1881* (Santa Cruz de Tenerife, 1976). The impact of the revolution on the Church in regional settings is discussed in Juan Bautista Vilar, *El obispado de Cartagena durante el sexenio revolucionario* (Murcia, 1973); and F. Rodríguez de Coro, *El obispado de Vitoria durante el sexenio revolucionario* (Vitoria, 1976).

Although the relationship between the Church and the liberal State has received considerable attention from historians, the social and economic role of the mid-nineteenth-century Church has not, with one exception. A substantial literature on the sale of Church lands from 1836 to 1859 has adequately described the disamortization process both at the national and regional levels. Francisco Simón Segura, *La desamortización española del siglo XIX* (Madrid, 1973) and F. Tomás y Valiente, *El marco político de la desamortización en España* (Barcelona, 1971) provide the best general assessments. Peter Janke has ably analyzed the political implications of the disamortizing legislation of 1836 in *Mendizábal y la instauración de la monarquía constitucional en España, 1790–1853* (Madrid, 1974. There are numerous regional studies of the sale of ecclesiastical lands. A good recent bibliography of the disamortization in local settings can be found in Vicente Cárcel Ortí, "El liberalismo en poder, 1833–1868," in *Historia de la Iglesia en España* (cited above), 137–138.

The extensive literature on the sale of Church property, although useful to the historian interested in the structure of ecclesiastical holdings in the Old Regime, is less valuable for the study of its impact on the Church itself. Little has been done on the financial state of the Church following disamortization, and less on how this revolutionary change in ecclesiastical financing transformed traditional social functions, such as charity. A recent article by J. M. Palomares Ibáñez, "La Iglesia española y la asistencia social en el siglo XIX," in *Estudios históricos sobre la Iglesia española contemporánea* (cited above), 119–149, begins to explore this topic, but more remains to be done.

Studies of the nineteenth-century clergy are still lacking. The hierarchy has received some attention, although as yet there is nothing comparable to the biographies of Cardinal Lorenzana and Bishop Tavira for the eighteenth century. Two biographies, however, are particularly useful: Julián Barrio Barrio, *Félix Torres Amat, 1772–1847: Un obispo reformador* (Rome, 1976); and Rafael María Sanz de Diego, *Medio siglo de relaciones Iglesia-Estado: El Cardenal Antolín Monescillo y Viso, 1811–1897* (Madrid, 1979).

There is even less on the lower clergy, although a recent article by Manuel Revuelta González, "Clero viejo y clero nuevo en el siglo XIX," in *Estudios históricos sobre la Iglesia española contemporánea* (cited above), 153–197, explores the topic in general terms. How effectively the Church conducted its religious mission is another topic left largely unexplored. There is a brief review from the standpoint of the Church in Baldomero Jiménez Duque, *La espiritualidad en el siglo XIX español* (Madrid, 1974). William Christian's fine study of religious devotion in contemporary Spain, *Person and God in a Spanish Valley* (New York, 1972), contains useful background information for the earlier period. The relationship of the Church to the new industrial working class of the period deserves much fuller treatment given the importance of the workers' alienation from the Church during the twentieth century. A collection of essays on Francisco Palau, a Carmelite active in attempts to preserve the Church's influence over the working class of Barcelona in the 1850's, suggests that there were at least some efforts to view the problem from a modern perspective: *Una figura carismática del siglo XIX: El P. Francisco Palau y Quer, O.C.D., Apóstol y Fundador* (Burgos, 1973).

The work of Mariano Peset and José Luis Peset, *La universidad española: Despotismo ilustrado y revolución liberal* (Madrid, 1974), is indispensable for the history of education before 1868, although its focus is primarily on higher education. Also useful for an appreciation of clerical attitudes toard intellectual freedom in education is Yvonne Turin, *La educación y la escuela en España de 1874 a 1902: Liberalismo y tradición* (Madrid, 1967).

Index

Harvard Historical Monographs

Out of Print Titles Are Omitted

1. *W. S. Ferguson.* Athenian Tribal Cycles in the Hellenistic Age. 1932.
3. *J. B. Hedges.* The Federal Railway Land Subsidy Policy of Canada. 1934.
9. *Crane Brinton.* French Revolutionary Legislation on Illegitimacy, 1789–1804. 1936.
11. *C. S. Gardner.* Chinese Traditional Historiography. 1938. Rev. ed., 1961.
21. *O. H. Radkey.* The Election to the Russian Constituent Assembly of 1917. 1950.
27. *Marius B. Jansen.* The Japanese and Sun Yat-sen. 1954.
31. *Robert L. Koehl.* RKFDV: German Resettlement and Population Policy, 1939–1945. 1957.
32. *Gerda Richards Crosby.* Disarmament and Peace in British Politics, 1914–1919. 1957.
33. *W. J. Bouwsma.* Concordia Mundi: The Career and Thought of Guillaume Postel (1510–1581). 1957.
34. *Hans Rosenberg.* Bureaucracy, Aristocracy, and Autocracy: The Prussian Experience, 1660–1815. 1958.
36. *Henry Vyverberg.* Historical Pessimism in the French Enlightenment. 1958.
38. *Elizabeth L. Eisenstein.* The First Professional Revolutionist: Filippo Michele Buonarroti (1761–1837). 1959.
40. *Samuel P. Hayes.* Conservation and the Gospel of Efficiency: The Progressive Conservation Movement, 1890–1920. 1959.
41. *Richard C. Wade.* The Urban Frontier: The Rise of Western Cities, 1790–1830. 1959.
42. *Harrison M. Wright.* New Zealand, 1769–1840: Early Years of Western Contact. 1959.
44. *Jere Clemens King.* Foch versus Clemenceau: France and German Dismemberment, 1918–1919. 1960.
46. *James Leiby.* Caroll Wright and Labor Reform: The Origin of Labor Statistics. 1960.
47. *Albert M. Craig.* Chōshū in the Meiji Restoration. 1961.
48. *Milton Berman.* John Fiske: The Evolution of a Popularizer. 1961.
49. *W. M. Southgate.* John Jewel and the Problem of Doctrinal Authority. 1962.
50. *Edward W. Bennett.* Germany and the Diplomacy of the Financial Crisis, 1931. 1962.
51. *Thomas W. Perry.* Public Opinion, Propaganda, and Politics in Eighteenth-Century England: A Study of the Jew Bill of 1753. 1962.
52. *Ramsay MacMullen.* Soldier and Civilian in the Later Roman Empire. 1963.
53. *Charles Montgomery Gray.* Copyhold, Equity, and the Common Law. 1963.

54. *Eugene Charlton Black.* The Association: British Extraparliamentary Political Association, 1769–1793. 1963.
55. *Seymour Drescher.* Tocqueville and England. 1964.
56. *Mack Walker.* Germany and the Emigration, 1816–1885. 1964.
57. *Stephen Lukashevich.* Ivan Aksakov (1823–1886): A Study in Russian Thought and Politics. 1965.
58. *R. C. Raack.* The Fall of Stein. 1965.
59. *Charles T. Wood.* The French Apanages and the Capetian Monarchy, 1224–1328. 1966.
60. *James Holt.* Congressional Insurgents and the Party System, 1909–1916. 1967.
61. *Keith Hitchins.* The Rumanian National Movement in Transylvania, 1780–1849. 1969.
62. *Louis M. Greenberg.* Sisters of Liberty: Marseille, Lyon, Paris and the Reaction to a Centralized State, 1868–1871. 1971.
63. *Alan B. Spitzer.* Old Hatreds and Young Hopes: The French Carbonari against the Bourbon Restoration. 1971.
64. *Judith M. Hughes.* To the Maginot Line: The Politics of French Military Preparation in the 1920's. 1971.
65. *Anthony Molho.* Florentine Public Finances in the Early Renaissance, 1400–1433. 1971.
66. *Philip Dawson.* Provincial Magistrates and Revolutionary Politics in France, 1789–1795. 1972.
67. *Raymond Callahan.* The East India Company and Army Reform, 1783–1798. 1972.
68. *Francis Godwin James.* Ireland in the Empire, 1688–1770: A History of Ireland from the Williamite Wars to the Eve of the AmericanRevolution. 1973.
69. *Richard Tilden Rapp.* Industry and Economic Decline in Seventeenth-Century Venice. 1976.
70. *Hock Guan Tjoa.* George Henry Lewes: A Victorian Mind. 1977.
71. *Marjorie O'Rourke Boyle.* Rhetoric and Reform: Erasmus' Civil Dispute with Luther. 1983.
72. *Jon Butler.* The Huguenots in America: A Refugee People in a New World Society. 1984.
73. *William J. Callahan.* Church, Politics, and Society in Spain, 1750–1874. 1984.